DANTE AND RENAISSANCE FLORENCE

Simon Gilson explores Dante's reception in his native Florence between 1350 and 1481. He traces the development of Florentine civic culture and the interconnections between Dante's principal 'Florentine' readers, from Giovanni Boccaccio to Cristoforo Landino, and explains how and why both supporters and opponents of Dante exploited his legacy for a variety of ideological, linguistic, cultural, and political purposes. The book focuses on a variety of texts, both Latin and vernacular, in which reference was made to Dante, from commentaries to poetry, from literary lives to letters, from histories to dialogues. Gilson pays particular attention to Dante's influence on major authors such as Boccaccio and Petrarch, on Italian humanism, and on civic identity and popular culture in Florence. Ranging across literature, philosophy, and art, across languages and across social groups, this study fully illuminates for the first time Dante's central place in Italian Renaissance culture and thought.

SIMON GILSON is Senior Lecturer in Italian at the University of Warwick. He is the author of *Medieval Optics and Theories of Light in the Works of Dante* (2000) and the co-editor of *Science and Literature in Italian Culture: From Dante to Calvino* (2004). He has published journal articles on topics related to Dante's scientific interests, the Dante commentary tradition, and his reception in the Italian Renaissance.

CAMBRIDGE STUDIES IN MEDIEVAL LITERATURE

General editor
Alastair Minnis, *Ohio State University*

Editorial board
Zygmunt G. Barański, *University of Cambridge*
Christopher C. Baswell, *University of California, Los Angeles*
John Burrow, *University of Bristol*
Mary Carruthers, *New York University*
Rita Copeland, *University of Pennsylvania*
Simon Gaunt, *King's College, London*
Steven Kruger, *City University of New York*
Nigel Palmer, *University of Oxford*
Winthrop Wetherbee, *Cornell University*
Jocelyn Wogan-Browne, *Fordham University*

This series of critical books seeks to cover the whole area of literature written in the major medieval languages – the main European vernaculars, and medieval Latin and Greek – during the period *c.* 1100–1500. Its chief aim is to publish and stimulate fresh scholarship and criticism on medieval literature, special emphasis being placed on understanding major works of poetry, prose, and drama in relation to the contemporary culture and learning which fostered them.

Recent titles in the series
J. A. Burrow *Gestures and Looks in Medieval Narrative*
Ardis Butterfield *Poetry and Music in Medieval France: From Jean Renart to Guillaume de Machaut*
Emily Steiner *Documentary Culture and the Making of Medieval English Literature*
William E. Burgwinkle *Sodomy, Masculinity, and Law in Medieval Literature*
Nick Havely *Dante and the Franciscans: Poverty and the Papacy in the 'Commedia'*
Siegfried Wenzel *Latin Sermon Collections from Later Medieval England*
Ananya Jahanara Kabir and Deanne Williams, eds. *Postcolonial Approaches to the European Middle Ages: Translating Cultures*
Mark Miller *Philosophical Chaucer: Love, Sex, and Agency in the Canterbury Tales*

A complete list of titles in the series can be found at the end of the volume.

DANTE AND RENAISSANCE FLORENCE

SIMON A. GILSON
University of Warwick

CAMBRIDGE
UNIVERSITY PRESS

PUBLISHED BY THE PRESS SYNDICATE OF THE UNIVERSITY OF CAMBRIDGE
The Pitt Building, Trumpington Street, Cambridge, United Kingdom

CAMBRIDGE UNIVERSITY PRESS
The Edinburgh Building, Cambridge CB2 2RU, UK
40 West 20th Street, New York, NY 10011-4211, USA
477 Williamstown Road, Port Melbourne, VIC 3207, Australia
Ruiz de Alarcón 13, 28014 Madrid, Spain
Dock House, The Waterfront, Cape Town 8001, South Africa

http://www.cambridge.org

First published 2005

Printed in the United Kingdom at the University Press, Cambridge

Typeface Adobe Garamond 11.5/14 pt   *System* LaTeX 2$_\varepsilon$ [TB]

A catalog record for this book is available from the British Library.

Library of Congress cataloguing in publication data
Gilson, Simon A.
Dante and Renaissance Florence / Simon Gilson.
p.   cm. – (The Cambridge studies in medieval literature; 56)
Includes bibliographical references and index.
ISBN 0 521 84165 8 (alk. paper)
1. Dante Alighieri, 1265–1321 – Homes and haunts – Italy – Florence.
2. Florence (Italy) – History – To 1421.   3. Florence (Italy) – Intellectual life – To 1500.
1. Title.   II. Series.   PQ4353.F6G55   2004   851'.1 – dc22[B]   2004058280

ISBN 0 521 84165 8 hardback

For my parents, Alan and Joan Gilson

Contents

Contents

Illustrations

Acknowledgements

I am grateful to a number of friends who were kind enough to read earlier drafts of this book and to make valuable suggestions for improvement, especially Zyg Barański, Steven Botterill, Pat Boyde, Catherine Keen, and Brian Richardson. I also wish to thank one anonymous reviewer for helpful comments. It goes without saying that any errors of fact or judgement and infelicities of style remain entirely my own. I would like to thank Jenny Burns, Ann Caesar, Loredana Polezzi, Sergio Sokota, and Josie Williams, my colleagues in Italian at Warwick, for their friendship and support during the years in which this book assumed its present form. My appreciation is also due to other friends and colleagues, both at Warwick and elsewhere, for their encouragement and comments on earlier papers and articles, especially Judith Bryce, Rhiannon Daniels, Jonathan Davies, Claire Honess, Prue James, Peter Mack, Martin McLaughlin, Steve Milner, Christian Moevs, and Linda Paterson. Chapter 6 of this book incorporates some material from two earlier articles, first published in *Italian Studies* 58 (2003), 48–74 and *The Italianist* 23 (2003.i), 5–53, and I am grateful to Judith Bryce and Zyg Barański, the respective Senior Editors of these journals, for permission to re-use relevant sections. I am grateful to my own university for a period of study leave that allowed the book to gain early momentum, and to Linda Bree for her enthusiastic response to the project at all stages. I would also like to record my debt to the late Peter Armour for encouraging me to explore Landino's *Comento*, and to thank Dick Andrews whose teaching first stimulated my interest in the Italian Renaissance. I owe most of all to my wife, Julie, for her love and patience during the writing of this book.

Abbreviations

Dante's Latin works are quoted from the second volume of *Opere minori* (Milan–Naples: Ricciardi, 1979). Dante's vernacular works are quoted from the editions by: Giorgio Petrocchi for the *Comedy*; Domenico De Robertis for the *Vita nuova*; Gianfranco Contini for the *Rime*; and Cesare Vasoli for the *Convivio*. Unless otherwise stated, all translations from Latin and Italian are mine.

Short titles are used in referencing in the notes; the reader is referred to the bibliography for full publication details. The following abbreviations are used in the notes and bibliography:

Works by Dante

Con.	*Convivio*
Dve	*De vulgari eloquentia*
Eg.	*Egloghe*
Ep.	*Epistole*
Inf.	*Inferno*
Mon.	*Monarchia*
Par.	*Paradiso*
Purg.	*Purgatorio*
VN	*Vita nuova*

Works by Dante commentators
(see bibliography for editions used)

Benvenuto	Benvenuto da Imola, *Comentum super Dantis Aldigherij Comoediam*

List of abbreviations

Buti	Francesco da Buti, *Commento di Francesco da Buti sopra la 'Divina Comedia' di Dante Allighieri*
Comento	Cristoforo Landino, *Comento sopra la 'Comedia'*
Pietro	Pietro Alighieri, *Comentum supra poema Comedie Dantis*

Journals, serials and encyclopaedias

ASI	*Archivio storico italiano*
CCSL	*Corpus Christianorum Series Latina*
DBI	*Dizionario biografico degli italiani*
DS	*Dante Studies*
ED	*Enciclopedia Dantesca*
GSLI	*Giornale storico della letteratura italiana*
IMU	*Italia medioevale e umanistica*
JHI	*Journal of the History of Ideas*
JWCI	*Journal of the Warburg and Courtauld Institutes*
LI	*Lettere italiane*
RELI	*Rassegna europea della letteratura italiana*
RQ	*Renaissance Quarterly*
SBoc	*Studi sul Boccaccio*
SD	*Studi danteschi*
SFI	*Studi di filologia italiana*
SP	*Studi petrarcheschi*

Other abbreviations

DC	Cristoforo Landino, *Disputationes Camaldulenses*, ed. Peter Lohe (Florence: Olschki, 1980)
LTQ	*Lirici toscani del Quattrocento*, ed. Antonio Lanza, 2 vols. (Rome: Bulzoni, 1973)
PLQ	*Prosatori latini del Quattrocento* (Milan–Naples: Ricciardi, 1952)
SCT	Cristoforo Landino, *Scritti critici e teorici*, ed. Roberto Cardini, 2 vols. (Rome: Bulzoni, 1974)

Introduction

This book is concerned with Dante's reception in Florence during a period that extends from the first meeting of Boccaccio and Petrarch in 1350 to Cristoforo Landino's commentary upon the *Comedy* which was first printed in 1481. During this time, all of Florence's main social groups make use of Dante, and he is present in its manuscript, print, and oral cultures. He is linked with the work, both Latin and vernacular, of humanists, scientists, philosophers, theologians, artists, and poets, and his name has especially close bearing upon the ways in which both Florentine identity and the Tuscan vernacular are developed and promoted. We will encounter Dante in various protean guises, as patriotic emblem, politically committed citizen, moralist, philosopher, theologian, Neoplatonist, and prophet. The book explores how several generations of Florentines fashion these 'Dantes', and how they affect, and are affected by, the cultural, political, and literary dynamics of the city. Its six principal chapters follow a chronological trajectory in order to investigate the nexus of factors that influence how individuals and groupings defined and redefined Dante's significance and placed him within their own fields of vision. As a first step this introduction provides an overview of Dante's reception in the period as a whole in order to clarify the varied forms and contexts in which Dante was assimilated, and to outline the main themes and preoccupations that will be explored in the chapters that follow.[1]

The view that Dante marks a pivotal moment in the revival of classical poetry and learning is first stated in the late 1320s by a Pisan commentator on the *Comedy*,[2] and it was to be widely repeated with differing emphases by later Florentines until at least the end of the sixteenth century. It is perhaps not surprising therefore that, in the last seventy years, several scholars have supported such formulations, by arguing that Dante either foreshadows or directly embodies 'Renaissance' forms and ideals, especially in his apparently humanistic veneration, cultivation, and imitation of classical antiquity.[3] It is true that Dante shows a strong predilection for classical writers and philosophers in all his writings, and most especially in the *Comedy*. After all, Virgil is his guide for much of the poem, and a place of honour is reserved for other pagan poets and philosophers in Limbo, the first circle of Hell. And yet, Dante's relationship to the classical world is quite a narrow one. His knowledge of Greek literature is confined to comments in Latin authors and his acquaintance with the Latin tradition is itself limited when compared to later humanist writers. For example, Dante never mentions the important Roman poets, Catullus, Lucretius, Martial; and he only has second-hand knowledge of other Roman poets and playwrights such as Persius, Propertius, Plautus, and Terence. He seems to have known little of the Roman historian, Livy; and he knew none of the authors and texts so enthusiastically rediscovered within his own life-time by Paduan contemporaries with strongly classicizing interests such as Lovato dei Lovati (d. 1309) and Albertino Mussato (d. 1329). These contemporaries also possess a sharper sense of historical consciousness and a closer concern with matters that were to become the hallmark of later students of the *studia humanitatis* such as the recovery of lost texts and the collation of manuscripts with a view to assessing the most authentic textual readings. By contrast, Dante's general conception of history might best be described as theological, since it is centred upon the Incarnation and the inscrutable unfolding of divine providence. Unlike some contemporaries and many later humanists, Dante is not motivated by philological preoccupations with textual accuracy and recovery, and his own omnivorous relationship to books is more often guided by compendia, excerpts, and commentaries than it is by texts that are read as integral works.

These considerations help to illustrate why earlier studies that have emphasized Dante's humanistic values underplay the profound differences between his outlook and the sensibilities of Florentine humanists from the late 1370s until the end of the sixteenth century. More importantly still, such studies often neglect the innovative nature of Dante's approach to antiquity. In the *Comedy* Dante may have Virgil born under the wrong Emperor, erroneously view Statius as hailing from Tolosa, and introduce some other glaring historical anachronisms.[4] These misapprehensions are often detected by later commentators on his poem,[5] and they are a sign that, as in many other areas of learning, he is a man of his time. Yet where he differs from his contemporaries is when, as the vernacular *auctor* of the *Comedy*, he consciously outdoes classical texts, sets about correcting and rewriting Virgil's poetry, and makes Virgil himself into the agent of Statius' conversion to Christianity.[6] One of the great paradoxes that lies at the heart of the *Comedy* is the fact that he is at his most radical and original when adapting traditional and often quite dated material. His richly transformative approach to classical literature is part of a still more audacious innovation – his exhaustively experimental use of the vernacular in a poem which offers a totalizing vision of the universe and incorporates a vast wealth of philosophical, theological, and scientific ideas. Dante was undoubtedly aware of the ferment in the Veneto where Mussato and others were developing new ways of approaching classical texts and cultivating a more refined style in Latin prose and verse.[7] His correspondence, between 1319 and 1320, in the form of Latin Eclogues with a Bolognese professor of poetry, Giovanni del Virgilio, is testament to this (as it is to Dante's own intimate knowledge of Virgil and indeed his ability to recover a lost classical genre). But when del Virgilio asks for a poem in Latin, which will be restricted to a narrow intellectual elite, Dante reaffirms his desire to use the vernacular in order to open up his message to a wider audience, and not merely the *pallentes*, those blanched from constant study of the Latin classics.[8]

A similar blend of backward-looking qualities and radical innovation emerges when comparisons are made between other features of Dante's *forma mentis* and the concerns of his contemporaries. While Florentine merchants are conquering European markets and the city is expanding, Dante denounces the activities that are making Florence the economic and cultural hegemon of Tuscany and longs instead for a return to a narrowly circumscribed civic space and a civic life characterized by feudal values.[9] While imperial ideology in Italy is in decline, as Florence and other Italian city-states increasingly assert their autonomy, and as national monarchies begin to emerge in France, Spain, and England, Dante presents a bold vision of the separation of spiritual and temporal powers in which a universal emperor rules the temporal sphere and receives his authority from the Pope.[10] As the first fissures start to appear in scholasticism, Dante remains a schoolman in doctrine and method and a follower of Aristotle.[11] As Duns Scotus and William of Ockham are unsettling the bonds between reason and faith, the *Comedy* produces its own supreme synthesis of Aristotelian science and Christian revelation. At a time when Latin is the language of learning and statecraft and increasingly the object of study and imitation by humanists in certain areas of the Veneto, Dante turns to the humble and unassuming vernacular, the language that 'even women use'.[12]

Some of Dante's later Florentine readers, especially the two generations of humanists that followed Petrarch and Boccaccio, were aware of the lacunae in his knowledge of antiquity and were often startled by his promotion of the vernacular, as well as by his political views and his decidedly unusual approach to certain classical texts. To this humanist avant-garde Dante did indeed appear outmoded, medieval even (because medieval was a term that they were coining and starting to use), when measured against its own standards of judgement in the second half of the fourteenth century and throughout the fifteenth. But not all Florentines adopted this critical approach, and most early humanists active in Florence did not regard his 'medieval' qualities as sufficient reason for discarding him. Indeed, it became difficult to ignore Dante, given that, by 1350, he had already acquired an imposing status as the city's supreme vernacular poet and leading civic patriot. By this date, a small-scale industry was producing manuscript copies of the *Comedy* in Florence, the city's authorities were being petitioned for public lectures to be held on the poem, and a cult of the author, complete with its own penumbra of legendary material, was establishing itself throughout Tuscany and in many other cultural centres on the Italian peninsula.

The preceding paragraphs help to explain why this book is not an attempt to define Dante's qualities using terms such as 'medieval' and 'Renaissance' which are at best rough and at worst arbitrary and tendentious periodizations (although Dante's reception does offer us a privileged point-of-view from which to consider how such labels originate and develop). In an intellectual climate that justified innovation in terms of renewal and restoration it was perhaps inevitable that Dante would get caught up with myths of rebirth. One major preoccupation of this book is rather to examine how and why Dante was distanced from, and associated with, these categories in later Florentine contexts that used and transmitted his name and works. In other words, the book deals with the ways in which later readers and writers responded to Dante and his legacy by tailoring him to their own contexts across at least six generations. The key point about such responses, or at least the most influential ones, is that it was his interlocutors who actively selected and interpreted the features that they then used to construct various visions of Dante and his poem. To understand more closely the factors involved in such reconstructions and to trace out more fully Dante's varied Florentine reception, one must first explore in greater detail the issues raised by the mediation and reception of his name and his texts.

Dante cared deeply about questions related to his fame and reputation. The writing of the *Convivio* was prompted by a desire to recover the good name that he had lost with exile; and in the opening lines of *Paradiso* xxv he indulged himself in the thought of being crowned as poet laureate in his beloved Florence.[13] Dante was fully conversant with the axiom that reception depends upon the nature of the recipient,[14] and, although he did not develop these ideas with explicit reference to literature, he was well aware of the ways in which an author may lose control over how his text is read, especially in matters of translation.[15] This may in part help to explain his tendency to interpret his own texts, commenting on some of his earlier lyric poetry in the *Vita nuova* and his *canzoni* in the *Convivio*, and also composing (at least in part) a Latin letter, the Cangrande Epistle, which offers a set of interpretative prolegomena to the *Paradiso*. In the *Comedy* he shows an awareness that his poem will have more than one audience. Indeed, his concern with the nature and effects of reading is such that he explicitly places within his poem scenes of reading which provide a critique of deficient approaches to literature, highlight the dangers and limitations of specific literary genres, and even promote certain ways of reading classical texts.[16] He repeatedly addresses his readers, calling upon them to engage in the intensely active series of processes that reading involves. An important strand in recent Dante scholarship has, moreover, suggested that the *Comedy* contains within itself its own auto-exegesis in a way that is designed to assist his readers and to close off the poem to misinterpretation.[17] It may well be that his very choice of *terza rima* reflects an awareness of how written texts can easily be distorted and subject to interpolation, and how this might be mitigated by the binding architecture of his rhyme scheme with its interlocking chain of rhyme words.

The study of Dante's reputation and influence developed in the age of positivist literary criticism and it considers why he and his work became famous, how that fame was perpetuated over time, and what factors increased or diminished it. Since the late 1960s, however, such an emphasis upon the author and his text has been reassessed by critics and theorists who prefer to view reading as an act which is socially situated and constructed. The branch of this field of study known as reception theory is particularly pertinent here, and it is most closely associated with the work of the German scholar, Hans Robert Jauss. By making readerly activity the ultimate source of meaning for a text and for lit-erary history itself, Jauss stresses how the evaluating subjects of a work bring their own social and historical situation to the text in a way which conditions interpretations of it. To privilege the reader is not, therefore, to disregard contextual factors: readers' perceptions are closely influ-enced by their own cultural background, and these perceptions issue into broader acts of interpretation. For Jauss, literary interpretation is unavoidably dependent upon the historical horizon of the interpreter: changing horizons of expectation, defined as the conventions and sys-tems of reference shared by a work's public(s), determine the ways in which readers approach and interact with particular works. It is thus the activity of the reader and changes in the manner of decoding texts that most clearly set off reception theory from studies of an author's reputation and his influence.[18]

The renewed exploration of the active role of the reader, of the reader's perspective, and of the conditions under which interaction with texts occurs has something to offer the kind of study proposed here. It opens up the possibility for different, and even conflicting, conceptions of Dante and interpretations of his work to co-exist without dismissing them as absurd or ancillary misreadings. It encourages further study of the reader's social, intellectual, and ideological background, and a closer appreciation of how such factors may in turn condition reading practices. It places history and literature into a more productive relation-ship, not within a hierarchy of value where literary works simply reflect history, but as discourses that are both constructed and that creatively

6

interact and overlap with one another. However, while this book draws some insights from concerns developed in reception theory, there remain several problems with Jauss' approach that have direct bearing on later 'readers' of Dante. Jauss tends to overemphasize the conformity of reading practices within designated periods (whose boundaries are in any case often arbitrary), whereas we will see that readers responded to Dante in a variety of ways and that interpretative screens may jostle and compete with one another in a single historical moment and even coexist within an individual reader. Jauss' approach posits, moreover, direct contact between reader and text, whereas we will witness a more complex situation, whereby later Florentines approach Dante in partial and selective ways and the very forms in which he is mediated are often crucial to their effect upon the reader.[19] Finally, within reception theory there is a danger of underestimating the legacy of tradition – a considerable one in the case of Dante, and even as early as 1350 – and of failing to take full account of how earlier critical vocabulary and paradigms are transmitted and re-used across generations.[20]

For these reasons, this book focuses upon how the history of Dante's reception is closely related to the construction of interpretative frameworks and filters by which his work, life, and reputation were approached. But it also considers how both earlier traditions and contemporary contextual issues shape these interpretative schemes. By covering an extended period of time and paying attention to both vernacular and Latin cultures, it should be possible to pinpoint elements of continuity, development, and disjunction in the reception of Dante over some 130 years during which he was shaped and re-shaped by his later Florentine readers.

Let us now examine the diverse ways in which information about Dante and his works was transmitted and outline the principal contexts in which such mediations took place. Of all the works of Dante that were available in our period the most important was the *Comedy*. Several of the individuals studied in later chapters are involved in the production of texts of the *Comedy*; and, in the period covered here, this was undertaken predominantly, but not exclusively, through the laborious copying of manuscripts.[21] As early as 1350, the heavy demand for the *Comedy* had led to processes of manuscript production on a mass scale in Florence, with one workshop owned by Francesco di ser Nardo da Barberino famously turning out a hundred copies of the poem, the so-called 'gruppo del Cento'.[22] It is a revealing index of Dante's growing popularity that more codices of the poem survive from the fifteenth century than from any other period, and of these extant copies more than fifty per cent are Florentine. The *Comedy* is also twice translated into Latin during the early fifteenth century, and there are several other partial translations, a number of them made in Florence.[23] The data from surveys of extant manuscripts reveal the great demand for the poem, and the material form of the Dante manuscripts described by Giorgio Petrocchi and Marcella Roddewig also helps to provide indications of its readership. Manuscript copies are found in all sizes, formats, and scripts,[24] but in Florence 'il Dante' (as the *Comedy* was known) is especially linked to a mercantile readership. Christian Bec's studies of library inventories and manuscript ownership of the *Comedy* confirm the popularity of the poem with this kind of reading public, especially in the first half of the fifteenth century.[25] However, the helpful inferences that can be made from statistical data and the material form of manuscripts still do not tell us anything qualitative about *how* their owners might actually have read Dante. For insight into the varied but elusive world of these readers of the *Comedy*, we must turn to the marginal annotations made by merchant readers and comments found in other written texts owned by them. For some merchants the poem seems to have been no more than a status symbol, a material possession; but there is also evidence from *libri zibaldoni*, the merchant book *par excellence*, that the *Comedy* was the privileged means by which Florentine men and women learned to write and then to read.[26]

The manuscript tradition of the *Comedy* brings with it several other layers of Dantean and non-Dantean material, all of which affected how his text was received. First of all, depending on their date, manuscripts of the *Comedy* frequently contain one or more of the many fourteenth-century or Trecento commentaries on the poem.[27] Several of these works are non-Florentine, but they circulated widely in the city and provided the conceptual and interpretative edifice upon which later Florentine constructions of Dante would be built. This tendency to extract earlier material (regardless of its provenance) and to fit it to a Florentine template is a feature of Dante's reception that we will meet in several later chapters. Later chapters will also deal with the influence of both non-Florentine commentaries and the main extant Florentine commentaries: Boccaccio's unfinished *Esposizioni* (1374); Filippo Villani's incomplete *Expositio* (*c.* 1400–04); and Landino's *Comento* (1481). The commentary, its modes of reading, re-reading, and re-presenting Dante, and the contextual issues it raises, will thus be a recurrent concern throughout this book. Here it is sufficient to stress that, for all its conservatism, Dante commentary, both in manuscript and in print, is valuable in its own right as a form of literary criticism and as an expression of a particular moment of interchange between past and present. The commentary can be usefully read as a revealing index of how Dante was adapted to later contexts, provided that sufficient discrimination is made between material which is traditional and glosses which elicit responses that arise from contemporary or personal concerns. Aside from commentaries, the manuscript tradition of the poem often includes biographies of Dante, especially Boccaccio's own life of the poet, various poems and other writings in his defence, and pseudonymous material sometimes erroneously attributed to Dante. One also frequently finds diagrams, illustrations, and illuminations in manuscripts of the *Comedy*, as well as layers of reactions from earlier readers in the form of marginalia.[28]

Apart from the manuscript tradition, with its accompanying commentaries and other paratextual material, our time frame sees the first printed editions of Dante's poem. The *editio princeps* is produced in Foligno in 1472, and it is followed by five more printed texts in Venice, Naples, and Milan between 1477 and 1478.[29] These printings are not, then, Florentine products, but in the late 1470s they play a part in provoking Landino to draw upon more than two decades of teaching and study of Dante in order to produce what was to become the most famous and influential Renaissance printed edition and commentary (see Part III).

As far as Dante's other poems are concerned, the *sestine* of the 'Rime petrose' and the moral *canzoni* seem to have been more popular than his other lyric production.[30] Florentine interest in the *Convivio* is notable in the second half of the fourteenth century – the work is not known to Dante's first commentators – and becomes very marked in the second half of the fifteenth century, especially at a time of heightened rediscovery of vernacular texts from the 1460s onwards. The *Convivio* is, in fact, the first of the 'minor works' to be printed after the *Comedy* and re-vealingly the first edition is produced in Florence.[31] The vernacular text that seems to have been transmitted most unevenly is the *Vita nuova*. It is mentioned by Dante's earlier commentators as well as by Boccaccio, who draws on it repeatedly in his fictional and exegetical work, but it seems to disappear from circulation in the early fifteenth century and it only became widely known again in the final third of that century.[32] The most interesting 'minor work' of all is the *Monarchia*. In spite of ecclesiastical censures in the 1320s and 1330s and significant later reser-vations about its Latin, the work begins to be copied again in Florence in the second half of the fifteenth century (see chapter 4, section 2). As for Dante's other Latin works, the *Egloghe* exchanged with Giovanni del Virgilio and several of his Latin letters, the *Epistole*, are not neglected throughout our period, but there are some significant omissions from his Latin oeuvre. The *De vulgari eloquentia*, Dante's unfinished Latin treatise on the illustrious vernacular, though well known to Boccaccio, dropped out of circulation and was only rediscovered in Florence at the beginning of the sixteenth century.[33] The cosmographical treatise, the *Questio*, re-entered circulation only in the early sixteenth century; and, except for its use by Filippo Villani, the *Epistle to Cangrande* did not circulate independently.[34]

Outside the textual tradition of Dante's own works, both in manuscript and printed forms, a vast array of information was relayed about him in a wide range of written sources, in prose and poetry, both vernacular and Latin. The traditions of commentary and lives of the poet have already been mentioned, since these were often connected with the textual tradition of Dante's works. But a variety of other prose writings also offers 'information' about his appearance and moral character, his role in the political life of the city, the nature and qualities of his poetry, and associated anecdotes, legends, and stories. None of this material can be taken at face value, since each strand of it is partial (in both senses of the word) and interpretative. These writings could be subdi-vided into Florentine historiography,[35] defences of poetry and works of poetics,[36] Latin epistolography,[37] mercantile production,[38] writings on artistic practice and theory,[39] and novelistic traditions.[40] But to employ such genre divisions is to mask the rich complexity of each tradition and to disregard the significant interconnections between many of them.

As regards Florentine poetry, Dante is a constant point of reference in the city's poetic tradition both as a *summa* of knowledge and as a literary model. His influence is less pronounced in the love lyric, where Dantean language often forms part of a common vocabulary. However, there are many interesting and direct adaptations, often in audaciously parodic form, of images and themes from the *Comedy* in the more popular currents of satiric Florentine poetry represented by Burchiello, Lo Za, and others.[41] And Dante is widely imitated in other genres and certain verse forms, in particular the dream-vision and didactic poetry, which were often written in *terza rima*. What is more, Dante is actively appropriated by poets writing in Latin, and his presence in Latin verse provides us with some of his more unexpected and intriguing adaptations. These intertextual uses of Dante are sometimes little more than passive imitation, but there are also many examples that show him to have been subject to critical re-reading. By viewing intertextuality, like commentary, as a mode of reading, this book will attempt to illustrate some of the areas of convergence between critical debates about Dante and literary adaptations of his writings in prose and verse, both Latin and the vernacular. For our purposes here, it is important to note that, even in writers who possessed an intimate knowledge of the *Comedy* and whose work is saturated with Dantean quotations, allusions, and echoes, there is often a high degree of selectivity and adaptation to new contexts.[42]

Despite its many forms, direct contact with Dante's texts, or with texts that provide information about him, is only one aspect of his reception. Between 1350 and 1481 most Florentines knew about Dante by having heard the *Comedy* read aloud or expounded in public and by having seen pictures of the poet. The most effective form that brought him to a very wide Florentine public indeed was the public lecture, a tradition which is instituted by the Florentine state in 1374 and continued, with some interruptions, throughout the following two centuries. As well as the appointments of Dante lecturers made by the *Signoria* (the official executive body of the Florentine government), the University of Florence or *Studio* played a key role in nominating individuals to read or give expositions of the *Comedy*, often specifically on feast days. Many of the names of the public lecturers are known, but although we have full commentaries by the Anonimo Fiorentino and Landino, partial ones by

Boccaccio and Villani, and some information about Filelfo's readings, little or no evidence has been found regarding the nature and content of the other lectures. What records of payments to these lecturers and the occasional comment on the size of their audience do reveal, though, is the immense popularity of Dante at all levels of society.[43] In his celebrated epitaph on Dante, written in the 1320s, Giovanni del Virgilio referred to him as 'the glory of the Muses, the most beloved author of the common people' ('gloria musarum, vulgo gratissimus auctor'). And even if Giovanni's later reference, in his first Eclogue, to a 'well-dressed wretch' ('comicomus nebulo') croaking out lines of the *Comedy*, is no more than a sophisticated piece of literary characterization,[44] the fact remains that the poem exercised a strong and perhaps unprecedented appeal across a wide range of lower social groups. The poem's links with popular culture are also exemplified to some extent in the *novella* tradition and in other writings.[45] In a pre-print and early print culture where there was a greater reliance on memory, there were close connections between the written Dante and a Dante known only by recitation. The written commentary on the *Comedy* is itself often based upon public or university lectures, and the particular inflection of the human voice is also to some extent preserved in sermons and other forms of public lecture that make use of him.[46]

Perhaps the least studied area of Dante's reception in fourteenth- and fifteenth-century Florence concerns the ways he was represented in the visual arts, which also reached a very wide audience. Dante's presence here offers a rich field of study that includes portraits, sculpture, painting, manuscript illumination, and printed illustrations. Florentine painterly tradition offered two main types of Dante portrait, that of the youthful dreamer represented in the Bargello in the Chapel of Santa Maddalena (*c.* 1333–7) and the more wretched, emaciated figure by Nardo di Cione in his *Ultimo giudizio* fresco (before 1357) for the Strozzi Chapel in the Church of Santa Maria Novella. Later portraits develop these two types, adding suggestions from Boccaccio's well-known description, and the most important fifteenth-century representations include: Andrea del Castagno's portrait in the refectory of S. Apollonia (1450–55); Domenico Michelino's fresco of Dante and his poem on the north wall of the Cathedral of Florence (1465) (see figs. 1–2); and the *intarsio* figure by Giuliano da Maiano on one of the wooden doors

1. Andrea del Castagno, portrait of Dante. Fresco. Refectory of S. Apollonia, Florence, *c.* 1450 (250 × 154 cm) Florence, Galleria degli Uffizi.

2. Domenico Michelino, *Dante and His Comedy*. Tempera on panel. Florence, Cathedral,
1465 © 1990, photo Scala, Florence. Crowned with the laurels and in the crimson robe
traditionally worn by poets, Dante holds open a copy of his poem to reveal the first six
lines of *Inferno* I. He stands outside the city walls; the principal civic buildings (the
Florentine Cathedral and Palazzo Vecchio) are displayed prominently. The panel also
provides a representation of the three realms of the Dantean afterlife: Hell with one group
of sinners (the *ignavi* of *Inferno* III) and a miscellany of demons; Mount Purgatory with its
gate and angelic gatekeeper, the terraces of Purgatory proper and their penitent souls, and
the Garden of Eden at its summit; Paradise with the planets and spheres.

leading to the Sala dei Gigli in the Palazzo Vecchio (1481).[47] These commissions can be closely linked to attempts to confer greater status upon
Dante and to use him in order to promote Florentine cultural excellence. In other artistic media, Dante is also an important visual type,
being named among several poets in an ordinance of 1396 calling for the
erection of statues in the cathedral.[48] Furthermore, manuscript illuminations of the *Comedy*, especially Tuscan ones, flourished throughout
the period. These pictorial responses fulfil a variety of functions by acting as interpretative guides, memorative aids, and devices for visualizing
Dante's text. They also offer additional information or interpretations

not directly elicited by the poem, may enter into critical debates on aspects of its reception, and be connected with the commentary tradition on the poem.[49] Printing sees the development of new forms of figurative representation, although the experience is at first rather unsatisfactory in the incomplete programme of *intaglio* engravings in Landino's 1481 edition and commentary (see fig. 3). One of the more important set of illustrations is by Sandro Botticelli, who provided the designs for the Landino engravings and whose own drawings for the poem, carried out between 1481 and the early 1490s, are now the area of Dante's Florentine visual reception that has been most widely explored.[50] The figurative reading of Dante as a subject in its own right lies outside the scope of this book, but relevant material will be used in order to provide parallels with the ways in which Dante is adapted in literary and critical writings and in other sources.

Having examined the ways in which Dante's texts and information about him were transmitted in Florence, let us now turn to the three major topics of interest with which this book is concerned. The first is the tendency to measure Dante, both positively and negatively, in relation to humanist values. Florence's leading role in the development of humanism is well known, and the varying reactions of humanists towards Dante represent one of the central themes in all the chapters of this book. A second key concern is the urge to make political and ideological capital out of Dante, in particular the keen interest in what might be called civic appropriations of his name, developing, that is, a vision of his personality, his writings, and even his visual type, in order to promote the interests of certain groups within Florence and to advance Florentine causes outside the city. As is the case with the humanist responses, we will see that Dante is used to support differing political positions and often quite disparate causes. A third cluster of adaptations is equally diverse and it relates to the re-use of Dante's teachings on theology, philosophy, natural science, history, morality, rhetoric, and other topics. Throughout the late fourteenth and fifteenth centuries, Dante is admired almost universally at the level of content (and such veneration continues well into the sixteenth century in Florence at least), notwithstanding Pietro Bembo's later and influential strictures in his *Prose della volgar lingua* (1525) against what he saw as the indiscriminate miscellany of material in the poem.[51] Of course, both contemporary critical debates and the tendency to situate Dante within new contexts inform the ways in which aspects of the poem's content are re-used. The occasional reservations expressed about him, when not voiced by theologians regarding matters of Christian doctrine, are addressed at his style and choice of language, although this is often counterbalanced by assertions of Dante's poetic inventiveness and doctrinal richness. Even Dante's use of the vernacular – one of the main areas of humanist unease – is regarded positively by many Florentines for whom the *Comedy* is a touchstone of what human language can achieve. These topics – the varied reactions to Dante by humanists, the ideological and civic values imposed upon him, and reworkings of his doctrine and language – do not of course remain constant. And it will be the burden of all later chapters to explore the interconnected ways in which Dante's name and writings are evaluated in relation to them. The appropriations and transformations of Dante are the result of active re-reading and conscious selectivity; they are indebted to earlier traditions and yet they are also contingent upon specific contemporary contexts, identifiable intellectual groupings, and often key individuals in close contact with one another.

In Part I, we shall see how Boccaccio and Petrarch assess Dante and how they refashion earlier traditions, pinpointing tensions between humanistic values and vernacular culture and establishing their own important evaluations, and, in Boccaccio's case especially, a specific Dantean legacy within Florence (chapter 1). The tensions between Latin and vernacular cultures become even more marked at the close of the fourteenth century and the beginning of the fifteenth, as Florentine humanists makes their own varying assessments of Dante, some of which are fiercely opposed by advocates of Tuscan vernacular culture (chapter 2). In Part II, we shall retain this focus on the humanist reception of Dante but consider how it affects biographies of Dante and attempts to assert the status of the vernacular in the 1430s and early 1440s (chapter 3). This section also assesses Dante's significance in the successful promotion of humanist vernacular culture in later Medici Florence, especially during the 1460s and 1470s (chapter 4). As the vernacular gains greater status, especially from the 1460s onwards, Dante plays an increasingly important part in the cultural and ideological strategies of Lorenzo de' Medici's Florence, culminating in Landino's commentary of 1481 which celebrates Florence and Florentine culture through Dante and presents the *Comedy* as emblematic of classical and contemporary values. Part III thus rounds off the chronological conspectus and draws together the themes of humanism, Florentine ideology, and Dantean language and content, by providing a detailed assessment of Landino's *Comento*. This commentary has recently been published in a critical edition, and this is the first time that the entire commentary will receive extended discussion. Chapter 5 pays close attention to the *Comento*'s background and its celebration of Florence and Dante in the lengthy prologue section; while chapter 6 examines its blend of innovation and tradition in mediating Dante in relation to topics of contemporary interest in the little-studied glosses in the commentary proper.

PART I

Competing cults: the legacy of the Trecento and the impact of humanism, 1350–1430

I

Boccaccio and Petrarch

By 1350, the year of the first meeting of Boccaccio and Petrarch, the early polemical responses to *Monarchia* had largely subsided, and the *Comedy* had become a compelling text for a varied early public belonging to most, if not all sections, of Tuscan society. The appeal of Dante's poem was related to such factors as its admixture of high and low cultures, its blend of eschatology and contemporary *cronaca*, its use of Tuscan vernacular (as opposed to Latin), and the ease with which the work could be memorized. From the 1340s up to Landino's printed edition, demand for manuscript copies of the poem remained constant, and from the 1370s public lectures on 'il Dante' became an established part of Florentine life. By 1350, too, interest in the *Comedy* had given rise to a number of commentaries which were – if one excludes Dante's own commentaries on himself – the first to be written on an Italian, or for that matter a European, vernacular text.[1]

This chapter aims to assess how Boccaccio and Petrarch interpreted and refashioned Dante in a close and intricate literary dialogue. It deals with Boccaccio's role in promoting Dante within Florence, with the interwoven ways in which he and Petrarch present their predecessor, and with the principal characteristics and forms of Dantean intertexuality in their own writings. The responses of Petrarch and Boccaccio to Dante and the *Comedy* are important in their own right, and, as we shall see in chapter 2, they provide many of the conventions and points of reference for Florentine debates, especially in the late fourteenth and early fifteenth centuries.

1 Boccaccio's cult of Dante

Boccaccio's role in establishing a cult of Dante in Florence is relatively well known, and it comprises his activities as copyist, biographer, literary artist, and exegete.[2] His youthful attachment to Dante was notably reinforced during his residence in Naples (1327–41) through contact with the Tuscan poets and intellectuals linked to the *Studio Napoletano* and the Angevin court. And in this way Boccaccio's absence from Florence, where in the 1320s and 1330s there was an initially slow and sporadic recovery of Dante's writings, served to develop his interests in the Tuscan literary tradition in general, and in Dante in particular. On his return to Florence in the early 1340s, Boccaccio's keen interest in Dante is evident above all in his work as a copyist and author of romance fictions. Having collected and copied texts of Dante's works in Naples, he repeatedly transcribed many of his vernacular and Latin writings.[3] There are three extant manuscripts of the *Comedy* which are copied in Boccaccio's own hand, and they date from the early 1350s to the early 1370s. The manuscripts testify to Boccaccio's attempt to create a collection of Dante's works and to the codicological complexity that we noted in the Introduction, since they include other anthologized material from Dante's works (the *Vita nuova* and fifteen *canzoni*), Boccaccio's own *terza rima* and short prose summaries of the *Comedy* (known as the *Argomenti* and *Rubriche* respectively), and redactions of his own biography of Dante (the *Trattatello in laude di Dante*).[4] Even the artistic realm is included, since Boccaccio provided his own illustrations of passages from the *Inferno* in one other manuscript he owned.[5] Apart from the collected 'editions' of Dante's works, Boccaccio also copied other Dantean texts in his personal notebooks – the *zibaldoni*. The *Zibaldone Laurenziano* 29, 8 is especially noteworthy for it preserves three of the Latin letters (*Epistole*, III, XI, and XII) not extant in any other known source. The Latin Eclogues exchanged between Dante and Giovanni del Virgilio are also transcribed here, and, while this is not the only source for their transmission, it remains the most important one.[6]

Further evidence of Boccaccio's profound admiration for Dante can be found in the complex forms of Dantean intertexuality or *dantismo* in Boccaccio's own fictional writings. This important subject has not received definitive treatment and some works still require close analysis.

However, since the late 1970s several critics have illustrated the centrality of Dante and the numerous gradations of intertexual reference to him throughout Boccaccio's vernacular works from the *Caccia di Diana* to the *Corbaccio*.[7] Dante is present in the metrical organization of many Boccaccian texts, in his adoption and development of certain key themes, and in a wide range of *topoi*.[8] Three general points can be made from an analysis of the recurrent features and patterns of appropriation. First, Boccaccio's interest in Dante is often displayed openly in his vernacular writings: he praises Dante among classical poets in the *Filocolo* (*c.* 1336–39), places him on the level of classical poets and addresses a paean to his poetic mastery in the *Amorosa visione* (*c.* 1342–43); and in all his works, including the *Decameron*, he produces moments of heightened accumulation of Dantean reference.[9] Second, he draws on the *Vita nuova*, the *Convivio*, and almost all of Dante's Latin writings, but above all he favours the *Comedy*, and reworks certain passages from it throughout his vernacular prose and poetry.[10] Third, even though the literary relationship is often one of enthusiastic imitation, especially in the earliest works, it is not without elements of critical reading and even parodic rewriting, as recent studies of the *Decameron* and the *Corbaccio* in particular have shown.[11]

Dante is also an important presence both as an *auctor* and a significant intertextual presence in Boccaccio's Latin works. In the *De casibus* (*c.* 1363), Dante is named as one of the illustrious men without an historian to give him posterity – a role which Boccaccio may well have sought to fill with his own biography of the poet.[12] And in the *Genealogie deorum gentilium* (*c.* 1350–75), Boccaccio's fifteen-book encyclopaedic repository of ancient mythology, Dante is used as an authority on the rivers of Hell. In the defence of poetry elaborated in the final two books of this work, it is highly significant that Dante and Petrarch – the pairing is significant – are the only vernacular examples to appear alongside Latin *auctores* in order to illustrate how certain kinds of poetry conceal theological truths beneath their fictive veil. The cross-fertilization between Boccaccio's view of poetry in the *Genealogie* and his Dantean interests may well be more pronounced than has been previously noted. The key elements of Boccaccio's poetics – finding new and unheard of arguments, eliciting virtuous deeds in the reader, poetry's privileged relationship to truth, and its use of the veil – all correspond to comments he makes about characteristics of the *Comedy*. In this way, Boccaccio provides one early example of how an understanding of Dante's poetry informs and is informed by the development of poetics in late fourteenth- and fifteenth-century Florence.[13]

Influential though the *Genealogie* was throughout the next 150 years, the works in which Boccaccio deals most directly with Dante are his biography of the poet, the *Trattatello*, and his unfinished commentary on the *Comedy*, the *Esposizioni*. These writings are also the most important means by which Boccaccio's 'Dante' was passed on to later Florentines. The *Trattatello* takes us to the heart of a series of fundamental questions about the relationship between Boccaccio and Petrarch, and the place of Dante within their own literary output and conceptions of culture.[14] As poets and intellectuals in the generation immediately following Dante, they were both obliged to come to terms with his imposing literary legacy. As we have seen, Boccaccio displayed his admiration for Dante and became his foremost Florentine advocate in the mid-Trecento and an enthusiastic, though far from passive, imitator of him in his many literary works. By contrast, we shall see that Petrarch outwardly expressed reservations about Dante and tried to mask his influence in his writings. Petrarch and Boccaccio met three times during the 1350s, briefly in Florence in 1350, at greater length in Padua in the spring of 1351, and again in Milan between March and April of 1359. It was during the second meeting that the question of Dante's value assumed particular significance and gave rise to a sustained literary dialogue *sub specie Dantis*. The first move was Boccaccio's. Having noted the absence of the *Comedy* from Petrarch's library, between the summer of 1351 and May 1353 Boccaccio sent Petrarch an exemplar of the poem – a nonautograph, but centrally important manuscript, now known as Vatican Latin 3199[15] – with his own epistolary poem in praise of Dante, 'Ytalie iam certus honos'. This short Latin *carmen*, written in the same period as the first redaction of the *Trattatello*, presents the *Comedy* as a learned work of popular appeal whose surface hides deeper meaning, while Dante is put forward as a *theologus* and *vates* who deserves the laurels but remains uncrowned.[16] There are strong echoes here of Giovanni del Virgilio's epitaph of Dante,[17] and the *carmen* thus shows how Boccaccio draws on earlier evaluations of Dante, but adapts them to new contexts and at the same time introduces new emphases. For example, he draws attention to Florence, calling her the great mother of poets ('grandis vatum Florentia mater', line 31). Boccaccio also uses this Latin poem to present a 'Dante' with some decidedly Petrarchan characteristics, revealing a concern with how Dante and Petrarch might be made to complement one another that permeates his work and is first made evident in his earlier biography of Petrarch, *De vita et moribus domini Francisci Petracchi de Florentia* (1342–43). In 'Ytalie iam', he also tackles the issue of the *Comedy*'s vernacular status by asking Petrarch to embrace Dante's poem even though it is written in vernacular verse, and he defends Dante from the charge that he avoided Latin due to ignorance.[18] Despite the evident differences in structure, tone, and overall purpose, many of the same arguments are developed at greater length in the first redaction of the *Trattatello* which also presents Dante in a form that owes much to his awareness of Petrarch's own literary predilections and sensibilities. Let us now turn in more detail to this important work.

2 Boccaccio's *Trattatello*, first redaction

The *Trattatello in laude di Dante* exists in three redactions that have been dated to 1351–55, 1360, and before 1372.[19] It represents a crucial point in the development of vernacular biography, both in Italy and in Europe, being the first biographical treatment of the life and works of Dante, or indeed any 'modern' author. Some biographical information about Dante had been recorded by *cronisti* as well as by his early commentators, but Boccaccio's work provides the first extensive account exclusively dedicated to his life. The *Trattatello* circulated widely in the late Trecento and throughout the fifteenth century, often accompanying the *Comedy* in Boccaccio's own manuscripts, in other manuscript copies, and in later printed editions;[20] and, as we shall see in chapters 2, 3, and 5, it is a point of reference for many later Florentine writers and biographers on Dante.

The first redaction of the *Trattatello* begins with a general introduction, which outlines Boccaccio's intentions in a thematic arrangement:

> E scriverò in istilo assai umile e leggiero [. . .] e nel nostro fiorentino idioma, acciò che da quello, che egli usò nella maggior parte delle sue opere, non discordi, quelle cose le quali esso [sc. Dante] di sé

onestamente tacette: cioè la nobiltà della sua origine, la vita, gli studii, i costumi; raccogliendo appresso in uno l'opere da lui fatte. (§ 9)

And so as not to be discordant from that style which he used in the majority of his works, I will write in a very humble and unadorned style [...] and in our own Florentine idiom. I will deal first with those things concerning himself about which Dante was modestly silent, namely, the nobility of his origins, his life, studies, and habits, and afterwards I will gather together all the works he wrote.

Boccaccio then proceeds to treat each of these themes in turn, describing Dante's ancestry, aspects of his life including his studies, and his relationships with Beatrice and Gemma Donati. After an account of Dante's marriage, there follows a misogynist invective and a description of his political career, exile, and wanderings. The 'biographical' narrative closes with an account of his death and the honours paid to him, quoting the full text of del Virgilio's epitaph. This is then followed by a lengthy invective against the city of Florence for exiling Dante, a celebrated physiognomical description of Dante's appearance, discussion of his personality, and a separate discursive section on the nature of poetry and its relationship to theology. The narrative now returns to Dante's 'costumi', describing his virtues and his faults, namely the sin of lust. There follows a description of his literary works and a justification of his decision to write the *Comedy* in the vernacular. The treatise closes with an expansion of the prophetic dream of Dante's mother, which was briefly mentioned in the section on his origins, and which makes use of Suetonius' account of the dream of Virgil's pregnant mother as transmitted through the biography of the fourth-century grammarian, Donatus.

As this outline suggests, Boccaccio's life of Dante is not a work of biographical documentation. It is rather an attempt to bestow a legendary aura upon his personality and activities while at the same time tackling some key preoccupations of early Italian humanism such as the defence of poetry, the most appropriate life for a scholar, and the relationship between the vernacular and Latin. Throughout the life, he draws closely on several earlier traditions, and, in this way, the *Trattatello* exemplifies the processes of adaptation that are so often prominent in Dante's reception, processes by which earlier formulations are revised under the influence of contemporary concerns. In Boccaccio's case, the issues brought to light in his life of Dante are redolent of what critics have referred to as the 'secondo Boccaccio', that is, the post-*Decameron* Boccaccio deeply influenced by his evolving relationship with Petrarch, one whose literary production is directed mainly towards Latin works of encyclopaedic scope on learned topics, and who indefatigably defends poetry from its detractors.[21]

The place of such concerns in the *Trattatello* has led Todd Boli to argue that the work is an attempt to recast Dante into a form attractive to Petrarch by incorporating Petrarchan responses to such questions as erotic love, the poet's vocation, and the pursuit of fame and glory. In this reading, the life is a form of defence in which Boccaccio attempts to secure Dante's transmission by 'accommodating the work's subject to Petrarchan standards, of forcing Dante, if necessary, into a Petrarchan mold'.[22] There is much evidence for this view in the *Trattatello*'s espousal of the scholarly life as requiring solitude, the importance of pursuing literary fame, and the dangers of civic participation.[23] Further support for this interpretation can also be found in 'Ytalie iam', as well as in Boccaccio's later redactions of the life (see section 4 below). The *Trattatello* most certainly does mediate Dante by responding to Petrarchan views, and, by extension, to emerging humanist values. But Boccaccio's responses are not simply reactive, and it is essential to note that he constantly attempts to juxtapose Dante and Petrarch and to make them complement one another, as he does earlier in the life of Petrarch and later on the pages of his Chigiano manuscript.

We should also not neglect the composite nature of Boccaccio's presentation of Dante and his use of a variety of other literary traditions, and in particular classical biography. In its open structure and movement between themes and significant biographical moments, Boccaccio models his life closely on the classical biographies of Virgil by Donatus and Servius. Thus, in all redactions Boccaccio explicitly portrays Dante as the vernacular and modern equivalent of the Latin poet.[24] This is an audacious move, anticipated in his vernacular fiction, especially the *Amorosa visione*, and later developed in the *Esposizioni* and his Latin works. In this way, Dante is placed within a poetic genealogy that stretches from antiquity to Boccaccio's present. And, by its very suggestion that Dante the vernacular poet can be compared with the language, thought, and culture of the Latin world, the *Trattatello* in effect works against Petrarch's views regarding both the relationship between Latin and the vernacular and that between his own poetry and Dante's (see next section). Boccaccio's most daring claim is found in the section on Dante's nobility where, reformulating *Purgatorio* I, 7–8 but perhaps with an echo of Guido da Pisa's commentary on the *Inferno*, he makes Dante the starting-point in a process of literary revival, and celebrates his attempts to demonstrate the value and beauty of the Florentine vernacular:

> questi fu quel Dante, il qual primo doveva al ritorno delle muse, sbandite d'Italia, aprir la via. Per costui la chiarezza del fiorentino idioma è dimostrata; per costui ogni bellezza di volgar parlare sotto debiti numeri è regolata; per costui la morta poesì meritamente si può dir suscitata. (§ 19)

> This was that Dante who was the first to open the way for the return of the Muses, who had been banished from Italy. Because of his efforts, the nobility of the Florentine idiom has been demonstrated, because of his efforts, the beauty of vernacular speech has been placed in proper metrical form; because of his efforts, one can justly say that dead poetry has been resuscitated.

This kind of commentary, which transfers humanist concepts and standards to Dante, is developed elsewhere in the first redaction, and it is an important feature common to both Boccaccio's biographical and his exegetical work on Dante. The view that Dante is to be closely linked with his classical heritage is stressed throughout the *Trattatello*, and despite subsequent erasures in later redactions the classical structure of the life remains. Florence itself 'ebbe inizio da' Romani' ('took her origin from the Romans': § 11); Dante traces his family back to a young nobleman from Rome at the time the city was refounded by Charlemagne (§ 13). And, in the first redaction, great emphasis is placed on Dante's own study and imitation of ancient literature:

> familiarissimo divenne [sc. Dante] di Virgilio, d'Orazio, d'Ovidio, di Stazio e di ciascuno altro poeta famoso; non solamente avendo caro il conoscergli, ma ancora, altamente cantando, s'ingegnò d'imitarli, come le sue opere mostrano. (§ 22)

he became most familiar with Virgil, Horace, Ovid and Statius, and every other renowned poet. Not only was it his heartfelt concern to know them, but he also strove to imitate them in his own high poetry, as his works show.

To associate Dante's achievements in the vernacular with Latin poets is a striking manoeuvre at a time when the learned elite was becoming ever more conscious of the distance between Latin literary culture and the vernacular. And Dante's familiarity with classical literature is under-scored later in the work when his founding a school of poetry draws favourable comparisons with the role of Homer and Virgil in raising the status of their own classical literary languages:

> e quivi [sc. in Ravenna] con le sue dimostrazioni fece più scolari in poesia e massimamente nella volgare; la quale, secondo il mio giudi-cio, egli primo non altramenti fra noi Italici esaltò e recò in pregio, che la sua Omero tra' Greci o Virgilio tra' Latini. Davanti a costui [...] niuno fu che ardire o sentimento avesse [...] di farla essere strumento d'alcuna artificiosa materia; anzi solamente in leggerissime cose d'amore con essa [sc. volgare] s'esercitavano. Costui mostrò con effetto con essa ogni alta materia potersi trattare, e glorioso sopra ogni altro fece il volgar nostro. (§ 84)

And here with his demonstrations he made many learned in poetry, above all in the vernacular. I believe he was the first poet who among the Italians exalted and elevated the vernacular in the way Homer did among the Greeks and Virgil among the Latins. Before Dante there was no-one who had the daring and will to make it an instrument of art. Indeed, [earlier Italian poets] only used the vernacular for trifling matters of love. He showed in reality that the vernacular could deal with all elevated subject-matter, and he made our vernacular glorious above all others.

In explaining the reasons for Dante having preferred the vernacular to Latin, Boccaccio first emphasizes – as Dante had done in the *Convivio* (I, ix, 2–3) – its usefulness to a wide range of fellow citizens and other Italians, including the illiterate, and reiterates the beauty and excellence of the Florentine idiom (§ 191). The second reason that Boccaccio gives for Dante's choice of the vernacular is also noteworthy and it again seems to rest in part upon views expressed in the *Convivio* (I, ix, 5). He says that Dante did begin his poem in Latin hexameters (and Boccaccio famously records the first three lines) but he returned to a 'stile conforme a' moderni sensi' ('style suited for modern understanding') because of the neglect shown by princes and other rulers for the work of Latin poets in his own lifetime (§ 192). As in 'Ytalie iam', then, Dante's choice of the vernacular is not taken as a sign of any deficiency in Latin.

The *Trattatello* is informed by other Latin and vernacular traditions in addition to classical biography. In particular, Boccaccio makes the prodigious qualities of the poet and poetry, already a prominent theme in Servius and Donatus, more resonant still by blending the comments of Macrobius and Martianus Capella with motifs taken from medieval lives of the saints. The life of Dante also includes misogynist invective, which will be developed with even greater verbal energy in the *Corbaccio*. And one can detect novellistic and popularizing traditions in the anecdotes that are told about Dante's moral qualities and failings, his learning, and his high-minded self-possession, as well as in the deliciously embellished stories concerning the obstacles to the composition of the 'divina *Comedia*' ('divine *Comedy*').[25] Finally, it is noteworthy that Boccaccio also echoes Dante's own language, from his poetry and prose works, throughout the life.[26]

In the *Trattatello* Boccaccio's lengthy discussion of the nature and worth of poetry shows his independence from Petrarch even at the points where Boccaccio borrows from him. The paragraphs devoted to a defence of poetry develop a cluster of concepts centred upon the idea of the poet-theologian (*poeta-theologus*). From the beginning of the fourteenth century, Dominican theologians in Italy had attacked poetry for its mendaciousness and corrupting influence, while early humanists such as Mussato had viewed it as a divine science and form of theology. The 'defenders' drew on a variety of traditions in order to argue that pagan poetry concealed Christian truth, and often adapted Aristotle by maintaining that certain ancient poets were *philomythai*, that is, lovers of myth, who were in some sense lovers of true wisdom. The term *poeta-theologus* has its distant origins here, but by the early fourteenth century it draws upon other traditions and the question of the status of poetry was the subject of repeated polemics.[27] Dante attaches great epistemological value to poetry in the *Comedy*, and stresses its links with theology, but the first to adapt the concept of the *poeta-theologus* explicitly to Dante seems to have been del Virgilio in his epitaph for Dante and he was followed by most of the Trecento commentators.[28] In the *Trattatello*, Boccaccio draws on this general context and on Petrarch's ideas regarding the analogies between biblical and poetic language as enunciated in a Latin letter, *Familiares* x, 4, dated 2 December 1349.[29] From this letter Boccaccio takes his account of how poetry can be reconciled with Christian teachings and theology insofar as they both involve language which is figurative and obscure. He also makes direct use of Petrarch for his views on the religious origins of poetry, its artificial style, the derivation of the name from the Greek *poetès*, and his examples of the affinities between biblical and poetic language. And yet, in his own defence of poetry, Boccaccio applies these Petrarchan formulations not to Virgil nor to his own Latin poetry (as Petrarch had done), but rather to Dante's vernacular poem. This presentation of Dante as the personification of the poet-theologian is re-emphasized in the *Esposizioni* and the *Genealogie*, but most significantly it is quite absent from Petrarch's discussion of Dante.

One final topic that remains outside the 'Petrarchan template' in the *Trattatello* concerns Florence and Dante's treatment by his home-city. By 1350 there was already a body of Tuscan poetry that condemned Florence for its unjust exile of Dante and its failure to recognize his true worth.[30] Boccaccio locates himself within such earlier traditions and marks out the importance of the theme by using his very first mention of Dante to introduce him as an individual who is defined by his exile (§ 4). The poet has been subject not only to the vicissitudes of Fortune, but also to active wrongdoing, principally on the part of Florence, and Boccaccio states that the aim of the *Trattatello* is to redress this injustice. He will make amends for the city's omissions, by tracing the nobility, life, studies, and habits of Dante. If his fellow Florentines have failed to erect a suitable monument in stone to Dante, Boccaccio will construct one in the words of his life (§§ 8–9).

The theme of Dante's worth and his disgraceful treatment by the Florentine state runs through the *Trattatello* but it is developed most emphatically following discussion of Dante's death, where Boccaccio launches a diatribe against the city for its ingratitude.[31] In this section Boccaccio strikes a number of Dantean chords, lambasting Florence for its merchant culture, its blind pursuit of riches, its vanity, and its cruelty to the city's dearest citizen, principal benefactor, and only poet. Boccaccio also uses classical examples in order to contrast Florence's neglect of Dante with the due reverence that Athens and other Greek cities paid to their most prominent citizens. Finally, in a clear allusion to contemporary Florentine discussions about recovering Dante's remains from Ravenna, the city is asked to recognize the wrong it has perpetrated and to 'riverlo morto', to 'have him back in death' (§ 102). In contrast with the city's behaviour, Dante's own Florentine identity and his keen sense of civic pride never desert him despite the travails of exile:

> In verità, quantunque tu [sc. Florence] a lui ingrata [cf. *Inf.* xv, 61] e proterva fossi, egli sempre come figliuolo ebbe in te reverenza, né mai di quello onore che per le sue opere seguire ti dovea, volle privarti, come tu lui della tua cittadinanza privasti. Sempre fiorentino, quantunque l'esilio fosse lungo, si nominò e volle essere nominato, sempre ad ogni altra ti prepose, sempre t'amò. (§ 103)

> In truth, although you were ungrateful and harsh towards him, he always held you in esteem like a son. Nor did he ever want to deprive you of that honour which was to come your way from his writings, as you deprived him of your citizenship. In spite of his long exile, he always called himself and wanted to be called Florentine, he always placed you above all others, he always loved you.

As we will see, Boccaccio's affirmation of the links between Dante and Florence (as well as the city's responsibility to recover Dante's remains) was to be repeated by Florentines for the next two centuries.[32]

3 Petrarch and Dante

After their meeting in Milan in the spring of 1359, Boccaccio sent a letter to Petrarch. The letter is now lost but some of its content can be deduced from Petrarch's reply in his own important Latin epistle, *Familiares* xxi, 15, written after 1359, in which he sets out his 'views' on the subject of Dante and Dante's influence upon his own poetry. In this letter Petrarch engages subtly and critically with the ideas presented in 'Ytalie iam' and especially in the first redaction of the *Trattatello*. Ostensibly, Petrarch defends himself against charges concerning his apparent disregard for the *Comedy* and his envious disposition towards Dante. But a closer reading of the letter shows that his 'praise' of Dante is constantly qualified in ways that emphasize the differences between the two poets and serve to stress Petrarch's superiority in literary and cultural terms. Let us look in detail at how he constructs his defence.

In order to demonstrate his lack of animosity towards Dante, Petrarch first observes how his own father, ser Petracco, and Dante were both exiled from Florence at the same time, and how they were well matched intellectually. He moves on to praise Dante's innate talent or *ingenium* and to express admiration for his ability to continue his studies despite the distractions of his life in exile:

> [. . .] in addition to a similar fate, they shared common interests and studies. But my father, compelled by other matters and by the concern for his family, resigned himself to exile, while his friend [sc. Dante] resisted and began devoting himself all the more vigorously to his literary pursuits, neglecting all else and desirous only of glory. In this I can scarcely admire and praise him too highly when nothing – not the injustice suffered at the hands of his fellow citizens, not exile, poverty, or the stings of envy, not his wife's love or his devotion to his children ['non civium iniuria, non exilium, non paupertas, non simultatum aculei, non amor coniugis, non natorum pietas'] – diverted him from his course once he had embarked upon it, when many other great talents, being weak of purpose, would be distracted by the least disturbance. This usually happens to writers of verse who need peace and silence more than other men since, beside the substance and words, they must also worry about style.[33]

Prima facie this passage stresses the affinities between Dante and Petrarch's family and offers praise of Dante's great erudition and indomitable pursuit of learning – one of the main themes of the *Trattatello*. But to equate Dante with Petrarch's father is to attach Dante to an earlier generation, and for Petrarch the act of delineating an earlier historical period brought with it judgements of value. As is well known, Petrarch was preoccupied with defining historical sequences precisely and thereby stressing his own prominent place in what he regarded as a moment of cultural and literary renewal.[34]

The passage quoted above also contains a veiled critique of Dante that is elaborated through a reworking of Dante's own language. A pointed differentiation is implied in Petrarch's emphasis upon how Dante pushed aside all matters, including family ones, in the ardent pursuit of fame. Not only does this contrast with ser Petracco's solicitude as *paterfamilias*, but it also echoes Dante's own presentation, ultimately a negative one, of Ulysses' unrestrained pursuit of knowledge of human vices and virtues to the detriment of his family commitments:

> né dolcezza di figlio, né la pieta
> del vecchio padre, né 'l debito amore
> lo qual dovea Penelopè far lieta,
> vincer potero dentro a me l'ardore
> ch'i' ebbi a divenir del mondo esperto
> e de li vizi umani e del valore. (*Inf.* XXVI, 94–99)

> neither the sweetness of a son, nor compassion for my old father, nor the love owed to Penelope which should have made her glad, could conquer within me the ardour that I had to gain experience of the world and of human vices and worth.[35]

Petrarch's adaptation of this passage is influenced by Boccaccio's use of these lines in discussing Dante's ardent pursuit of his studies in the first redaction of the *Trattatello*.[36] But whereas both Boccaccio and Petrarch use the passage to comment upon Dante's studious resolve, it is only Petrarch who mentions a lack of *pietas*, and thereby gives his own presentation a distinctive negative charge. Petrarch's portrait of Dante's restless post-exilic years and other poets' inability to work under conditions other than silence and repose distantly echoes other passages from the *Comedy* (*Inf.* XXIV, 46–54; *Purg.* V, 10–18). But given his predilection for viewing the poet-intellectual as best suited to the contemplative life, that of *otium* rather than *negotium*, the passage again suggests the distance that separates him from Dante.[37] Petrarch now adds a further restriction that narrows the value of Dante's use of the vernacular (implicitly measured against the greater worth of the Latin language): 'as you see, there are no reasons for hatred and many for love, including our fatherland, our family's friendship, his talent and style, the best of its kind, which must always raise him far above contempt'.[38] One should here recall Boccaccio's earlier and ardent praise, in the first redaction of the *Trattatello*, of Dante's efforts in raising the vernacular to a level of excellence comparable to that of Homer's Greek and Virgil's Latin. Such an absolute judgement of value is narrowed by Petrarch to a circumscribed kind of poetry ('in suo genere optimus').

Petrarch recognizes the truth of the other principal charge levelled against him by his detractors, namely that he does not possess a copy of the *Comedy*. Such neglect is only apparent, however; it is due to his desire not to be influenced by Dante when he was composing his own earlier vernacular poetry. Now, far removed from his youthful experiments in the vernacular, he has no fear of being influenced by others, and he can safely turn to Dante. He cannot envy someone who dedicated his whole life to studies which Petrarch says he outgrew very quickly:

> Today I have left these scruples far behind; and with my total abandonment of such productions and the waning of my earlier fears, I can now welcome wholeheartedly all other poets, him [sc. Dante] above all. I used to submit my work to the judgement of others, whereas now I judge others in silence, varying in my opinion of them but deeming him the one to whom I would readily grant the palm of vernacular eloquence.[39]

Petrarch may thus award Dante the 'palm of vernacular eloquence', but the superiority of Latin over the vernacular is implied, and, as such, Petrarch suggests that his own cultivation of other literary concerns is of a higher order.

Having answered these charges, Petrarch now turns on the ignorant herd who accuse him of detracting from Dante's glory, and he draws attention first of all to their lack of judgement in matters of poetic understanding. His line of argument brings with it the same difference in value between Latin and the vernacular (and implicitly between himself and Dante). If the educated minds of ancient Greece and Rome failed to appreciate Demosthenes, Homer, and Virgil, then the situation can only be far worse with Dante's own illiterate and dissolute audience.[40] The association between Dante's poetry and the popular throng is not original to Petrarch: as was noted in the Introduction, it has antecedents in Giovanni del Virgilio, and is famously recorded in two of Francesco Sacchetti's *novelle*.[41] It is also a theme that Boccaccio develops in both the 'Ytalie iam' and the *Trattatello* in order to assert Dante's excellence and universality. In Petrarch, however, the emphasis is not only more focused and vehement, but conceals a very different judgement from Boccaccio's comments that the *Inferno* was 'conosciuto da molti e uomini e donne' ('known by many men and women') and that the *Comedy* 'con la dolcezza e bellezza del testo pasce non solamente gli uomini, ma i fanciulli e le femine' ('with the sweetness and beauty of its text nurtures not only men but children and women').[42] In the next few lines of 'praise', Petrarch further develops this point and inserts a comment upon Dante's own moral failings (most probably the lustfulness referred to by Boccaccio):

> I would venture to say in all honesty that, had he been allowed to live into our times, there would have been few with whom I would have been friendlier – provided his character matched his genius. On the other hand, there are none by whom he would have been more disliked than these silly admirers who never know why they praise or censure, who so mispronounce and mangle his verses that they could do no greater injury to a poet; and if my many concerns were not so pressing, I might even strive to the best of my powers to rescue him. As it is, I can only express my reprehension and disgust at hearing them befouling with their stupid mouths the noble beauty of his lines. Here may be the proper place to mention that this was not the least of my reasons for abandoning his style of composition to which I devoted myself as a young man.[43]

Unlike Boccaccio's enthusiastic response to Dante's popular appeal, Petrarch vents his scorn towards popularizing recitations of Dante in this passage and several others that are redolent with a humanistic and Horatian contempt for the common herd. By paying attention to this aspect of the *Comedy*'s reception, Petrarch presents the use of the vernacular as a form of writing which, because of its very mode of reception, involves factors beyond the author's control and falls prey to ignorant and debased responses. Petrarch is, in other words, building upon the precedent of del Virgilio, in order to associate Dante's vernacular poetry with popular culture and thereby to divorce it from the aristocratic world of Latin verse. In this highly partial construction, the *Comedy* is a verbal artefact liable to suffer mangling by the mouths of the uneducated. Petrarch's best-known statement on the subject, that he cannot envy a poet who is the darling of manual workers from lower social groups, now follows in a passage that rests upon classical *topoi* and is found in one of the most rhetorically wrought sections of the entire letter:

> how can someone who does not envy Virgil, envy anyone else, unless perhaps I envied him [sc. Dante] the applause and raucous acclaim of the fullers, or tavernkeepers, or woolworkers who offend the ones whom they wish to praise, whom I, like Virgil and Homer, delight in doing without?[44]

Petrarch's final qualified judgement on Dante is more directly related to issues of language, although it remains shrouded within a sequence of praise. And it also continues the dialogue with the *Trattatello* by addressing Boccaccio's earlier view that Dante had started the *Comedy* in Latin before deciding that the present-day neglect of Latinity was such that a vernacular poem would be the best means of ensuring longevity for his work. For Petrarch, Dante's *ingenium* and style are most delectable (although delectability is itself a way of locating Dante's poetry within the realm of unreflective, popular responses),[45] but he was not equal to himself in writing in Latin:

> You will accept my solemn assurance that I delight in our poet's talent and writing, and never refer to him except with the greatest admiration. I have at times said only one thing to those who wished to know my exact thoughts: his style was unequal for he rises to nobler and loftier heights in the vernacular than in Latin poetry or prose.[46]

This letter and a further comment on Dante's vernacular excellence in *Seniles* v, 2 are the only documents in which Petrarch puts forward his views about Dante. But in his earlier vernacular poetry Petrarch shows a similar desire to present Dante as the leading vernacular love poet of his generation. In the collection of anecdotes that make up the *Rerum memorandarum libri* (*c.* 1344), Petrarch includes two *novelle* about Dante at the court of Cangrande della Scala, and though emphasizing his excellence in vernacular poetry, they essentially modulate some traditional motifs of novelistic literature on the 'proud and disdainful poet' also present in the *Trattatello*.[47] The two other direct references to Dante in Petrarch's *oeuvre*, which both occur in his vernacular poetry and date from the late 1340s and early 1350s, reflect more closely the critical stance to be found later in *Familiares* XXI, 15. In the *Canzoniere*

Dante is directly mentioned in a way that suggests he belongs to an earlier generation of vernacular love poets by his being placed alongside Guittone d'Arezzo and Cino da Pistoia in the 1349 sonnet composed on the death of Sennuccio del Bene.[48] Similarly, the presentation of Dante in the *Trionfi* (*c.* 1352) is guided by a desire to place him within a previous generation and specific kind of poetry. Petrarch does not project an image of Dante as a poet of a philosophical or theological stamp as del Virgilio and the early Trecento commentators had done, nor does he associate him with classical poets as Boccaccio had in the *Amorosa visione* and the *Trattatello*. Instead he presents him as a vernacular love poet accompanied by a throng of other lyric poets: Dante is the *rimatore* of the *Vita nuova* and not the *auctor* of the *Comedy*:

> Così, or quinci or quindi rimirando,
> vidi gente ir per una verde piaggia
> pur d'amor volgarmente ragionando:
> ecco Dante e Beatrice, ecco Selvaggia,
> ecco Cin da Pistoia, Guitton d'Arezzo,
> che di non esser primo par ch'ira aggia;
> ecco i duo Guidi che già fur in prezzo.[49]

And so, gazing around now here and now there, I saw people moving along a green field, speaking only of love in the vernacular: here is Dante and Beatrice, here is Selvaggia, here is Cino da Pistoia, Guittone d'Arezzo, who seems to be angry that he is not the first; here are the two Guidos who were once held in esteem.

As in the later *Familiares* letter, Petrarch here deliberately echoes the *Comedy*, especially Dante's own judgements in *Purgatorio* on his predecessors in the lyric tradition (*Purg.* XI, 97–99; XXVI, 124–26), but, as in that letter, he also in effect gives his own judgement on Dante by resolutely assigning him to the ranks of vernacular love poets.

Both the *Canzoniere* and the *Trionfi* present Dante in ways that offer a selective and polemically charged vision of the poet's value. Although Petrarch claimed never to have read the *Comedy* before receiving the manuscript copy from Boccaccio, he undoubtedly did have a detailed knowledge of the poem, and his first sustained contact with it most probably came during his time as a student in Bologna in the 1320s.[50] Subtly disguised echoes of the *Comedy* reverberate through the linguistic texture of the *Canzoniere* from the prologue sonnet until the closing *canzone*; and the very idea of a collection of poetry, especially compositions on the death of the lady, owes much to the precedent set by the *Vita nuova*.[51] The view that Petrarch had outgrown the vernacular by the late 1350s is thus patently false. At times, the Dantean echoes may indeed be unconscious ones, but there is much that is conscious and carefully crafted in accordance with Petrarch's own highly innovative form of *ars imitandi*. The status of Dante within the vernacular literary tradition is such that, like Boccaccio, he can only define his own role within that tradition in relation to him. In Petrarch's case, the relationship is especially complex and agonized, and, as Roberto Mercuri in particular has argued, it is characterized by emulation and competition.[52]

Petrarch's other major vernacular work, the *Trionfi*, is written in *terza rima*, and even if the Dantean verse form may actually owe more to Boccaccio's precedent in the *Amorosa visione*, the work contains repeated reminiscences of the *Comedy* and several passages that treat Dante's poem agonistically.[53] In particular, Petrarch affirms the worth of Plato, Dido, and Ulysses in ways which recall yet overturn Dante's presentation of them in *Inferno* IV, V, and XXVI.[54] What is more, Petrarch's rewriting of Dante is especially pronounced at the very opening of the *Trionfi* which alludes to several sections of *Inferno* I, but places the echoes within a radically different context. Both authors mention spring, the place of the sun in Aries and the power of love, but Dante evokes the spring equinox as the pivotal moment in both universal history and Dante the pilgrim's spiritual life, whereas the poet-protagonist Petrarch establishes a personal frame of reference which does not allow his existence to transcend its earthly dimensions.[55] More disguised and still more intriguing is the transfigured presence of Dante's Latin and vernacular works in Petrarch's own production in Latin, where imitative emulation can also be identified, although in contrast to Boccaccio nowhere is Dante cited as an *auctor*.[56]

As these examples suggest, Petrarch's intertextual use of Dante includes a critical reading of him that has much in common with his more 'direct' statements in *Familiares* XXI, 15. Later readers of Petrarch seem rarely to have appreciated the critique of Dante implicit in such emulative strategies in his poetry. But there is interesting evidence that contemporaries attributed to Petrarch views that are critical of Dante's learning, such as the latter's belief in the incompleteness of Statius' *Achilleid* and his problematic use of the term *Comedia* as the title for his poem.[57] Like the rewritings of Plato, Dido, and Ulysses in the *Trionfi*, the relevant texts suggest that Petrarch entered directly into a subtle polemic with Dante's knowledge of the ancient world, and in effect signalled his predecessor's deficiencies by measuring them against his own standards. In this sense, too, Petrarch anticipates some of the later humanist critiques of Dante's classical erudition that will be explored in later chapters. Yet what matters most here is the effects that the more explicit pronouncements had on Boccaccio. For Boccaccio the problem of how to reconcile Dante with a more developed humanist culture as embodied in his *praeceptor* Petrarch, above all of how to resolve the conflicts between Latin and the vernacular, remained pressing throughout his life. He could not simply separate off his Latin production from his vernacular interests as Petrarch often does,[58] even if the second half of Boccaccio's career, post-1350/53, is marked by close emulation of Petrarch's example, and sees him move away from vernacular fiction towards works written in Latin. It is not fair to say that the influence of Petrarch distanced Boccaccio from his love of Dante, but rather that Boccaccio constantly attempted to reconcile Petrarch's influence with his own earlier intuitions and estimates about Dante. Too much has often been made of Boccaccio's passivity in what amounts to a dialogue, both with one another's own views on Dante and with earlier estimates. The later phases of this dialogue and Boccaccio's further attempts to accommodate Dante to humanist concerns lead us to the later redactions of the *Trattatello*.

4 Boccaccio's *Trattatello*, second redaction

As we have seen, Petrarch's pronouncements on Dante in *Familiares* XXI, 15 enter into dialogue with the first redaction of the *Trattatello*, endorsing certain aspects of Boccaccio's potrayal, but eliminating or reinterpreting many others, especially with regard to Boccaccio's presentation of Dante as scholar-poet and vernacular agent of a classical revival. This dialogue between Boccaccio and Petrarch continues in the later redactions of Boccaccio's life; for, as Carlo Paolazzi has shown, many of his modifications are governed by an attempt to refine his earlier claims in response to Petrarch's letter.[59] Such reactions are particularly noticeable in the evolution of Boccaccio's thinking on the status of vernacular poetry, on Dante's classical knowledge, and on the relationship between Latin and the vernacular. There are of course tensions even in the first redaction between Dante's use of the vernacular and the greater prestige of Latin.[60] But in the second redaction of the *Trattatello* Boccaccio revises previous statements that seemed to ally Dante too closely with a revival of classical literature. He excises, for example, the passage quoted earlier (see p. 29) regarding Dante's revivification of the Florentine idiom and his association with Homer and Virgil; and he also modifies his assertion of Dante's classical learning and imitation of ancient poets which is now reduced to the brief statement that 'familiarissimo divenne di tutti, e massimamente de' più famosi' ('he became most familiar with all of them, and especially with the most renowned': § 18). Boccaccio attenuates, too, his earlier emphasis on Dante's Latin works: no mention is made of the Latin *Epistole*, and both the *Monarchia* and the *De vulgari eloquentia* receive abbreviated commentary.[61] Petrarch also influences one modification where Boccaccio expands his earlier praise of Dante as a vernacular lyric poet and author of the *Vita nuova* – the one area of poetic activity in which Petrarch had acknowledged Dante to be pre-eminent.[62] On more than one occasion, Boccaccio also gives less emphasis to his earlier enthusiastic celebration of Dante's use of the vernacular. Instead of praising the *Comedy* as an unprecedented work that is testament to the beauty and excellent artistry of the Florentine language, it is merely said that Dante honoured it marvellously (§ 130).

It seems clear, then, that by the early 1360s, and under the influence of Petrarch, Boccaccio no longer found it acceptable to relate the classical canon as directly and emphatically to a work of vernacular poetry as he had a decade earlier. One witnesses here the evolving responses of a sophisticated reader of Dante as earlier reactions are shaded and even elided by other concerns made salient by the *Familiares* letter. And we are also observing the difficulties experienced by a devotee of Dante who is nonetheless increasingly aware of, and influenced by, the perceived supremacy of Latin literary culture.

5 Boccaccio's *Esposizioni*

In June 1373, a number of Florentine citizens petitioned the authorities in the city for the election of a skilled and wise man 'to read the book which in the vernacular is known as "the Dante" in the city of Florence to all those who want to hear it'. The petition recognizes the value of the *Comedy* as a source of ethical teachings, by asking for the reading of the 'book of Dante' to be made available for all citizens, including those not literate in Latin, who aspire to virtue, shun vice, and cultivate eloquence.[63] Following approval of the petition, on 25 August Boccaccio was nominated and appointed for a period of one year, with his first reading beginning on Sunday 23 October 1373 in the church of Santo Stefano di Badia. After about sixty lectures, in January 1374, the readings were suspended at the opening lines of *Inferno* XVII because of Boccaccio's ill-health but perhaps also as a result of the polemical responses to his *lecturae dantis* that are echoed in his four late sonnets which offer a *retractatio* of them.[64] Boccaccio did not resume the task, and he died on 21 December 1375.

Boccaccio's notes for the lectures are not in final form and they are replete with additions and corrections written in the margins – these are the *Esposizioni sopra la Comedia*, an incomplete commentary which nonetheless provides Boccaccio's most direct and detailed judgement on Dante's poem. Despite its unfinished state, this work is an important source for any assessment of Boccaccio's relationship to Dante, and it is also valuable because of its popularity with later Florentine *dantisti*. Many of the features found earlier in the *Trattatello* – biographical and anecdotal elements, the ingratitude of Florence, moralizing critiques of avarice, women, and mercantilism, the theme of the poet-theologian and digressions on poetry, controversies over Dante's use of the vernacular – are developed in the *Esposizioni*. But the hybrid nature of this work – which mixes oral and written commentary, relies on the earlier Dante commentary tradition, and responds to contemporary preoccupations – endows it with a very particular form and content. To illustrate these qualities and to give a sense of how the text draws together both past interpretations and present-day concerns, one must distinguish areas of the commentary that rely closely on previous traditions from matters which represent new departures informed by contemporary and personal issues. Like other medieval commentary texts, including earlier exegesis on the *Comedy*, the *Esposizioni* contain an academic *accessus ad auctores*, that is, a formalized way of introducing an author and his text which relates the latter to certain pre-established literary and philosophical categories. Boccaccio's *accessus* begins with a proem in which he states his intention to 'spiegare l'artificioso testo, la moltitudine delle storie e la sublimità de' sensi nascosi sotto il poetico velo della *Comedìa* del nostro Dante' ('explain the refined artistry of the text, the multitude of stories and the sublime quality of the senses hidden under the poetic veil of our Dante's *Comedy*': *accessus*, § 3). This statement is itself revealing of Boccaccio's preferences for historical narratives and the status he confers on allegorical reading. It is followed by a description of the threefold task to be undertaken in the *accessus*: to demonstrate the four causes of the poem, to discuss its title, and to classify the branch of philosophy to which it belongs. Boccaccio describes the four causes, and he discusses the etymology of the title 'Comedìa', noting with some perplexity that it is an unsuitable designation by which to describe the poem's stylistic qualities.[65] He then provides a short biographical sketch of Dante's life and a discussion of his name, echoing his earlier treatment of these topics in the *Trattatello*. This is followed by a brief comment on the poem's relationship to ethical teaching, a lengthy exposition on Hell, and finally a justification of Dante's decision to write the *Comedy* in the vernacular. From the above summary, it can be seen that many of the concerns of the 'secondo Boccaccio' are again addressed in the prologue. Certain features are nonetheless part of the critical idiom of the *accessus* form itself and, in accordance with this tradition, Boccaccio places especial emphasis on the ethical value of literature and the importance of its doctrinal content.

After the *accessus*, Boccaccio's glosses to the first seventeen cantos of the *Inferno* have much in common with the exegetical modes of earlier non-Florentine commentaries upon Dante. As in Guido da Pisa's *Expositiones*, each canto is given first a literal and then an allegorical exegesis, although Boccaccio omits the allegorical interpretation in cantos x–xi and xv–xvi and restricts it severely in canto viii. Like much earlier and later Dantean allegoresis, Boccaccio's own allegorical exposition often goes to unusual lengths: for example, the worms and blood that torment the *ignavi* (*Inf.* iii, 67–69) receive lengthy expositions in order to

43

moralize every aspect of this punishment and bring it to bear upon the sin itself. Within the literal exposition, each canto receives (as it does in Guido) a detailed division into parts or *divisio textus* according to the technique developed by Dominican commentators on the Bible and widely used in the teaching of legal and other texts at Italian universities. At the level of literal exposition, Boccaccio includes a considerable body of paraphrase, normally preceded by markers such as 'cioè', 'quasi voglia dire', 'quasi voglia dinotare'. Earlier Trecento commentators employ similar techniques, but in comparison to them Boccaccio, reveals a very keen interest in the literal sense throughout the *Esposizioni*, as is shown by the following example in which he elucidates Dante's description of Cerberus (*Inf.* VI, 16–18):

> *Con tre gole*, per ciò che tre capi avea, *caninamente latra*; e in questo atto dimostra lui essere cane, come i poeti il discrivono; *Sopra la gente che quivi è sommersa*, sotto la grandine e l'acqua e la neve. *Gli occhi ha vermigli*, questo Cerebro, *e la barba unta ed atra*, cioè nera. *E 'l ventre largo*, da poter, mangiando, assai cose riporre, *e unghiate le mani*, per poter prendere e arrappare; *Graffia gli spiriti*, con quelle unghie, *e ingoia*, divorandogli, *e squarta*, graffiandogli. (VI, i, §§ 6–7)

> *With three throats*, because he had three heads, *barks doglike*; and he shows himself to be a dog by this action, as the ancient poets describe him; *over the people submerged there*, under the hail, water, and snow. *His eyes are red*, this Cerberus, *his beard greasy and black*, that is, black. *His belly large*, so as to be able to hold, when eating, many things, *and his hands have talons*, in order to take and grab violently; *He claws the spirits*, with those claws, *and swallows*, devouring them, *and quarters them*, scratching them.

Boccaccio's close engagement with Dante's text in many such passages is not, however, uninterrupted by other more personal concerns. He uses the open and hybrid structure of the commentary form to insert his own narrative sequences, often employing techniques and rhythms that are strongly reminiscent of the *Decameron*.[66] Nor is his preoccupation with Dante's text matched by his attempts to judge between different variant readings. On the few occasions when Boccaccio outlines his reasons for favouring a certain reading he makes judgements on the basis of personal preference or else he draws distinctions between different *lectiones* that rest on notions of perceived logical consistency.[67]

Like almost all earlier Dante commentators, Boccaccio's longer glosses pay particular attention to topics that lend themselves to encyclopaedic digression, although such tendencies are often coloured by his own interests. Boccaccio develops the technique of learned compilation in the *Esposizioni* with particular reference to classical culture (history, literature, and mythology), medieval law, theology, geography, and various branches of natural science (medicine, meteorology, astrology, and astronomy).[68] In many such glosses there is also a clear and considerable overlap between the *Esposizioni* and material found in Boccaccio's Latin encyclopaedias, the *Genealogie* and the *De montibus* (1355–7).[69]

Throughout the commentary, Boccaccio also discusses, borrows, and adapts specific glosses found in earlier Dante commentators. It is common to find him examining the different views of earlier commentators on a given passage, and at times doing no more than report them. But he also disputes and overturns the interpretations offered by earlier Trecento commentators. In particular, he denies – in polemic with Guido's interpretation of the poem – that the *Comedy* is to be read as a supernatural revelation. Boccaccio insists instead on its literary and rhetorical qualities, that is, the very features where points of contact with classical models can be established, and in this respect his most important precursor is Pietro Alighieri.[70]

In spite of the conventional *topoi* and techniques that align Boccaccio quite closely with the earlier tradition of Dante commentary, the *Esposizioni* remain a particularly interesting document in providing insight into Dante's Florentine reception in the early 1370s. In the *accessus* Boccaccio attempts to downplay the differences between vernacular and classical culture, but the tensions between the two cultures are very much in evidence; and he goes further than ever before in affirming the superiority of Latin by commenting that:

> quantunque in volgare scritto sia [sc. Dante's poem], nel quale pare che comunichino le feminette, egli è nondimeno ornato e leggiadro e sublime, delle quali cose nulla sente il volgare delle femine. Non dico però che, se in versi latini fosse, non mutato il peso delle parole volgari, ch'egli non fosse più artificioso e più sublime molto, per ciò

che molto più d'arte e di gravità ha nel parlare latino che nel materno. (*accessus*, § 19)

Although it is written in the vernacular in which women communicate, it is nonetheless ornate, graceful, and sublime, and none of these qualities are found in the vernacular used by women. However, I believe that were it written in Latin verse, without changing the weight of the vernacular words, it would have more refined artifice and be much more sublime, because there is much more artistry and gravity in Latin than in our maternal language.

But the most revealing comment of all is found in his literal exposition to canto XV, where one senses a contemporary situation of humanist unease when Boccaccio comments on Petrarch's literary reputation and observes that the light of Dante's value 'è per alquanto tempo stata nascosa sotto la caligine del volgar materno' ('has for some time been hidden under the cloud of the maternal vernacular': XV, i, § 97).

In the closing section of the *accessus*, Boccaccio also discusses Dante's reasons for using the vernacular, and repeats arguments made earlier in the *Trattatello*: Dante's choice of the vernacular as the *corteccia* or outer-shell of his poem is governed by the need to make it intelligible to the rulers of his time (*accessus*, § 77). Boccaccio returns to this notion of the *corteccia* in the first allegorical exposition of *Inferno* I, where Dante is said to conceal the precious jewel of catholic truth under the vernacular shell of his poem ('sotto la volgare corteccia del suo poema': I, ii, § 18). The learned use their intelligence to uncover the wisdom hidden beneath the literal sense; the simple take delight in the literal sense. And, in a simple but profound analogy, Boccaccio borrows an expression that Saint Gregory had earlier applied to the Book of Psalms in order to compare Dante's poem to a river that is shallow enough for a lamb to pass yet deep enough for an elephant to swim through:

> intorno al senso allegorico si possono i savi essercitare e intorno alla dolceza testuale nudrire i semplici, cioè quegli li quali ancora tanto non sentono che essi possano al senso allegorico trapassare [...] dir si può [...] questo libro essere un fiume piano e profondo, nel quale l'agnello puote andare e il leofante notare, cioè in esso si possono i rozi dilettare e i gran valenti uomini essercitare [...] è da dimostrare la seconda [sc. allegorical part], intorno alla quale si possano gl'ingegni

più sublimi essercitare: la qual cosa si farà aprendo quello che sotto la crosta della lettera sta nascoso. (I, ii, §§ 23–25)

> the wise can exercise themselves with the allegorical sense and the simple (that is, those who feel that they cannot yet move on to the allegorical sense) feed themselves with the sweetness of the text itself [...] one can say that this book is like a stream which is both shallow and deep: the lamb can cross it and the elephant can swim in it. In other words, rustic people can take delight in this book and the wise exercise their intelligence upon it. We must now demonstrate the second part in which the highest intellects may exercise themselves and this will be done by opening up what is hidden beneath the crust of the letter.

In these passages, Boccaccio retains his interest in Dante's popular appeal but shows how his vernacular verse accords with a humanist conception of poetry as a learned work, which is intended for a refined and classically educated elite. In this way, he broadens and revises Petrarch's earlier view that had characterized the *Comedy* in terms of its reception by the illiterate masses.

The *Esposizioni* also provide evidence of Boccaccio's own classicizing interests and his attempt to use them in ways that bring Dante into line with incipient humanist values. Boccaccio uses a vast repertoire of classical mythology in glossing individual lines and single words, often in a way that goes far beyond clarification of the literal sense of the text. Boccaccio often uses Dante's own allusions to figures from classical myth as the starting-point for expounding the 'moltitudine delle storie' that are stored in his knowledge of classical (but also romance) history and literature. The mention of the word *poeta* in *Inferno* I, for example, prompts a digression of forty-one paragraphs, the *muse* of *Inferno* II receive eighteen, and Dante's own parade of virtuous pagans in *Inferno* IV spawns a succession of micro-commentaries which amount to nearly 200 paragraphs and make the literal exposition to this canto the longest of all. Extracts from classical texts, including little-known ones, are also cited as *auctoritates* in discussing points of doctrine as varied as the location of Hell, the sinful inclinations of souls, and the physiology of sleep.[71] But Boccaccio's most significant use of his classical erudition is to provide analogies between Latin *auctores* and Dante the vernacular poet. In the allegorical exposition to the first canto, Boccaccio tells us that Virgil treated the same material as Dante though with another meaning (I, ii, § 148); and in canto II, after a long description of classical invocations and their varying forms, Dante is said to have followed the Virgilian model, and it is noted that 'il nostro autore s'acostò più allo stilo di Virgilio, come in ciascuna cosa fa' ('our author came closer to the style of Virgil, as he does in all things': II, i, § 15). Like Pietro Alighieri before him, Boccaccio comments on numerous passages where Dante has taken words, characters, and comparisons from Virgil's *Aeneid*, and he also often transfers his earlier exegesis of Virgilian figures in his Latin works to those that reappear in the *Comedy*. The belief that Dante closely imitated Virgil's literary example is even used to justify passages in the *Comedy* that are either historically inaccurate or potentially heretical.[72] Boccaccio's concern with Greek culture is another area of classicizing interest – he comments on Homer, shows some knowledge of *topoi* found in the *Odyssey*, and discusses Greek etymologies.[73] Such background knowledge is not always used in pro-Dantean ways, however; for Boccaccio does on occasion point out inconsistencies in Dante's classical references. 'Non veggo come esser potesse' ('I do not see how it can be') is his incredulous comment on *Inferno* I, 70 which erroneously implies that Virgil was born towards the end of the rule of Julius Caesar (I, i, § 59). In all these ways, Boccaccio provides an important precedent for later Florentine writers and Dante commentators who repeatedly measure the *Comedy*'s classical content and allusions against humanist standards.

The question of Dante's religious orthodoxy also runs through Boccaccio's commentary in a manner that suggests that the poem was still subject to polemical responses in late Trecento Florence. In the early 1320s, Cecco d'Ascoli was the first to seize upon the notion that Dante's teachings might be potentially heretical, although his attack remained very much *ad personam*. Other early challenges to the poem on religious grounds came from the Dominican Order in Florence and its objections seem to find some echo in the solicitude with which the early Trecento commentators justify Dante's more controversial passages in the *Inferno* and elsewhere.[74] In the *Esposizioni*, Boccaccio develops such concerns as he attempts to neutralize Dante's less orthodox passages. He is perplexed by some of the figures found in Limbo, in particular

Ovid and the Islamic philosophers, Avicenna and Averroës (IV, ii, § 49). In his commentary to *Inferno* IX, 22–27, he avoids the necromantic associations implicit in this passage, by disputing the historical claims of this story and digressing on biblical precedents (IX, i, §§ 18–20). *Inferno* XIII is the most problematic canto of all. First, Boccaccio observes that it is 'dirittamente contrario alla verità catolica' ('directly contrary to Catholic truth') to assert that the suicides will not arise from the dead and recover their bodies at the Universal Judgement (XIII, i, § 69). But rather than charge Dante with such an error, he argues instead that the poet has expressed an erroneous view through one of his characters, and he devises a subtle scholastic distinction that allows Dante to have written like a Christian poet (§§ 76–83). In the same canto, Boccaccio also resolutely states that to believe that a statue of Mars has power over the bellicose temperaments of the Florentines (as an unnamed character suggests in lines 146–50) is to indulge not only in stupidity but also in heresy (§ 104).

As these preoccupations show, Boccaccio frequently adopts a strongly moralizing tone in the *Esposizioni*, and in so doing he draws at least in part upon earlier commentators, especially Guido da Pisa. He digresses at length on favourite moral themes such as avarice and its effects (VII, ii, §§ 45–82) and takes verbal delight in condemning certain vices, as is shown by the following example of lexical assault upon the gluttonous which is worthy of some comparison with his descriptions of the dissolute lifestyles of Cepparello and Frate Cipolla in the *Decameron* and is not surpassed in European vernacular literature before Rabelais:

> Questi adunque tutti, ingluviatori, ingurgitatori, ingoiatori, agognatori, arrappatori, biasciatori, abbaiatori, cinguettatori, gridatori, ruttatori, scostumati, unti, brutti, lordi, porcinosi, rantolosi, bavosi, stomacosi, fastidiosi e noiosi a vedere e ad udire, uomini, anzi bestie, pieni di vane speranze, sono vòti di pensier laudevoli e strabocchevoli ne' pericoli, gran vantatori, maldicenti e bugiardi, consumatori delle sustanzie temporali, inchinevoli ad ogni dissoluta libidine [. . .] (VI, ii, § 41)

> All these, then, are guzzlers, gorgers, gulpers, yearners, grabbers, sloberers, bitchers, twitterers, howlers, belchers; they are intemperate, oily, dirty, filthy, foul, wheezing, dribbling and nauseating men

who are disgusting and harmful to see and hear. No they are not men, but rather beasts. They are full of vain hopes, bereft of all laudable thoughts, and overflowing with dangerous ideas; they are great self-flatterers, backbiters, liars, and devourers of earthly things; they tend towards every kind of dissolute act of lust.

All in all, the *Esposizioni* are an intriguing blend of moral and religious conservatism with more innovative tendencies in the use of classical literature, history, and myth. They bring together characteristic features of the later Boccaccio: a strong sense of religiosity, the inclinations of a compiler, and an openness to a more distinctive humanist mentality. Boccaccio's commentary reveals traces of its oral context, and addresses a varied audience which includes both the Latin-educated elite and the vernacular literate. Boccaccio relies quite extensively on the Trecento commentary tradition, but he also fashions his own innovative responses, and often associates Dante's poetry with preoccupations that arise from a contemporary context which bears the imprint of Petrarchan and other values. In all these ways, the *Esposizioni* provide us with a particularly interesting example of how it is possible for past and present and for tradition and innovation to come together in a single work.

6 Conclusion

One is tempted to define the forms of Dante's reception discussed in this chapter in terms of conflicting allegiances, perhaps as Boccaccian enthusiasms and Petrarchan reservations. And yet, what is most significant is the way in which these two authors, by far the most important of their generation, engage with one another in a series of calculated attempts to establish the historical, literary, and cultural value of the *Comedy* and of Dante as a writer in vernacular and Latin. Their intensely literary exchange of views (replete with echoes of one another's writings) owes something to earlier judgements on Dante, but it is based above all upon a reading of him against one another's responses. The importance of this dialogue to the later history of Dante's reception rests upon the way in which Boccaccio and Petrarch associate Dante and his poetry with questions concerning the establishment of literary authority, his relationship to Florence, the nature and value of the vernacular, and the significance and purposes of a renewed interest in the classical world. Even in Boccaccio's case, allegiance to Dante in no way excludes the active reinscribing of him within a new conception of literary culture and the role of the poet.

Boccaccio, copyist, editor, imitator, biographer, and commentator of Dante, takes the leading role in attempting to align the *Comedy*, a 'modern' vernacular text (but one which the *literati* who admire and promote classical letters perceive as historically dated), with a set of contemporary values that are defined by reverential engagement with the ancient world. Despite some tensions, Boccaccio constantly attempts to emphasize Dante's links with the classical tradition. He also casts a powerful mythologized vision of Dante as scholar, contemplative, pre-eminent Florentine citizen, and *poeta-theologus*. In so doing, he may borrow elements taken from earlier judgements on Dante, but he is the first to fashion a mythological framework upon which he articulates his life and works, and it is the one against which all his subsequent Florentine biographers situate themselves.

As we have seen, Boccaccio is himself an important catalyst for Petrarch's own views on Dante. The recipient of a prized manuscript of the *Comedy* and of other Boccaccian works of Dantean apology, Petrarch is teased into breaking his silence on the subject. The qualified reflections in *Familiares* XXI, 15 present Dante as member of an earlier generation, and establish a series of distinctions that emphasize how Petrarch and Dante cannot be placed on the same level, and that thereby reduce Dante's overall cultural dimension. Petrarch probably felt his 'otherness' from Dante at several levels: he shared neither his totalizing ambitions nor his prophetic tendencies, and he had no interest in theoretical reflections upon language and the intrigues of city-state republicanism. Indeed, given Petrarch's cosmopolitan outlook and the fact that he only spent a few days in Florence itself, the construction of Petrarch's own *fiorentinità* by later writers is an operation which is even more manipulative than that performed on Dante. It is Dante's linguistic choice that Petrarch finds particularly difficult to digest, as it will continue to be for later generations of Florentine humanists until the relationship between the vernacular and Latin is set on new foundations (see chapter 4). Petrarch relegates Dante to a provincial dimension by insisting upon Dante's vernacular status, and crucially the form of reception attributed to it. Such judgements are developed through Petrarch's own acute understanding of how texts are transmitted and read.[75] Within such a perspective, his approach to Dante in the *Familiares* letter is highly original: he delimits Dante on the basis of his reception by reifying one facet of it. It is, then, one of the more delicious ironies in the history of Petrarch's own reception that under his name there circulated pseudonymous defences of Dante, including a Latin poem in praise of him and even a commentary on the *Comedy* (a text which, unlike Boccaccio, Petrarch never wrote). The sixteenth-century humanist Girolamo Claricio forged a letter which relates how Petrarch requested Benvenuto da Imola to write his own commentary; and an apocryphal story tells how Petrarch attributed Dante's own writing of the *Comedy* to the initiative of the Holy Spirit.[76] These are colourful and extreme examples, but they nonetheless reveal how Petrarch is himself swept along in the Dantean tide of popularity he tried to redirect for his own ends. Authors lack control not only over their own texts, but also over their attempts to direct the reception of other authors.

From the 1350s onwards Boccaccio himself moves towards a more humanist conception of culture of the kind advocated by Petrarch, but Dante and through him the question of the value of poetry remain central to his activities. Even if concerns such as the role of the vernacular and Dante's popular reception are modified, the classical form of the *Trattatello* is largely retained, the defence of poetry remains firmly attached to the figure of Dante, and the Latin works treat him as an *auctor* on the same level as classical writers. Nor does Boccaccio abandon Dante at the level of literary imitation in the vernacular, and he composes his last vernacular fiction, and arguably his most Dantean work, the *Corbaccio*, in the 1360s. Boccaccio may move towards Petrarchan positions on the superiority of Latin and develop a more aristocratic conception of poetry, but he strives repeatedly towards complementarity, a form of literary concordism between Dante and Petrarch. This is evident in his copying of both their works in the Chigiano manuscript and in his linking of them in various ways in his writings, and it has a counterpart in the visual arts in later Florentine representations of them face-to-face. He does not share the distinctions that govern Petrarch's attitude to the vernacular and Latin cultures and that are used by him to develop a very particular vision of Dante's value as opposed to his own. Boccaccio's concern with Dante's reputation is most explicit in his Florentine lectures and commentary notes on the *Comedy*. His public expositions on the *Comedy* mark a crucial turning-point in Dante's Florentine reception. The finest and most critically acute Trecento commentator on Dante, Benvenuto da Imola, was present at Boccaccio's lectures and he developed this oral testimony, both in his own lessons at Bologna and Ferrara and in his own important commentary (*c.* 1375–83).[77] The posthumous manuscript diffusion of Boccaccio's *Esposizioni* provides a further point of reference for all later commentators on Dante,[78] and an example of how the *Comedy* might be legitimized by means of techniques usually reserved for classical authors. The 'classicization' of Dante's poetry through the exegetical modes of the commentary is a topic to which we will return in later chapters. The following chapter deals directly with the legacy of Boccaccio and Petrarch in examining how Dante was interpreted at a time when humanist values exercised a stronger influence in Florence, but Dante is still vigorously supported by proponents of vernacular culture who, like Boccaccio, assert the excellence of their city through its most celebrated poet.[79]

2

Florentine humanism and vernacular culture: perspectives on Dante, 1375–1430

The revival of classical antiquity in Italy takes place outside Florence for much of the Trecento, but in the final years of that century several factors, both internal and external, coalesce to make the city into the leading centre of humanist activity on the peninsula. During the first half of the fifteenth century, Florence will remain at the forefront of the recovery of ancient letters and civilization: important new discoveries of classical Latin texts are made and these works are copied and studied; techniques of textual emendation and criticism are developed; Latin composition is put on a new footing through the use of classical grammatical structures and the development of regular humanist and italic script. The activities of visiting teachers, resident translators, and book-collectors enable the language and cultural heritage of ancient Greece to be assimilated with a level of expertise that goes far beyond the earlier imperfect efforts of Petrarch and Boccaccio to acquire Greek. Florentine humanists make their own distinctive contributions to moral philosophy, historiography, and patristic studies; and their highly developed skills in Latin epistolography and oratory help them to assume positions of importance within the Florentine government and civil service. By the end of the first decade of the fifteenth century, humanist ideals have become an established part of the patrician culture of Florence, and familiarity with Latin language and culture represents one way of determining participation in the social elite.[1]

And yet, in spite of the incursions made by early humanist culture into Florentine public and intellectual life, the foothold gained for Dante as an object of Florentine civic pride is strong, especially among those Tuscan *literati*, who, from the 1380s, are members of the ruling oligarchy, and are active in the city as notaries, teachers, and scholars. The tradition of public lectures on 'il Dante' continues throughout the period covered by this chapter, gaining impetus following the re-organization of the *Studio* in 1385. Dante is widely imitated in the Tuscan tradition of vernacular poetry, not only by members of the oligarchy, but also in the audacious and irreverent world of burlesque poetry. And, as a visual 'type' designed for public consumption he is included with other illustrious Florentines in artistic commissions for the Florentine cathedral, the Palazzo del Proconsolo, and the Palazzo della Signoria.[2]

This chapter assesses the complex and often competing claims made both for and against Dante by supporters of Florentine vernacular culture, on the one hand, and the principal representatives of the early Florentine humanist movement, on the other. Its primary aim is to assess the debates about Dante's worth that are prompted by his being evaluated in relation to a sharpened sense of historical perspective at a time when the classical world was being rediscovered as a source of authoritative models for literary pursuits and much else. Several earlier studies have stressed how cultural conflict between humanists and traditionalists characterizes much of the Florentine cultural environment in the late fourteenth and the early fifteenth centuries.[3] This point of view is not disputed here, but it will be seen that the various assessments and uses of Dante cannot always be conveniently separated by distinguishing between vernacular and Latin cultures. The debates are complex and finely differentiated and they include some of the best-known writings by important figures in Florentine public and literary life. The defenders of Dante have much in common with Boccaccio, especially the Boccaccio of the first redaction of *Trattatello* and the minor works, and they often build upon his earlier attempts to affirm Dante's status as an authoritative writer, worthy of close association with the ancients. It is, however, also the case that Petrarch's comments in *Familiares* XXI, fifteen remain – at least implicitly – very much alive in Florentine humanist disputations regarding both the relative worth of the ancients as compared to the moderns and the value of the vernacular. In the rest of Italy, the cult of Latinity is such that fifteenth-century humanists tend either not to discuss the vernacular or else to deny it any potential as a language capable of attaining higher literary and cultural status. The distinctive legacy of Florence's vernacular literary culture, as embodied in the three crowns or 'tre corone' (Dante, Petrarch, and Boccaccio), means that the city's own humanists are less able to avoid the questions raised by assessment of the *volgare* and its comparison to Latin. As we shall see, in such a context, Dante is repeatedly used as a sounding-board for political and civic themes that exalt the primacy of Florence and defend its political traditions.

The five sections of this chapter examine how these topics are developed in the judgements on Dante, and related writings and activities, of a number of individuals. As in the previous chapter, a prominent emphasis is placed throughout on the dialogical nature of the relationships between individuals and groupings as they present Dante in new forms, often echoing and borrowing one another's arguments, and on occasion overturning them.

1 Coluccio Salutati

A notary by training and profession, Coluccio Salutati (1332–1406) played an important part in the idealization of Petrarch, and, following his example, became deeply involved in the cultivation and defence of classical literature. Salutati's preoccupation with the classical world first developed during his student years in Bologna, but it was intensified by his later contact, from the early 1360s, with a Petrarchan circle of scholars and poets in Florence whose members included Boccaccio. Like Petrarch, Salutati was interested in relating classical studies to moral and religious problems, and he was closely concerned with improving the textual tradition of ancient Latin authors. He was one of the first humanists to write about techniques of textual criticism, establishing a set of methods which he passed on to his younger followers. Salutati's own literary output was focused primarily upon Latin prose and was characterized by an intense interest in rhetoric and close obedience to the standards of Cicero, Seneca, and Quintilian. Unlike Petrarch, however, Salutati married and spent much of his life involved with the affairs of the Florentine state, and, as Chancellor of Florence between 1375 and 1406, he was charged with writing letters to foreign powers and delivering public orations to visiting dignitaries. It was through his public missives, especially during the Florentine wars, first with the Papacy (1375–78) and then with the Visconti of Milan (1389–1402), that he gained a reputation for classical style and learning within his own lifetime. In addition to his duties as chancellor, he also participated in a range of other activities which helped to make Florence the leading centre of humanism in Italy: he established lines of communication throughout Italy and beyond with his private correspondence; he built up one of the largest libraries of ancient texts in Europe; and he played a pivotal role in restoring the study of Greek to the Latin West by bringing to Florence, in 1397, the Byzantine scholar, Manuel Chrysoloras. Under Salutati's aegis, there developed a form of Florentine classicism that helped to confer intellectual prestige on the city and to make its humanist scholars the envy of the other main centres of power and culture in Italy. In the final decade of his life, Salutati was a key point of reference for all literary and scholastic figures, whether natives of the city or visitors to it. And several of his students were to become key figures in the next generation of the humanist movement in Italy, in particular Pier Paolo Vergerio of Capodistria, Antonio Loschi of Vicenza, and the Tuscans, Leonardo Bruni and Poggio Bracciolini.[4]

But Salutati did not cultivate Latin letters to the exclusion of Florentine vernacular culture. He was a strenuous defender of Dante, and despite his ambiguous relationship with the vernacular (see pp. 60–61), he wrote some vernacular verse and had close links with many of the Tuscan notaries and merchants who most strongly defended Florentine literary culture. Salutati did not write a commentary on Dante, but he did engage in exegesis upon lines of the *Comedy*, and he showed a particularly strong interest in translating sections of the poem into Latin. In almost all of his writings that deal with Dante, Salutati builds upon the precedent of Boccaccio, as well as other non-Florentine commentators on the *Comedy* such as Pietro Alighieri and Benvenuto da Imola, by viewing Dante through the lens of classicizing considerations. As Boccaccio had done, Salutati also appropriates Dante's ideas on a wide range of doctrinal subjects and shows a keen interest in using Dante's name to promote Florentine interests. To illustrate these facets of Salutati's relationship with Dante, let us examine four of his more important works: the various judgements expressed about Dante in Salutati's Latin epistolography; the *De laboribus Herculis*, a work of poetics that deals extensively with the interpretation of classical myths; the *De fato et fortuna*, a treatise on astrology, fate, fortune, and predestination; and the *De tyranno*, a work which takes its starting-point from Dante's treatment, in *Inferno* XXXIV, of the assassins of Julius Caesar, Brutus and Cassius.

(a) *'Iterum atque iterum de Dante rogo': Salutati's epistolography*

Throughout his Latin letters, Salutati lavishes fulsome praise on Dante the poet. He is 'our most divine Dante'; he is treated as an authority on topics such as embryology and nobility; and his learning in the *Comedy* receives some notable encomia.[5] Salutati's earliest judgement on Dante comes in a particular context as part of a eulogy to Petrarch, written following his death in August 1374. Salutati takes up Petrarch's own comments in *Familiares* XXI, 15, § 25 about the impossibility of excelling in more than one genre and affirms Petrarch's exception to this rule. In marking out Petrarch's pre-eminence as a vernacular poet, Salutati reverses Petrarch's own view that Dante holds the 'palm of vernacular eloquence': Dante is a divine and valiant man who is nonetheless surpassed by his younger compatriot.[6] This letter should not be taken as evidence of an early ambivalence towards Dante, for, in later judgements Salutati either refers to the two vernacular *auctores* as equals or, as is more often the case, he assigns primacy to Dante. The later assessments may well have been influenced by Benvenuto da Imola's own formulation of the Dante–Petrarch comparison in his important commentary on the *Comedy*, where Petrarch is praised as a great orator, but Dante is celebrated as the supreme poet. Salutati received a copy of Benvenuto's *Comentum* in 1383 and this work clearly helped to focus, catalyse, and to some extent shape Salutati's interest in Dante. As we will see, Salutati does not adhere slavishly to Benvenuto's commentary, but he makes use of it for specific arguments in his Latin epistolography and in other works. Benvenuto may also have guided Salutati's attempts to relate the *Comedy* to classical culture, since he, like Salutati in later letters, repeatedly contends that Dante is the equal of the ancients and at times even implies that he is their superior.[7]

A letter of June 1383 in which Salutati thanks Benvenuto for receipt of his Dante commentary is important for what it reveals about the Florentine chancellor's own efforts to develop the study of the *Comedy* through a form of commentary that articulates Dante's poem upon a classicizing framework and tangles it within a web of classical references. Despite praising Benvenuto's commentary, Salutati initially chides him for a lack of requisite Latinity in dealing with the 'dignity of the divine and human matters, such a series of noble stories, so many highly subtle allegorical senses, such unprecedented and such ordered doctrines'.[8] Following this general comment (which in part recalls 'the multitude of stories and the sublimity of the hidden senses' in the *accessus* to Boccaccio's *Esposizioni*), Salutati deals with the interpretation of *Inferno* 1, 70 – a line which, because of its erroneous suggestion that Virgil was born under the rule of Julius Caesar, had drawn a perplexed response from Boccaccio and seems to have provided something of a *banc d'essai* for later classicizing readers of the poem. Benvenuto had noted the historical inaccuracy, but he had refused to believe that Dante was ignorant of a fact familiar even to young boys, and hence he had argued that the line referred to Caesar not as an Emperor but as a private citizen.[9] Like Benvenuto, Salutati notes the apparent error and defends Dante from the many who, he says, condemn him in an unlearned way. His own solution is rather different from Benvenuto's insofar as it shows a greater concern to reconcile Dante's text with the current state of humanist knowledge regarding the ancient world. Having established Virgil's date of birth as 58 BC, Salutati notes that in this year Caesar exercised proconsular control over both Gaul and Transalpine Gaul in which Mantua was included. It is now a simple matter for him to conclude that the Mantuan Virgil was born under Caesar's consulate, albeit an external one.[10] By using an ingenious argument constructed out of a patchwork of ancient sources, Salutati demonstrates his own erudition, but also – and more importantly – he classicizes and updates Dante's reference. Other letters reveal similar techniques of reading Dante in order to rebuff either charges that he was ignorant of classical sources or claims that he was guilty of historical inaccuracies.[11]

It has often been noted that Salutati's interest in Dante becomes more pronounced in the mid-1390s and that his most important judgements on Dante are found in letters from this period. Ronald Witt has seen this heightened interest in Dante as a sign of Salutati's personal development towards religious matters, especially in the final decade of his life and following the death of his second wife.[12] But rather than personal and religious crisis, it is perhaps more relevant to stress how Salutati's attentiveness to Dante during this period arises at a time of growing humanist unease both with vernacular culture and with Dante. At the close of the fourteenth century some younger humanists and students of Salutati, including most notably Leonardo Bruni, Poggio Bracciolini, and Niccolò Niccoli, became increasingly critical towards the legacy of Boccaccio and Petrarch and openly rebellious to the cult of Dante. This group of humanists perceived Dante's use of the vernacular, his Latin style, and many of his teachings as remote from, and even discordant with, their own interests and values. By contrast, Salutati tends towards a synthesis that draws together features of Dante's vernacular poetry and the new concerns of Florentine humanism. Preoccupied with preventing a rupture between humanists and traditionalists, Salutati attempts to ensure a degree of continuity with Dante's heritage that is nonetheless proportionate to the preoccupations of the new age.[13] Salutati's conciliatory role may well reflect personal fears about fissures between Christianity and early Florentine humanism, but it is also conditioned by his awareness that to affirm Dante's excellence is to claim literary and cultural primacy for Florence.

Salutati's defence of Dante is characterized by a wholehearted endorsement of Dante's learning and inventive powers, even though he does at times share contemporary humanist reservations over Dante's use of the vernacular. Such ambivalence with regard to the *Comedy*'s linguistic cover is implicit in Salutati's interest in translating passages from the *Comedy* into Latin hexameters, first in a letter from the mid-1390s (translating *Inferno* II, 91–93),[14] and then more extensively in the *De fato et fortuna*. Salutati's reservations over Dante's use of the vernacular are made more explicit elsewhere. In a letter of 1 August 1395 which describes and evaluates a succession of literary periods from Cicero to the fourteenth century, Salutati exalts ancient writers over the moderns, but some exceptions are noted from his own century, first Albertino Mussato and Geri of Arezzo, and then Dante, Petrarch, and Boccaccio. Although the written style of the *moderni* is of a different order from that of the ancients, Dante is singled out as possessing 'that highest honour of vernacular eloquence to which no-one who flourished in our time nor anyone in ancient times is to be compared in terms of knowledge and genius'.[15] Such a judgement represents an intriguing synthesis of the views of both Petrarch and Boccaccio outlined in chapter 1 and probably owes much to Benvenuto's *Comentum*. Salutati implicitly recognizes that there is a distinction to be made between Dante's great erudition and his use of a lesser linguistic form, yet he celebrates Dante's excellence in a way that takes him beyond even the classics. Dante is also held up as a model of poetic perfection in a letter from 1401 that associates him with the leading poets of Latinity. It is here, however, that Salutati comes closest to Petrarch's position in *Familiares*, XXI, 15, and expresses some reservations about the fact that the *Comedy* had been written in the vernacular. If Dante, he comments, had written in Latin with the elegance which he demonstrated in his mother tongue, he would have surpassed all the ancient poets.[16] The hypothetical construction is revealing. In spite of all his enthusiasm for the *Comedy*, and notwithstanding his appreciation of the vernacular within certain limits, Salutati seems never to have fully reconciled his devotion to Dante with a humanist's preference for Latin eloquence.[17] Salutati shares Boccaccio's enthusiasm for the poem and he develops further analogies between it and classical culture, but he also asserts that Dante chose an inferior linguistic medium – a view which, as we saw in the previous chapter, had been so skilfully manipulated by Petrarch and anxiously negotiated by Boccaccio.

The most important letter of all, and the one that gives the most extensive and detailed judgement on Dante, is that to Niccolò da Tuderano which dates from October 1399. Salutati is aware that Niccolò has recently acquired books from the library of Menghino Mezzani, a poet and close acquaintance of Dante during his years in Ravenna, and seemingly the first to coin the term *dantista*.[18] And it is for this reason that Salutati petitions Tuderano in the hope of obtaining a codex of the *Comedy*:

> I am anxious to have an uncorrupted copy of our Dante's most divine work ['correctum opus divinissimum Dantis nostri']; believe me no poem so far is loftier in style or more elegant in invention or of greater weight when you consider the subject, the diction or the treatment. Where is there more fully and clearly a reasoned differentiation of the three-fold style? Where do you find so many great things joined more finely and more beautifully? Where do you find more important matters expressed in more fitting words? In brief, Niccolò, we can find nothing more embellished, nothing more polished, and nothing more profound in knowledge than those three *cantiche*. He has comprehended fully and simultaneously things that are separate and single in others. There moral, philosophical, and theological precepts shine

in wonderful fashion; there rhetorical figures of thought and language are evident in such splendour that it would be difficult to find such great elegance elsewhere, even in the most supreme authors. There the laws and habits and languages of all ages and peoples, and a wonderful compendium of historical matters, blaze like stars in the firmament with so great a majesty that no-one as yet has been able to surpass or equal him in that style.[19]

The letter is, of course, important for the general judgements expressed about the *Comedy*. For Salutati, the poem is a most divine work ('opus divinissimum'), a designation employed by Boccaccio and some earlier commentators on the poem.[20] Moreover, like almost all the Trecento commentators, Salutati considers it to contain morality, philosophy, theology, and history. Once again, a series of close correspondences with Benvenuto's *Comentum* suggests that his commentary played some part in shaping both Salutati's general judgements and specific categories.[21] However, it is also the case that Salutati pays greater attention to humanist ideals of classical form and expression. He is in fact quite clearly selective in underlining the *Comedy*'s harmony and elegance (rather than the roughness to be detected by some later humanist writers) in line with the best Ciceronian standards and the tradition of *ornate dicere*. In this respect at least, he anticipates Leonardo Bruni's later 'judgements' on Dante's poetry in Book II of the *Dialogi ad Petrum Histrum* (see below section 4).

   What is not found in Benvenuto, and is perhaps more significant still about this letter, is Salutati's anxious concern to obtain a better exemplar of the poem as the first step towards its textual emendation. This provides another good example of how Salutati applies incipient humanist methods to Dante; for, as Witt has shown, it was Salutati's practice to collate classical texts in order to emend them, and, in so doing, to identify and follow the oldest and best manuscripts of a particular text.[22] The letter goes on to discuss the corrupt textual tradition of the poem, which is attributed to the inexpertise of the scribes responsible for copying it. Petrarch had made similar comments regarding the work of Latin *auctores* in his letters, but this is the first time that, with reference to the *Comedy*, scribal inadequacy had been noted, and an attempt made to remedy the situation.[23] Salutati's close attention to textual accuracy in matters pertaining to Dante even extends as far as the spelling of his family name: in his annotations to the first redaction of Filippo Villani's *De origine civitatis Florentie et eiusdem famosis civibus*, he protests against any confusion with 'Aldigherius' and spells the family name 'Alagherie'.[24]

In addition to his humanistic approach to the *Comedy* at the level of exegesis, translation, and textual criticism, Salutati also promotes Dante in his letters as a patriotic emblem and a motif of civic pride. Such preoccupations are implicit in several letters but they are addressed most openly in a late letter (26 March 1406) to his student and fellow humanist, Poggio Bracciolini. Salutati writes to defend Petrarch's reputation from the acerbic and derogatory comments made by Bracciolini,[25] yet in so doing he also mentions Dante whom he places higher than Petrarch. What is most notable, though, is his concern that Florentines should not denigrate a primary locus of Florentine fame: 'believe me, after Dante and his harmonious vernacular, our excellent city has no-one more illustrious and eloquent than Petrarch, so that neither you nor anyone else, who are Florentine, should lightly take away from the reputation of our city'.[26] Within Salutati's writings, perhaps the most important work that uses Dante's reputation as part of a defence of the city is the *Invectiva in Antonium Luschum Vicentinum*. The invective, completed by 1403, but begun earlier, responds to a pamphlet by Antonio Loschi, humanist and chancery employee of the Duke of Milan, written at the opening of renewed hostilities between Florence and Milan in the spring of 1397. Loschi had presented Florence as the oppressor of Italy and a most cruel tyranny. In his own *Invectiva*, Salutati states that, although he omits the names of Florentine soldiers and statesmen, he cannot pass over in silence those of Dante, Petrarch, and Boccaccio.[27] As we will see later in this chapter, Salutati's use of Dante in order to promote Florence is a feature common to many defenders of the poet in Tuscan vernacular culture and to some fellow humanists.

(b) Dante and the De laboribus Herculis

The *De laboribus Herculis* exists in two redactions both of which are incomplete and date respectively from the early 1380s and from the mid-1390s until Salutati's death. The work provides a lengthy allegorical treatment of the vicissitudes of Hercules' life, from conception and birth through to his eventual apotheosis on Mount Oeta, and its ostensible aim is to resolve the contrast between Seneca's presentation of Hercules both as the murderer of his wife and children and as a god in his tragedies, *Hercules furens* and *Hercules oeteus*. By the use of allegorical interpretation and the etymological analysis of names, Salutati presents Hercules as overcoming the assaults of vice by the force of his own will, and he suggests that the Senecan tragedies, like the work of other classical poets, have inner recesses of meaning that are in close contact with Christian verities. The second draft is the more ambitious and important work, and it adds an introductory book, which offers general considerations regarding the origin, nature, and purpose of poetry.[28] In this book, as in several of his letters, Salutati defends classical poetry from its scholastic and ecclesiastical detractors, using many of the familiar *topoi* that had been rehearsed by Boccaccio, Petrarch, and other earlier writers.[29] In his own way, Dante had opened up the possibility for viewing some classical texts as containing Christian truth and had considered pagan myths to be in accordance with Christian revelation. But the key passages in which he develops these ideas (*Purgatorio* XXII, 67–72; XXVIII, 139–44) do not seem to have influenced Salutati in his defence of poetry.

Prima facie, then, Dante appears to have only a marginal role in this influential treatise; he is mentioned directly only once, as an authority on teachings related to the generation of human beings.[30] Dante is nonetheless an important, but submerged, influence on the discussion of poetry provided in the first book, where Salutati's definition of its characteristics rests upon contemporary interpretations of the *Comedy*'s own poetics. Salutati repeatedly aligns poetry with the central objective of epideictic rhetoric in such a way that poetic discourse is defined as pertaining to criticism or praise; and he also notes on several occasions how its defining characteristics are the use of fictions, metric melody, and figurative expressions.[31] Poetry, Salutati continues, brings together and transcends all the liberal arts as well as philosophy and theology; it reflects earthly and celestial harmony, and it is intrinsically related to arithmetic. The poet requires doctrine, art, and innate capacity; and his poetry, if he is to attain true eloquence, requires propriety, variety, and sweetness. Finally, one of the chief characteristics of poetry is its allegorical quality.[32]

There are, of course, many possible antecedents that help to under-gird Salutati's discussion here, including most notably Cicero's *Pro Archia*, Bernard Silvestris' allegorical commentary on the *Aeneid*, and Boccaccio's *Genealogie*. Moreover, the link between poetry and epide-ictic rhetoric, as well as the emphasis upon figurative expression and metre, derive from Aristotle's recently discovered *Poetics*.[33] But it is dif-ficult not to be reminded of Salutati's presentation of the *Comedy* as a work of vast learning and elegant artistry in the letter to Tuderano. And the connections between Dante and the theoretical formulations in Book I of the *De laboribus* are, in fact, more specific still and reveal once again how Salutati assimilates and adapts critical judgements from Benvenuto's commentary on Dante. In the preface to Benvenuto's *Co-mentum*, there are strong parallels for all of Salutati's arguments, from his quotation of the praise and blame theme in Aristotle's *Poetics* to the importance of metric harmony, figurative language, and allegorical techniques.[34]

(c) De fato et fortuna

Salutati's treatise on astrology, written *c.* 1395, has already been men-tioned in the context of his attempts to translate sections of the *Comedy* into Latin,[35] but it is worth paying further attention to it for two reasons: the role of Benvenuto's commentary in transmitting Dante to him; and Salutati's use of Dante as a doctrinal source. The *De fato* is ostensibly written in order to probe the causes of bloody warfare destroying the peace of Perugia. Although Salutati is interested in the political and social repercussions of astrological belief, he also uses the treatise to offer a detailed treatment of fate, fortune, and chance by collating dif-fering arguments on the subject. In so doing, he surveys a variety of theological and philosophical themes, and draws upon a wide range of scientific, theological, and literary authorities. Witt has perhaps over-stated the case in claiming that Dante is Salutati's principal source, but it is nonetheless true that he devotes quite a substantial section of the tractate on fortune to Dante and that his ultimate position on this topic, that it is an agent of God's providential design which does not impact upon human free will, is Dantean.[36] As far as Benvenuto's mediation is concerned, Concetta Bianca, the editor of the critical edition of the *De fato et fortuna*, has shown precise points of contact with his *Comentum*, including not only Salutati's quotations of *auctoritates*, but also a large segment of the fourth tractate which is given over to defending Dante from Cecco d'Ascoli's attack upon him in the 1320s.[37] At a time when the intellectual and literary climate is dominated by Latin, it is notable that Salutati chooses to endow a vernacular poet such as Dante with the authoritative status usually only reserved for ancient writers. Some now familiar themes are re-elaborated, including Dante's vernacular excellence, the divine quality of his poem, and the patriotic associations evoked by his name:

> Our most divine compatriot Dante Alagheri, although he was stupidly and rashly criticized in some matters, dealt with fortune in a most decorous way in the first *cantica* of his most sacred and celestial poem [. . .] Our Dante wrote this about fortune in the vernacular hendecasyllables in which he composed his divine poem, making use of that elegant Florentine idiom which alone, better than all the languages of the world, is fitted to poetic rhythms through its own elegance and sweetness. I translated his hendecasyllables into Latin hexameters, but in a humble style and one very distant from the majesty of Dante's language; it is a hasty translation, albeit a faithful one. And from its roughness let no-one claim to have an idea of the refined style, the sweetness, and the incomparable richness of such a great poet.[38]

(d) De tyranno

Even more than the *De fato*, the *De tyranno* (*c.* 1400) takes Dante as its starting-point and argumentative core, and it is best located within a climate of growing humanist dissatisfaction with Dante at the turn of the century. The *De tyranno* is quite clearly a work of polemic with all the distortions and exaggerations that befit such writings, but it nonetheless illustrates how closely connected the realms of literary culture and politics were for Salutati and his contemporaries.[39] Salutati defends four theses but it is the fourth, that Dante unjustly condemned Brutus and Cassius as traitors for assassinating Julius Caesar, which is the most important. Dante's own mature political thought developed away from the preoccupations of Florentine municipal politics and had at its centre an overriding conviction in the divinely ordained nature of the Roman Empire. As such, its various manifestations in the *Comedy* and elsewhere were not easily reconciled with the intense local patriotism and strong Republican sentiments of the Florentine state. Such sentiments had been a part of the communal heritage of Dante's Florence, but in the closing decades of the fourteenth century they acquired a new level of intensity as the ties loosened between the city and the institutions of Empire and Papacy. The Florentine Republic now viewed Brutus and Cassius as heroic figures (Salutati is no exception and he repeatedly praises Brutus as an agent of Roman freedom in his letters).[40] By contrast, Caesar's position of personal power in the Roman Republic was interpreted as having precipitated the final phase of the civil wars which marked the end of the relative political freedom of the Romans and the beginning of a more autocratic imperial administration (Salutati also condemns Caesar in other contexts in his later letters). Yet for Dante, Caesar is not only one of the virtuous pagans in Limbo, but more significantly he is held up as an instrument of divine providence and the emperor *par excellence*. And, in *Inferno* xxxiv, 55–67, Dante condemns Brutus and Cassius as the lowest form of traitors for their assassination of Caesar, placing them – in a parodically unholy Trinity – on either side of Judas Iscariot and having all three traitors eternally mangled by Lucifer's three mouths.[41]

How does Salutati deal with this passage in the light of the revitalized Republicanism and vehement anti-Caesarism of his contemporary Florentine context? First, he establishes that Caesar is a legitimate monarch in part iii of the *De tyranno*, and then emphasizes his magnanimity in part iv, as well as his efforts to bring peace and justice to the state. Second, he defends monarchy as the ideal form of government by arguing, as Dante had done in *Monarchia*, that human affairs better replicate the divine order when there is a single ruler. Salutati thus views Caesar as a legitimate ruler and the saviour both of the Roman state and of justice. It follows that Dante is right to condemn the two conspirators, since they assassinated a just prince, acted against the will of God who had established a single monarch, and were responsible for the ensuing civil wars. Third, he seals his argument with an exquisitely humanistic touch, quoting Virgil's condemnation, in the *Aeneid*

(VI, 612–13), of those who do not fear to betray their lord, and he sup-poses that Dante drew inspiration from here:

> It is clear that Caesar was most wickedly killed. For, as we have most clearly proven, he was not a tyrant by title insofar as he was freely chosen as prince by his homeland, and he was not proud insofar as he ruled with clemency and humanity. Thus, with regard to the spiritual life, our Dante – who was aware that murder (which is the gravest of all sins) is a violation of faith – assigned Caesar's assassins to the lowest reaches of Hell, frozen in ice, in the area where tricephalous Lucifer is located at the centre of the universe [. . .] And who can criticize Dante for thrusting into the depths of hell and condemning to extreme punishment those men who sinned so grievously in their treacherous murder of Caesar, father of his country, when he was administering with such clemency the government, which, in a moment of desperate crisis, the Senate and the people of Rome had conferred upon him so as to put an end to the evils of civil war? In short, the authority of Virgil is more than sufficient for he [sc. Dante] proposes him as a leader and master [*Inf.* 1, 85]. And among those whom Virgil places lowest are those 'who followed the standard of treason and feared not to break allegiance with their lords' [. . .] And so we may conclude that, in condemning Brutus and Cassius in the way he did, our Dante made no mistake in this matter either theologically or morally, and still less poetically – rather, not only did he make no mistake but without question he rendered a just judgement.[42]

Salutati's attempt to justify Dante's outmoded condemnation rests first and foremost upon the need to defend the poet from attack. Indeed we might well legitimately question how far the treatise is an accurate reflection of Salutati's mature thought on Caesar and the Empire, and ask instead whether he is not arguing in a calculated way for a specific cause. In his letters, Salutati was after all the key figure in transposing Florentine political consciousness on to the template of civic patrio-tism associated with ancient Republican Rome; and, as we have already noted, he also wrote epistles that praise Brutus and condemn Caesar. What is more, in his *Invectiva in Antonium Luschum*, a work that post-dates the *De tyranno* but was first drafted during the same period as it, he used his extensive knowledge of classical sources in order to overturn the traditional view – endorsed by Dante – that Florence was founded by Julius Caesar at the time of the Catilinarian rebellion. The Caesarean foundation of Florence was difficult to reconcile with a renewed emphasis upon the city's Republican traditions; and, on the basis of his studies of Sallust and Cicero's second oration, Salutati argued instead that Florence was founded by soldiers of the veteran Sulla in Republican Rome of the first century BC before the beginning of the Empire. It may well be, therefore, that Salutati's oscillations between the pro-republican tone of some letters and the *Invectiva*, on the one hand, and the imperialism of the *De tyranno*, on the other, stem from the need to argue in different contexts and to different audiences. Such tergiversations were not, however, shared by Salutati's younger humanist followers, who reserved the concept of *libertas* almost exclusively for republican forms of government and retained no residual admiration for the Empire. As we will see in section 4, one of these younger contemporaries, who notably developed the theory of the Republican origins of Florence, was to treat the question of Dante's anti-Caesarism in a very different light.

2 Filippo Villani

A friend and correspondent of Salutati, Filippo Villani (1325–*c.* 1405), was a member of the family of Florentine chroniclers, and continued the *Cronica* of his father, Matteo. Within Dante studies today, he is perhaps best known as the first commentator to refer to the Cangrande Epistle as a Dantean work and to note that Dante's name is a syncopated form of Durante.[43] But within his own lifetime he showed an interest in Dante as biographer, textual critic, and commentator of the *Comedy*. Villani was also employed as a public expositor of Dante at the Florentine *Studio* (1391–1405), an appointment which, like Boccaccio's, was officially linked to the moral teaching of the city's populace.[44] The period spent at the *Studio* and the close contacts Villani cultivated with several of its leading figures, as well as with the city's other intellectual and literary circles, inform his unfinished commentary on the *Comedy* which only extends as far as the first canto of the *Inferno*.[45] Like Salutati, Villani also paid attention to the textual tradition of the *Comedy*, although unlike the chancellor, his attempts to emend the poem survive in one extant manuscript (now known as Laurenziano S. Croce, XXVI, sin 1) which is considered to be an important work of textual reconstruction.[46] Villani's efforts in this regard continue in his

Dante commentary, where he repeatedly discusses variant readings, and this provides further evidence of how, at the close of the Trecento in Florence, evolving techniques of textual philology were being applied to the *Comedy*. After Salutati and Villani, Florence will have to wait until a revitalized cult of Dante, beginning in the 1460s, for further refinements in the textual recovery and transmission of Dante's texts (see chapter 4, section 1).

Our main concern here rests with the two other facets of Villani's engagement with Dante where he develops several strands of the late fourteenth- and early fifteenth-century effort to accommodate Dante to humanist standards and values. In a different way from Salutati, Villani emphasizes Dante's *fiorentinità*, attempts to reconcile his vernacular heritage with the rise of ancient studies, and defends the poet from humanist censure. We shall start with the biography of Dante contained in his *De origine* which Villani himself deemed to be an essential prerequisite to the exegesis of his poem.

(a) De origine civitatis Florentie et eius famosis civibus

The *De origine* is extant in two redactions (1381–88 and 1395–97), both of which provide an evocative portrayal of Florence in two parts. The first part narrates legends concerning the foundation of Florence, echoing many of the familiar *topoi* on the city's links with ancient Rome through its foundation by Caesar and refoundation by Charlemagne that formed an established part of the city's mythology as early as 1300 and are found in Boccaccio's *Esposizioni*.[47] Having established the Roman origins of Florence in Book I, Villani exemplifies how such an august inception is related to the virtue of Florentine citizens. The second book, which is of most interest here, provides a patriotically charged catalogue of distinguished Florentines, by giving a series of biographical elogia of poets, theologians, jurists, physicians, orators, astrologers, musicians, painters, and even buffoons. It was this part of the book that helped to establish a genre that was to be widely imitated throughout the fifteenth century in Florence. Book II contains, moreover, one of the most important documents of the growing cultivation of the literary traditions of the city, and probably the most direct application of the language and imagery of cultural rebirth to Dante. In its bare details, Villani's biography of Dante owes much to Boccaccio's *Trattatello* and it adapts the now traditional *topoi* regarding Dante's excellent style, profound learning, and high moral value. But Villani's life of Dante reveals its originality, and draws its deeper significance, from what amounts to a programmatic attempt to present the native Florentine literary tradition, with Dante at its head, as the direct inheritor of ancient traditions.

For Villani, Florence's poets inherit the achievements of ancient Rome in a genealogical continuity which is made possible by transforming the late Roman poet Claudian (d. 408) into the last Florentine poet of antiquity.[48] Dante plays a pivotal role in the rebirth of ancient letters, by bringing back to the light the cult of poetry after it had fallen into an abyss of darkness:

> After Claudian, who was almost the last poet that ancient times pro-
> duced, the greed and weak-mindedness of the Emperors resulted in
> the decline of poetry; and, because the catholic faith started to deni-
> grate the figments of poets as a most pernicious and vain thing, poetry
> was not an art held in esteem. With poetry lying without any cult or
> elegance, a great man, Dante Allagherii, almost as if tearing it out of
> an abyss of darkness, returned it to the light, and by his hand brought
> it to its feet again. He harmonized the fictions of the poets pertaining
> to natural and moral philosophy with Christian letters, so that he
> showed that the ancient poets, as though inspired by the Holy Spirit,
> prophesized certain mysteries of our faith.[49]

In their commentaries, Guido da Pisa and Boccaccio had used similar language with reference to Dante, but Villani formulates more clearly the notion that Dante presides over a new cultural dawn, and he gives a stronger sense of the dark centuries which preceded it. Rather than being relegated to this earlier period, Dante becomes the motive force behind the new cultural initiatives in contemporary Florence. Dante is, in short, the *fons et origo* of cultural and literary renewal in the city; and Villani's attempt to fit Dante to the values of humanist culture shows how he views Dante's excellence to be intertwined with the primacy of Florence.[50]

The biographical details that follow gain force from, and add tex-
ture to, this opening comment. Villani now describes Dante's Roman origins (significantly confirmed by his own family's links with Dante), his imitation of Virgil's poetry, his general love for classical poetry, and

his Christianizing reading of the classics.[51] If we are to discriminate adequately between Villani's life and Boccaccio's earlier version, we must also consider Villani's discussion of Dante's political activism. Boccaccio had emphasized the distractions placed in the way of study by Dante's civic duties; but Villani does not suggest that there is anything remiss about Dante being a 'dutiful citizen' ('offitiosus civis') who 'strove with all his being for the glory and exaltation of the homeland', and who is preoccupied with reforming the republic even in exile.[52]

Not surprisingly, this presentation of Dante was well attuned to the sympathies of a late fourteenth- and fifteenth-century Florentine public and the *De origine* circulated widely in the city and was translated into the vernacular in the 1470s. Villani sets an important precedent both for his contemporaries and for later Florentine writers by affirming that Florence's immediate cultural past is the precursor to modern humanist culture, and by promoting the idea that Dante had inaugurated the city's return to the ideals of classical antiquity.[53] Villani's life also affects the selection of Dante as a figure in the visual arts. The four principal Florentine poets – Dante, Petrarch, Boccaccio, and Zanobi da Strada – whom Villani mentions are the very ones named in the 1396 provision for statues to be erected in the Florentine Cathedral that we mentioned in the Introduction. And the *De origine* also guides the choice of poets, including Dante, found in a series of *viri illustres* frescoed in a minor hall of the Palazzo della Signoria with accompanying epigrams composed by Salutati.[54]

(b) Expositio seu Comentum super Comedia Dantis Allegherii

According to Villani's own account, after publishing a commentary (now lost) to canto xxx of *Purgatorio*, and at the request of his audience, he began the *Expositio seu Comentum super Comedia Dantis Allegherii* (*c.* 1400). This commentary comprises a lengthy preface and an exegetical commentary on the first canto of the *Inferno*. The *prefatio* includes many features associated with the *accessus*, and, like the commentary proper, it strongly foregrounds allegorical modes of reading. Indeed Villani has left many later readers of the work exasperated by the relentlessness with which he applies the exegetical categories of the Cangrande Epistle to the *Comedy* in order to provide a sustained allegoresis of the canto (and many other sections of the poem). The text of the commentary can now be consulted in Saverio Bellomo's critical edition which has valuable notes and an introduction that offers a useful account of the *Expositio*'s relationship to its context. In particular, Bellomo shows that the commentary presupposes an educated public (it is written in Latin and largely without literal exposition), and argues that its central theme is the defence of classical literature, continuing the polemic with ecclesiastical authorities that so animated Florentine intellectual life in the decades around 1400.[55]

Like many other commentary texts, however, the *Expositio* is as much a blend of tradition as it is a purveyor of innovation. It draws repeatedly on Boccaccio's biography and commentary on Dante, and makes use of other commentators on Dante, on Virgil, and on the Bible.[56] It repeats the familiar themes that we noted earlier in Salutati and which make Dante's poem a divine work, a fount of moral teachings, and a *summa* of all things human and divine. Like earlier Dante commentators, including Boccaccio, Villani uses the technique of *divisio textus*, and he offers glosses that contain notes on points of grammar, rhetoric, and language.[57] Like Benvenuto, he directs a number of broadsides against the more extreme currents of Aristotelian science that had developed at Padua and Bologna and whose representatives, known as Averroists, had been the target of some celebrated Petrarchan invectives.[58] Like Pietro Alighieri, Benvenuto, and Francesco da Buti, he makes use of the distinction between a Hell that is 'essential' (that is, the actual realm of the Christian afterlife) and a 'moral' one which betokens the sinful state of human beings in this life.

In spite of these and other such borrowings, Villani often attempts to emulate Dante's Trecento commentators. Throughout the *Expositio* he indirectly counters views that can be identified with a given commentator – and this tendency is particularly marked in the *cruces* from *Inferno* I, where Villani takes great delight in providing new solutions to such enigmas as the 'passo' of line 26 and "'l piè fermo' of line 30. Emulative strategies are also apparent when he makes unusual or more extensive applications of suggestions and exegetical devices found in earlier Dante commentators. He picks up, for example, comments made earlier by Pietro and Boccaccio regarding the analogies between Dante's poem and the epics of Homer and Virgil, and develops these into a fundamental imitative principle. According to Villani, Homer and Virgil provide the allegorical model for Dante's conception of the entire poem, and all three poems are taken to represent the journey of man in this life towards happiness.[59] The *Expositio* also goes beyond earlier commentaries in the level of attention it pays to variant readings, although the preference for a given *lectio* is frequently motivated by allegorizing interests.[60]

Where Villani departs most significantly from earlier commentators, and especially from Boccaccio's *Esposizioni*, is in his lack of interest for the literal sense of the *Comedy*. In his glosses, Villani delights in allegorization to such an extent that on occasion he distorts the syntax and grammar of Dante's text. Of course, almost all the Trecento commentators use allegory, but Villani, armed with the exegetical canons of the Cangrande Epistle, is more assertive than any of his predecessors (or for that matter than commentators on Virgil for whose *Aeneid* he also gives anagogical as well as moral readings). In fact, Pietro, Boccaccio, Benvenuto, Buti, and the Anonimo Fiorentino all quote (as Dante had done in *Monarchia*, III, iv, 6–11) a passage from Augustine on the dangers of searching for allegorical senses in every part of a composition. By contrast, Villani criticizes commentators who do not go beyond the literal sense and readers who only follow the harmony of his verse (for Salutati, as we have seen, this is an important feature of Dante's poem).[61] And he is quite explicit in noting that whenever Dante uses a time-reference or a periphrasis such passages are to be interpreted as concealing a mystical sense.[62]

A good example of Villani's disinterest in the literal sense of the poem is his treatment of *Inferno* I, 70. Villani reports Salutati's solution, but although he shares Salutati's general concern to defend classical letters, his own approach is to offer not a classicizing response, but a de-historicized reading which presents Caesar as an allegory of the devil:

> Saint Gregory in his *Moralia* says that when the literal meaning cannot be upheld then one is to make use of the allegorical sense. This [line 70] cannot be upheld by the letter, as you see, although someone [i.e. Salutati] maintained that, at the same time as the aforementioned consuls held the senate, Julius Caesar was made senator and consul of both Gauls, and that therefore he [sc. Virgil] was born under Caesar. But wishing to expound the allegorical sense, we say that Caesar

subjugated the world to himself by the power of war; hence, the violent empire of Caesar stands for the empire of the duplicitous devil.[63]

It is not necessary to go into the precise details of each allegorical interpretation: this example illustrates how such an approach leads to distortions both of the *Comedy*'s textual surface and a total disregard for Dante's views on the providential role of the Empire. In this way, Villani provides an interesting and extreme example of one reader's capacity to free himself from any determinacy imposed by the text, and to fashion new meanings for Dante's poem.

Despite such emphases, in the *prefatio* Villani does nonetheless pay some attention to the issue of Dante's relationship to Florence and his choice of the vernacular. Villani shows less interest in Dante's civic qualities than in the *De origine*, but there are still some revealing moments such as his excision of the words 'florentinus natione non moribus' ('a Florentine by birth not custom') from the title of the Cangrande Epistle (*pref.*, § 55). A further example of Villani's municipal patriotism is found at the close of the preface when he discusses Dante's decision to write the *Comedy* in the vernacular. At first, Villani follows Boccaccio in noting that Dante had originally started his poem in Latin but that he changed to the vernacular after having reflected upon the decline of liberal studies and the ignorance of rulers. Villani's closing observation, however, has no precedent in Boccaccio. Here, he purports to draw on the testimony of a contemporary and friend of Dante, his own grandfather, Giovanni Villani, in order to show that the poet was acutely conscious of the gulf between his own Latin style and the standards of ancient poetry:

> I heard from my grandfather, Giovanni Villani, who was a friend and companion of Dante, that the poet sometimes said that, having placed his own verse next to that of Virgil, Statius, Horace, Ovid and Lucan, it seemed to him to have put rough cloth together with purpura. And since he understood himself to be more capable in vernacular verse, he fitted his genius to this. He would say, moreover, that he did this so as to ennoble his idiom and to develop it further; and he added that he did it in such a way as to show that vernacular eloquence was able to deal with the most difficult intellectual matters ['ut ostenderet etiam elocutione vulgari ardua queque scientiarum posse tractari'].[64]

The closing consideration, which Dante himself never raised, reflects the viewpoint of a late fourteenth-century reader whose judgements of literary value are determined by the rise of Latin literature. We have already seen that similar value judgements are operative in Boccaccio, but there is no precedent for Villani's suggestions that Dante believed himself to be more capable in vernacular verse and that he was intent on making the vernacular able to deal with the most arduous intellectual matters.

3 Dante and Florentine vernacular culture

We now turn to the writings of two figures who were promoters of Dante and the Florentine vernacular tradition and who responded in rather different ways to the challenges made to Dante following the emergence of a humanist school in Florence.

The first, Giovanni Gherardi da Prato (1367–1442?), a notary and poet, lectured publicly on Dante in Florence and imitated him widely in his own works of poetry and prose. On 29 May 1417 he was nominated as public lecturer on both the *Comedy* and Dante's moral *canzoni* by reformers of the Florentine *Studio*, a post which he held until 1425. By 1426, however, he had been passed over as reader of Dante and withdrew to Prato where he continued to work on his best-known composition, *Il Paradiso degli Alberti*, a series of five vernacular prose dialogues interspersed with *novelle*, which are set retrospectively in 1389 at the villa of the poet-merchant, Antonio degli Alberti. Apart from the *Paradiso*, Giovanni also left a substantial body of vernacular writing that includes a number of works that draw closely on Dantean themes and language, as well as on the vernacular output of Boccaccio and Petrarch.[65] Here we are especially concerned with his use of Dante in the *Paradiso*, since it provides evidence of yet another gradation in the positioning of Dante between vernacular and classicizing interests that we have examined in Salutati and Villani. Giovanni's intention to exalt and ennoble the vernacular is clear from the very beginning of Book 1, where he uses and perhaps coins the term the 'three Florentine crowns' ('tre corone fiorentine')[66] with reference to Dante, Petrarch, and Boccaccio. Within this perspective, it is also revealing that the humanists, especially Salutati and Luigi Marsili, who are admitted to the debates at Alberti's villa have vernacular interests. The form of the work itself attests to such a merging of interests, since it creates a new narrative genre from a range of precedents, and seems to be devoted principally to demonstrating the versatility of the vernacular to humanists.[67] In the *Paradiso*, especially the incomplete fifth book, Giovanni applies the new critical methods of humanists to Florentine history, by asserting the Roman origins of the city on the basis of evidence of supposed Roman ruins and monuments, and using arguments derived from the humanist historiography of Salutati and Bruni.[68]

Dante's significance within the work lies not only in the programmatic association between the 'tre corone' and the composition of the book, but also in his use both as a doctrinal source and as a prominent intertext, especially in Book I.[69] In this book, 'nostro divino Dante' ('our divine Dante') is also held up as a supreme authority on love in line with passages from *Purgatorio* XVIII, 19–21 and 52–60.[70] What is more, the transformations described in the central *novella* of Book II evoke Dantean language, both from the *Rime petrose* and the *Inferno*.[71] The remaining three books continue to blend *novelle* with doctrinal discussions on a miscellany of topics. Giovanni's discussion of human generation in Book IV makes explicit use of Dantean teachings, drawing on a doctrinal sequence from *Purgatorio* XXV that was much admired by Tuscan writers, including Salutati and Villani.[72] The extracts selected from Dante reveal Giovanni's keen interest in making use of Dante as the basis for a vernacular prose able to deal with scientific and philosophical subjects. This particular point is made explicit by one of the non-Florentine protagonists, the Paduan Marsilio da Santa Sofia, a teacher of medicine at the *Studio*:

> l'edioma fiorentino è sì rilimato e copioso che ogni astratta e profonda matera si puote chiarissimamente con esso dire, ragionarne e disputarne. E bene omai voglio credere quello che io sento del vostro Dante, poeta teolago, che tante alte sentenza d'ogni disciplina elli ponghi sotto il velame della sua leggiadrissima invenzione.[73]

> the Florentine idiom is so polished and abundant that one can use it to speak, reason, and dispute about every abstract and profound subject. And now I truly believe what I have heard said about your Dante, the poet-theologian, who places so many high thoughts from all disciplines under the veil of his most graceful invention.

In this way, the *Paradiso* seems to mark an attempt, at least in its doctrinal sections, to use Dante's example in order to deal with what Villani, in his *Expositio*, had referred to as the difficult matters of human knowledge, the 'ardua [. . .] scientiarium'.

Our second vernacular defender of Dante is Cino Rinuccini (1350–1417), a wealthy Florentine merchant and founder of an important school of rhetoric, who was the author of a collection of vernacular verse, a defence of Republican Florence, and an invective written in defence of Dante, Petrarch, and Boccaccio.[74] His defence of Florence, the *Risponsiva*, is a work of political polemic in which, like Salutati, he replies to Loschi's own invective of 1397.[75] Rinuccini illustrates the greatness of Florentine *virtù*, by giving a number of biographical sketches of 'nostri uomini illustri' ('our illustrious men') arranged by professions. Dante is celebrated as a supreme poet and theologian in an encomium that makes him superior to Greek and Latin poets for his powers of *inventio* and more worthy than Peter Lombard, the medieval theologian *par excellence*, for his subtlety in matters of theology:

> Dalla divina filosofia alla morale discendendo, m'occorre l'onore dei poeti, il teolago Dante degli Alighieri, il quale tutti i poeti, così greci come latini <avanza>, e di amirabile invenzione e di sottiglieze d'ingegno i nodi teologichi dissolvendo, Piero delle Sentenzie avanzò, tutte le cose infernali, purgatorie e celesti cercando.

> Moving from divine to moral philosophy, I speak of the honour of poets, the theologian Dante Alighieri, who, as he searches through all things infernal, purgatorial, and heavenly, surpasses all Greek and Latin poets in his remarkable invention and goes beyond Peter of the Sentences in untying the knots of theology with the subtlety of his intelligence.[76]

For our purposes, however, the most important text of all is that of the *Invettiva* (*c.* 1400) which is only now extant in a vernacular translation from the Latin original. The vernacular text addresses directly the humanist criticism of Dante that, as I have argued, plays an important part in Salutati's own defences in the 1390s. The *Invettiva* opens with its author fleeing Italy on a voyage throughout the known world in order to escape a 'brigata di garulli' ('group of garrulous men') whose maniacal obsession with antiquity takes the form of vain disputations upon the minutiae of classical culture (such as diphthongs and orthography) to the neglect of real knowledge. Within a vigorous, strongly caricatured attack on the values of avant-garde humanist culture, there is a lengthy excursus on Dante which follows an account of the criticisms that the 'brigata' level against Boccaccio and Petrarch, and against the immoral and mendacious qualities of poetry. The passage is worth reading in full:

> Poi, per mostrarsi littcratissimi al vulgo, dicono che lo egregio e onore de' poeti Dante Alighieri essere suto poeta da calzolai. Non dicono che 'l parlar poetico è quello che sopra agli altri come aquila vola [*Inf.* IV, 96], cantando con maravigliosa arte e fatti groliosi dell'ignominiosi uomini e pognendo per nostro ben vivere innanzi agli occhi tutte le storie, mescolando alcuna volta ne' loro poemi sottile filosofia naturale, alcuna volta la dilettevole astronomia, alcuna volta l'ottima filosofia morale, alcuna volta e santi comandamenti delle leggi, alcuna volta la vera e santa teologia. Lo illustre ed esimio poeta Dante, il quale, sia detto con pace de' poemi greci e latini, niuna invenzione fu più bella, più utile e più sottile che la sua, trattando tutte le storie, così moderne come antiche, così de' benfatti come de' mali fatti degli uomini per nostro essempro con sì maravigliosa legiadria che più tosto è miracoloso che umano, i pecati d'ogni maniera punisce e i purgati rimunera, gli umani fatti dipinge in vulgare più tosto per fare più utile a' suo' cittadini che non farebbe in gramatica. Nè tonando deridano e mali dicenti, però che 'l fonte della eloquenza, Dante, con maravigliosa brevità e legiadria mette due o tre comparazioni in uno rittimo vulgare che Vergilio non mette in venti versi esametri, essendo ancora la gramatica sanza comparazione più copiosa che 'l vulgare. Il perché tengo che 'l vulgare rimare sia molto più malagevole e maestrevole che 'l versificare litterale. Ancora aguaguliando a Vergilio, rispondano con verità: non ha narrato nel suo poema Dante più istorie antiche che Vergilio? No·llo possono negare, con ciò sia cosa che lo 'Nferno solo abbi più istorie antiche che tutto Vergilio. Delle moderne non ha lasciato cosa degna di fama che non abbi recitata; raguardino l'undecimo capitolo di Dante, dove tratta le tre disposizione che 'l cielo non vole: incontinenza, malizia e la matta bestialità [*Inf.* XI, 81–83]. Di fizioni e favole poetiche tutte le passate ornando e sufulgendo suo poema racconta, e con maraviglioso artificio delle nuove compone, quivi e altrove: 'Taccia di Cammo e d'Arrettusa Ovidio' ecc [*Inf.* XXV, 97]. E troveràvi più moralità che in tutto Vergilio, il quale per umiltà e per ornare suo poema, fingendo sé pella sensualità e lui per la ragione nominò suo maestro di filosofia naturale.[77] Come l'attivo

seme dell'uomo sopra il passivo sangue della donna caggia e d'animale sensibile divenga intellettuale [*Purg.* xxv, 43–75], dichiarando che sia l'ombra della luna [*Par.* ii] e molte altre cose filosofiche sottili, fisicamente e sottilissimamente pertratta nel capitolo come d'animale divenga infante [*Purg.* xxv, 61]. Ancora d'astrologia tanto legiadramente descrive quanto a stile poetico si richiede [*Purg.* xxv, 1–3], qui e altrove per tutto il libro: 'Velando i Pesci ch'erano in sua iscorta' ecc [*Purg.* i, 21]. Della verace e santa teologia è tanto verace maestro che tutti e sottili nodi teologichi disolve disputando, e con invenzioni tanto maravigliose gli ostinati peccati di cerchio in cerchio con varii dimoni esaminatori de' peccati punisce, e per simile modo quegli che pentuti si sono rafina purgando, e ultimamente gli mette in cielo di pianeto in pianeto con tanta legiadria e suavità e sentenzie che a pena si potrebbe narrare. La grolia celeste ci mostra, narrando nell'ultimo com'è fatta la Trinità e la visione beatifica [*Par.* xxxiii]; per che maestro Piero delle Sentenze in sottiglieze trapassa, e sanza aguaglio ogni poema così greco come latino avanza. Ora, lasciando il maraviglioso poema del grolioso Dante, il quale chi lo leggerà con intelletto troverrà d'ogni arte, d'ogni iscienza, d'ogni filosofia le conclusioni e fioretti, tornando a mia materia [. . .].[78]

Then, in order to show themselves to be highly literate to the people, they say that Dante, the most excellent and worthiest of poets, was a poet for shoemakers. They do not say that his poetry soars above all others like an eagle, by singing with marvellous artistry about the noteworthy deeds of ignominious men, and, for our own well-being, by putting before our eyes all stories, and adding to their poems now the subtleties of natural philosophy, now the pleasures of astrology, now the excellence of moral philosophy, now the holy commandments of law, and now true and holy theology. The illustrious and distinguished poet Dante, who (without any protestation on behalf of Greek and Latin poems, let it be said that nothing is more beautiful than his invention, nothing more useful and subtle), treating all stories, both modern and ancient ones, and for our example dealing with both good and evil deeds with such marvellous grace, that it is a thing more miraculous than human, punishes sins of all kinds and rewards the purgating souls, and describes human dealings in the vernacular in a way that is more useful to his citizens than it would be in Latin. Without thundering let the spiteful deride, for Dante, the fount of eloquence, with marvellous brevity and grace places two or three comparisons in a vernacular rhyme where Virgil would take more than twenty hexameters. For Latin is incomparably more copious than the vernacular. For which reason, I hold that vernacular verse is much easier to handle and more authoritative than Latin verse. And still keeping the comparison with Virgil, let them respond with truth to this question: has not Dante narrated in his poem more ancient stories than Virgil? They cannot deny it, for the *Inferno* alone has more ancient stories than one finds in all of Virgil. And Dante has not omitted among modern stories one that was not worthy of gaining reputation. Let them look at the eleventh chapter of Dante, where he deals with the three dispositions that heaven does not want: incontinence, malice, and mad bestiality. His poem recounts all earlier poetic fictions and fables making them ornate and resplendent, and with amazing artifice he composes new ones, here and elsewhere: 'Let Ovid be silent about Cadmus and Arethusa', etc. And you will find there more moral teaching than in all of Virgil. Out of humility and to ornament his poem, pretending that he is sensuality, Dante calls Virgil reason as his master of natural philosophy. Scientifically and with the greatest subtlety, he deals with how the active seed of man falls upon the passive blood of the woman and how a sensitive soul becomes intellectual, showing what the shadows on the moon are and treating many other subtle philosophical matters, in the chapter about how an animal becomes a child. He also treats astronomy with the elegance required of poetic style, and here and elsewhere he does this throughout the poem: 'Veiling the Fish which were escorting her', etc. He is such a true master of true and holy theology that he unties all the subtle knots of theology when he engages in disputation, and he uses such marvellous inventions in punishing the obstinate sinners from circle to circle with various demons who are examiners of their sins, and in a similar way, he refines those who have repented and are purging themselves, and finally he places them in heaven from planet to planet with such grace, consummate skill, and sententiousness that one can hardly relate it. He shows us celestial glory, narrating at the end what constitutes the Trinity and beatific vision. For this reason he goes beyond Peter of the Sentences in subtlety, and, being without equal, he surpasses all poems both Greek and Latin. Now, leaving behind the marvellous poem of glorious Dante, for whoever reads with intelligence will find that it possesses the conclusions and flowers of all art, science, and philosophy, and returning to my subject [. . .].

This passage provides a sprawling but compelling overview of the competing projections of Dante in debates between vernacular and humanist culture at the turn of the century. For a start, the view of Rinuccini's opponents, that Dante is a 'poeta da calzolai' ('poet for shoe-makers'), recalls Petrarch's view that Dante's poem is lauded by 'fullers, or tavernkeepers, or woolworkers'. Rinuccini celebrates Dante's poetry at several levels. Not only is Dante praised for his inventive capacity and his learning in almost all the fields traditionally associated with the scholastic curriculum of Italian universities (the liberal arts, moral and natural philosophy, law, and theology). But he is also held up as a model of language and style in what amounts to the most extreme statement in favour of the vernacular and against Latin that is known from the history of Dante's Florentine reception: 'sanza aguaglio ogni poema così greco come latino avanza'. The vernacular is not simply more useful to his fellow citizens (a point which, as we have seen, is made by both Boccaccio and Villani), but Latin verse is technically and artistically inferior to its vernacular counterpart. It is intriguing that Dante is praised for his concision and Virgil derided for his prolixity, especially when one notes how earlier and later commentators single out this very quality as a feature common to their poetry.[79] What is more, Dante's modernity takes him beyond the ancients, for he is able to bring together ancient stories and contemporary ones (one recalls again Boccaccio's 'moltitudine delle storie'). In his letters, Salutati singles out Dante's learning as being equal or even superior to that of the ancients, and celebrates his stylistic elegance, but he never devalues Latin letters. Quite the opposite. Salutati's interest in translating Dante and other occasional comments suggest a very different set of linguistic values. Both Salutati and Villani are interested in accommodating Dante to an elite public keenly conscious of classical standards and values. And it is this which helps to motivate their attempts to bring Dante's life and poetry into line with many of the key features of early Florentine humanism. By contrast, Rinuccini reveals a strong aversion to humanism, and makes Dante, as the embodiment of scholastic knowledge, immeasurably superior to classical authors in both style and subject-matter. As has been recognized, the principal target of the invective is Niccolò Niccoli renowned by his own contemporaries for a militant classicism that sought a complete break with the vernacular legacy of the Trecento.[80] Niccoli left only a handful of writings. However, from comments in the letters of Bruni, Poggio, and the Greek translator and General of the Camaldolensian Order,

Ambrogio Traversari, it is clear that he played a central role as an arbiter of taste in the early Florentine humanist movement, as well as being an important collector and copyist of manuscripts.[81]

4 Leonardo Bruni's *Dialogi*

We now turn to Leonardo Bruni's *Dialogi ad Petrum Histrum*, the work of the most original and incisive interpreter of the growing humanist polemic regarding Dante at the beginning of the fifteenth century. Born in Arezzo, an important centre of learning and classical studies, Bruni came to Florence to study civil law in the early 1390s, where he fell under the influence of Salutati and was schooled in Greek under the tutorship of Chrysoloras. After a period of employment in the Papal Curia, he returned to Florence in 1415 and was granted citizenship in 1416, eventually becoming its second humanist chancellor from 1427 until his death in 1444. He was one of the most productive writers of his day, publishing translations, many from the Greek, as well as independent humanist treatises on historiography, pedagogy, and moral philosophy.[82] The *Dialogi* is one of his most celebrated works and it stands as a manifesto of early humanism, marking a return to the Ciceronian dialogue and lambasting the excesses and stupidities of scholastic culture, above all through the figure of Niccolò Niccoli. Before examining its presentation of Dante, it may be helpful to provide a brief summary of the content and argumentative framework of the *Dialogi*.

After a *proemio* dedicated to Pier Paolo Vergerio, Bruni narrates how during the Easter festivities of 1401 he and his friends, Niccolò Niccoli and Roberto de' Rossi, visited the house of Coluccio Salutati. The debate that takes up the rest of the work is prompted by Salutati's invitation to cultivate the art of disputation. Niccoli, who is the main protagonist of work, ostensibly refuses and launches instead into an extended critique of contemporary cultural standards in which he attributes responsibility for the current parlous state of learning to the culture of medieval scholasticism. Ancient texts have been lost, classical Latin has been allowed to corrupt, and, as a consequence, a monstrous miscellany of 'knowledge' has been produced and transmitted. Aristotle has become the absolute standard yet his works have undergone a degrading transformation at the hands of their incompetent translators. The

83

principal theme developed by Niccoli is thus the unbreachable distance between present-day Florence and the classical past. Not goaded by this remarkable attack on contemporary culture, Salutati replies merely by extending once more the invitation to Niccoli to exercise disputation. In order to show the excellence attained by some contemporaries, Salutati mentions the example of Dante, Petrarch, and Boccaccio, who receive widespread approval and are the glory of the city. Salutati even ventures to say that if Dante had employed another style of writing, he would be content not merely to compare him with the ancients but to place him before the Greeks themselves.[83]

Niccoli rises to the challenge and supports his general argument about the moribund state of classical learning in contemporary Florence by demonstrating the specific deficiencies of the 'tre corone' in classical matters. There now follows the most polemical section of text in which Niccoli pronounces harsh judgements on all three Florentine poets. Dante had shown himself to be a bad interpreter of Virgil, and he anachronistically referred to Cato as an old man. Worse still he had un-justly condemned to Hell Marcus Brutus, the just assassin of the tyrant Caesar. The distance here between Salutati and Bruni's Niccoli is espe-cially marked, and it recalls the daring conceptualization of republican liberty put forward in Bruni's own panegyric of Florence, the *Lauda-tio florentine urbis*, composed in the summer of 1404.[84] Turning more directly to what Niccoli calls 'our studies', he observes that Dante had taken pleasure in the scholastic treatises of friars, and was not able to draw on the ancient works then available. Dante is, in short, accused of clumsiness and ignorance in Latin. In a statement that harbours echoes of Petrarch's *Familiares*, xxi, 15, § 22, but in a context of openly polemical attack which makes no mention of Petrarch's praise of Dante's *ingenium*, the poet of the *Comedy* is distinguished from those who exercise literary discernment: he is left instead to his plebeian public of belt-makers, bakers, and the like:

> Dante read the quodlibeta of the friars and other such annoying things, but of the books of the gentiles, on which his art especially depended, he had no contact even with those that are left. In short, granted he had every other endowment, he surely lacked Latinity. Will we not be ashamed to call him a poet, and even prefer him to Virgil, when he could not speak Latin? I recently read some letters of his, which he

seemed to have written very carefully, for they were in his own hand and signed with his seal. But by Hercules, no-one is so uncultivated that it would not shame him to have written so awkwardly. On this account, Coluccio, I shall remove that poet of yours from the number of the lettered and leave him to belt-makers, bakers, and the like; for he has spoken in such a way that he seems to have wished to be familiar to this sort of men.[85]

Book II opens the following day, but in a new setting – the gardens of Roberto de' Rossi, a professor of Greek at the *Studio* and favourite of Salutati – and it is prefaced by an evocation of the beauties of Florence in the spirit of his *Laudatio florentine urbis*. Niccoli now states that the only reason for his attack on the 'tre corone' was to provoke Salutati into defending them. Salutati refuses to do so, and, after some urging and with Bruni as the arbiter of the dispute, it falls to Niccoli to reverse his earlier judgements and to offer a retraction (although one rightly seen by many critics as artificial and ambiguous). The *Comedy* is now referred to as 'great and brilliant poem' ('magnum ac luculentum poema'), and Dante is said to possess the qualities of a great poet: the power to make fictions, elegance, and knowledge of many things. He proffers amazing fictions of the three realms of the afterlife as well as showing skill in translating subtle theological and philosophical truths into verse. He is praised for his representation of the human passions, for his astronomical descriptions, and for his ability to praise and blame. The three specific criticisms of Dante's lack of classical knowledge made in Book I are not strictly retracted but rather are explained away as being figurative expressions. The general point about Dante's medieval scholastic interests is also left unanswered. By contrast – and here the difference between Bruni and Villani is significant – Petrarch is singled out as the one who opened up the pathway towards the *studia humanitatis*: 'this man was the one who revived humane studies that had by now been extinguished, and who opened up for us the way by which we might reacquire them'.[86]

In Book I, all the characters' views seem to correspond to what is known of them historically. There is contemporary evidence for Niccoli's views on Dante in the works (albeit mostly polemical ones) studied in sections 3 and 5 of this chapter, as well as in a later invective that Bruni himself wrote against Niccoli.[87] The very nature of Niccoli's tirade against Dante, which is closely concerned with matters of literary decorum and historical accuracy, also seems to reflect Niccoli's well-known predilection for textual and philological questions. As is clear from section 2 of this chapter, moreover, Salutati's brief comments fit closely with his judgements on Dante. That Dante possesses a faulty knowledge of antiquity is clearly a notion that had been circulating in Italy for some time, since it motivates Salutati's various defences of the poet's classical erudition. We have already met criticisms of Dante's abilities as a Latinist in Petrarch, Villani, and to a lesser extent in both Boccaccio and Salutati. But there is no direct precedent within the earlier traditions of Florentine intellectual and literary culture for Niccoli's full-scale diatribe against Dante's ignorance of Latin language and culture.

The key question is how one is to assess the relationship between the harsh judgements on Dante made in Book I and their 'retraction' in Book II. This issue could not be more controversial and critics are divided over a series of questions, involving often quite intricate issues of dating. The most influential, but now widely contested, interpretation is that the work is written at two separate moments and is closely related to a set of changed historical circumstances which impact on Bruni's thought and help to explain the differences between the two books. This is the thesis of Hans Baron who dates the first book to 1401 and the second to 1404–05 and relates the palinode in Book II to the experience of the years of crisis in which the Florentine Republic was threatened by the Visconti Lordship of Milan. For Baron, the threat to Florentine *libertas* acted as a catalyst for the birth of an intensely republican philosophy that he termed civic humanism, one developed in relation to Cicero's ethical and political thought and concerned with the active life, wealth, military valour, and the family. In Book II, Baron argues, Bruni reflects such new matters of interest by celebrating the city and its most famous poets and marking his distance from the militant and politically uncommitted classicism of Niccoli.[88] For a variety of reasons, Baron's dating and general argument are no longer tenable. It is clear that the *Dialogi* is indeed a unitary work from studies of its Ciceronian model, the *De oratore*; codicological evidence indicates that there are more earlier extant manuscripts with both books and the textual tradition that contains only the first book is relatively late; and social and intellectual historians have shown that the values Baron associated with civic humanism not only predate the apparently pivotal year of 1402, but that they are also found in other humanists working outside Republican Florence.[89]

Jerrold Siegel is the principal modern originator of the opposite thesis to Baron's: that the *Dialogi* is a unitary work which, rather than being determined by its historical context, is instead a rhetorical exercise closely modelled on the *De oratore* and motivated in part by Bruni's desire to promote his candidature to succeed Salutati as chancellor.[90] The importance of the *De oratore* has been further substantiated by subsequent work which has shown the great care and considerable originality Bruni demonstrates in building the structure and thematic arrangement of the *Dialogi* upon Cicero's work.[91] But a more nuanced reading of the work has been put forward by a number of other scholars, especially Antonio Lanza, who has argued that the *Dialogi* is better viewed in relation to a Florentine context characterized by the opposing literary and intellectual programmes and the related rivalries of an established vernacular literary culture, on the one hand, and an emergent Latin humanist one, on the other.[92] Rather than simply reflecting the tensions of the time, such scholars prefer to see Bruni as fighting a rear-guard action in the growing belief that Dante's stature and close ties with oligarchic culture are such that it would be politically foolish to deride him in the manner of the more extreme Niccoli. Thus, Dante's popularity is re-interpreted positively as being that of a poet who writes for the entire city. Lanza also suggests that one reason for Bruni's change of focus was his reading of Rinuccini's *Invettiva* and *Risponsiva*.[93] This is ultimately difficult to verify, but it is clear that, in the *laudatio Dantis* of Book II, Bruni echoes earlier judgements on Dante such as Rinuccini's praise of the poet's capacity to weave subtle knots of theology into his poetry, and Salutati's similar comments in the letter to Tuderano and the *De fato et fortuna*. From this perspective, it is possible to recognize the highly literary and rhetorical quality of the *Dialogi*, as well as possible motivations of personal ambition, and yet not to deracinate Bruni's work from its historical context. It is, however, perhaps overly restrictive to view the *Dialogi* as being significant merely as an exercise in damage-limitation, albeit in a highly sophisticated literary form. The *Dialogi* may more usefully be viewed as being concerned at several levels with questions related to hierarchies of value and authority, between scholasticism and the new humanist culture, between Dante and the classics, between Bruni and Salutati, and between Bruni and Niccoli. All these questions – cultural, epistemological, literary, and personal – hinge on the assessment of Dante. It is not simply the case that Dante is reinstated in Book II, but that, with Bruni as arbiter, his authority is refounded, although not without certain ambiguities and tensions. Dante's inelegant Latin and the close link posited between him and scholastic culture are conveniently not addressed in Niccoli's retraction, and it would seem that Dante's authority in these areas is still open to dispute. What is more, despite the echoes of Salutati's views on Dante, as well as other defences,[94] in Book II Bruni continues to stake his distance from the Florentine Chancellor's own approach to Dante (and the general premises of the *De laboribus Herculis*), by giving far less emphasis to the allegorical and moral content of his poetry.[95] Bruni may in part rehabilitate Dante along Trecento lines, but he does not bestow upon him the cultural centrality that had been stressed by Salutati, Villani, and Rinuccini, and the question of the relationship between the *volgare* and Latin is not even broached in Book II. Dante is, in short, more used than celebrated. The defence of Dante in Book II can therefore be seen at one level as a humanist's desire for reconciliation with supporters of the vernacular tradition, a rear-guard action aimed at recuperating a Dante who stands for the best traditions of the city. Bruni's interest in using Dante in this way to assert Florentine cultural supremacy is confirmed by his comments in several later works (see chapter 3). But at another level, *Dialogi* II can also be viewed as an attempt to project new lineaments and values upon Dante. Indeed, that Bruni continued to harbour suspicions over Dante's response to Latin literature seems to be borne out by evidence presented in the next section. In this respect, it is also significant that when Bruni himself, in his *Historiae florentini populi*, first introduces the term 'middle age' into historical terminology, he does so in order to mark a political renaissance in Florence following its refounding by Charlemagne, and not, as Villani had suggested, to inaugurate a moment of cultural and literary rebirth which takes its origins from Dante.[96]

5 Domenico da Prato

A defender of vernacular culture, poet, and notary, Domenico da Prato (1375–1433) modulates many of the themes and issues developed in

Rinuccini's *Invettiva* in his dedicatory letter or *prefazione* to his own collected vernacular verse, which was first composed *c*. 1409 and re-drafted some twenty years later.[97] In the *prefazione*, Domenico levels his sights at a Latin letter by Bruni from the spring of 1418 which expresses perplexity at the account of the founding of Mantua in *Inferno* xx, where Dante clearly and purposefully contradicts the account of the city's origins given in the *Aeneid* in order to dissociate its foundation from the Virgilian seer, Manto. Bruni first comments that all ancient writers, including Virgil, had attested to the fact that Mantua was founded by Tuscans; he then states:

> Nor is there any author who argues against this, except for one, Dante, about whom I am compelled to great bewilderment. For he seems never to have read or to have noted what so many and such eloquent authors have written about the power of Tuscans, and he goes so far as to contradict Virgil, who affirms the Mantuans to have been born from Tuscan blood and names Ocnus as founder of the city. And yet, almost ignorant of all things, Dante assigns another origin to it without producing any author or argument to support his view [. . .] Dante says this daughter of Tiresias [i.e. Manto], who is trained in the magical arts, is a virgin, but Virgil by contrast more truly and more learnedly calls her a mother. Unless this passage is to be taken poetically, it is, then, vain and puerile to believe that Manto was a virgin and came to Italy with servants to a place removed from all human commerce [*Inf.* xx, 82–85].[98]

In contemporary Dante studies, *Inferno* xx tends to be viewed as an original Dantean rewriting of the Virgilian text that is motivated by his need to excise any association between Virgil and the magical arts practised by Manto.[99] Bruni, however, reads the passage against a different set of priorities, both literary and ideological: for him, Dante's treatment of Manto not only violates the letter of the *Aeneid*, but it also reveals his ignorance of Mantua's Etruscan origins in other classical sources. In this way, Bruni sets his own knowledge of ancient history and classical literature against Dante's imperfect poetic myth, thereby pinpointing the latter's deficiencies in the realm of classical erudition. There are also patriotic motives for Bruni's critique, since the ancient Etruscans were identified by Bruni and other pro-Florentine writers with the present-day Tuscans and, as such, they offered a prime example of the cultural vitality of Tuscany long before the foundation of Rome.[100]

Domenico's *prefazione* underlines the contentious nature of rival readings of Dante in the late 1420s. He is especially enraged by the fact that one member of the humanist vanguard has dared to write down his criticisms of Dante's failings with regard to the origin of Mantua. Let us read the full list of charges made against Dante:

> Ed altri di loro dicono il libro di Dante esser da dare alli speziali per farne cartocci, overo più tosto alli pizzicagnoli per porvi dentro il pesce salato, perché vulgarmente scrisse. O gloria e fama eccelsa della italica lingua! Certo, esso volgare, nel quale scrisse Dante, è più autentico e degno di laude che il latino e 'l greco che essi hanno. Vero è che alcuno di questa setta più ignorante che gli altri, ed al quale pare essere il più prudente, simulando avere compassione della intelligenzia di Dante, quella biasima espressamente, e se stesso d'avere inteso commenda, quando dice esser nociuto alla fantasia di Dante il non avere vedute molte opere fatte, e greche e latine, le quali molto sarebbono state favorabili alla sua Commedia, come se in essa discernesse grandissimi mancamenti. Ed un altro di lor dice, anzi l'ha scritto che è peggio, Dante non avere nella origine mantuana Virgilio inteso. E tutte queste cose dicono dimostrando, overo volendo mostrare, se essere eccellenziori e più intelligenti di lui.[101]

And others among them say that Dante's book, because he wrote it in the vernacular, is to be given to apothecaries to be used as wrappings, or rather to purveyors of street-food for wrapping up salted fish. Oh the glory and highest renown of the Italian language! Certainly, this vernacular in which Dante wrote is more authentic and worthy of praise than the Latin and Greek that they have. It is true that there is one of this sect who is more ignorant than the others, yet he believes himself to be more prudent. This person, feigning to have sympathy for Dante's intellect, condemns the latter's understanding openly, and commends his own powers of understanding, when he says that Dante's poetic inventiveness has been damaged by his not having seen many works, in both Greek and Latin, that would have been helpful to his *Comedy*, as if he saw in that work very great failings. And another one of them says that – indeed, far worse, he has written about it – Dante did not understand Virgil regarding the origin of Mantua. And they say all these things in order to demonstrate, or rather to attempt to show, that they are more excellent and more intelligent than him.

This passage has of course many features in common with Rinuccini's *Invettiva*. Domenico takes issue with the irreverence of those who view Dante's poem as lacking classical erudition and dismiss it – with a subtle allusion to classical *topoi* on comic poetry – as only of use to apothecaries and vendors of food as a paper wrapping for their wares.[102] Like Rinuccini's *Invettiva*, Dante's vernacular is upheld as more authentic and worthier of praise than either Greek or Latin. The classicists are so extreme in their views, Domenico continues, that they believe nothing can be said or done that has not been better expressed or produced by the ancients. Yet these self-proclaimed judges and arbiters of present and future tastes produce nothing of worth or originality. Their cult of the antique is such that they spend the whole day running after the derivation of a word or a diphthong; and their lack of interest in doctrine is shown by the fact that they give false judgement of 'Dante, messer Francesco Petrarca, messer Iohanni Boccacci, messer Coluccio ed altri' ('Dante, sire Francis Petrarch, sire Giovanni Boccaccio, sire Coluccio, and others').[103] The appending of Salutati to the 'tre corone' here fits closely with what can be gleaned about the relationship between the aged Salutati and his former students from the letters exchanged between them in the final years of his life; and such an addition may even be a response to the way Bruni undercuts Salutati's authority in the *Dialogi*. The targets of this attack are, as in Rinuccini, not named but they are quite clearly identifiable, and, as should now be clear, the *prefazione* closely associates Bruni with the arch-classicism and zealous ultra-humanism prevalent in Florence in the first third of the fifteenth century.

Conclusion

This chapter has explored how Tuscan writers active in Florence connected Dante with their own incipient constructions of a 'Renaissance' and how some others relegated him to the scholastic culture of the 'Middle Ages'. For the more avant-garde humanists, Dante displayed obvious points of weakness: from deficiencies in his knowledge of antiquity to an imperfect Latin style, from a strong attachment to scholastic modes of thought to an ardent imperial politics. For the supporters of Dante, by contrast, the stress falls repeatedly on his example as a moral teacher, Florentine citizen, cultivator of the city's native idiom, and authoritative writer, especially in matters of ethics, natural philosophy, and theology. The extreme points in these sites of Dante's reception are represented by the polemicists of vernacular culture, Cino Rinuccini and Domenico da Prato, on the one hand, and the equally polemical, staunch classicism of Niccolò Niccoli, on the other. All the other figures dealt with in this chapter take up more nuanced positions on Dante that owe much to their reading of him in the light of both vernacular and humanist concerns. Salutati attempts to realign Dante with humanist preoccupations in matters of philology, classical erudition, and poetics; and his very interest in doing this at all reveals his strong sense of the symbolic significance of Dante in projecting a certain vision of the Florentine state and its cultural heritage. The fact that his most intense activity related to Dante takes place in the decade around the year 1400 strongly suggests that he is motivated into a pro-Dantean, apologetic stance by a growing humanist polemic against Dante with which he finds little sympathy. Villani aligns Dante with some of the humanist interests shared by Salutati, but he is far more direct in associating Dante with the notion of Florentine cultural renewal and the defence of poetry. Like Salutati, he recognizes Dante's inadequacy in Latin, but he has less of Salutati's ambiguity in justifying Dante's choice of the vernacular, even though his incomplete commentary is itself in Latin and addressed to a select audience. One might say that Salutati is closer to the mature Boccaccio of the *Esposizioni* and *Genealogie*, that Villani's positions come nearer to the Boccaccio of the first redaction of the *Trattatello*, and that they both share Petrarch's hesitations over Dante's Latin.

Giovanni Gherardi da Prato and Cino Rinuccini are both concerned to hold the *Comedy* up as a work to be imitated as a literary model and studied as a source of doctrinal authority. With force and fury, Rinuccini takes a stand against the humanist polemic against Dante, derogatorily dismissing Dante's opponents for their narrow interests and complete disregard for civic responsibility. Similar themes are modulated by Domenico da Prato but at a later date when Bruni's *Dialogi* had begun to circulate widely and Florentine humanists, including Bruni himself, were still bent upon pointing out inaccuracies, or what Domenico calls 'grandissimi mancamenti', in Dante's classical knowledge. The *Dialogi* offers the most problematic 're-interpretation' of contemporary debates regarding Dante, and it represents an original attempt to re-read Dante by means of select interpretative categories, even in the retraction and apparent endorsement of the poet in Book II.

PART II

New directions and the rise of the vernacular, 1430–1481

3

Dante as a civic and linguistic model, 1430–1441

The innovations of Florentine humanism were carried forward and developed in the 1420s and 1430s by Niccoli, Bruni, and Poggio, as well as by Traversari, and the humanist polymath, Leon Battista Alberti. The 1430s in particular witness a number of developments that are formative both for the evolution of humanist studies in Florence and for that of the vernacular. What is more, Florence's economic wealth helps to make her as much the capital of Christendom as Rome, by facilitating the prolonged residence of Pope Eugenius IV there (1434–6, 1439–43) and the decision to move to the city the Council of Union (1439), an ecumenical council convened to resolve the schism separating the Roman Catholic and Greek Orthodox Churches. The presence of the pope with his humanist entourage and the council itself further enhanced the cultural prestige of the city and opened up new avenues of intellectual exchange. This decade also sees the rise of Cosimo de' Medici to power in 1434 and inaugurates a period of increasing Medicean control, and ultimately dominance, over the political fortunes of Florence that was set to last until 1494.

The enduring value of employing Dante in order to promote Florence was not lost on intellectuals linked to the Medici party from the mid-1430s onwards. And the Medici preoccupation with raising the status of the vernacular, as well as adapting Dante to fit its own purposes will be explored in the following chapter. These later developments are not straightforward, however. For, as we have seen in Part I, Dante is preeminently associated with the cultural patrimony of the *literati* close to the ruling Florentine oligarchy before the rise of the Medici. For this oligarchy, the cult of Dante brings with it the civic connotations whose forms we have examined in the previous chapter. To criticize

97

or to ignore the vernacular (and by implication Dante) remains characteristic of humanists such as Niccoli and Bracciolini who are most closely associated with Cosimo and assist in projecting a vision of him as the prime mover in the Florentine revival of antiquity. Within such a set of contexts, this chapter explores the activities and writings of four individuals who lay claim to Dante's inherited cultural prestige while at the same time fashioning him into new forms and fitting him to new contexts. Three of these writers go further than the authors studied in the previous chapter in transposing Dante on to a civic template and in reinterpreting him as an emblem and ideal model of active and politically committed Florentine citizenship. The first, Francesco Filelfo, offers the most extreme and overtly ideologized treatment, one which is directed against the Medici party and its supporters. The next two, Leonardo Bruni and Matteo Palmieri, cast Dante along Ciceronian lines as an *optimus civis* who plays a leading role in administering and preserving the Republic. Bruni is also significant both for the judgements he expresses about Dante's use of the vernacular and for his involvement in a humanist debate on the language spoken in ancient Rome that affects assessments of the *volgare*. The chapter closes with an examination of Alberti's vernacular writings and related activities in which Dantean interests, though not wholly absent, are far less prominent.

1 Francesco Filelfo

'Mia fatichevole et pericholosissima impresa', 'My exhausting and most dangerous enterprise'.[1] With these words, the Tolentine humanist, bibliophile, and Greek scholar, Francesco Filelfo (1398–1481), summed up his early experiences of lecturing on Dante in Florence.[2] Filelfo had been brought to the city at the instigation of one of the leading figures in the ruling oligarchy, the humanist patrician, Palla Strozzi, although his appointment was also supported by Cosimo, Traversari, Niccoli, and Bruni. He arrived in April of 1429 and by the autumn of that year had been elected to teach rhetoric and poetry at the *Studio*. Initially, Filelfo appears to have been welcomed by the leading elements of Florentine public and literary life. But his relationship with Niccoli had already soured by 1430 and this year also marks the end of his relations with the Medici, as well as with other prominent intellectuals, including most notably Carlo Marsuppini, a Medici favourite who was his rival for key positions at the *Studio*. In the academic year 1431–32, Filelfo was reappointed to his university post and also elected to lecture on Dante on feast days, resuming a tradition that had been interrupted since 1425 and becoming the first humanist (if one excludes Boccaccio, Villani, and Giovanni Malpaghini) to hold the Dante chair. It is clear from the reaction of the university's governing officials, whose members included Lorenzo di Giovanni de' Medici, Cosimo's brother, that this move was in large part ideologically motivated, and widely interpreted as such. The officials removed Filelfo from his positions in October 1431 and assigned new posts to several individuals, including Marsuppini, who were known for their pro-Medici sympathies. In early December, however, Filelfo's supporters succeeded in obtaining an ordinance re-instating him to his post and also to the task of reading Dante in the Florentine Cathedral. A later ordinance of 21 December, which guar-antees him access to a hall for his *Studio* teaching and to a *cattedra* in the cathedral for his Dante lectures, suggests that Filelfo was subject to intimidation from his opponents. He continued his Dante readings for the remainder of the academic year to considerable popular approval, and taught at the *Studio* until 1434.[3] The official documents give some sense of the manoeuvring and rivalries, but we need to turn to another source, Vespasiano da Bisticci's life of Filelfo, for further insight into the appeal of his oral teachings in the Florentine Cathedral (known as Santa Liperata), and into his training of the youth from the city and elsewhere in public oration:

> Venuto [sc. Filelfo] a Firenze, sendo di prestantissimo ingegno, ebbe tutti i figliuoli degli uomini da bene alle sua letioni. Aveva del continovo dugento iscolari o più. Fece, nel tempo che vi lesse, molti giovani dotti et in latino et in greco. Legeva non solo allo Studio, ma in casa faceva molte exercitationi; et per contentare gli appetiti delle lettere lo condusono a legere Dante in Sancta Liperata il dì delle feste.[4]

After his arrival in Florence, Filelfo's outstanding powers of mind meant that he had all the sons of the upper classes attending his lessons. He constantly had two hundred students or more. During the period in which he lectured there, he made many young men learned in both Latin and Greek. He would lecture not only at the *Studio*, but he also taught a lot in his home; and to satisfy the appetite for literature he was led to read Dante in Santa Liperata on feast days.

In 1432–33, as tensions mounted between the Medici and the ruling oligarchic party, led nominally by Rinaldo degli Albizzi and Niccolò da Uzzano, Filelfo became ever more closely tied to the oligarchic faction.

It is against this climate of heated rivalries and vitriolic factionalism that one needs situate the extant orations on Dante, both by Filelfo and his students. From such a perspective one can appreciate the reasons for the controversy and recognize what Bec has called the ideological background implicit in humanistic interpretations of Dante's work and name.[5] In the oration that precedes Filelfo's reading of the poem, Dante is praised in what are now standard terms as the 'nobilissimo e illustre poeta, lo eruditissimo filosofo e sublimissimo matematico e prestantissimo teologo Dante Alighieri' ('most noble and illustrious poet, the most erudite philosopher, most subtle astrologer, and most learned theologian, Dante Alighieri').[6] Filelfo goes on to tailor Dante more explicitly to the traditional views of the poet's oligarchic defenders in his subsequent assertions, by affirming the value of the vernacular and comparing him favourably with the paragons of modern humanist culture. According to Filelfo, Dante is to be placed above the ancients and his eloquence in Italian is such that all peoples benefit from the harmonious melody of his divine poem.[7]

In a later oration that Filelfo delivered in the Florentine Cathedral on 26 December 1431, before he resumed the readings on Dante, he adds further texture to this oligarchic defence of Dante by attacking Niccoli's well-known views on the poet:

> vedendo il divino poeta Dante Alighieri essere da voi meritamente et amato et avuto in reverenza e divozione [. . .] senz'alcun altro o pubblico o privato premio a ciò fare indotto, cominciai quello poeta pubblicamente a leggere [. . .] Et avvegnadioché il leggere di questo divino poeta, chiamato da miei ignorantissimi emuli leggere da calzolai e da fornai, quanta benevolenza e favore m'ha acquistata presso la vostra magnificenza, in tanto odio e persecuzione ha me indotto

presso de' miei invidi, non però mi ritrarrò né scosterò dal mio onesto e laudibile principio.[8]

seeing that you [Florentines] deservedly love, revere and are devoted to the divine poet, Dante Alighieri [. . .] I began to read that poet in public without being induced to do so by any public or private reward [. . .] And given that in reading this divine poet – whom my most ignorant antagonists call reading matter for shoemakers and bakers – I have gained as much benevolence and favour from your magnificence as I have secured hatred and persecution from those who are envious of me, I will not withdraw or remove myself from my honest and praiseworthy first undertaking.

As the earlier comments on Dante as philosopher, theologian, and supreme exponent of the vernacular suggest, it is clear that Filelfo had resolutely aligned himself with the traditionalist view of Dante that we studied in the previous chapter. There is not the same ardour that we find in Rinuccini, nor is the defence of Dante made, like those by Salutati, Rinuccini, and even Bruni, through arguments based on the literary features of the *Comedy*. Filelfo's orations have a rhetorical patina and formulaic quality, yet they are nonetheless a remarkable testimony to the way in which 'Dante' is used as a point of demarcation between opposing factions who define themselves in relation to their own constructions of the poet. In the early 1430s competing interpretations of Dante's value are being used to draw out the battle-lines in political and ideological struggles within Florence.

A later oration of 29 June 1432, delivered by one of Filelfo's students in the civically charged space of Florence's cathedral, and probably composed under his master's guidance, provides the most markedly 'ideologized' reading of Dante. In this oration the poet is imbued with all the values of civic patriotism associated with the Republican oligarchy. Of course, this vision is a selective one that ignores Dante's own repeated condemnations of Florence and its violent factionalism. The oration also echoes yet overturns Boccaccio's *Trattatello* (and perhaps even the very language in that work) by emphasizing the value of civic activism that Boccaccio had viewed as so detrimental to Dante's pursuit of learning:

Lui [sc. Dante] nei governi della republica fiorentina a ciascuno giustizia amministrava, lui nelle cose comuni e particulari, che a trattare avesse, la giustizia predominare sempre voleva, lui non meno al povero che al ricco la santa giustizia dispensare desiderava [. . .] Non nei pericoli della sua republica, quantunque grandi fossino, mai gli ardiri, mai le forze, mai l'amoroso suo core per la difension d'essa poté mancare. Anche più animoso in quella difendendo continuamente perseverava. Molte furono le persecuzioni, molte le insidiazioni, molti i tradimenti, da che lui questa inclita città di Firenze più volte liberò. Quante guerre la città vostra perseguitanti, con sapere, con forza, con industria rimosse et al tutto estinse! O divino più tosto che umano! o ardentissimo della patria difensore! o liberatore della amplissima tua republica, che la vera corona per li tanti beneficii che alla tua patria desti, più che altro uomo mortale meriti! Tu solo infinite persecuzioni d'uomeni per difension della patria incorresti; tu nelle crudeli invidie di molti scelerati per difension de la patria intrasti; tu tra gli apuntati coltelli e tra le taglienti spade più volte ti trovasti, per difension della patria; tu finalmente in esilio fosti mandato per difension della patria. E più ancora dirò io degno di gran memoria, che nello esilio Dante ritrovandosi, sempre la patria lodava, sempre la magnificava, sempre la difendeva.[9]

He would administer justice to all in the governments of the Florentine Republic. He always wished for justice to prevail in the things, both common and individual, with which he dealt. He desired to dispense holy justice as much to the poor as to the rich. During the dangers – however great they were – faced by his republic, his ardour, his forces and his amorous heart never failed to act in its defence. In defending the republic he was even more full of spirit and constantly persevered. Several times he freed this great city of Florence from many persecutions, many plots, and many acts of treachery. How many wars threatening your city did he remove and completely extinguish with wisdom, strength and industriousness! Oh divine more than human! Oh most ardent defender of the homeland! Oh liberator of your most ample republic, who, more than any man, deserves the true crown for the countless benefits you brought to the homeland! You alone were subject to infinite persecutions in defence of the homeland. In defence of the homeland you became embroiled in the cruel acts of envy many evil men commit. In defence of the homeland, you often faced drawn daggers and razor-sharp swords; and finally in defence of the homeland you were sent into exile. And I will add yet something else which is worthy of being long remembered: for, Dante always praised the homeland, always applauded it, always defended it.

As if this were not clear enough, Filelfo's student calls on Florentines to imitate Dante in defence of the *patria* at a time of attack: 'Ora è il tempo, civi pregiati, ora è il tempo che per difensione della patria non solamente le vostre ricchezze conjuniate, ma in sino alla morte, se bisogna, vi mettiate' ('Now is the time, worthy citizens, now is the time for us, in defending the homeland, to join together not only our wealth but our very selves, until death if needs be').[10] The enemy, of course, is within and Filelfo's attack is directed at the family whom the ruling oligarchy views as threatening to assume power to the detriment of the city's freedom and its best political traditions. Dante has, in short, become a Republican rallying-cry in a manipulation of his name which is, on Filelfo's part, an especially cynical one. An outsider, professional rhetorician, and astringent controversialist, who is clientelistically linked to the anti-Medici faction, he seizes on the opportunity to make use of Dante as a politically charged symbol at a time of tumultuous factional rivalry. Indeed the controversy was to become so turbulent that attempts were made to expel Filelfo from the city, to imprison him for debt, and finally, in May 1433, he was disfigured by an assailant's knife. According to the magistrate's records that relate the legal proceedings which followed this incident, the assailant was an employee of Girolamo Broccardi, *rettore* of the *Studio* and a Medici partisan, who had earlier opposed Filelfo's employment at university. The link with the Medici family becomes clearer still when one notes that it was Lorenzo di Giovanni de' Medici who paid Broccardi's eventual fine.

The hostile situation towards Filelfo was temporarily overturned when the Medici and their allies were forced into exile on 7 September 1433. Yet Filelfo was left isolated and outmanoeuvred when the Medici returned on 6 October 1434; leading figures in the oligarchic party were now exiled, and Marsuppini was appointed to a Chair at the *Studio*. Filelfo left Florence in December, and, burning with resentment, dispatched an assassin to the city to kill Marsuppini, Broccardi, and Cosimo's brother, Lorenzo. The plot failed and he was sentenced *in absentia* to have his tongue cut out were he to return to Florence or its subject territories – a fitting *contrapasso* perhaps for someone whose eloquence had been so threatening to the Medici.[11]

2 Matteo Palmieri's *Vita Civile*

Matteo Palmieri (1406–75), a Florentine merchant and politician, was closely associated with the Medici and occupied several high offices in the state.[12] He shows a close engagement with Dante which in the 1460s also takes the form of an intriguing, yet little-studied *terza rima* poem, the *Città di Dio* (see chapter 4, section 3a). Here we are concerned with the *Vita civile*, an earlier vernacular work written in dialogue-form c. 1433–36.[13] Composed with the aim of educating the citizens of the political class, this dialogue has close structural and thematic links to Cicero and Quintilian, as well as to the tradition of Florentine humanism represented by Bruni and Alberti. And our attention is focused principally on the remarks Palmieri gives in the *proemio* on Dante's use of the *volgare*, his discussion of the first line of *Inferno* I in Book I, and his presentation of Dante as a protagonist in the dream-vision sequence found in the closing section of the fourth and final book.

The *Vita civile* is set in 1430 and recounts the educational and moral guidance given by Agnolo Pandolfini to Palmieri and two other Florentine protagonists, Franco Sacchetti and Luigi Guicciardini. Its principal objective is to describe the best kind of life, that lived by a virtuous citizen in a good commonwealth, and to offer the advice to be found in Greek and Latin writers on the arts and disciplines appropriate to such a life. The *proemio* sets out these aims and observes that many are deprived of these teachings because they are without Latin; few writers, Palmieri notes, have written in the vernacular, but the first among these is Dante:

> Il primo et sopra a ogni altro degnissimo è il nostro Dante poeta: costui in ogni parte excelle qualunche altro volgare, che non si degna assimigliarsi a essi, però che fuor della lingua poco si truova drieto a sommi poeti latini. In nelle cose grandi sempre si monstra sublime et alto; nelle piccole è diligente dipintore della vera proprietà; lui si truova lieto, rimesso, jocondo et grave; ora con abondanza, altra volta con brevità mirabile, et non solo di poetica virtù, ma spesso oratore, philosopho et theologo si conosce excellente. Sa lodare, confortare, consolare, et è copioso di tante lode che è meglio tacerne che dirne poco. Ma pe' velami poetici è in modo oscuro ché, dove nonn-è grande ingegno et abondante doctrina, più tosto può dare dilecto che fructo.[14]

First and worthy above all others is our poet Dante. In every manner he surpasses all other vernaculars that it is unfitting to compare him with them; for, if one excepts language, he is found only a little behind the greatest Latin poets. In great things, he always shows himself to be sublime and lofty, and in small ones he is a diligent painter of true characteristics; he is happy, humble, jocund, and serious; now he shows abundance, now remarkable brevity. And he excels not only in poetic prowess but also as an orator, philosopher, and theologian. He knows how to praise, comfort, and console, and he is so full of praiseworthy qualities that it is better to be silent than to say little about them. But on account of his poetic veils, he is somewhat obscure so that where there is not great intelligence and abundant doctrine he is more likely to give delight rather than fruit.

There are several points that call for further commentary here. First, in spite of the praise lavished on Dante, one notes the equivocal stance that Palmieri shows towards his use of the vernacular – one that reflects earlier Florentine humanist assessments, beginning with Petrarch, that rest upon an implicit dichotomy between his worth as a poet *tout court* and the inferior value of his chosen linguistic medium. The restrictions of a humanist reading of Dante are also evident in a later discussion, in Book I, of the revival of the arts in Florence, where Palmieri mentions Giotto and the contemporary revival of sculpture, but, unlike Villani in his *De origine*, he associates the Florentine literary renaissance exclusively with Latin literature and Leonardo Bruni.[15] That Dante is nonetheless worthy of association with the ancients in all matters except language is a judgement that we have already found in subtle variations in Boccaccio, Salutati, and Bruni. And Palmieri reinforces such links by modelling his celebration of Dante's poetic qualities upon Quintilian's praise of Homer in the *Institutio oratoria*, although he also establishes a point of contact with earlier Florentine judgements on Dante by insisting on his philosophical and theological qualities.[16] Palmieri's more unusual point – the obscurity of Dante's language – rests upon another dichotomy in earlier critical approaches to the *Comedy*, that between the poem's delectable surface and the doctrinal riches of its inner-meaning. We have already met this distinction in Boccaccio's *Trattatello* and *Esposizioni*, where it is used to emphasize the poem's universality and the hidden learning that can be unlocked by a learned literary elite. By contrast, Palmieri pays homage to Dante as poet but also expresses some concern that his use of poetic veils means that he speaks obscurely and therefore only to the learned few. This judgement is directed exclusively at the *Comedy*; Palmieri either does not know or perhaps chooses to ignore Dante's own preoccupation in the *Convivio* (I, ix, 3–5) with a vernacular that 'servirà veramente a molti' ('will truly serve many'). Palmieri's comment is primarily motivated by a need, like the Dante of the *Convivio* (I, i, 13), for the vernacular to be made useful to a wide public. And public utility is also the criterion against which Palmieri judges the limited value of the vernacular in Petrarch and Boccaccio. He concludes by noting the necessity to fashion a form of Tuscan prose for the well-disposed citizen that is able to impart moral and civic lessons:

> Per tali cagioni in me stessi più volte considerando nostra lingua volgare non avere auctori atti a inviare il bene vivere di chi si volesse sopra agli altri fare degno, mi disposi comporre questi libri della *Vita Civile*, coi quali io potessi giovare il bene diritto proposto de' ben disposti civili.[17]

> For these reasons, considering repeatedly that our vernacular language did not have authors capable of imparting good living to those who wish to be worthier than others, I decided to compose these books of the *Vita civile* with which I might assist the good upright aim of well disposed citizens.

Dante is discussed at length for different purposes on two more occasions in the *Vita civile*. In Book I, Palmieri gives an account of the upbringing and education of the citizen, and in so doing, he discusses the importance of the transition from adolescence to youth. This topic leads him into a discussion of the first line of *Inferno* I which he relates to the moral crossroads that, according to Pythagorean tradition, is represented by the letter *y*:

> in Virgilio Enea non può vivo andare allo inferno, se prima non coglie i dorati frutti di questo *y*, cioè le virtù della nostra vita. E 'l ritrovare tali fructi molto gli è faticoso, perché sono posti nel mezo d'una selva [...] Da questo luogo di Virgilio prese il nostro glorioso poeta Dante il principio della sua honorata opera, la quale è assai grossamente intesa da chi dice averla cominciata nella età d'anni trentacinque, dove è il mezo di nostra vita corporea, però che il suo fine è trattare della vita

dell'anime et non della sua propria, ma di tutti gli stati animali: onde se il suo primo verso si riferisce solo alla prima cantica, chiamata *Inferno*, certo intende il mezo della vita fra l'età della ignoranzia e quella della cognitione, secondo la divisione fatta in su il *y*, o veramente, secondo più alta scientia di Platone, se si riferisce a tutta l'opera, intende dell'anime, le quali, fatte da Dio eterne, infondendosi ne' corpi mortali trascendono per certo cerchio dell'universo, il quale coniunto alla superficie della rotondità lunare è termine mezo di tutte le vite spiritali, et è vero confine tra la vita et la morte, perché da indi in su è tutto eterno et, di sotto, ogni cosa è caduca et mortale. Questo cerchio come è mezo delle vite dell'anime, così è principio dello inferno et di tutta morte: onde Dante, considerando per questo cerchio, posto nel mezo delle vite spiritali, cominciarsi a scendere in inferno, disse: *Nel mezo del cammino di nostra vita.*[18]

In Virgil, Aeneas cannot go to Hell while alive unless he first gathers the gilded fruit of this letter *y*, that is, the virtues which pertain to our life [...] From this Virgilian passage our glorious poet Dante took the beginning of his most acclaimed work. This work is most grossly understood by those who say that he started it at the age of thirty-five, which is the middle of our corporeal life, because his objective is rather to treat the lives of souls, not his own, but all the states of the human soul. And so, if his opening line refers only to the first *cantica*, which is called the *Inferno*, he undoubtedly means the middle of life between the age of ignorance and that of knowledge according to the division made by the letter *y*. If, however, according to the higher wisdom of Plato the line refers to the entire work, he means souls which, after God has created them as eternal and after they have entered into mortal bodies, pass through a certain sphere of the universe which is joined to the surface of the sphere of the moon. This is the middle term of all spiritual lives and the true dividing-line between life and death, because from here upwards all is eternal and from here downwards all is mortal and prone to decay. Just as this circle is the middle-point in the souls' lives, so is it the beginning of Hell and of death. For this reason, on considering that one begins to descend to Hell through this circle which is placed in the middle of our spiritual lives, Dante said: *In the middle of the journey of our life.*

Palmieri's tone of explicit polemic has some justification, since most early commentators had indeed accepted the interpretation that he criticizes.[19] However, there are also several points of contact with the earlier commentary tradition. Buti, for example, relates this line to the Pythagorean *y* and notes that it marks a transition from sensuality to the judgement of reason. Villani interprets the passage as applicable to the state of man universally and reads the poem as a vernacular version of the descent to the underworld (*descensus ad inferos*) found in Homer and Virgil. Pietro Alighieri also adapts this concept to the *Comedy* and he is the first to present the analogies between the forest of *Aeneid* VI and that of *Inferno* I.[20] In spite of these possible debts, it is important to note that Palmieri is the first to interpret Dante's opening line in this manner and to suggest connections with the Platonic doctrine of the descent of souls. Such a reading is made possible by distorting the poem's textual surface so as to understand 'mezo' as referring to the circle of the moon, the final celestial sphere through which souls pass in their descent to the corruptible, sublunar realm. We shall return to later and more extensive Platonizing interpretations of *Inferno* I in subsequent chapters, but this example reveals that the concern is not entirely absent from earlier Florentine discussions of Dante.

Palmieri makes more extensive use of Dante, both as a narrative protagonist and intertext, when describing his 'historical' role during the Battle of Campaldino (1289) in the closing section of the final book. Here Palmieri reveals the rewards that await the souls of those who have served the Republic and have lived according to the precepts set out in the dialogue. The literary precedents for the account are, as Palmieri himself observes, Plato's myth of Er in Book x of the *Republic* and Cicero's *De re publica*, but these are refashioned around the figure of Dante, who is presented as Florence's supreme poet and an ardent servant of his beloved republic:

> mi torna a memoria un caso che più volte ho udito essere miracolosa-
> mente adivenuto a Dante, nostro poeta, dopo quella singulare victoria
> che ebbono i fiorentini in Campaldino; onde per conforto di chi se
> exercita ne' facti publici intendo narrare quanto ho di quello caso in-
> teso, acciò che certo possiate et vedere et conoscere quanto sia optimo
> il fine de' buoni governatori delle republiche; e poi sia fine dell'opera
> nostra. Dante, poeta giovane et disideroso di gloria, apparechiandosi
> in Casentino grave battaglia fra gli Aretini et gli exerciti fiorentini,
> electo un suo fedelissimo compagno studioso di philosophia et, sec-
> ondo que' tempi, de' primi eruditi di lettere et di studi di buone arti,

se n'andò in el campo de' suoi. Ivi più tempo fermatisi, con optimi consigli molto giovorono a' conducitori degli exerciti [. . .] In quella battaglia Dante, quanto più fortemente poté, s'aoperò; et perseguitando gli sparti et fugitivi nimici, pochissimi scampare poterono le loro mani victoriose, et con quello empito Bibiena et più altre castella del contado d'Arezo acquistorono.[21]

There comes to my memory an incident about which I have often heard and which is said to have happened miraculously to Dante, our poet, after that singular victory which the Florentines had at Campaldino. Thus, in order to give succour to those involved in public life, I intend to tell what I have understood about this incident. I do this so that you may certainly see and understand how excellent is the goal of good governors of our republic; and this will then be the end of our work. As there approached the hour of a great battle between the Aretines and the Florentine armies, Dante, a young poet and most desirous of glory, first chose a most faithful companion, a student of philosophy who in those times was one of the most learned men in letters and in the noble arts. He then ventured into the enemy camp. Having remained there for some time, they greatly assisted the leaders of the armies. Dante fought in this battle with all his might; and pursuing the divided and fleeing enemy, few were able to escape the hands of the victors. With this attack the Florentines acquired Bibbiena and several other castles from the district of Arezzo.

The attention given to Dante's participation at Campaldino on the winning Guelph side (a detail derived from Book IV of Bruni's *Historiae Florentini populi*) imbues his figure with qualities of civic devotion that are paralleled in both the oration quoted in the previous section and in Bruni's later treatment of the same episode in his *Vita di Dante* (see section 3).[22] Palmieri's treatment of Dante's participation in the battle differs from that found in Bruni's historical and biographical works in that he extends the episode to include legendary material, connected in part to Virgil's narrative of the attack on the enemy camp by the Trojans Nisus and Euryalus in *Aeneid* IX, 241–711, as well as to Dante's own fictional account of the death of Buonconte da Montefeltro at the Battle of Campaldino in *Purgatorio* V, 85–129. Dante's 'fedelissimo compagno' is killed in battle, and his body is initially lost; however, when Dante finds his remains after three days of searching, the companion miraculously returns to life and there ensues a dialogue between him and Dante. This section of Palmieri's dialogue is textured with strong reminiscences of the *Comedy* and the idea of seeing things 'between the two lives' over a three-day period provides obvious parallels with the fictional timescale of Dante's poem and its Christological implications:

> il fedito gli disse: 'Ferma l'animo et lascia ire ogni sospetto [*Purg.* v, 10–14], però che non sanza cagione [*Inf.* vii, 10] sono per speziale grazia mandato da un lume dello universo [*Par.* iv, 49–50] solo per narrare a te quello che infra le dua vite ho in questi tre dì veduto: siché ferma lo ingegno et recati a memoria [*Inf.* xviii, 63] ciò ch'io dirò, però che per te è ordinato che il mio veduto segreto sia manifesto alla humana generatione'. Dante, udito questo, in sé riavuto, postpose il terrore et cominciò a parlare et disse: 'E' mi fia bene caro ogni tuo dire [*Purg.* xxii, 27]; ma se non t'è grave, sodisfammi prima di tuo stato, acciò ch'io intenda che gratia t'abbia questi tre dì con tante fedite mortali sanza nutrimento o subsidio conservato con tanto valore.' Rispuose lui: 'Assai mi pesa non potere in tutto sodisfare alla tua domanda [*Par.* xxi, 93] et volentieri mi t'apirrei tutto, potendo, ma piglia da me quel ch'io posso, ché più non m'è lecito promettere [...] con empito spronai pel mezo de' piu spessi nimici, ritto a Guglielmino [sc. Guglielmo degli Ubertini], capo di tutti: et come a Dio piacque [*Inf.* xxvi, 141], lui con mortale fedita aterrai [...] infine, mancando alle mia membra vigore, forato come tu mi vedi [*Purg.* v, 98], lasciai loro di me sanguinosa et bene vendicata vittoria. Qui comincio io ora a inombrare in me medesimo, né so bene alla tua domanda sodisfare, se io rimasi nel corpo o se fuori del corpo viveva in altro' [*Par.* i, 73–74].[23]

the wounded one said to him: 'Take heart and put away all suspicion because it is not without reason that out of special grace I am sent by a light of the universe to tell you about what I have seen in a state between the two lives in these three days. So hold your wits and bring to memory what I will tell you, for it has been willed that through you humankind is to be shown openly what I have seen in secret.' Upon hearing this, Dante collected himself. He held back his fear, and started to speak, saying: 'Everything you say will be dear to me; but if it does not offend you, satisfy me first about your state, so that I may understand what kind of grace has conserved you so vigorously for these three days, given that you have such mortal wounds and have been without any food or help.' He replied: 'It weighs on me greatly not to be able to respond fully to your question, and I would openly reveal all if I were able, but take from me that which I can give [. . .] with force I spurred into the enemy where they were thickest, right up to Guglielmino, the leader of them all; and, as it pleased God, I brought him to the ground with a mortal wound [. . .] finally with my mortal members lacking strength, wounded as you see me, I let them have bloody and well avenged victory over me. At this moment, I started to enter into shadow, nor do I know how to satisfy your question whether I remained in the body or if out of the body I lived in another.'

Further strong echoes of the language of the *Comedy* are also found in the remainder of the book where the companion gives an account of his meeting with the Holy Roman Emperor, Charlemagne, who instructs him about the afterlife. The choice of Charlemagne as guide reflects a particular Florentine tradition (one established by Giovanni Villani, endorsed by Boccaccio, and opposed by Bruni in his *Historiae*) which assigned to him, and by extension to the French monarchy, a decisive role in the history of the city as its second founder following its alleged destruction by Totila.[24] Palmieri's Charlemagne goes on to describe the realms of the afterlife in a sequence which is rich in reminiscences from Virgil, Cicero, Macrobius, and Dante.[25] In line with Cicero's account in the *De re publica* and Macrobius' commentary, Charlemagne stresses the radical separation between the celestial and sublunar realms, and draws attention to the degradation of the soul as it descends to the Earth.[26] The ultimate message is clear: no human activity is finer than to provide for the well-being of the *patria* and to maintain unity and concord in the city: the citizen who devotes himself to this cause will live eternally with the blessed in the heavenly realm. The message is well understood by Palmieri's Dante: 'Dante inteso con maraviglia tutte queste cose volle rispondere: "Poi che tu m'hai significato tanto excellente premio, con ogni diligentia io mi sforzerò seguire in questo" ' ('Having understood with astonishment all these things Dante wanted to reply: "Since you have explained to me such an excellent reward, I will strive with all my efforts to follow it"').[27]

What is perhaps most remarkable about this section of the *Vita civile* is that the repeated echoes of the Dantean afterlife – which are not noted in Belloni's edition – are reassembled in order to justify in Dante's name and on his example a form of civic patriotism which, as in Filelfo's orations, is very remote from the political message of the *Comedy* itself. It is hardly surprising therefore that Palmieri's echoes of the *Comedy* are almost entirely decontextualized and that he makes no reference whatsoever to Dante's own repeated criticism in the *Comedy* of the excesses of Florentine civic activism, municipal politics, and self-aggrandizement.[28]

3 Leonardo Bruni and his *Vita di Dante*

The Republican ideology into which Palmieri casts Dante in his *Vita civile* also informs Leonardo Bruni's *Vita di Dante* of May 1436. The *Vita* stands out as the most sophisticated and important Renaissance life of the poet, and, like the *Dialogi*, it again reveals how closely Dante was tied to the cultural politics of Renaissance Florence. The thirty years between the *Dialogi* and the *Vita* had been intensely active ones for Bruni. On his return to Florence in 1415, his literary output became ever more prolific, with translations from Greek authors as varied as Xenophon, Plato, Plutarch, Demosthenes, and Aristotle, as well as a wide range of independent works. Bruni's aversion for scholasticism led him to engage in an important attempt to revitalize Aristotle, making a new translation from the Greek of his *Nicomachean Ethics* (1417).[29] And until the end of his life, he devoted himself intermittently to his history of Florence which was presented to the *Signoria* on 6 February 1439 in a ceremony charged with civic significance, given that it took place on the same date as the act which transferred the Council of Union from Basel and Ferrara to Florence.[30]

We have already seen that Dante was not forgotten after the *Dialogi* insofar as Bruni made further criticism of him as reader of classical texts in his letter on the foundation of Mantua (see above chapter 2, section 5). But apart from this negative judgement, Bruni also showed a positive interest in Dante at two further levels. First, Dante is mentioned as an historical figure on several occasions in Book IV (completed *c.* 1424) of the *Historiae*, where he is recorded as present at the Battle of Campaldino, praised for his exceptional intellect and learning, and his exile is discussed in some detail.[31] The other and perhaps more significant document of Bruni's ongoing interest in Dante is an official letter of 1 February 1430 which petitions Nastasio da Polenta, the Lord of Ravenna, for the return of Dante's remains. As we saw in chapter 1, Boccaccio had shown his concern, in the *Trattatello*, to recover Dante *post mortem* from Ravenna. Bruni's own letter is closely connected to an ordinance of 1396 which calls for the return of the remains of five illustrious Florentine citizens, including Dante, Petrarch, and Boccaccio. The provision mentions the erection of a tomb and statuary monuments for the poets in the Florentine cathedral in order to satisfy 'the perpetual fame and celebrated memory of all the aforementioned and the city and republic of Florence'.[32] Bruni's letter calls for the return of the 'ossa' of Dante and Petrarch – Boccaccio is, in a move that anticipates his later life, passed over – and he offers a small-scale panegyric of Dante's literary qualities:

> Neither you nor anyone else should be astounded if we and all our people have a singular and overwhelming affection and love for the glorious and unfailing memory of Dante Alagherii, the excellent and most renowned poet. This man's glory is such that he undoubtedly adds to the splendour and renown of our city and the light of his intellect illuminates the homeland. Who today has greater celebrity and a more immortal name than this poet, and as far as we can conjecture, it will be so forever in posterity? Whose books are written with such elegance that nothing can be thought of more quickly? Whose books have such wisdom, doctrine, variety, and abundance that they can delight the illiterate, teach the most learned and quick-witted of men, and give instruction and direction to the entire community? [...] Since therefore there exists a decree for their ashes and remains to be brought back to the homeland and for monuments to bury them, and given that in your city of Ravenna there are the ashes and remains of Dante, we ask your excellency most affectionately not to oppose their return.[33]

Such a judgement (and a related comment on Florentine literature in a public oration of 1436)[34] contrasts both with the silence Bruni expresses over Dante's literary qualities in the *Historiae* and with his direct criticism in the letter on the origin of Mantua. The contrast helps to show how Bruni's use of Dante shifts according to genre and context, and reveals how it is possible for an individual to lay alternate claims upon Dante. It also illustrates how Dante continued to be appropriated in order to promote a certain vision of Florence as a pre-eminent capital of culture and learning, one which encompasses both the contemporary revival of classicism and the earlier legacy of Trecento vernacular poetry.

The *Vita di Dante*, like the *Dialogi*, thus draws together elements of two modes of reading Dante – the critical, humanist approach and that of enthusiastic, civic promotion in his name. The *Vita* can be linked to the letter to Nastasio da Polenta, as well as to comments in *Dialogi* II, insofar as all these works celebrate Dante's literary powers as part of an attempt to assert the cause of Florentine primacy. As with the *Dialogi*, the wider historical context to the *Vita* is one of intermittent conflict with the Duchy of Milan, since it was composed in a period of renewed hostility with the Visconti dynasty, now led by Filippo Maria Visconti; and the work may well respond in part to the literary provocation of Pier Candido Decembrio's pro-Visconti tract, the *De laudibus mediolanensium urbis panegyricus* of 1436.[35] The *Vita di Dante* has often been interpreted, along with the funeral oration for Nanni Strozzi, as the clearest expression of Bruni's civic humanism. And even if one may question how helpful this term is in defining the specific nature and contribution of Florentine humanism, it cannot be disputed that Bruni's life develops almost all the principal motifs of Florentine patriotism and Republican ideology in the first third of the fifteenth century. After all, the *proemio* to the work makes clear the intention to celebrate Florence through the lives of Dante and Petrarch: 'la notitia et la fama di questi due poeti grandemente reputo appartenere alla gloria della città nostra' ('I firmly believe that the renown and fame of these two poets belongs greatly to the glory of our city').[36]

The *Vita di Dante* is also an important work for several other reasons, however. First, the *Vita* represents Bruni's most direct attempt to appropriate Dante to a specific political and ethical programme by means of a fascinating admixture of classical and vernacular elements: it is written in the vernacular but its structure and general approach are underpinned by classical sources. Thus, the *Vita* draws on an ideology of the Florentine citizen that owes much to Bruni's keen interest in Aristotle and Cicero (for whom Bruni also wrote lives) and it is fashioned with a biographical method and related set of techniques that follow the example of heroic narrative and biographical selectivity found in Plutarch's *Lives*. Second, it provides a running critique of Boccaccio's *Trattatello* which is revisited and criticized, not only with regard to points of detail but also in relation to its general method. Bruni distances his 'Dante' from the hagiographical scheme so prominent in Boccaccio and places the poet's life, studies, and habits under an alluring veil of historical 'objectivity' and exemplary narrative. In this way, the *Vita* offers a critical reflection on the arts of historiography and biography. And third, Bruni's life provides an important new evaluation of poetry and Dante's choice of vernacular, which once again breaks with the legacy of the poet-theologian and the long-standing humanist unease regarding Dante's linguistic preferences. With the general context outlined above and these key elements of innovation in mind, let us look more closely at the life itself.[37]

The *proemio* to the *Vita di Dante* relates how Bruni, in need of mental repose after completing a long work, turned to a vernacular work and came across Boccaccio's biography of Dante. Having read the biography with due diligence, Bruni comments that Boccaccio had written the life and habits of such a sublime poet in the same manner as he had his works of prose romance: all full of love, sighs, and burning tears ('tutta d'amore et di sospiri et di cocenti lagrime').[38] Boccaccio's emphasis on amorous dalliance is such, Bruni continues, that serious and substantial aspects of Dante's life are passed over in silence. As we have noted, this explicit polemic with Boccaccio informs much of the life which follows, and, though Bruni refers to his own life as being written for recreation ('per spasso'), this literary pose should not mask what is in fact a major landmark in Dante's critical reception.

From the beginning, Bruni adopts a tone of circumspect, historical analysis as he weighs up the life, habits, and deeds of Dante against contemporary evidence and raises objections to Boccaccio's account. Thus, Bruni notes that it is very uncertain that Dante had Roman origins: the most that is known is that he was the great-great-grandson of a Florentine knight, Cacciaguida. Brunetto Latini is introduced as an early teacher (perhaps because of Latini's own interests in civic teachings and Cicero), and Dante's studies are presented in a markedly different light either from the self-absorbed, abstracted scholar of the *Trattatello* who seeks solitude or from Giovanni Villani's Dante who is presumptuous and disdainful and unable to converse with the 'laici':

> Né per tutto questo si racchiuse in ozi, né privossi del secolo, ma, vivendo et conversando con gli altri giovani di sua età, costumato et accorto et valoroso ad ogni esercitio si truova; intanto che in quella battaglia memorabile et grandissima, che fu a Campaldino, lui giovane et bene stimato si trovò nelle armi, combattendo vigorosamente a cavallo nella prima schiera [. . .] dico che Dante virtuosamente si trovò a combattere per la patria in questa battaglia; et vorrei che 'l Boccaccio nostro di questa virtù più che dello amore di nove anni avesse fatto mentione [. . .] Doppo questa battaglia tornasi Dante a casa et agli studii più ferventemente che prima si diede; et niente di manco, niente tralasciò delle conversazioni urbane et civili [. . .] Nella qual cosa mi giova di riprendere l'errore di molti ignoranti, e quali credono niuno essere studiante se non quelli che si nascondono in solitudine et in otio.[39]

> And for all this, he did not close himself up in studious leisure or separate himself from the times, but living and talking with his contemporaries he found himself well adapted and aware and hardy in all youthful activities. In that memorable and great battle fought at Campaldino, the young and highly regarded Dante fought vigorously on horseback in the first rank [. . .] I say that Dante fought valorously for his native land in this battle, and I wish that our Boccaccio had mentioned this valour rather than the nine years of love [. . .] After this battle, Dante returned home and gave himself over to studies even more than before. Nonetheless, he left aside nothing of cultural and civic affairs [. . .] On this point I am happy to correct the error of many ignorant people who believe that there is no student who does not hide himself away in solitude and leisure.

Even allowing for the rhetorical flourishes, we have come a long way from the *otium*-seeking poet-scholar so idealized by Petrarch and under his influence by Boccaccio. The same is true of the comments that follow concerning the legitimacy of Dante's taking a wife – once again Boccaccio is upbraided for arguing that marriage is contrary to study, and the counter-examples are provided in the personages of Socrates, Aristotle, and Cicero, as well as other classical poets and philosophers. Aristotle and Cicero, as reinterpreted by Bruni in his own earlier biographies, are key figures in the ideation and design of the *Vita di Dante*, which reworks many of the themes that he had earlier elaborated in relation to them.[40] With important passages in mind from Cicero's *De officiis* and Aristotle's *Nicomachean Ethics* and *Politics* (Bruni had rendered these Aristotelian works into elegant Latin in 1416 and 1435–37), he goes on to laud the procreative function of marriage as essential to the growth of the city and the fulfillment of man's nature as an 'animale civile' or 'social animal':

> perdonimi il Boccaccio, i suoi giudicii sono molto fievoli in questa parte et molto distanti dalla vera oppinione. L'huomo è animale civile, secondo piace a tutti i philosophi: la prima congiuntione, dalla quale multiplicata nasce la città, è marito e moglie; né cosa può essere perfetta dove questo non sia, et solo questo amore è naturale, legittimo et perfetto.[41]

> May Boccaccio pardon me – his opinions are very frivolous on this topic, and very distant from correct judgment. Man is a social animal, according to what the philosophers say. His first joining, from the multiplication of which is born the city, is husband and wife, and nothing can be perfect where this is lacking, for only this love is natural, legitimate, and permissible.

Bruni's Aristotelian and Ciceronian emphases on human community, responsible citizenship, and man's intimate connection with the *polis* also motivate his account of Dante's political career: 'tolta donna et vivendo civile et honesta et studiosa vita, fu aoperato nella repubblica assai' ('having taken a wife and living his honest and studious life in society, he was frequently employed in affairs of the Republic').[42] Bruni discusses at considerable length the events leading to Dante's exile, quoting from 'documentary' sources in the form of one of Dante's own letters which was not known to Boccaccio and is now lost. Bruni tells his reader that he has come across the letter during his research as the official historian of Florence ('per cagione della *Storia* che abbiamo scritta'); and in this section in particular he condenses details from Book IV of his *Historiae* into the *Vita*.[43] The innovation in method is considerable and it allows Bruni to present his life of Dante as an accurate piece of historical writing grounded in primary sources from Dante's own time. Of course, the *Vita* resembles the *Trattatello* in one key respect: it is an interpretative enterprise grounded in pre-established ideological and literary categories, and, as such, it entails a selective reading of Dante's life and works (as it does a partial interpretation of the *Trattatello*). There is perhaps no better example in Dante's Florentine reception of my earlier observations in the Introduction about how varying interpretative frameworks are built around Dante and how these interact with earlier traditions to re-present him within new contexts. Such considerations apply to Bruni's treatment of Dante's exile, where, with none of Boccaccio's scorn for the city's unnatural antipathy to the poet, Bruni is careful to point out how, even at his most anti-Florentine, Dante showed 'reverentia della patria' ('respect for his homeland').[44] Like Boccaccio, Bruni inserts details of Dante's economic situation, lineage, and physical bearing, although his account is highly abbreviated and has clear differences in tone and emphasis compared to the *Trattatello*. Dante's youthful familiarity with love poetry is, for example, put down to his noble heart, not his lustfulness.[45]

After the lengthy historical excursus on the background to Dante's exile, Bruni's main preoccupation for the rest of the *Vita* is to offer an extended discussion of poetry. He starts with a succinct definition of the nature of Dante's poetry, which he then clarifies further by discussing the two main species of poetry, one based upon mental abstraction and agitation (the *furor poeticus* of Plato's *Phaedrus*),[46] the other upon intense study and mental application. Dante is of the second kind:

> Lo studio suo fu poesia, ma non sterile, né povera, né fantastica, ma fecundata et inricchita et stabilita per vera scientia et di moltissime discipline. Et per darmi a intendere meglio a chi legge, dico che in due modi diviene alcuno poeta. Uno modo si è per ingegno proprio agitato et non mosso da alcuno vigore interno et nascoso, il quale si chiama furore et occupatione di mente [. . .] l'altra spetie è per scientia, e per istudio, per disciplina et arte et prudentia. Et di questa seconda spetie fu Dante, per che per studio di philosophia et di teologia et astrologia, aritmetica et geometria, per letione di storie, per revolutione di molti et varii libri, vigilando et sudando nelli studi, acquistò la scientia, la quale doveva ornare et explicare co' li suoi versi.[47]

His principal study was poetry, but it was not of the sterile, impoverished or fantastic kind; his poetry was fecund and enriched, built upon true knowledge and great learning. In order that the reader may understand me better, let me say that one may become a poet in two ways. One is through the incitement and motion of personal genius by some inner and hidden force, which is called 'furor' – having one's mind possessed [...] the other sort comes through knowledge and study, through learning and art and prudence, and Dante was of this second sort. For he acquired the knowledge with which he was to adorn and exemplify his poetry through attentive and laborious study of philosophy, theology, astrology, arithmetic, geometry, through the reading of history and through the turning over of many different books.

Bruni then considers the definition of the word 'poet' itself, making an implicit criticism of the arguments and etymologies adopted by Boccaccio, Petrarch, and Salutati in their attempts to elevate poetic discourse by drawing on analogies with biblical language.[48] Bruni knows the correct Greek etymology of the word:

[...] Con tutto che queste sono cose che male si possono dire in vulgare idioma, pure m'ingegnerò darle ad intendere, perché, al parer mio, questi nostri poeti moderni non hanno bene intese; né è maraviglia, essendo ignari della lingua greca. Dico adunque che questo nome 'poeta' è nome greco, et tanto viene a dire quanto 'facitore' [...] de' libri et delle opere poetiche alcuni huomini sono leggitori delle opere altrui et niente fanno da sé, come addiviene al più delle genti; altri huomini sono facitori d'esse opere, come Vergilio fece il libro dell'*Eneida*, et Statio fece il libro della *Thebaida*, et Ovidio fece il libro *Metamorphoseos*, et Homero fece l'*Odissea* et l'*Iliade* [...] Poeta è adunque colui che fa alcuna opera, cioè autore et componitore di quello che altri legge.[49]

[...] even though these things can only be said poorly in the vulgar tongue, yet I shall exert myself to offer them to be understood, because in my opinion these modern poets of ours have not understood it well – but that is not surprising because they are ignorant of Greek. I say then that this name of 'poet' is a Greek word and means 'maker' [...] some men are readers of others' books and works of poetry, and they do nothing themselves, as happens with most men; other men are makers of these works, as Virgil made the book of the *Aeneid*, and Statius made the book of the *Thebaid*, and Ovid made the book the *Metamorphoses*, and Homer made the *Iliad* and the *Odyssey* [...] The poet then is he who makes any work, that is to say, the author and composer of what others read.

The examples of Virgil, Statius, and Ovid in this discussion of Dante-*poeta* are not incidental, since they help to foreshadow Bruni's account of the relationship between the vernacular and Latin which now follows in a centrally important passage that is worth reading in full:

> Or questa è la verità certa et assoluta del nome et dell'effetto de' poeti: lo scrivere in stilo litterato [i.e. Latin] o vulgare non ha a fare al fatto, né altra differenza è se non come scrivere in greco o in latino. Ciascuna lingua ha sua perfetione et suo suono et suo parlare limato et scientifico; pur, chi mi domandasse per qual cagione Dante piuttosto elesse scrivere in vulgare che in latino et litterato stile, risponderei quello che è la verità: cioè che Dante conosceva sé medesimo molto più atto a questo stile vulgare in rima che a quello latino o litterato. E certo molte cose da lui leggiadramente in questa rima vulgare sono dette che né arebbe saputo, né arebbe potuto dire in lingua latina ed in versi heroici. La prova sono l'*Egloghe* da lui fatte in versi exametri, le quali, posto sieno belle, niente di manco molte n'abbiamo vedute più vantaggiatamente scritte. Et a dire il vero, la virtù di questo poeta fu nella rima vulgare, nella quale è excellentissimo sopra ogni altro; ma in versi latini o in prosa non aggiunge appena a quegli che mezzanamente hanno scritto. La cagione è che il secolo suo era dato a dire in rima; et di gentilezza di dire in prosa o in versi latini niente intesero gl'huomini di quel secolo, ma furono rozzi et grossi et senza peritia di lettere, dotti, niente di meno, in queste discipline al modo fratesco e scolastico.[50]

Writing in literary or vernacular style has nothing to do with the case, any more than the difference between writing in Greek or in Latin. Each language has its own perfection and its own sound, and its polished and learned diction. Yet if someone should ask me why Dante chose to write in the vernacular rather than in Latin and the literate style, I would reply that the truth is right here, that is to say, that Dante knew himself much better adapted to this vernacular style in rhyme than to that Latin and literate style. Certainly he says many things graciously in this vulgar rhyme, which he could not have said and would not have known how to say in Latin and heroic verses. The proof of this is the *Eglogues*, done in hexameters; agreed they are beautiful, but nonetheless we have seen many that are better written. To speak the truth, the virtue of our poet was in vernacular rhyme, in which he is more excellent than any other; but in Latin verse, or in prose, he barely comes up to the average. The reason for this is that his century was given to rhymed speaking; the men of that time understood nothing of speaking in prose, or in Latin verse, for they were coarse and heavy and unskilled in letters, even if nonetheless learned in these disciplines according to the monkish scholastic manner.

Although Latin and the vernacular are not given complete parity here as some critics have suggested, the parallelism is strong and goes far beyond anything that Boccaccio and Salutati (both more enthusiastic 'defenders' of Dante than Bruni) had written about the *volgare*. For Bruni, both languages are capable of perfection, have their own sound structure, and can be polished and scientific. Dante's choice of the vernacular stems from his own recognition of his greater ability in this language (the only source to anticipate this assertion is Filippo Villani's *Expositio*). Such a view reworks the association that Bruni had made in the *Dialogi* between medieval scholastic culture and Dante, as well as the perceived gulf between Dante's vernacular poetry and his Latin writings. This point is made explicit in the *Vita del Petrarca* with which Dante's biography is paired. In Latin verse and prose, Bruni argues, Dante writes in the same rough, coarse, and unlettered way as his contemporaries, who, like him, were steeped in the scholastic texts of the friars. As in the *Dialogi*, Bruni's discussion frees Dante's poetry from the allegorical qualities praised by Boccaccio, Salutati, Villani, Rinuccini, and others. However, compared to the earlier work, the *Vita* also broadens and refines the praise of Dante's poetry in new ways, and in particular it eliminates almost completely the mythologized account of Dante as *poeta-theologus*, whose traces can still be detected in Book II of the *Dialogi*.

Bruni's views on the vernacular here can be related in part to arguments he elaborated a year before the *Vita di Dante* during a dispute among a group of apostolic secretaries held in Florence in the antechamber of Pope Eugenius IV. The debate concerned the question of whether the ancient Romans delivered their orations in Latin or in a *sermo vulgaris*. In a letter to Flavio Biondo dated 7 May 1435, Bruni favoured the view (which is Dante's own) that ancient Rome was a time of diglossia with Latin as a grammatical language which was distinct from the variable and agrammatical vernacular. The opposite (and correct) thesis – that classical Rome was essentially a monolingual culture, though one which was stylistically highly differentiated, and that the vernacular derived from this at a later date – was advanced by Biondo and expressed in his *De verbis Romanae locutionis ad Leonardum Arentinum* of 1 April 1435. Bruni's reliance upon Dantean arguments and positions is well known and has been studied in detail by both Angelo Mazzocco and Mirko Tavoni.[51] The debate on which language was spoken in ancient Rome had implications for the modern vernacular, even though Bruni did not explicitly state them. As Tavoni has shown, Bruni's view conferred some status upon the vernacular by projecting it back into antiquity, but it also meant that he endorsed the medieval view that it was agrammatical and inferior by its very nature; and this meant in turn that the vernacular was far from being reconciled with classicism as Baron and others have maintained.[52] It is rather a question of endorsing the legitimacy of the vernacular poetic tradition within certain contexts, while recognizing that Latin was required for higher subjects of a historical and philosophical nature. That this is indeed Bruni's attitude to the vernacular finds support in his comments on Latin and the vernacular in the *Vita*, not only in the important passage quoted above but also in his earlier observation on the difficulty of discussing the nature of poetry in the vernacular: 'queste sono cose che male si possono dire in vulgare idioma' ('these things can only be said poorly in the vulgar tongue').

The remainder of the *Vita* offers a succinct overview of Dante's place in the vernacular poetic tradition and of his own works. Following Dante's view in chapter 25 of the *Vita nuova* that poetry in Italian preceded him by relatively few years, Bruni lists some of Dante's predecessors and notes how far he surpassed them in his use of *sententiae*, polish, elegance, and grace. Poetry's allegorical qualities are not mentioned and the stress falls instead on Dante's variety and abundance, knowledge of philosophy, and familiarity with ancient and especially modern history (once again Dante is being celebrated by means of literary categories that are pre-eminently humanistic). Dante's *canzoni* are singled out for praise, but, still faithful to the distinction between his ability in the vernacular and his Latin production, the Latin works are dismissed as lacking the appropriate style, and the *Monarchia* in particular is singled out as 'scritto al modo fratesco, sanza niuna gentilezza di dire' ('written in the monkish style without any nobility of language'),[53] in a judgement that also echoes the general condemnation of Dante's scholastic culture found in the *Dialogi*.

As we have seen, then, a central feature of Bruni's life is the attempt to make Dante into an emblematic figure who embodies the ideal Florentine citizen – learned, politically active, and conscious of how all spheres of human activity may best serve the city. It is not therefore surprising that critics have often spoken in general terms of Bruni's Dante as a prototype of the civic humanist, and have noted the propagandistic quality of the *Vita* as a celebration of Florentine pre-eminence. But the oscillations in Bruni's political orientations and his known ties to the pre-1434 oligarchy have led some to suggest that the work may have a more specific ideological underpinning. As Arthur Field in particular has argued, given the pro-Dante and vernacular leanings of the oligarchical faction, Bruni's life may, in its very choice of subject-matter and language, be a form of defiance to the Medici regime.[54] Field's thesis is lent some support by the general similarities between Bruni's sober observations on Dante's political activism and the impassioned rhetoric of Filelfo's Republican Dante. But Filelfo's Dante is a far less subtle creation whose partisan allegiances are openly displayed in ferocious polemic. It may well be that Bruni was intent on keeping his options open amidst the ambiguities and fluctuations of Florentine political life, but we cannot say any more than that, especially given his links with Cosimo and a letter from 1436 which suggest his detachment from the exiled oligarchic party by petitioning the Sienese authorities, on Cosimo de' Medici's behalf, for measures to be taken against Filelfo. Indeed, it may be possible that a further motivation for the *Vita* is one that the Medici were themselves keen to endorse – the desire to promote Florence externally, at a time when the first attempts were being made for the city to be the venue for the Council of the Church.[55] In this light, the *Vita* can be viewed as a potent example of how the evocative force of Dante's name and its value for maximizing the 'gloria della città' help to overturn ideologized cultural preferences that had previously militated against him.

4 Leon Battista Alberti

A Florentine by family but not formation, the bastard son of an exiled banker, Leon Battista Alberti did not visit Florence until after 1428 when the city lifted the ban on his family. By this date, he had received an exemplary humanist education in Padua and Bologna and was employed in the Papal Curia. The residence of Pope Eugenius IV in Florence brought Alberti to the city for a period of at least eight years between 1434–36 and 1439–43. During this time, Alberti produced several major vernacular works which are all in different ways reactions to the literary, artistic, and social dimensions of contemporary Florence: a vernacular dialogue on Florentine social attitudes; the first grammar of an Italian vernacular; technical compositions, in both Latin and the vernacular, on painting and sculpture, and mathematics; and vernacular treatises that survey the philosophical traditions of antiquity. In all these works, as well as in a small but important corpus of vernacular poetry produced mainly in the early 1430s, he experimented constantly with the possibilities of the Italian language and attempted to bring it into fertile contact with the conceptual riches of the classical tradition and the lexical and syntactic resources of the Latin language. In Florence of the 1430s and early 1440s, Alberti thus provides one of the most important and sophisticated attempts to ennoble the vernacular by using it to deal with humanist themes and topics.

In the *proemio* to Book III of his *Libri della famiglia* (*c.* 1437), Alberti quite clearly takes sides against Bruni by maintaining that there was an original Latin language which barbarian invasions caused to degenerate. He insists that modern Tuscan is a language with its own grammar (the inability of servants to vary tenses and cases appropriately is sufficient testimony to this):

> Fu Italia più volte occupata e posseduta da varie nazioni [. . .] di dì in dì insalvatichì e viziossi la nostra prima cultissima ed emendatissima lingua [. . .] Non vediamo noi quanto sia difficile a' servi nostri profferire le dizioni in modo che sieno intesi, solo perché non sanno,

né per uso possono variare casi e tempi, e concordare quanto ancora nostra lingua richiede?[56]

Italy was repeatedly occupied and ruled over by different nations [. . .] from day to day our once most refined and polished language became rustic and degenerated [. . .] Do we not see how difficult it is for our servants to use the right words so that they are understood simply because they do not know how, and cannot make, words agree due to their lack of knowledge and practice in varying cases and tenses?

In this way, Alberti seizes on the potentialities in Biondo's thesis concerning the forms of Latin spoken in ancient Rome in order to argue that the vernacular is itself a language that has grammatical regularity, and that it can be developed into a medium of higher literary expression. This kind of militant approach to the vernacular is completely absent from Biondo's original formulation of the question, and it bypasses some of the hesitations and residual prejudices which remain in the vernacular works of Palmieri and Bruni.

In this *proemio*, Alberti goes on to argue that if ancient writers wrote in one language so as to be understood by many then there is no reason to disparage or condemn those who write in Tuscan. In other words, to use Tuscan vernacular is to establish a relationship with all the citizens of the city, and to provide a means of affirming the identity of the *patria*. Moreover, the Tuscan language has, like Latin, its own 'ornamenti' ('ornaments'); and, if it lacks the authority of Latin, this is due to the absence of learned writers in the vernacular who through study and effort will polish and perfect it:

stimo niuno dotto negarà quanto a me pare qui da credere, che tutti gli antichi scrittori scrivessero in modo che da tutti e' suoi molto voleano essere intesi [. . .] Più tosto forse e' prudenti mi loderanno s'io, scrivendo in modo che ciascuno m'intenda, prima cerco giovare a molti che piacere a pochi, ché sai quanto siano pochissimi a questi dì e' litterati [. . .] Ben confesso quella antiqua latina lingua essere copiosa molto e ornatissima, ma non però veggo in che sia la nostra oggi toscana tanto d'averla in odio, che in essa qualunque benché ottima cosa scritta ci dispiaccia. A me par assai di presso dire quel ch'io voglio, e in modo ch'io sono pur inteso, ove questi biasimatori in quella antica sanno se non tacere, e in questa moderna sanno se non biasimare chi non tace. E sento io questo: chi fusse più di me dotto o tale quale molti vogliono essere riputati, costui in questa oggi commune troverrebbe non meno ornamenti che in quella, quale essi tanto prepongono e tanto in altri desiderano. Né posso io patire che a molti dispiaccia quello che pur usano, e pur lodino quello che né intendono, né in sé curano d'intendere. Troppo biasimo chi richiede in altri quello che in sé stessi recusa. E sia quanto dicono quella antica apresso di tutte le genti piena d'autorità, solo perché in essa molti dotti scrissero, simile certo sarà la nostra, s'e' docti la vorranno molto con suo studio et vigilie essere elimata e polita.[57]

I believe that no wise man will deny what I believe is the case here, namely, that all the ancients writers wrote in such a way as to be understood by all their people [...] Indeed, the wise are more likely to praise me if, by writing in a way that all can understand, I at first attempt to be useful to many rather than to please a few, for you know how very few people are literate these days [...] I readily admit that the ancient Latin language was most abundant and ornate, but I do not see why our own Tuscan is so odious that anything written in it, no matter how excellent, fails to please us. It seems to me enough if I can say more or less what I want to say and do so in a way that can be understood; meanwhile these critics only know how to be silent in the ancient language and to condemn those that speak in the modern one. And I believe that if someone else were more learned than I, or were what many would like to be thought to be, he will find no fewer ornaments in our common language than the one they so much prefer and wish everyone to use. I cannot stand the fact that many people show contempt for what they themselves speak, and praise what they neither understand nor attempt to cultivate. It is reprehensible to ask others to do what you yourself refuse. And as for the great authority among all peoples which they say is in the ancient language, this is because learned men have written in it: our own language will be similar to it if the learned would refine and polish it with labour and study.

In this passionately charged passage, which is run through with a strong opposition to the narrow, vituperative attacks against the vernacular made by some fellow humanists (Niccoli, Bracciolini, and Marsuppini are the obvious candidates), Alberti envisages a refounding of Tuscan in a conscious attempt to bridge the chasm that has come to separate the *studia humanitatis* from the vernacular.

For Alberti, then, Italian provides a proper medium for the learned debates that were carried on in classical Latin, and in the four books that make up the *Libri della famiglia* he shows how the vernacular is able to treat complex moral teachings and a variety of other topics. And yet, despite the revolutionary quality of these statements and their influence on later Florentine attempts to promote the vernacular, especially from the 1460s onwards (see above chapter 4, section 1), it is intriguing that throughout the *proemio* Alberti maintains a notable silence over Dante and other earlier Italian writers. It would seem that the vernacular is not to be refounded upon their example but through the efforts of modern writers drawing on different models. It is certainly true that Alberti's own Italian prose is closely modelled, both lexically and syntactically, upon Latin and remains to a large extent independent of Trecento precedents (this is illustrated by the passage quoted earlier from Alberti's *proemio* with its Latinizing constructions such as 'suo' for 'loro' and 'confesso [...] essere').[58] In the 1430s Alberti uses his classical reading to create a Tuscan language able to deal with the technical and terminological demands of writing about painting, sculpture, and mathematics, moral philosophy, and ancient philosophy. This kind of classicizing approach to the vernacular also informs his innovative grammar of Tuscan, the *Grammatichetta della lingua toscana* (*c.* 1438–41), which is founded on the conviction that Latin and contemporary Tuscan are underpinned by a shared grammatical structure and hence that the *volgare* can be analysed according to the precepts and terminology of classical grammars such as Priscian's *Institutiones*.[59]

Prima facie, such neglect for the Trecento tradition is also apparent in Alberti's own vernacular poetry which is perhaps best known for its use of the metrical structures of Latin poetry, especially the hexameter and the sapphic strophe, as well as for the invention of the vernacular eclogue.[60] However, as a seminal article by Emilio Pasquini and Guglielmo Gorni's notes to his critical edition of Alberti's Italian poetry make clear, Dante occupies a centrally important presence throughout this poetic corpus of nineteen compositions.[61] One of Alberti's sonnets contains his only direct reference to Dante in all his writings, when, following a lament of injustices suffered, Alberti the poet contemplates a future moment of redistributive justice:

> La tu' iustitia, ché tanto s'aspecta?
> Ben dice Dante, ond'io prendo vigore:
> La spada di lassù non taglia in fretta.[62]

> What about your justice, which is so long awaited? Dante – from whom I take strength – rightly says: the sword from on high does not cut in a hurry.

This quotation is only the most direct form of Dantean intertextuality at work in Alberti's vernacular poetry, and it seems that the Dantean matrix forms a key model for his own poetic experimentalism which tries out eight verse forms, and constantly seeks to reconcile ancient models with more contemporary ones.

Dante's legacy also has some part to play in the *Certame coronario*, a public contest in vernacular poetry, which Alberti organized and which represents his most daring attempt to demonstrate the excellence of the vernacular, by having it assimilate the structures of classical poetry. The idea of a singing contest, or *certame*, is itself a classical archetype being a device of the pastoral mode, and the linkage with a memorable classical model is integral to Alberti's aim of gaining humanist recognition for the vernacular. The entrants to the *Certame* were called upon to write in Tuscan vernacular on the theme of friendship, a Ciceronian motif *par excellence*, and one which was evidently chosen to show how topics from classical moral philosophy could be handled in vernacular poetry. The contest was supported financially by Piero de' Medici, and its victor, as the title of the contest suggests, was to be awarded a laurel crown. Alberti sought a seal of legitimacy for the enterprise by choosing humanist critics as judges of the compositions. The adjudicators were in fact the ten secretaries to Pope Eugenius, and they included Bracciolini, Biondo, and several other humanists who had been involved in the earlier debate on Latin in the pope's antechamber.[63]

The contest took place on 22 October 1441 in the Florentine Cathedral with eight contestants either reading their poetry aloud or having it read for them. The participants developed a wide range of themes and drew on a multiplicity of sources, from ancient mythology to classical philosophy, from Neoplatonic thought to patristic theology. But in contrast to the classical framework, upon which Alberti articulates the contest, Dante is never far removed from the linguistic texture of most of the compositions. Indeed, two *certatori*, as the contestants were known, invoke Dante's name so as to establish the authority of the vernacular by direct reference to him. In his *canzone* 'Benché si dica nel volgar parlare', Anselmo Calderoni mentions Dante, and, perhaps echoing Boccaccio's *Trattatello*, makes the standard comparison with Homer and Virgil:

> Così come del greco fu Omero
> solo, simil Vergilio nel latino,
> e Dante fiorentino
> nobilitò questo nostro idïoma.

> As Homer was without peer in Greek, and Virgil similarly in Latin,
> and so too the Florentine Dante ennobled this language of ours.

As well as other reminiscences of the *Comedy*, this *canzone* adopts Dantean metres, employing the same metrical structure and *congedo* used by Dante in one of his *Rime petrose*, 'Così nel mio parlar'.[64] Another contestant, Mariotto Davanzati, places his *capitolo* under the dual influence of the 'duo sacri lumi' ('two sacred lights'), Dante and Petrarch, 'senza i qua' di parlar non sare' oso' ('without whom I would not dare to speak').[65] Almost all the compositions contain strong verbal echoes of the *Comedy*, and this is particularly true of Francesco d'Altobianco Alberti's *capitolo* 'Sacrosancta, immortal, celeste e degna' and Ciriaco d'Ancona's sonnet 'Quel Sir, che socto l'idëale stampa'.[66] By contrast, the composition which most closely measures up to Alberti's militant approach to a vernacular enriched by classical exemplars is that by his fellow humanist, Leonardo Dati. Dati's contribution, 'I' son Mercurio, di tutto l'olimpico regno', audaciously adapts the vernacular to classical metres, such as the hexameter and sapphic strophe, as Alberti himself had done in his own vernacular elegies and eglogue.

The outcome of the *Certame* could not have been more disappointing for Alberti. The adjudicators acknowledged that the vernacular poets had displayed rhetorical skill, but they refused to award the crown, since the *certatori* fell short of the ancient works from which their contents were drawn. Alberti wrote an impassioned *protesta* in which he denounced the judges and reiterated his belief in the expressive capacities of the vernacular. As in the *proemio* to Book III of *Libri della famiglia*, he made historical parallels with the situation of Latin in ancient Rome and asserted that learning was compatible with vernacular expression; and he also stressed the utility of the vernacular to Florentine citizens and its value to the *patria*. The *protesta* is again reticent about the role of Dante and the earlier Florentine vernacular tradition, but another contemporary document, which laments the outcome of the *Certame*, is less circumspect:

> Che se il nostro celebrato poeta Dante, o 'l Petrarcha, o 'l Bocchaccio ànno tanto conseguitato di gratia et di gloria solamente innelle loro dolcissime e suavissime rime, certamente maggiore degnità che quella meritano odierni poeti, i quali non solamente le rime ànno avute ardire di cantare, che non sono composte se none del numero delle sillabe, ma ancora ànno avuto ardire non solamente di cantare l'eroico verso esametro e 'legorico, ma anchora di cantarllo con grandissime lode.[67]

> For if our celebrated poet Dante, or Petrarch and Boccaccio, have gained grace and glory by the sole means of their most sweet and delectable rhymes, surely contemporary poets today deserve greater dignity. These poets have not only dared to sing rhymes which are entirely composed according to the number of syllables, but they have, moreover, dared to sing in heroic hexameters, and not only to sing but to receive great praise for so doing.

With its emphasis upon the way that contemporary poets have surpassed Florence's own 'tre corone', the anonymous author of this prose *capitolo* provides an important glimpse into the emulative and classicizing designs of vernacular poetry in one section of Florentine society in the early 1440s. The view expressed may well provide us with an insight into Alberti's motivations, and his sense of the distance between his Tuscan and the language of Dante.

What the outcome of the *Certame* reveals most directly are the strong reservations that continued to bedevil attempts to use the vernacular as a learned, literary language on a par with humanist Latin: the humanists in the papal entourage simply did not accept that the vernacular had attained sufficient stature to be placed alongside Latin. Indeed, the very attempt to draw classical forms into the vernacular and to use it to deal with humanist themes was probably an affront to humanists of the stamp of Poggio and Biondo for whom the vernacular by its very nature was a bastardized, plebeian, and medieval offshoot of Latin. Dati himself returned to producing works in Latin. Alberti attempted to stage a second contest, appropriately enough on the theme of envy, but this did not come to fruition and in the early 1440s he was to leave Florence: his great period of vernacular experimentation was largely over and he was only to return to the city for brief periods.

The *Certame* may have been a resounding failure and a sign of Alberti's misjudgement of the criteria of judgement employed by many of his fellow humanists. Yet in spite of this, at other cultural levels, the Tuscan poetry of the competitors met with success, as is shown by the popularity of manuscripts of the *certatoris'* poetry in the second half of the fifteenth century. During this later period there emerges a reinvigorated attitude to Dante and the Trecento vernacular tradition under the aegis of Cosimo's grandson, Lorenzo de' Medici. And, as we will see in the next chapter, it is within this context that Alberti's ideas about the vernacular were to be recast in an effort to establish the vernacular as a language and literary form of equal worth to Latin.

4

Dante and Florentine vernacular humanism: critical judgements and literary experiments

After the failure of the *Certame coronario* to gain official recognition for a revalorized vernacular modelled upon classical precedents, in the 1440s and early 1450s the literary and scholarly activities of Florentine humanists are concerned predominantly with Latin and Greek. Of course, the vernacular is still used in a wide range of contexts from civic orations to university lessons, from letters to family records and onto poetic works of various kinds, and there are numerous examples of cross-fertilization between it and Latin. The Tuscan vernacular begins, moreover, to gain a stronger foothold in other cultural centres due to the interest shown in it by Italian princes. And yet, humanists in Florence and elsewhere continue to devalue the vernacular, reaffirming its links with lower cultural levels in a way that is prejudicial to the reputation of Dante. The life of Dante written in the early 1440s by Gianozzo Manetti (1396–1459), a Florentine humanist with close ties to residual elements in the city's communal and oligarchical culture, is a revealing document of such reactions. Gianozzo's life is itself composed in Latin as part of his *Vitae* of Dante, Petrarch, and Boccaccio, and the preface compares unfavourably (as Salutati and Bruni had done) their use of Latin not only with the ancients but also with contemporary writers. However, this preface also laments a situation in which the three crowns 'come to be little esteemed by the erudite and learned, who regard them as trifles or nothing at all', and 'as a result they are praised mostly by the ignorant and the unlearned, but none of the erudite take up their poems, or tales, or other writings of theirs, except maybe for the sake of a laugh or a jest'. The ghost of Niccolò Niccoli, who had died in 1437, lives on.

Manetti distinguishes his lives from Villani's earlier treatment of illustrious Florentines in the *De origine*, by restricting himself only to poets, and describes his main purpose as to bring the 'tre corone' 'at last to the knowledge of learned men, who have always set small value on vernacular writings such as form our poets' chief claim to fame'.[1] In his own life of Dante, Manetti shows a tendency to compile from earlier Florentine biographies, by borrowing details from Bruni's *Vita di Dante* such as Dante's participation at Campaldino, and giving renewed expression to Villani's view that Dante brought poetry back to life after centuries of somnolence.[2] But Manetti's principal source is Boccaccio's *Trattatello*, which he follows closely in both structure and tone throughout his account. Thus, Manetti celebrates Beatrice, praises the *Comedy* as a divine poem, uses legendary material, presents Dante as a book-devouring, solitary scholar, and engages in invectives against Florence's treatment of him. As we will see, this is not an isolated example of how Boccaccio's work on Dante continues to provide points of reference for Florentines even after Bruni's withering attack in his *Vita di Dante*.

By 1450, relatively few individuals remained from the oligarchical grouping whose allegiances to Dante have been explored in earlier chapters. Manetti was himself exiled in 1453, and, in the same year, that renowned deprecator of the vernacular, Poggio Bracciolini, returned to Florence as Chancellor. Dante plays a minor role in his writings, except for the light-hearted treatment of him in three stories within a collection of Latin *novelle* – one is reminded of Manetti's allusion to laughter and jests.[3] In Florence, there were also now few humanists of the generation of Bruni, and contemporaries sensed that the city had begun to lose its cultural standing in Italy following the rapid development of Rome as a centre of humanist scholarship under the pontificate of Nicholas V (1447–55). The 1450s were fractious and turbulent years for the Medici and their control over the city was far from absolute. In this context, after a period of closure, the Florentine *Studio* began to play an increasingly important role in developing new cultural initiatives, and acted as a site in which the anti-Medicean faction asserted itself. The most important initiative occurred in 1457 when prominent figures within this faction such as Donato Acciaiuoli and Alemanno Rinuccini were successful in bringing a Byzantine scholar, John Argyropoulos, to the *Studio* to lecture on Aristotle.[4] Aristotle's name brought with it a civic inflection since his ethical and political writings had been popular with earlier Florentine humanists, who, as we saw in the previous chapter, had used his teachings in order to analyse the active life and the proper role of the citizen in the *polis*. As translator and scholar, Bruni had earlier notably revised how the medieval Aristotle was presented, rendering his works into good humanist Latin. Argyropoulos, who held his post until 1471, was unusual in teaching an enlarged Aristotelian corpus that went beyond the ethical and political writings, and his lectures gained wide circulation through the manuscript publication of lecture-notes by his students.[5] Aristotle thus remained an essential component of the classical heritage studied by humanists in Medici Florence, even though the second half of the fifteenth century is best known for a revitalized concern with Plato and the Platonic tradition, most notably through the efforts of Marsilio Ficino (1433–99).[6]

From the 1460s onwards, and especially after the death of Cosimo de' Medici on 1 August 1464, we witness the first stirrings of a renewed movement towards employing the vernacular at higher cultural levels. There are various attempts to promote interchange between the ancient and Tuscan languages in the fields of philosophy, theology, and classical studies. Lorenzo de' Medici, Cosimo's grandson, assumes power in 1469 at the age of twenty-one, and he plays a key role in intensifying efforts to promote Tuscan in what amounts to a cultural project that linked the *volgare* to the political standing and intellectual prestige of the Florentine state. The vernacular now comes to be used for subjects which had previously been almost the sole preserve of Latin. After a considerable interlude, there are new vernacular versions or *volgarizzamenti* of classical and humanist texts. Various attempts, both practical and theoretical, are made to enrich the lexicon and syntax of the vernacular by bringing it into closer contact with the Latin tradition. And much energy and insight are devoted to collecting and re-evaluating vernacular works.[7] Dante represents an important figure within this intellectual and linguistic ferment, and his name and writings often underpin efforts to classicize vernacular literary culture that will reach a high-point in Landino's commentary on the *Comedy* (see Part III).

This chapter explores the ways in which Dante's *Comedy* and other writings are transmitted, reinterpreted, and imitated in Florence during the 1460s and 1470s. It assesses in particular the contributions of Lorenzo de' Medici, as well as Angelo Poliziano and Cristoforo Landino, the humanists most closely linked to him, in promoting what is often known as vernacular humanism. The chapter also takes into account three other figures who pay close attention to Dante: the philosopher and prime mover in the revival of platonism, Marsilio Ficino; the merchant and copyist, Antonio Tuccio Manetti; and Matteo Palmieri. These individuals offer us a rich variety of material related to Dante which is developed in a number of different directions and contexts. For convenience, in what follows this subject-matter has been organized into three principal categories – literary judgements on Dante and the recovery of his texts; *volgarizzamenti*; and various forms of poetic experimentation that bear markedly Dantean echoes. As we will see, the categories contain several overlapping strands, and many of the individuals considered are active under more than one heading, as well as having close relations with one another.

1 Literary judgements and the recovery of vernacular texts

At some time between 1467 and 1470, Cristoforo Landino decided to lecture upon Petrarch's vernacular poetry from his Chair of Rhetoric and Poetry at the Florentine *Studio*.[8] Landino was fully aware that this was a radical move: no-one had previously read a vernacular author from this *cattedra* – the tradition of Dante lectures being, as we have often seen, a special category of lecture with a moralistic purpose, reserved for wider public consumption and generally held in civic spaces on feast days. Anticipating his critics, Landino used his inaugural lecture or *prolusione* to set out a defence of the *volgare* as a language of both poetry and prose. In so doing, he offered a programmatic statement about how to ennoble Tuscan as a literary language, whose present-day deficiencies are not related to anything intrinsic to its nature or origins, but rather to the negligence of those who use it:

> se e' considerassino [sc. detractors of the *volgare*] diligentemente non solo quello che insino a ora di lei [sc. 'la fiorentina lingua'] si vede, ma e quello che in essa ancora imperfetto e quasi rozo si potrebbe elimare e con molto ornato ripulire, intenderebbe non la natura di essa lingua, ma la negligenza di chi l'usa essere in colpa.[9]

If they considered diligently not only what until now we have seen of the Florentine tongue, but also those parts of it which, still imperfect and almost coarse, could be polished and cleaned with much ornament, they would understand that the fault lies not with the nature of this language but with the negligence of those who use it.

In this way, Landino follows a line of argument very similar to that adopted by Alberti, his friend and mentor in the *proemio* to Book III of *Libri della famiglia*. Landino goes on to give an account of classical languages that emphasizes how they have been perfected by the talent, artistry, and sedulity of generations of Greek and Latin writers. And he then extends this notion of perfectibility to what he calls 'la fiorentina lingua' ('the Florentine language'), developing two important theses. The first is that, in order to enrich the lexical patrimony of the Tuscan vernacular and to enhance its stylistic elegance, it is necessary to study and imitate Latin models of style and thought and to transfer these into the vernacular:

> il nostro patrio sermone non avere avuto più debile principio che gli altri, e per niente altro essere rimaso indietro se non per carestia di dotti scrittori [...] dico che niuno potrà essere nonché eloquente ma pure tollerabile dicitore nella nostra lingua, se prima non arà vera e perfetta cognizione delle lettere latine. Il che mentre che in brievi parole vi pruovo, vi priego che con attenzione mi ascoltiate. Niuno di voi dubita che ogni sermone ha di bisogno di parole e di sentenzie. Le parole sanza arte sempre fieno inette, perché mancheranno d'eleganza, mancheranno di composizione, mancheranno di dignità. Le sentenzie, le quali non saranno tratte da veri studi di umanità, sempre fieno e frivoli e leggieri, né mai potrà avere lo scrittore gravità e buon suco o nervi nello stile quando non sia, se non al tutto dotto, almanco alquanto introdotto in filosofia [...] Se adunque fa di bisogno l'arte, fa di bisogno la dottrina, e queste sanza la latina lingua non s'acquistano, è necessario essere latino chi vuole essere buono Toscano. Aggiungete a queste due ragioni la terza. Ognuno si vede che volendo arricchire questa lingua, bisogna ogni dì de' latini vocaboli, non sforzando la natura, derivare e condurre nel nostro idioma.[10]

The language of our homeland has not had a less stable beginning than others and it has remained behind for no other reason than the lack of good writers [...] I say that no-one can be a tolerable writer in our language, still less an eloquent one, if he does not first have a true and perfect knowledge of Latin letters. And whilst I prove this to you in a few words, I beg that you listen to me attentively. Now, none of you doubt that every language needs words and thoughts. Words expressed without artistry will always be ineffectual, because they will lack elegance, composition, and dignity. Ideas which are not taken from true studies of humanity will always be light and frivolous. Nor will any writer have gravity and robustness or daring in his style unless he is, if not learned in philosophy, at least instructed in it. If therefore good writing is a matter of artistry and learning and these things are only acquired through the Latin language, whoever wants to be a good writer of Tuscan must be a good Latinist. Add to this a third reason: everyone sees that if we want to enrich this language we must every day take Latin words and, without forcing the nature of Tuscan, bring them into our idiom.

This passage encapsulates the essence of Landino's ideas on the vernacular, emphasizing how through the key concept of 'transferimento' or 'transference', it can be made continuous with the classical tradition and raised up to the level of Latin. In his later lectures and writings, Landino further develops the notion of using Latin as a model from which to detach lexical items and bring them into the vernacular, while at the same time respecting the nature of Tuscan. The second key idea that Landino elaborates in this *prolusione* regards the status of the vernacular as a patriotic language: love of the vernacular is tantamount to love of the city itself:

> se amate adunque la patria, suvvenitela in questa parte, acciò che, come in molte altre cose tutte le italiche terre avanza, così in questa ottegna il principato.[11]

> if therefore you love the homeland, help it in this respect, so that just as it surpasses all the Italian states in many other things, so may it obtain primacy in this matter.

One could not wish for a clearer expression of the civic and patriotic connections between the status of Florence and the development of its language.

As several critics have recognized, the *prolusione* on Petrarch represents perhaps the most decisive text in the refounding of literature in Italian along humanist lines. In his ardent passion for the vernacular Landino distinguishes himself from many other humanists of the time, with the exception of Alberti. What Landino in effect promotes is a new form of literature, no longer municipal and backward-looking, but nurtured by the *studia humanitatis* and anchored to the Latin classics, on the one hand, and to both Petrarch (especially the poet of the *Canzoniere*) and Dante, on the other.[12] In this way, Landino takes a very different stance from Alberti's guarded silence over Dante, and adopts a far more refined approach to the vernacular than that represented by the contestants at the *Certame*. Landino only mentions Dante in passing in this lecture, although significantly he uses the language of rebirth, commenting that 'La poetica, ognun vede che resuscitò Dante, uomo per certo degno che la natura avesse prodotto immortale. Ma non è ora tempo di raccontare sue laude' ('Everyone knows that poetry was revived by Dante, a man certainly worthy that nature had made him immortal. But now is not the time to recount his praises').[13] Such praise of Dante comes in Landino's later *prolusione* (c. 1474) to his lectures on the *Comedy*, and above all in the *proemio* to his Dante commentary of 1481, where he reworks all the principal themes of the *prolusione* on Petrarch in order to assert that the *volgare* is a literary language and that Dante is its initiator (see below chapter 5, sections 1 and 3).

A decade after Landino's *prolusione* in 1477, two of his best-known former students, Lorenzo de' Medici and Angelo Poliziano, produced a codex known as the *Raccolta Aragonese*. The original exemplar of the *Raccolta* is not extant, but later copies indicate that it was a wide-ranging collection of vernacular poetry which contained some 480 compositions across a span of over 200 years, from the Sicilians and Guinizelli to the poets of the *Certame*, and on to contemporary Tuscan poets, including Lorenzo himself.[14] The collection was prefaced by an introductory *Epistola*, now established as being written by Poliziano,[15] which dedicates the work to Frederick of Aragon, the younger son of the King of Naples, Ferrante or Ferdinand I. In its entirety the *Raccolta* and accompanying epistle mark the beginning of more systematic attempts to search out and collate manuscripts of the vernacular lyric tradition, and to place them within an historical perspective, with some of the fervour that had been applied to classical texts a century earlier.[16] This kind of approach to vernacular texts is strongly suggested by the analogies that Poliziano himself makes in the *Epistola* between Pisistratus' recomposition of the

Homeric corpus and the 'grandissima fatica' ('very great effort') he has expended in discovering 'gli antichi esemplari' ('ancient exemplars') for the vernacular collection.[17] Poliziano's prefatory letter sets out a series of positive judgements on earlier literature in Italian; and, as its dedication suggests, it is subtended by the broader political and patriotic implications of Tuscanization. The letter thus echoes some of the themes dealt with by Landino, especially the need not to scorn the Tuscan language but rather to appreciate its riches and ornaments. Yet, as Roberto Cardini has shown, there are also major differences between Landino's earlier *prolusione*, with its narrow view of what constitutes vernacular excellence, and the more eclectic approach to the earlier Tuscan poetic tradition advocated by Poliziano.[18]

Dante is an important facet within the extant manuscripts based upon the *Raccolta*, and he is given pride of place insofar as he is the first poet whose works are included in the collection. It is Dante's *Vita nuova*, nineteen of his *canzoni*, and nine other compositions that are transcribed, and as such the *Raccolta* marks the first serious attempt at recovering the minor works of Dante since Boccaccio. The *Convivio* also formed part of earlier versions of the *Raccolta* and it may even have been part of the codex presented to Frederick.[19] As Michele Barbi and Domenico De Robertis in particular have demonstrated, there are close links with Boccaccio's work as copyist, since both the *Vita nuova* and fifteen of the *canzoni* derive from the textual traditions established by him through a late autograph manuscript now known as Chigiano L. V.176. It is significant, too, that, in the *Raccolta*, Boccaccio's *Trattatello* precedes the bloc of Dantean material. This reveals not only the enduring popularity of the work in Florence, and a further point of contact with Chigiano L. V.176, but it also shows how Dante's works were transmitted with earlier exegetical and encomiastic texts attached to them.[20] What is more, the *Epistola* echoes the language of the *Comedy*, and offers some especially interesting judgements on Dante's poetry. Poliziano recognizes Dante's centrality within the Tuscan tradition of vernacular poetry, and this may well have motivated the inclusion of Boccaccio's life within the *Raccolta*.[21] In the *Epistola*, Poliziano refers to both Dante and Petrarch as 'two wonderful suns' in what is a subtle, decontextualized allusion to *Purgatorio* XVI, 107: 'Risplendono dopo costoro [sc. Bonagiunta da Lucca, Jacopo da Lentini, Pier delle Vigne] quelli dui mirabili soli, che questa lingua hanno illuminato: Dante, e non molto drieto a esso Francesco Petrarca' ('After them shine those two wonderful suns who have illuminated this language: Dante and not much behind him, Francis Petrarch').[22] Poliziano goes on to allude to Dante's own judgements in the *Comedy* on his predecessors in the lyric tradition (as we saw in chapter 2, Petrarch had echoed and reversed these judgements in the *Trionfi*), but he also makes a highly personal evaluation of Dante's language:[23]

> Il bolognese Onesto e li siciliani, che già i primi furono, come di questi dui [sc. Dante and Petrarch] sono più antichi, così della loro lima più averebbono bisogno, avvenga che né ingegno né volontà a alcuno di loro si vede essere mancato. Assai bene alla sua nominanza risponde Cino da Pistoia, tutto delicato e veramente amoroso, il quale primo, al mio parere, cominciò l'antico rozzore in tutto a schifare, dal quale né il divino Dante, per altro mirabilissimo, s'è potuto da ogni parte schermire.[24]

> The Bolognese Onesto and the Sicilians were in fact the first; but as they were more ancient than these two, so they would have had more need of their file, although one can see that neither of them lacked talent or willingness. Cino da Pistoia, wholly refined and truly a poet of love, lives up to his reputation very well. In my opinion, he was the first who began altogether to avoid the antique coarseness which the divine Dante, most marvellous in other respects, could not completely avoid.

Landino describes Tuscan as being 'rozo' ('coarse'), in need of smoothing and polishing through the example of Latin, but he never applies the term to Dante, and in his 1481 commentary he reaffirms how opposed he is to such a view of Dante's language. Nor, indeed, had earlier Florentine humanist writers failed to praise Dante's vernacular style for its elegance, harmony, and grace (his Latin is, of course, quite a different matter).[25] Equally notable is Poliziano's use of the adjective 'antico' which projects Dante backwards into an earlier age. Such judgements on Dante's language are, then, innovative, as is Poliziano's sense of the breadth and potentialities of the earlier poetic tradition in the vernacular. The *Epistola* reveals that his predilections lie with Guido Cavalcanti, who, though only a shadowy semi-poet in Villani's *De origine*, now receives the lengthiest commentary of all the poets mentioned. All in all, in his attitude to the Tuscan poetic tradition, as well as in his subtle but peremptory judgement on Dante's harsh and medieval qualities, he polemically distances himself from Landino's *prolusione*.

The textual reconstruction and renewed vision of earlier Florentine culture involved in the *Raccolta Aragonese* did not arise *ex novo* and it had important precedents in earlier collections of vernacular texts produced by Florentine copyists. A key figure here is Antonio di Tuccio Manetti (1423–97), whose scribal role in the *Raccolta* has been studied in some detail by De Robertis.[26] Manetti contributed in no small measure to the revitalized interest in Dante in Florence during the 1460s and 1470s, and he is closely connected not only to Poliziano's enterprise, but also to the Dantean activities of Ficino and Landino. As copyist, his transcriptions of Boccaccio's *Trattatello*, of Dante's vernacular poetry, and of other later vernacular poetry, all correspond closely to the materials included in the *Raccolta*. Manetti is also responsible for manuscript copies of the *Convivio* and the *Comedy*, and his own annotations to his 'private' edition of the *Comedy*, transcribed in 1462, reveal the scientific and cosmographical preoccupations that he brings to his reading of the *Comedy*.[27] Manetti did not himself publish his cosmographical studies, but they are outlined under his name by Landino in his *Comento* (see chapter 5, section 5), and later still in Girolamo Benivieni's dialogue which precedes his 1506 Giuntine edition of the *Comedy*.[28] Manetti also composed the *Notizia*, a prose dream-vision in imitation of Dante, which includes reminiscences of Dante the lyric poet, and details the historical research he has undertaken to recover Guido Cavalcanti's writings and other texts related to him.[29]

2 *Volgarizzamenti*

A shift towards employing the vernacular in subjects previously reserved for Latin is especially evident in the renewed interest both in vernacular versions of classical works and in the tendency of Florentine humanists to translate their own Latin writings into the vernacular. In the early 1470s Landino made an important and influential *volgarizzamento* of Pliny's *Historia naturalis*, in an attempt to reinforce the linguistic structure and lexicon of Tuscan through his notion of 'transferimento', especially with regard to scientific and technical words, where the limitations of the vernacular were most keenly perceived.[30] Other important vernacular versions in the 1470s are made of 'patriotic' texts such as the humanist histories of Florence by Bruni and Bracciolini, as well as Villani's *De origine* (*c.* 1478).[31] But the first important vernacularizations in Florence date from the early 1460s and include Donato Acciaiuoli's *volgarizzamento* of his own *Vita Caroli Magni* (1461), a celebration of Cosimo de' Medici modelled upon the template of Charlemagne. Ficino is the most important force behind the movement towards vernacularization in the 1460s, especially in the more avant-garde sectors of Florentine intellectual culture.[32] For four decades from the late 1450s, Ficino is occupied with translating Plato's *Dialogues*, neoplatonic authors, and hermetic texts, and with adapting the Platonic tradition to a Christian context in his own philosophical and theological writings. In the early phases of these activities, he devoted much energy to the vernacular, and his earliest writings in Tuscan date from the mid-1450s. In the 1460s, moreover, his keen interest in Dante is evident at several levels, in echoes of Dantean language, in his decision to copy Dante's Eclogues, and in his best-known vernacular work – the *volgarizzamento* of Dante's *Monarchia*.[33] As Giuliano Tanturli has shown, such interests gain impetus through Ficino's contacts with important Florentine copyists, most especially Antonio Manetti and the Benci brothers, who provided him with vernacular codices, transcribed vernacular versions of humanist texts, and made *volgarizzamenti* of some of Ficino's own Latin translations of Greek philosophical writings. Manetti, for example, tell us in his *Notizia* that he was asked to draw up a codex of Cavalcantian works and commentaries 'per satisfare alla esortazione del nostro dottissimo platonico Marsilio Fecino' ('to satisfy the exhortation of our most learned platonist, Marsilio Ficino').[34] These vernacular copyists form an important strand in Florence's divergent vernacular culture in the mid-fifteenth century. The seminal product of this growing interchange is Tommaso Benci's 1464 *volgarizzamento* of Ficino's Latin translation of the *Pimander* – a series of fourteen hermetic Greek texts attributed to Hermes Trismegistus.[35] Underlying the choice of this text is Ficino's belief in a *prisca theologia* or ancient theology, a kind of universal religion which was the ancestor of Christianity, contained its revelations, and numbered among its adherents Zoroaster, Hermes Trismegistus, and Plato.[36] Not since the *volgarizzamenti* of Aristotle in the thirteenth century had Florence witnessed Greek philosophical culture being accommodated to a vernacular audience in this way.[37] The innovation and something of the ideological charge implicit in such initiatives are evident not only in the fact that one of the most recent products of the recovery of classical civilization is made available to a vernacular audience, but also in the dedication of the *Pimander* to the Medici favourite, Francesco del Nerone.

Apart from the *Comedy*, there is also evidence that Florentine vernacular copyists had developed a keen interest in Dante's minor works from the 1450s onwards. As well as Manetti's copy of the *Convivio*, Bernardo del Nero, a politician closely linked with the Medici, made transcriptions of this vernacular treatise and of an anonymous *volgarizzamento* of *Monarchia* which he finished on 27 October 1456. Dissatisfied with the accuracy of his vernacular version, Bernardo suggested that Ficino undertake a new translation. Ficino's own elegant rendering of Dante's political treatise was completed in 1468, and its *proemio* jointly dedicates the work to Manetti and Bernardo.[38] In an important study, Cesare Vasoli has explored the circumstances surrounding Ficino's vernacular works and his relations with their dedicatees. Vasoli shows how a specific political conjuncture, in which there was considerable conflict between Florence and the Papacy under Paul II, gave new significance to Dante's passionate thesis, in the *Monarchia*, that authority in the temporal sphere should be concentrated in a single secular ruler.[39] It is clear that such a conception of the temporal ruler could readily be extended to the position of the Medici in Florence during a particularly turbulent time (in addition to the troubles with the Papacy, a conspiracy to assassinate Piero de' Medici had been uncovered in 1466). One should also note that, in the late 1460s, there were notable tensions in the Ficino's relationship with the Medici.[40] With all these factors in mind, Ficino's vernacular *Monarchia* emerges as an emblematic episode in the Florentine appropriation of Dante. It provides an excellent example of how a particular historical conjuncture affects not only the presentation of Dante, but also the very text chosen. It reveals how personal motives may be interwoven within a larger order of political motivations, and it shows how Dante, for so long attached to the pre-1434 oligarchy, could be reinterpreted so as to offer support for the Medici regime.

In his *proemio* to the work, Ficino shows a strong desire to reconcile Dante with contemporary Florence when he notes how Dante gave such lustre to his homeland that his name and that of the city are interchangeable ('ccosì bene Firenze di Dante, come Dante da Firenze, si può dire'). What is more, Ficino also brings philosophical associations to bear on Dante in a manner calculated to make him more acceptable to contemporary Florence: he modernizes Dante as a poet-philosopher by making him into a platonist. To do so, he regards Virgil as a platonist and asserts that Dante himself drank in deep drafts of platonism through the cup furnished by the Virgil of the *Aeneid*:

> Dante Alighieri, per patria celeste, per abitatione fiorentino, di stirpe angelico, in professione philosopho poeticho, benché non parlassi in lingua grecha con quel sacro padre de' philosophi, interpetre della verità, Platone, nientedimeno inn-ispirito parlò in modo con lui che di molte sententie platoniche adornò e libri suoi; et per tale hornamento massime inlustrò tanto la ciptà florentina che · ccosì bene Firenze di Dante, come Dante da Firenze, si può dire. Tre regni troviamo scripti dal nostro rettissimo duce Platone: uno de' beati, l'altro de' miseri, el terzo de' peregrini. Beati chiama quelli che · ssono alla ciptà di vita restituti; miseri quelli che per senpre ne sono privati; peregrini quelli che fuori di detta ciptà sono, ma none iudicati in senpiterno exilio. In questo terzo ordine pone tutti e viventi, e de' morti quella parte che a tenporale purgatione è deputata. Questo hordine platonico prima seguì Virgilio; questo sequì Dante dipoi, col vaso di Vergilio beendo alle platoniche fonti.[41]

> Dante Alighieri, divine by homeland, Florentine by dwelling, angelic by race, and poetic philosopher by profession, though he did not speak in Greek with that sacred father of philosophers and interpreter of the truth, Plato, nonetheless spoke with him in spirit in such a way that he adorned his books with many Platonic thoughts. And by means of such ornamentation he so greatly illuminated the city of Florence that one can just as well say the Florence of Dante as Dante of Florence. We find three realms described by our very upright leader Plato: one of the blessed, the other of the suffering, and the third of the pilgrims. He calls blessed those who are restored to the city of life, suffering those who are forever deprived of it, and pilgrims those who are outside the city but who are not judged to be in everlasting exile. In this third order he places all the living, and those of the dead who have been assigned to temporal purgation. This Platonic order

was first followed by Virgil; it was then followed by Dante, drinking at the Platonic well-springs with Virgil's cup.

It has become traditional to note the originality of Ficino's interpretation and how it anticipates Landino's tendency to offer Platonic interpretations of Dante in his later commentary. There is a long-standing tradition for viewing Virgil as a platonist which finds some echo in earlier Dante commentaries, especially Benvenuto's *Comentum*; and, as we saw in chapter 3, Palmieri had interpreted *Inferno* I, with reference Plato in his *Vita civile*.[42] But Ficino's comments are most unusual in emphasizing the pervasive influence of platonism in the *Comedy* and suggesting that Dante's predilection for Plato arises from his familiarity with Virgil. As recent archival findings indicate, Landino was the first to make this connection in lectures on the *Aeneid* at the *Studio* in the early 1460s,[43] and this suggests that Landino provides the foundation for Ficino's own interpretation. While not unprecedented Ficino's view that Dante is a platonist is important not least because it projects Dante through a lens which updates his legacy in terms of one of the latest innovations of Florentine intellectual life – the renewal of Platonic studies.

As well as the *volgarizzamento* of *Monarchia*, further insight into Ficino's involvement with vernacular culture is provided by his Latin treatises, *De christiana religione*, *De raptu Pauli*, and *De amore*, which were rendered into the vernacular in the 1470s with the titles *Della christiana religione*, *Il rapimento di Paolo*, and *Il libro dell'amore*. These Ficinian texts all have religious goals and reflect a fervent attempt to enrich contemporary Christianity, enhance its intellectual credibility, and win people of intelligence over to the faith. The fact that they are all dedicated to Bernardo del Nero (and the *Dell'amore* to both Bernardo and Manetti) allows us to appreciate that Ficino's preoccupation with vernacular versions was borne out of a desire to divulge his apologetic programme to an educated but non-Latin literate public of merchants, skilled artisans, and members of the political class. As we noted in the introduction, this is the very section of Florentine society which showed an especially keen interest in Dante and his writings throughout the time-span of this book.

Plato's place in God's providential design for humankind is most clearly expressed in the *Della christiana religione*, where contemporary religious decline is related to the absence of a *religio docta*, of a religion which joins *pietas* and *sapientia*. The treatise makes some use of Dantean doctrine: it conflates the angelic hierarchies and the orders of blessed souls; it presents an afterlife with has Dantean lineaments; and it distinguishes between the spiritual power of popes and their limited political power.[44] *Il rapimento di Paolo* describes how St Paul ascends through the planetary spheres to the Primum Mobile and onto the Empyrean in a process of deification that presents some analogies with Dante the pilgrim's own progress through the heavenly spheres towards the Empyrean in the *Paradiso*.[45] However, Ficino echoes Dante most directly in the *proemio* to the *Dell'amore*, a highly original re-elaboration of the *Symposium* which interprets Plato with a strong emphasis upon religious motifs. In this *proemio*, Ficino quotes the opening lines of *Inferno* I as he explains how the work is designed to lead its readers away from the 'selva obscura' ('dark wood') of loving badly and back to the 'diritta via da noi smarrita' ('the straight way which we have lost').[46] In the text of the *Dell'amore*, there are further Dantean reminiscences and general links with his doctrinal teachings, although the poet who receives most emphasis is Guido Cavalcanti whose philosophical *canzone* 'Donna me prega' is radically reinterpreted in order to emphasize the analogies between it and Socrates' account in the *Symposium*.[47] At one level, Ficino refashions both Dante and Cavalcanti in his own image, but his exploitative reading of them also conceals a general tendency that is not exclusive to him in the 1460s – to emphasize the intellectual vitality of Trecento vernacular culture and to draw organic connections between it and contemporary Florence.

3 Poetic experimentation

The field of Florentine poetry in the 1460s and 1470s is many-sided and eclectic. Not only do these decades witness the imitation and reworking of existing Tuscan traditions of didactic and lyric poetry, but they also see the emergence of new forms in the vernacular such as the chivalric epic and unusual genres such as the epyllion or mini-epic. Latin and Greek sources are imitated extensively, renewing the link with the vernacular poetry of Alberti and Dati. Almost all Florentine poets writing in the vernacular participate in the tendency to update Dante in line with new cultural prerogatives, the recovery of texts, and the political climate that we have studied in the first two sections of this chapter. Limitations of space have meant that there is no room for the vernacular production of all the Pulci brothers in whom there is a high degree of Dantean intertextuality, nor for the Latin poetry of Ugolino Verino whose *Paradisus* and *Carlias* have close links, both structurally and thematically, with the *Comedy*.[48] In the very selective examples that follow the aim is to sketch out some of the forms that literary re-use of Dante takes and to illustrate how this often invests many of the topics that have been explored earlier in this chapter.

(a) Matteo Palmieri's Città di Dio

As we saw in chapter 3, Matteo Palmieri, in his *Vita civile*, was deeply conscious of the ambiguities inherent in using the vernacular at a time when Latin was the pre-eminent language of literature and culture. After this vernacular dialogue, Palmieri was in fact to publish only humanistic works in Latin for the next two decades. In the late 1450s, however, he returned to the vernacular with a lengthy *terza rima* poem in three books entitled the *Città di Dio*, which he completed in 1464 and revised in 1466. The poem has been little studied because of its length, its complexity, and the lack of a critical edition, but it is nonetheless an important document in the revalorization of the vernacular and the re-use of Dante. The fact that it was the subject of a learned Latin commentary by Palmieri's friend, the humanist and poet, Leonardo Dati, is itself revealing of a context in which earlier assessments of the gulf between Latin and the *volgare* are beginning to be reformulated.[49]

The *Città di Dio* provides one of the more intriguing episodes in Dante's Florentine reception, since it imitates and emulates the *Comedy* at metrical, structural, thematic, and doctrinal levels. The poem describes an imaginary journey that Palmieri the poet himself undertakes in 1455 while acting as Florentine Ambassador at the court of King Alfonso of Naples. Under the guidance of the Cumaen Sibyl, Palmieri traverses the heavens of the physical universe, and reaches the Elysian fields. Here, he sees the neutral angels – who neither sided with Lucifer nor affirmed their allegiance to God – and learns how they descend to Earth and take on human bodies as a punishment for their corrupt nature. During their descent, this category of angels passes through the seven spheres of the planets (from which they receive various influences) and the sublunar spheres (from which they acquire bodies and start to suffer). On Earth, the angels are free to choose whether to follow the path of good or that of evil (the Pythagorean crossroads that we have already met in the *Vita civile*): the left-fork takes them through the eighteen mansions of vice and towards perdition; the right one ascends through various virtues to celestial beatitude. Throughout his journey, Palmieri receives instruction from his guide on matters of theology, philosophy, ethics, and astrology, and the choice of pathways permits numerous digressions on vices and virtues that take up much of Books II and III respectively. With its strong suggestions of Origen's doctrine regarding the return of the neutral angels to Earth and echoes of Pythagorean and Platonic teachings on the soul, the poem presents some heady and heterodox doctrine. It is perhaps not surprising therefore that, in spite of Dati's best efforts to explain away potentially heretical passages in his accompanying Latin commentary, the work was roundly condemned as heretical by ecclesiastical authorities, as was Francesco Botticini's fig-urative representation of its teachings in his *Assumption of the Virgin* (*c.* 1475–76).[50]

The general structure of Palmieri's poem and its rhyme scheme are quite clearly motivated by Dante's precedent. With its division into 100 cantos in three books the *Città di Dio* closely follows the macrotextual features of the *Comedy*, although it is also characterized by a range of variations on, and departures from, the Dantean model. In Book II, for example, the concatenation of the rhymes is not interrupted by the close of each canto, as is always the case in the *Comedy*; it is the final book, rather than the first *cantica*, which has 34 cantos; and there is far greater uniformity in canto length (50 tercets are devoted to each *capitolo* in Books I and III, and 51 in Book II). Palmieri's poem is replete with verbal reminiscences and even direct, though almost always decontextu-alized, quotations from the *Comedy*.[51] Thematically, too, there are many general parallels in the *topos* of the allegorical journey towards philosoph-ical and spiritual enlightenment which is set in a cosmological frame that borrows imagery and stock situations from Dante. What is more, throughout the poem, Palmieri displays his erudition, by indulging in doctrinal disquisitions, especially on matters related to astrology, the soul, and human vices and virtues.[52] However, more than the apparent points of contact with the *Comedy*, what is most notable is the extent to which Palmieri distances himself from Dante's language and his ideas. Palmieri's imitation of Dante is constantly fused with regionalisms and Latinisms of the most varied kind, and this often makes the poem's linguistic surface quite obscure (one recalls with no small irony that this is the very complaint that Palmieri had made against Dante's poetry in the *Vita civile*). Palmieri's divergence from Dante's doctrine is especially notable with regard to some of the central teachings of the *Città di Dio* – the nature of the soul before and after death, its relationship with the body, and the status of the neutral angels. In the *Comedy*, Dante treats this rank of angels with the utmost contempt because of their inability to make any kind of choice, and relegates them to a zone outside Hell proper (*Inf.* III, 34–69). By contrast, in *capitolo* V of Book I, Palmieri follows Origen in allowing the neutral angels to keep their free will; Palmieri's angels are far removed from the 'cattivo coro' ('wicked chorus') for whom Dante reserves a foul and degrading punishment in *Inferno* III:

> La parte terza ad dio non fur nemici
>   ne seguaci della divina voglia
>   ma stetton dubii ad chi si fare amici.
> merito alcun non hanno ancor ne doglia
>   perche riman lor libero el volere
>   fin che loro election non ne gli spoglia.
> [. . .]
> El padre che non fu da questi udito
>   quando da tutti domando risposta
>   nella lor purita nel primo invito,
> Ad la seconda pruova vuol sia posta
>   lor liberta ma sia con tal compagno
>   mostri la voglia channo in lor riposta.
> Per questo el creatore eccelso & magno
>   anime felle accio co corpi uniti
>   perdita eterna faccino o guadagno.
> (capitolo V, 34–35, 44–46)[53]

The third group were not enemies of God, nor followers of the divine will, but were uncertain over whom to make friends with. They have no reward or punishment yet, because their will remains free until

their choice deprives them of it [...] They did not listen to the
Father when He demanded a response from all in their purity at the
first invitation, and He wishes their free will to be tested a second time
and that this happens with such a companion that it shows the will
that is in them. For this reason, the excellent and high creator made
them souls, so that, united with bodies, they attain either salvation or
eternal damnation.

In the same chapter, moreover, Palmieri gives a lengthy account of
the creation of souls in which he supports Platonic views regarding
the pre-existence of souls, thereby endorsing an opinion with which
Dante evidently has little sympathy (*Par.* IV, 49–63). Palmieri's doctrines on the fallen angels and pre-existence of the souls are decidedly
heterodox and not shared by his contemporaries, but the poem does
contain many other passages based upon classical history, mythology,
and literature that owe much to its immediate Florentine context. And
in this sense, the *Città di vita* offers an updated vision of the afterlife
and a set of teachings that are permeated by contemporary concerns,
texts, and ideas, as well as being imbued with the poet's own personal
philosophy.[54]

All in all, Palmieri's work partakes of the tradition of structural *dantismo*, albeit an intellectually sophisticated one, that is found in Tuscan
verse imitation of Dante throughout the late fourteenth and fifteenth
centuries. He makes use of Dante's verse form, elements of his narrative
scheme, important themes and situations, and his language constantly
bristles with echoes of the *Comedy*. And yet, this is done almost exclusively in an extrinsic manner, as a kind of framework upon which the author articulates his own philosophical, historical, and religious positions.
In short, Palmieri presents one kind of approach to Dante's *Comedy* that
is common to imitations of his masterpiece in much *terza rima* poetry
produced in late fifteenth-century Florence, and that is found in works as
varied as the verse *volgarizzamento* of Ptolemy's *Geographia* by Francesco
Berlinghieri and the dream-vision by Tommaso Sardi.[55]

(b) Angelo Poliziano's Stanze per la giostra *and* Sylva in Scabiem

We have already examined Poliziano's role in promoting the Tuscan
language, his interests in the textual recovery of the early vernacular

tradition, and his judgements on Dante. Here we are concerned with his unfinished vernacular epyllion, the *Stanze per la giostra di Giuliano de' Medici*, where his use of Dante is more marked than in any of his other vernacular works. We will also examine Poliziano's creative re-use of Dante in the *Sylva in Scabiem*, an experimental Latin poem which dates from the same period.

The *Stanze* are contemporary to the *Raccolta Aragonese* and they show the intensely active ways in which Poliziano rewrites Dante in his poetry in the late 1470s. The tourney alluded to in the title was won by Giuliano de' Medici, Lorenzo's younger brother, on 29 January 1475, even though the poem itself breaks off early in Book II, and consequently does no more than relate the background to the event. That background is a refined mythological one, steeped in classical reminiscences, and its nominal theme is the revenge taken by Venus through her son, Cupid, on the poem's central protagonist, Iulio. An ardent devotee of the hunt, Iulio so spurns love and its adherents that he prompts Venus to demonstrate her powers through the intermediary of her son. So it is that Cupid descends to Earth and conjures a white doe to entice Iulio away from his hunting companions; the doe miraculously transforms itself into a beautiful young woman who reveals herself to be Simonetta Cataneo. Iulio the hunter is himself enraptured and ensnared in the net of love, and Cupid returns, victorious, to Venus. The remainder of Book I (some 87 *ottave*) is then devoted to describing the goddess's luxuriant realm, gardens, and palace, and the incomplete Book II describes how Iulio and his fellow Florentines are incited to take part in the joust.

In the last twenty years, the *Stanze* have been the subject of important critical re-evaluations which have highlighted its political implications and philosophical undercurrents, as well as its almost obsessive concern with intertextuality.[56] The poem is self-evidently linked to the promotion of the Medici whom it celebrates in encomia at the beginning of Books I and II; and it puts forward an account of Iulio's development that passes through a series of triumphs (on the model of Petrarch's *Trionfi*) and owes much to the classificatory schemes of Florentine platonism. Poliziano, like other poets in Lorenzo's circle during the 1470s, cultivates both the most recently discovered classical models and older Tuscan poetic traditions. Thus, the *Stanze* not only constantly echoes the 'three crowns', Cavalcanti, and some more recent Tuscan poets, but it also draws upon an extraordinarily wide range of Latin and Greek writers, makes erudite use of Greek mythology, and shows a predilection for rare and technical terminology. The poem's remarkable intertextuality means that almost every line has a wide range of literary models, Greek, Latin, and vernacular, in accordance with Poliziano's own literary credo of *docta varietas*, a theory of imitation based upon variety and a multiplicity of poetic models. Indeed, one of the most remarkable features of the work is the way that Poliziano engenders dynamic forms of contamination between vernacular and classical sources. Poliziano uses the poetry of Dante, Boccaccio, and Petrarch as linguistic media for transforming classical figures, situations, and *topoi*, thereby recreating them in the vernacular. The appearance of Simonetta, for example, echoes both classical descriptions of Proserpina and Dante's own of Matelda in *Purgatorio* XXVIII, whereas the description of Venus' realm draws upon both a wealth of classical sources (especially Claudian), as well as the ekphrastic passages in *Purgatorio* X–XII. Poliziano even recreates individual lines of his favourite Latin authors in Dantean language, and in this way he helps to refashion the vernacular by modelling it upon the linguistic template provided by the *Comedy*. Such processes of cross-fertilization between classical and vernacular literature are sophisticated and highly-crafted, and they reveal the extent to which Dante functions as a means of recreating classical writings in contemporary Tuscan poetry.

Two important recent studies of Dante's presence in Poliziano by Daniela Delcorno Branca and Elisa Curti have shown how extensive and skilful Poliziano is in his adaptation of the *Comedy*.[57] The *dantismo* found in the *Stanze* is most marked in Book I, especially during the presentation of Iulio and the hunt (I, 26–33), the appearance of Simonetta (I, 42–47), and the ekphrastic descriptions of Venus' palace (I, 97–119). The echoes of Dante are never passively mediated and they include general reminiscences of Dantean images and themes, as well as precise echoes of similes, individual words, rhyme-words, syntactic structures, and syntagms. Such allusions and recalls are characterized by the most subtle forms of *variatio*. Although Poliziano makes use of *dantismi* from almost all sections of the *Comedy*, the presence of *Purgatorio* is especially marked, and this can in part be attributed to some general analogies in thematic development – in particular, a process of development that involves ascent and purification – between the *Stanze* and Dante's second *cantica*.[58] A single example, stanza 90 of Book 1, which forms part of the extended description of the Realm of Venus, must suffice to illustrate Poliziano's handling of the *Comedy* in the *Stanze*:

> Li augelletti dipinti intra le foglie
> fanno l'aere addolcir con nuove rime,
> e fra più voci un'armonia s'accoglie
> di sì beate note e sì sublime,
> che mente involta in queste umane spoglie
> non potria sormontare alle sue cime;
> e dove Amor gli scorge pel boschetto,
> salton di ramo in ramo a lor diletto.

The brightly painted little birds among the leaves make the air sweet with new rhymes. And from their several voices gathers a harmony made up of such sublime qualities and such blessed notes that a mind wrapped up in these human coils would not be able to rise up to its heights. And where Love guides them through the wood they hop at their pleasure from branch to branch.[59]

This entire stanza is modelled upon several *terzine* from the opening of *Purgatorio* XXVIII where Dante describes the 'divina foresta' ('divine forest') of Earthly Paradise:

> Un'*aura dolce*, sanza mutamento
> avere in sé, mi feria per la fronte
> non di più colpo che soave vento;
>   per cui le fronde, tremolando, pronte
> tutte quante piegavano a la parte
> u' la prim' ombra gitta il santo monte;
>   non però dal loro esser dritto sparte
> tanto, che li *augelletti* per le *cime*
> lasciasser d'operare ogne lor arte;
>   ma con piena letizia l'ore prime,
> cantando, ricevieno *intra le foglie*,
> che tenevan bordone a le sue rime,
>   tal qual *di ramo in ramo si raccoglie*.
> (*Purg.* XXVIII, 7–19; italics mine)

A sweet breeze, unchanging in itself, struck my brow with no greater force than a gentle wind, by which the pliant branches, trembling, were bent, all of them, toward where the holy mountain casts its earliest shadow, but not parted so much from their straightness that the little birds in the treetops left off exerting their every art, but with full gladness they welcomed the first hours, singing among the leaves, which kept the bass note to their rhymes.

A closer comparison of the two texts reveals the full extent of Poliziano's *ars imitandi*. Not only does Poliziano radically recontextualize certain reminiscences ('cime' in line 8 is made metaphorical), but he also inserts other Dantean syntagms taken from elsewhere in the *Comedy* (*Par.* VI, 124–26: 'Diverse voci fanno dolci note [. . .] rendono dolce armonia tra queste rote') and rhyme words ('nove rime': *Purg.* XXIV, 50; 'foglie', 'spoglie': *Inf.* III, 112 and 114).

In the *Stanze*, Poliziano adapts *dantismi* from all three *cantiche* of the *Comedy*, but one linguistic register that he does not exploit is the comic-realist style which is particularly pronounced in the cantos Dante devotes to Malebolge (*Inferno* XVII–XXX). That Poliziano the poet was nonetheless attracted by the full range of Dante's poetic experimentalism is clear from his use of this section of the *Inferno* in his innovative Latin poem, the *Sylva in Scabiem*. Despite their apparently divergent subject matter – the *Sylva* describes in anatomical detail the ruinous physical degradation of its poet-protagonist – critics have argued persuasively that this poem and the *Stanze*, rather than being antithetical visions, constitute parts of a single reality, a poetic universe regulated by literary memory and underpinned by a shared theory and practice of poetry.[60] Although *dantismo* is less pronounced than in the *Stanze*, the Latin poem transmutes Dantean language into Latin, mirroring the way in which the vernacular epyllion uses the *Comedy* as a medium for rendering Latin texts into the vernacular. Hence, the 'marcite membre' ('rotting limbs': *Inf.* XXIX, 51) to which Dante alludes in the *bolgia* of the falsifiers become Poliziano's 'marcida [. . .] } membra' (*Sylva*, 84–85).[61] Poliziano's imitation of Dante is especially noticeable in a number of sequences that describe the degrading effects of the protagonist's disease through successive and often violent images that strongly recall the afflictions suffered by Dante's falsifiers. Perhaps the most interesting passage of all – and the one that best illustrates Poliziano's approach to Dante's text – is his transformative rewriting of a simile used in *Inferno* XVII in order to describe the reactions of usurers to the flames that torment them. In Dante, the comparison rests upon an analogy between these sinners and dogs that lash out with their tails and snouts when afflicted in summer time by fleas, flies, and horse-flies:

> non altrimenti fan di state i cani
> or col ceffo or col piè, quando son morsi
> o da pulci o da mosche o da tafani.
> (*Inf.* XVII, 49–51)

> dogs do the same in the summer, now with muzzle, now with paw, when they are bitten by fleas or flies or horseflies.

Poliziano radically recontextualizes the simile in order to convey the reactions of the diseased poet. There are precise echoes of Dante's enumeration of three kinds of insect in the rare and non-classical Latin words *muscas*, *pulices*, and *tabanos* (the only Latin precedent here is Benvenuto's commentary which Poliziano knew well),[62] as well as in the reactions of the dog ('nunc pede, nunc rostro'). However, what one notes above all is the way Poliziano enriches the comparison through a variety of insertions that owe much to precise echoes of, and subtle variations on, passages from Hesiod, Virgil, and Statius:

> Non secus, Icarii quotiens iuba fulgurat astri,
> cernimus in triviis villosum saepe molossum
> nunc pede, nunc rostro, tremulae nunc verbere caudae
> pellentem obscoenas furiali murmure muscas
> aut pulicis dentem aut pregnantem sanguine tetro
> tabanum et morsus frustra intentare crepantes.
> (*Sylva*, 73–78)[63]

> Likewise, when the crest of Icarus' star flashes forth, we often see in the streets a hairy Molossian hound, growling in rage as, now with its paw, now with its muzzle, now with its quivering tale, it beats away the foul flies, biting fleas, and the horsefly gorged with blood, or tries in vain to bite and swipe.

These 'translations' of Dante bring the violent imagery and linguistic tension of certain areas of Dante's *Inferno* to Latin verse, and they provide one of the more fascinating examples of the richly creative fusion wrought by a sophisticated reader and rewriter of the *Comedy* who is at the vanguard of learned humanist culture in the late 1470s.

(c) Lorenzo de' Medici

Lorenzo de' Medici's first experiments in vernacular verse date from the period 1464–68, and although these early sonnets, *canzoni*, and *sestine* frequently echo Dantean language, the reminiscences are often subsumed within a frame of reference that owes much to rhetorical and situational *topoi* associated with Petrarch and Luigi Pulci.[64] There is some playful inversion of Dantean language in these compositions, but the most interesting example of Lorenzo's early use of Dante is the *Simposio*, an unfinished *terza rima* composition in *capitoli* which dates from the late 1460s. The very title of Lorenzo's *Simposio* parodies Ficino's commentary on the eponymous Platonic dialogue, and on more than one occasion the poem makes light of the doctrine of divine fury by punning on the word 'di-vino' ('divine' and 'of wine'). In the form of a mock dream-vision, Lorenzo's work presents a procession of Florentine drunkards, and it falls into a distinctive vein of poetic caricature whose most notable precedents include Lo Za's poems, the *Buca di Montemorello* (1407–09) and the *Studio d'Atene* (1411–12). As we noted in the Introduction, parodic rewriting of Dante is a notable feature in this tradition, and it is clear that Dante is subject to similar playfulness from Lorenzo's inversion of certain markedly Dantean motifs. One contrasts, for instance, the way that Dante enumerates souls in the *Inferno* and *Purgatorio* for exemplary and moralizing purposes with Lorenzo's sprawling catalogue of individuals who make headlong pursuit to a place where a hosteller has spilt a 'botticello' of wine. Similarly, Lorenzo uses the figure of the guide, yet his own escorts are far removed from the personal and figural value of Dante's Virgil and Beatrice: they are Bartolino Tedaldi and Nastagio Vespucci, two of the heaviest drinkers or *beoni* in the city. In contrast to the providential roles of Dante's guides, and the courteous yet rigidly defined spiritual hierarchy within which they operate, Lorenzo's own guides replace one another in the most unwilling and haphazard manner:

> Ma io scorgo da lungi ser Nastagio,
> che ti potrà mostrar lui questo resto;
> ma per farmi dispetto, e' vien adagio
> (v, 12–15)[65]

But I spy from afar ser Nastagio who will be able to show you what is left; and to spite me he is coming along slowly.

Apart from its playful handling of structural devices from the *Comedy*, the *Simposio* makes unrestrained comic use of Dantean language, especially in the dialogue and gestures between the guides and the poet-protagonist.[66] The opening nine lines of the second *capitolo*, for example, describe the reactions of Lorenzo to the first grouping of *beoni* he sees, and in so doing, he echoes yet inverts the seriousness of exchanges between Beatrice and Dante in *Purgatorio* XXXIII and the dramatic appearance of Virgil to Dante in *Inferno* I:

> Parte da riso e parte da vergogna
> per quel vedevo e udivo occupato,
> mi stavo quasi a guisa d'uom che sogna; [*Purg.* XXXIII, 31–33]
>   quando mi sopragiunse qui da lato
> un che per troppo ber era già fioco; [*Inf.* I, 63]
> conobbil presto, perch'era scianciato;
>   allor mi volsi e dissi: "Ferma un poco,
> o tu, che vai veloce più che pardo;
> fermati alquanto meco in questo loco!"
> (*Simposio*, II, 1–9)[67]

Caught up in part by laughter and in part by shame on account of what I saw and heard, I was almost like one who dreams, when there came upon me from a side one who seemed weak from too much drinking. I quickly knew who he was because he was lame; then I turned and said: "Oh you, stay a little, you who move quicker than a leopard; stay with me a little while in this place."

Critics have often noted the contradictory qualities of Lorenzo's poetry, his capacity for engaging almost simultaneously in both the burlesque and the serious. And if we turn to some of Lorenzo's works from after 1473, we find a very different use of Dante as part of what is often viewed as a second phase in his literary *iter*, which sees a growing interest in philosophical and theological subject-matter. The shift in emphasis seems to have brought with it a fundamental rethinking of Lorenzo's approach towards Dante, probably under the influence of Landino and Ficino, who had both earlier reinterpreted Dante as a poetic philosopher with a Platonizing orientation. In line with such estimates of Dante and of the earlier Tuscan poetic tradition, Lorenzo uses poetry as a tool for intellectual discovery and debate. Such concerns are particularly evident in another incomplete *terza rima* poem, the *De summo bono* (c. 1473), which draws closely but not slavishly upon one of Ficino's technical treatises in order to consider the question of the primacy of will and intellect and to debate the relative merits of the active and contemplative lives. The *De summo bono* is not without echoes of Dantean language, but unlike the verbal and structural *dantismo* of the *Simposio*, Lorenzo owes most to Dante (or a contemporary view of Dante) for his general approach to poetry's cognitive value, its capacity to expound profound theological truths.[68] This kind of reading also informs several sonnets and *canzoni* included in the *Raccolta Aragonese*, where Lorenzo uses the *Comedy* and the *Convivio* as a linguistic and conceptual model for developing the themes of the lady's beauty and the effects of her absence.[69]

As we saw in earlier sections of this chapter, the 1470s are a key decade for the development of literary production in the vernacular. As initiatives such as the *Raccolta Aragonese* reveal, the vernacular is used as a political tool for promoting a vision of Lorenzo as the cultural guide of his city, and as the inheritor and continuator of its language and traditions. In his own poetry and that of his circle, moreover, Lorenzo seizes upon the political value latent in efforts to promote vernacular culture in areas outside Medici control. Another important document in such appropriations of the vernacular is Lorenzo's *Comento de' miei sonetti*, a prose commentary to his own earlier poetry. In the *proemio* to this self-commentary, Lorenzo makes clear both his sympathies with the linguistic theories of Landino that we studied in section 1 and his heightened sense of the bond between the vernacular and *fiorentinità*:

> E potrebbe facilmente, nella iuventù e adulta età sua, [sc. of 'nostra lingua'] venire ancora in maggiore perfezione; e tanto più aggiugnendosi qualche prospero successo e augumento al fiorentino imperio,

come si debbe non solamente sperare, ma con tutto lo ingegno e forze
per li buoni cittadini aiutare.[70]

And our language could easily, in its youth or adulthood, become
more perfect still; and all the more if we add some prosperous success
and increase to the Florentine empire – something for which one
must not only hope but also help to carry out with all one's mind and
forces through the efforts of good citizens.

The *Comento*, first conceived in the mid-1470s, is strongly influenced by
both the *Vita nuova* and the *Convivio* and, as such, it provides further
evidence of a reawakened interest in these texts. Book I of the *Convivio*
in particular underscores much of Lorenzo's opening discussion in the
proemio, where Lorenzo provides mitigating reasons for indulging in
self-commentary (§§ 8–13), for being so preoccupied with amorous material (§§ 14–39), and for writing in the vernacular (§§ 40–71). In the
argumento, Lorenzo's exposition of the first four sonnets draws closely
on the precedent of the *Vita nuova* in speculating upon death as the
beginning of a new life. Aside from analogies in genre and structure,
there are also precise echoes of the language and ideas of these minor
works throughout the *Comento*.[71] Unfinished and bedevilled by issues
of dating, the final form of this work takes us beyond the time-frame
of this book. It is nonetheless worth recording the direct judgement
that Lorenzo makes on Dante, for here one finds a careful amalgam of
earlier ideas about his value as a poet-theologian, his affinities to ancient
writers, and his power to surpass them:

> chi legge la *Commedia* di Dante vi troverrà molte cose teologiche e
> naturali essere con grande destrezza e facilità espresse; troverrà ancora
> molto attamente nello scrivere suo quelle tre generazioni di stili che
> sono dagli oratori laudate, cioè umile, mediocre e alto; e in effetto,
> in uno solo, Dante, assai perfettamente assoluto quello che in diversi
> auttori, così greci come latini, si truova.[72]

> whoever reads Dante's *Comedy* will find expressed there many the-
> ological and natural matters expressed with great skill and facility.
> He will find most aptly employed in its language those three kinds
> of style which are praised by orators, the humble, the middle, and
> the high styles. And, in effect, one poet alone, Dante, has perfectly
> brought together that which is found in various authors, both Greek
> and Latin.

This judgement not only contrasts with Poliziano's earlier criticism (one voiced in Lorenzo's name) of Dante's 'rozzore', but, as we shall see in the next chapter, it also owes much to Landino's commentary to the *Comedy*.

To conclude, then, we have seen that, in the 1460s and 1470s, a number of influential writers in Florence attempted to promote the *volgare* by recovering earlier vernacular texts, by composing vernacularizations of Latin and Greek texts, and by experimenting in prose and verse. In spite of the differing motivations and personal emphases, all these initiatives have in common the urge to raise up Florentine achievements, both past and present, to classical standards, as well as a desire to elicit linguistic interchange between Latin (and to some extent Greek) and the vernacular. Of course, the re-use of the vernacular heritage takes place at a multiplicity of levels and it is far from being focused exclusively upon Dante – there is also a strong growth of interest in Petrarch and Cavalcanti. However, we have seen that Dante occupies a growing presence at higher cultural levels and in strongly politicized contexts, and that the 1470s in particular are a key decade in which he and the vernacular become central objects of attention for leading Florentine poets, intellectuals, and humanists.[73] The example of Poliziano's poetry, in both vernacular and Latin, demonstrates how the early Tuscan tradition with Dante as its principal representative, is assimilated to the highest and newest levels of Florentine culture. Lorenzo de' Medici also plays a significant role in encouraging civic patriotism and the reputation of Florence abroad, through his involvement in a range of activities that might be termed cultural patronage and his exaltation of the vernacular and its most excellent writers. He promotes the *Raccolta Aragonese*, actively redeploys Dante's minor works and the *Comedy*, and becomes increasingly conscious of the ties between Florence's status and the Tuscan language. It is this immediate background which, as we shall see in Part III, helps to underpin Cristoforo Landino's 1481 edition and commentary of Dante's *Comedy*.

Cristoforo Landino and his *Comento sopra la Comedia* (1481)

5

Cristoforo Landino on Dante and Florence:
the prologue to the *Comento*

Cristoforo Landino (1425–98) had many guises in fifteenth-century Florence. A Florentine by birth, he studied law at Pavia, and returned to the city in 1439, perhaps as a scribe at the Council of Florence. His close links with the Alberti family are well known: he read the tercets of Francesco d'Altobianco degli Alberti at the *Certame coronario*, dedicated the first redaction (*c.* 1443–44) of his own collected Latin poetry to Leon Battista Alberti, and married one of Leon's cousins in 1459. Best known until his mid-thirties as a Latin poet, he was appointed to the Chair of Rhetoric and Poetry at the Florentine *Studio* in 1458, and for almost the next forty years he taught classical and vernacular literature at the university. In the late 1460s he began to engage closely with philosophical ideas, and from this period he also assumed several other important institutional and civic offices, becoming the Chancellor of the Guelph Party and the writer responsible for drafting public letters in the secretariat of the *Signoria*. He was acquainted with all the major cultural figures in Florence during the second half of the fifteenth century, and tutored Ficino, Poliziano, and Lorenzo. His literary output in Latin, in addition to his poetry, includes three dialogues on philosophical themes related to action and contemplation, the human soul, and nobility, as well as printed commentaries on Horace (1482) and Virgil (1488). As far as the vernacular is concerned, as we saw in the previous chapter, he played a central role in refounding Tuscan as a literary language able to develop humanist concerns and themes. And he composed a wide range of vernacular works such as *volgarizzamenti* of Latin texts, academic prolusions, and orations, and even a guide to writing letters in the vernacular.[1]

The two chapters in Part III of this book outline and assess Landino's most important vernacular work as a *dantista* – his commentary on Dante's *Comedy*, the *Comento di Christophoro Landino Fiorentino sopra la Comedia di Danthe Alighieri poeta fiorentino*, which first left the presses of Niccolò Tedesco's print-shop on 30 August 1481 in a large print run, possibly of 1200 copies.[2] The commentary is made up of two distinct sections: a lengthy prologue or *proemio* to which this chapter is devoted; and an extensive body of commentary in the form of glosses or *chiose* on all three *cantiche* of the *Comedy* that will form the subject of chapter 6. As its full title suggests, a central theme in Landino's presentation of Dante is that of *fiorentinità*. That the *Comento* is connected to the Florentine state is clear from the fact that Landino delivered a dedicatory oration to the representatives of the *Signoria* in a ceremony which marked their receipt of a sumptuous presentation copy of the work.[3] Apart from being linked with the Florentine government, Landino's commentary also contains the direct imprint of Florence's leading platonist, Marsilio Ficino, who composed a Latin letter on Dante's symbolic return to the city that is incorporated in the *proemio*. What is more, one of the city's most famous artists, Sandro Botticelli, provided the original illustrations from which the incomplete series of copperplate engravings or *intagli* to the first nineteen cantos of the *Inferno* were made (see fig. 3).[4]

The significance of this prestigious commentary can hardly be overstated, both at the time of its first printing and through the fifteen subsequent reprints that were made before the end of the sixteenth century. It is without doubt the most celebrated and widely influential commentary on the *Comedy* to be printed in Renaissance Italy. It marks a pivotal moment in the Florentine cult of Dante, in commentary literature upon his poem, and in the book market for printed 'Dantes'. As a document in Dante's Florentine reception, Landino's commentary deals critically with almost all the themes that we have met in this book. Landino imbues Dante with ideological and civic values that celebrate him as the embodiment of Florence's best traditions, and this preoccupation is especially pronounced in the *proemio* which heralds Dante, the undeserved exile, as returning symbolically to the city in the form of the commentary itself. The Florence with which Dante is reunited is, of course, a Laurentian one whose values, concerns, and innovations Landino often projects on to the poet and the poem alike, although

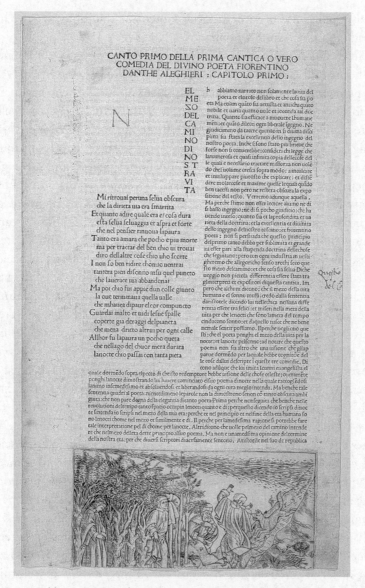

3. Baccio Baldini, engraving after Sandro Botticelli to *Inferno* 1. Printed in Cristoforo Landino, *Comento di Christophoro Landino Fiorentino sopra la Comedia di Danthe Alighieri poeta fiorentino*, Niccolò della Magna, 30 August 1481 (folio). The folio also contains the first twenty-one lines of *Inferno* 1 (left-hand column) and part of Landino's opening gloss on line 1 'Nel mezo del camino' (right-hand column and left-hand column below Dante's text).

he also makes use of several earlier Florentine traditions that we have already examined in this book.

Given its centrality, it is not surprising that Landino's commentary has been studied in some depth, especially in the last thirty years. After the pioneering work of Michele Barbi, the studies of scholars such as Carlo Dionisotti, Manfred Lentzen, and Roberto Cardini, as well as more recent work by Paolo Procaccioli, Arthur Field, Deborah Parker, Craig Kallendorf, Francesco La Brasca, and others, have contributed to a better understanding of the commentary's genesis and ideological dimensions, the nature of its *proemio* and its *chiosa*, its place in contemporary debates on Dante and vernacular humanism, its linguistic and doctrinal concerns, and its relationship both to the tradition of earlier Dante commentary and to its own contemporary Florentine context.[5] These contributions have recently been complemented by Procaccioli's critical edition of the *Comento* in four volumes (Rome: Salerno, 2001) which also contains a valuable introduction and critical apparatus. I have incurred various debts to the work of these scholars and critics in attempting to provide the first discussion in English of the *Comento* that gives close consideration both to the *proemio* and to the *chiosa*. However, earlier studies have not been able to set Landino against the wider background of Dante's earlier Florentine reception to the extent that is possible here as a result of the assessments already provided in Parts I and II. And a major preoccupation in Part III as a whole will be to illustrate how Landino constructs a 'Dante' who is a conscious and critically refined synthesis of earlier Florentine (and to some extent non-Florentine) traditions, as well as of issues of contemporary concern. The following chapter substantiates this general point by examining three important areas of interest in the *chiosa* – Landino's use of Plato, scientific doctrine, and classical sources – that have received little, if any, critical attention. The present chapter has a two-fold aim. First of all, it discusses the background to the *proemio* and examines the cultural, ideological, and patriotic factors that Landino brings to bear upon his reading of Dante. It then provides a running commentary on the thirteen chapters that make up the prologue, exploring in particular the ways in which Landino reinterprets Dante in relation to Florentine traditions, both past and present, both civic and humanist.

1 Contexts

There are several distinct, but overlapping, contexts which influence the genesis of the *Comento*. The immediate background is that of Medici Florence in the late 1470s and the aftermath of the conflicts brought about by the Pazzi conspiracy which saw the assassination of Giuliano de' Medici on 26 April 1478 and the ensuing war that pitted Florence against Pope Sixtus IV and Ferdinand of Aragon, the King of Naples. Following Lorenzo's dramatic and successful resolution of this crisis in March 1479, there is a climate of heightened patriotic sentiment within Florence that is directed towards promoting the primacy of city in the Italian peninsula by means of cultural initiatives and related projects. As we saw in the previous chapter, several attempts were made in the late 1460s and 1470s to use the vernacular, often with reference to Dante, in order to treat subjects previously reserved for Latin. Within this context, the fact that the first printings of the *Comedy*, in the 1470s, were not Florentine products can only have been interpreted as a shocking provocation, especially following the 1478 Milanese edition of the *Comedy* prepared by Martino Paolo Nibia (known as Nidobeato) which was accompanied by the Bolognese Trecento commentary of Jacopo della Lana. Nidobeato's edition is notable in its own right for interventions in historical and political matters, where it updates Lana and revitalizes the *Comedy*, bringing it into line with the vernacular tastes of a readership based in the northern courts.[6] The very choice of Lana, however, implied a judgement on the value of his Bolognese dialect in opposition to Tuscan, and in the Latin preface to the edition, Nidobeato made quite explicit his view that Bolognese surpassed all other Italian vernaculars:

> But Jacopo della Lana on account of his maternal Bolognese language seemed to excel: this city [i.e. Bologna] is in fact situated exactly in the centre of Italy, so that by assiduous commerce it has words that are not only polished, but also common to all provinces. Bolognese has no less grace and dignity in Italy than the *sermo Laconicos* once had in Greece.[7]

It is clear from the opening section of the *proemio* that such comments goaded Landino since here he says that he will leave the merits of his own commentary for others to decide, but he affirms his innovation in freeing Dante from the barbarity of other foreign idioms to such an extent that the text of his edition has brought the poet back from exile to his homeland:

> Questo solo affermo, havere liberato el nostro cittadino [sc. Dante] dalla barbarie di molti externi idiomi, ne' quali da' comentatori era stato corropto; et al presente chosì puro et semplice è paruto mio offi- cio apresentarlo ad voi illustrissimi signor nostri, accioché per le mani di quel magistrato, el quale è sommo nella fiorentina rep., sia dopo lungo exilio restituito nella sua patria, et riconosciuto né Romagnuolo essere né Lombardo, né degli idiomi di quegli che l'hanno comen- tato, ma mero fiorentino. La quale lingua quanto tutte l'altre italiche avanzi manifesto testimonio ne sia, che nessuno nel quale apparisca o ingegno o doctrina, né versi scripse mai né prosa, che non si sforzassi usare el fiorentino idioma.[8]

> I only affirm this: that I have freed our citizen from the barbarisms of many foreign idioms with which commentators had corrupted him. And in the present day it seemed my duty to offer him to you, our most illustrious lords, so that, through the hands of that magistrature which is supreme in our Florentine Republic, he is returned to his homeland after a long exile, and he is recognized to be a pure Florentine, and not to be either from Romagna or Lombardy, nor to belong to the idioms of those who have commented upon him. We see clear evidence of how much this language surpasses all other Italian ones in the fact that no writer endowed with genius and learning ever wrote either verse or prose without trying to use the Florentine idiom.

This passage is permeated by tones of patriotic self-affirmation and the strong assertion that Tuscan is the pre-eminent Italian vernacular, and it provides one of the best examples of Landino's own skilful attempt to raise Tuscan to the status of what might be called hegemonic vernacular. As we saw in the previous chapter, Landino was deeply conscious of the advantages that would accrue to Florence from further widespread diffusion of Tuscan to other areas of Italy. The idea of Dante's return from exile will be developed later in the *proemio*.

The motivations for the *Comento*, then, are related to pressures ex- ercised in the late 1470s by the cause of Florentine self-promotion, Landino's programmatic awareness of the political value of Tuscan- ization, and the particularities of the earlier print history of Dante.

But aside from such factors, closer analysis of Landino's *Comento* itself shows that both the *proemio* and *chiosa* are composed of material compiled over a number of years prior to the rapid drafting which internal references indicate to have taken place between March 1480 and 30 August 1481.[9] Throughout his commentary, Landino reworks motifs related to Dante that he had earlier developed in letters and especially in his courses and inaugural lectures at the *Studio* between the late 1450s and the late 1470s.[10] These points of contact between the *Comento* and Landino's earlier teaching and writings show that his commentary is not merely the product of the immediate circumstances that precipitated its publication. Landino alludes directly to this fact in his oration to the *Signoria* when he draws attention to the close relationship between his lengthy teaching career and the publication of the *Comento*.[11] In the *Comento*, Landino's expository technique as a lecturer can often be felt, especially in the *chiosa* to the commentary, where he relies heavily on paraphrase and does not always disguise traces of the oral form of the lessons themselves.[12] His experience as a teacher of Dante also informs the way in which he distinctively tailors the poem for a wide vernacular readership that is educated but not necessarily erudite. In its openness to such readers and its pragmatic eclecticism, the *Comento* bears many of the hallmarks of Landino's professional background, and provides an interesting example of how institutional parameters influence the way he presents Dante's text.

In the *Comento*, Landino also makes extensive use of his two earlier philosophical dialogues in Latin, the *De anima* and the *Disputationes Camaldulenses*. The *De anima* (*c*. 1471), with its encyclopaedic examination of the human soul and its operations, is the ultimate source of many of the psychological categories (see below chapter 6, section 1) that are used to explain the allegorical significance of Dante's journey and the relationship between the characters of Dante and Virgil. In the *Comento*, Landino also draws upon this dialogue in order to expound specific points of doctrine (see below chapter 6, section 3). The *Disputationes Camaldulenses* (*c*. 1474) is an even more important antecedent.[13] The first two books of this dialogue debate the relative merits of *otium* and *negotium* and action and contemplation, and the final two provide a philosophical commentary on the first six books of the *Aeneid*. In the Virgilian exegesis provided here, as in his earlier lectures on the *Aeneid* from 1462–63, Landino presents Virgil's epic as an allegorical work deeply informed by platonism. According to Landino, Aeneas' journeys from Troy to Carthage to Sicily and on to the Italian mainland, betoken the man who leaves behind sensuality, overcomes the obstacles of the active life, and follows the path towards perfection that ends in contemplation of divine ideas.[14] In two important passages, one from the beginning of Book IV, the other near to its close, Landino directly extends the main contours of this reading to Dante's poem, the 'divine poem of our city', as he calls it:

> Among our writers do we not have Dante, an important man endowed with all learning, who imagines that man [sc. Virgil] is his guide on a journey in which he traverses the entire universe from the depths of Tartarus to the heights of heaven? Searching for the *summum bonum* of man, does he not select – with remarkable genius – the *Aeneid* as his only model, and although he seems to excerpt very few things from it, do we not see that, if we look with rather more attention, he never departs from it? Are not those things which he wrote from the very beginning (concerning the midpoint of life, the forest, the three beasts, the high mountain-top already illuminated by the sun's rays) derived from here? I pass over other things which are so concealed in Dante's poem that they cannot be discovered except by a few very learned men. The fact is, then, that Dante chooses Virgil as his leader in a matter which looks to the *summum bonum* and not to anything relating to the physical world [...] While you [sc. Alberti] were attempting to make Virgil clear for me [sc. Lorenzo], you were at the same time leading into a discussion of that divine poem of our own city. For now I finally see what Dante meant: first he descends to the underworld, then he comes out and finds no other way to heaven except through purgatory [...] Now [...] when I run through the entire argument in my mind, I have the greatest admiration for the genius of the man [sc. Dante]. For although in weaving his own work he was to borrow only a very few threads of the Virgilian pattern, in actual fact nearly all of them come from there. And now I finally understand what Landino, following the teaching of Cicero, used to warn us: that great care must be used in imitation. It must not be done as if we were exactly the same as those whom we are imitating; we must be similar to them – and in such a way, in fact, as can hardly be understood by anyone except the learned.[15]

In the opening chapter of the *proemio* to his Dante commentary, Landino stresses the close connections between this earlier reading of the *Aeneid* and that of the *Comedy*:

> Ora perché havevo novellamente interpretato, et alle latine lettere mandato l'allegorico senso della virgiliana *Eneide*, giudicai non dovere essere inutile a' miei cittadini, né ingiocondo, se con quanto potessi maggiore studio et industria, similmente investigassi gl'arcani et occulti, ma al tutto divinissimi sensi della *Comedia* del fiorentino poeta Danthe Alighieri; et chome el latino poeta in latina lingua havevo expresso, chosì el toscano in toscana interpretassi.[16]

> Now because I had recently interpreted and written in Latin an allegorical reading of Virgil's *Aeneid*, I judged that it would not be unprofitable nor displeasing for my citizens, if, with as much learning and industry as I could, I made a similar investigation into the arcane, occult, but most wholly divine senses of the *Comedy* of the Florentine poet, Dante Alighieri; and as I had expounded the Latin poem in Latin, so I interpreted the Tuscan one in Tuscan.

In both the *proemio* and in his glosses to many passages from the *Comedy*, Landino adapts the allegorizing and philosophical interpretation that he had elaborated earlier in the *Disputationes Camaldulenses*; and he also makes use of other themes and motifs from that dialogue. The key point to note here is that Landino firmly believes that the *Aeneid* and the *Comedy* share a single underlying structure, and it is the structural homology between them that allows him to read Dante's language and thought on the same level as Virgil's. The *Comedy* has, in effect, become a classic in its own right: it is a profound imitation of the *Aeneid*, an *imitatio* that contains hidden, but highly meaningful, analogies to the Latin poem that can be decoded by the learned reader and the commentator. The passages quoted above from the *Disputationes* mark an end-point in the many-sided Florentine debate on Dante's value as a vernacular poet in relation to classical standards. Landino resolves the tensions between vernacular and Latin found in Boccaccio, Salutati, and others, and he overturns earlier and contemporary Florentine views that suggested Dante had little or no grounding in the Latin classics. Through the concept of *imitatio*, Landino asserts that the literary relationship between Dante and Virgil is not merely a question of passages in the

Comedy being understood as the conscious imitation of Virgil (the kind of reading that is made by many earlier Dante commentators).[17] It is rather a matter of both works sharing the same deep structure and fundamental core of meaning. This is perhaps the best example that we have met so far of how a later Florentine reader of Dante created new forms of literary authority for his poet, by suggesting filiations between him and an ancient writer.

2 Dante and Florence (chapters I–VIII)

Having examined the conditions affecting the genesis of the work and its prehistory in Landino's own earlier career and writings, let us now return to the *proemio* itself and consider in detail its thirteen chapters. The general structure of the *proemio* departs significantly from the traditional format of the medieval *accessus* that is found in almost all earlier Dante commentaries.[18] Landino follows instead a pattern common to many humanist commentaries on classical texts in later fifteenth-century Italy, whereby the commentator emphasizes the divinity and excellence of poetry, makes observations on its sacred nature, and provides information about the life of the author.[19] With his own emphases, Landino follows this kind of outline at the beginning of the prologue, by comparing Dante favourably to Greek and Latin writers who nonetheless fail to equal the Florentine poet 'et per profondità, et varietà di doctrina, et per elegantia, et copia, et sublimità di stilo' ('for depth, variety of doctrine, elegance, abundance, and sublime style'). Such concerns show how Landino views the style of the poem in terms of humanist literary predilections and related categories. He then goes on to exalt Dante's use of doctrine, and comments on his ethical teachings in a way that can be quite closely linked to earlier Florentine vernacular traditions that viewed Dante as a wellspring of doctrinal teachings and a poet-theologian.[20] Civic traditions co-exist with classicizing preoccupations in Boccaccio, Salutati, and Bruni in whom there are nonetheless some unresolved tensions between a strong sympathy for Dante as a poet and patriotic emblem, on the one hand, and a more critical approach to Dante's choice of the vernacular and the limits of his classical erudition, on the other. Landino enacts a fuller synthesis than any previous writer, and in so doing he bridges the divisions between the two cultures, Latin and vernacular, in a way that Alberti was unable or unwilling to do.

After describing the qualities of Dante's poetry and the purified linguistic form of his own edition (see previous section), Landino does not immediately relate the life and customs of Dante, nor does he discuss the nature of Dante's poetry and questions of poetics. He defers treatment of such concerns, and further departs from the tradition of the *accessus*, by inserting a defence of Dante and Florence. The relevant chapter is entitled 'Apologia nella quale si difende Danthe et Florentia da' falsi calumniatori' ('Apology in which one defends Dante and Florence from false calumniators'), and it deals principally with the problem raised by Dante's own fierce and ostensibly calumnious attitude towards his home-city and its inhabitants in the *Comedy*. This is not, of course, a new issue in Dante's Florentine reception, and it had elicited a variety of earlier responses. Jacopo Alighieri, one of Dante's own sons and the first commentator on the *Inferno* (1322), had softened some of the charge of Dante's more anti-Florentine passages. By contrast, Giovanni Villani and Boccaccio had embraced, and at times even extended, Dante's vituperative outbursts against Florentine decadence and excesses. Boccaccio's condemnation of Dante's exile, in the first redaction of the *Trattatello*, circulated widely throughout the Italian peninsula, and his charges received new emphasis with the printing of this life in Vindelino da Spira's 1477 Venetian edition of the *Comedy*. Filippo Villani, by contrast, had exalted Dante's preoccupation, even in exile, with reforming the Florentine Republic. Bruni had taken a more subtle defensive line, excusing Dante's antagonism to Florentines in *Epistola* VI on the grounds that such pique was characteristic of the age in which Dante lived.[21] And in the visual arts, Michelino had shown a Dante wearing the laurel crown, but still outside the walls of Florence, in his 1465 fresco of the poet and his poem for the Florentine Cathedral (fig. 2, see p. 14). However, no Florentine writer before Landino had dealt at such length with the question, nor attempted to give an *in bono* reading of Dante's views on the city in his 'acerrime invective contro a' Fiorentini' ('bitter invectives against the Florentines') and 'riprensioni acerbissime di varii et scelestissimi loro vitii' ('harsh criticism of their many wicked vices'). To deflect the weight of potential criticism of Dante in this regard, Landino adopts a two-fold strategy. First, by quoting selected lines from the poem (*Inf.* x, 26; *Par.* xv, 97–99; *Par.* xxv, 5), he attempts to show that Dante did not condemn the city, but rather that he revered it. There is some basis for such a reading in the *Comedy* itself, but the relevant passages are double-edged, since they go on to mete out bitter criticism of contemporary Florentine behaviour and politics. Landino thus provides only partial references, because full or contextualized quotations from the poem would undermine his line of argument. The second, and equally selective, prong in Landino's defence of Dante and Florence is to argue that, where the *Comedy* condemns Florentines, such passages only refer to specific groups of citizens. Landino closes his defence by stating that at times Dante may indeed have overstepped the mark but that he deserves to be excused given the unjust exile that he suffered:

> [. . .] non vitupera e Fiorentini, e quali chome habbiamo mostro altrove chiama sobrii et tranquilli, chiama gloriosi et giusti [*Par.* xv, 97–99], perché sarebbe gran levità in tanto poeta scrivere chose repugnanti, et tra se stesse contrarie; ma vitupera quegli Fiorentini, e quali per ambitione, et factione, erano divenuti ingiusti, rapaci, crudeli, et avari [. . .] Vitupera adunque gli scelerati governatori, o più tosto raptori del suo popolo Danthe [. . .] Arrogi anchora che facto ingiustamente exule et rebelle da lloro della la sua patria, merita scusa se alquanto per giusto sdegno excede el modo; et questo basti in difensione del poeta.[22]

> He does not condemn the Florentines whom, as we have shown elsewhere, he calls sober and tranquil, glorious and just, because it would be a sign of great levity in such a poet to write things which are repugnant and self-contradictory; but he condemns those Florentines who through ambition and factionalism had become unjust, rapacious, cruel, and avaricious. Dante thus condemns the wicked rulers, or rather those who have usurped power from his people. I add further that, having been unjustly exiled by them and made a rebel from his homeland, he deserves to be excused if sometimes out of righteous zeal he goes too far; and let this be enough in defence of the poet.

Such solutions are clearly rhetorical and partial but no less interesting on that account, and they reveal Landino's keen desire to bring about a *post-mortem* reconciliation between Dante and his home-city, strategically placating Boccaccio's earlier outbursts against the cruelty of the city. It is instructive to compare Landino's comments here with his glosses on Dante's invectives against Florence in the main body of the commentary. In such glosses, Landino does not in every case mitigate the polemical charge of the original passages, and this in itself provides some support for Procaccioli's view that the *proemio* with its strongly pro-Florentine ideology has markedly different finalities from the *chiosa*. For example, on at least two occasions Landino paraphrases Dante's condemnations without attempting to moderate or excuse them, while in two further passages he provides a rhetorical annotation, observing how Dante uses the figure of *ironia* against Florence. Yet there are at least four glosses on Florence in the *chiosa* where Landino relies on the techniques that he had used in the *proemio* in order to limit Dante's 'invective' and 'reprensioni' either to a specific category of Florentines or to the corruption of an earlier historical period. And there are two passages which in effect argue against the view of Boccaccio, Bruni, and Manetti that Dante always showed reverence for his homeland, and openly criticize the poet for *not* speaking with greater discretion about the city.[23]

Within the structure of the *proemio*, Landino's *apologia* serves a further important purpose – it allows room to assert the virtues and achievements of those Florentines that fall outside both the Dantean condemnations and the time-frame of the *Comedy*. In the next six chapters, Landino celebrates his illustrious fellow-citizens whose worth has been displayed in doctrine, eloquence, music, painting and sculpture, law, and mercantile pursuits. Rather than reaffirming, in the traditional manner of the *accessus*, how his text and author are related to conventional literary and philosophical categories, Landino is concerned to inscribe his commentary, and by extension his Dante, within the best traditions of Florence itself. In the remainder of the *apologia* and the subsequent chapters, Landino draws on a variety of sources, and in particular on Filippo Villani's catalogue of Florentines in the *De origine*. He actively reorders details from Villani, and adds information from a subsidiary set of texts which had presented earlier eulogies of the city. In this way, Landino brings Villani up to date, and in effect transcends the earlier literature in defence of Florence in order to provide his own highly sympathetic vision of the city. He also draws together Florence's humanist and vernacular cultures and attenuates their differences so as to place emphasis upon a common Florentine patrimony.

In the remainder of chapter ii, no opportunity is missed to praise Florence through its associations with Rome and the excellence of its inhabitants in all spheres of human activity, from the contemplative to the active life. If Landino's contemporaries are not familiar with the prudent men who in the past advised and ruled Florence, this is only because the city has lacked good writers, as is shown by its chronicles which are read by few because of their rough style. The Athenians, like the Florentines, performed many great feats, but the ancients seem greater still because of the eloquence of their writers.[24] Landino eagerly takes up this very task – the parallel with Athens will be further developed later – as he charts selected events from the Trecento in order to demonstrate the city's fortitude in the face of tyranny in an account that owes much to Bruni's *Historiae* but which also updates this text in the light of recent events.[25] As well as rulers and advisers, Landino mentions Florentine soldiers, whose prowess in war is given a mythical veil and ascribed to the influence of Mars in a manner that is closer to some medieval Florentine chroniclers than it is to Bruni.[26] Landino proudly evokes Florentine conquests in Tuscany during the fifteenth century, and mentions several episodes and military figures whose endeavours are compared with classical examples.

Leaving behind the realms of war and politics, chapters iii and iv of the *proemio* deal respectively with Florentines who excelled in doctrine and eloquence. The pairing is derived from Cicero, and Landino views it as being especially pertinent to Dante.[27] Landino uses chapter iii to comment upon themes that were often included in earlier eulogies of Florence which linked the splendid opulence of its churches with both the piety of its citizens and the patronage of Cosimo de' Medici. Chapter iii also illustrates how Landino revises earlier Florentine sources, in particular Villani's own catalogue of Florentines in the *De origine*.[28] The most distinctive feature of Landino's account is his keen interest in affirming the continuity and harmony present in the entire cultural tradition of Florence. Thus, in addition to the Florentine theologians, physicians, and astrologers mentioned by Villani, Landino discusses scholastic philosophers alongside humanist polymaths such as Leon Battista Alberti and Antonio Manetti and a scientist with humanistic interests such as Paolo Toscanelli. In so doing, he draws together selected but richly varied components of political, literary, intellectual, artistic, and professional activity in Florence, both past and present. We find little trace in the *Comento* of the Petrarchan critique of scholastic culture that is present in the Dante commentaries of Benvenuto and Villani and that is directed against Dante himself in Bruni's *Dialogi* and *Vita di Dante*. Quite the opposite. Landino's interests in doctrine and science are evident throughout the *Comento*, and behind them lies not only the earlier tradition of Dante commentary but also a veritable explosion of contemporary interest in classical and medieval scientific texts in Florence during the fifteenth century (see below chapter 6, section 3).[29]

The following chapter ('Fiorentini excellenti in eloquentia') opens in a markedly Ciceronian key with a paean to the uniquely human nature and civilizing virtues of eloquence, and it goes on to emphasize the close links between the orator and the poet.[30] According to Landino, the fortunes of these 'due spetie di scriptori' ('two kinds of writers') follow the pattern of rise and decline traced out by the Roman Empire, which reached its pinnacle in Cicero and Virgil. Following Bruni's lead, Landino relates the decline of Latin eloquence to the end of Empire,[31] but he also asserts that eloquence has only recently been brought back to life by Dante and Petrarch. The chronological limits of this cycle are set by two Florentines – the last true Latin poet, Claudian, and the first modern one to receive the laurel crown, Petrarch:

> [. . .] l'ultimo poeta laureato, che in prezo rimanessi in lingua latina, fu el fiorentino Claudiano, et dipoi perché el primo che dopo la res- urrexione della facultà poetica prendessi laurea corona fu el Petrarca, perché Dante dinegò prendere tale honore se non lo prendessi nel baptisterio fiorentino [cf. *Par.* xxv, 4–6]. Fu adunque la nostra città l'ultima, nella quale si spegnessi tale facultà, et la prima nella quale si raccendessi [. . .] Merita adunque la nostra rep. buona gratia da tutta Italia, poiché in quella nacquono e primi che l'una et l'altra eloquen- tia, non solo morta, ma per tanti secoli sepulta in vita riduxono, et dalle tartaree tenebre in chiara luce rivocorono.[32]

the Florentine Claudian was the last poet-laureate who was held in esteem in the Latin language. And there then followed Petrarch who was the first to take the laurel crown after the resurrection of the poetic faculty, because Dante refused to take such an honour unless he received it in the Florentine baptistery. Our city, then, was the last in which this faculty was extinguished and the first in which it

was rekindled [. . .] Our republic thus deserves the benevolence of all
Italy since it was the birth-place of the first poets to bring back to life
both Latin and vernacular eloquence which had been not only dead
but buried for so many centuries, and to bring back to the light both
forms of eloquence from the Tartarean shadows.

Dante is not strictly the final link in this genealogical chain, but Landino
makes it clear that he would have been the first to take the laurel
crown had he not been intent on doing so in the Florentine Baptistery:
'the resurrection of the poetic faculty' is most directly associated with
Dante. In this way, Landino echoes the earlier judgements of Guido
da Pisa and Boccaccio on Dante's role in resurrecting poetry. He also
adapts Florentine uses of Claudian in this kind of context, especially
that by Filippo Villani, and revises earlier humanist estimates regarding the worth of the vernacular, from Palmieri's *Vita civile* where the
literary revival is associated exclusively with contemporary Latin literature to Bruni's *Dialogi* and *Vita di Dante* which had placed Dante's
achievements in the vernacular on a different level from the revival
in Latin.

Landino's catalogue of eloquent Florentines excludes, like his earlier
prolusione to Petrarch, many earlier vernacular poets. It includes Guido
Cavalcanti, who is nonetheless placed on a lower level than Dante and
Petrarch in what represents a pointed response to Poliziano's *Epistola* to
the *Raccolta Aragonese*. After brief references to Boccaccio and Zanobi da
Strada, which parallel those found in the *De origine*, Landino considers
several Florentines who fall outside the chronology of Villani's work,
but had gained renown as Latin stylists. Salutati is included in the
catalogue of names despite contemporary judgements against the quality
of his Latin. Brief mentions are made of Bruni and Bracciolini, and
more extended notices of Traversari, Leonardo Dati, Alberti, Donato
Acciaiuoli, Palmieri, Lapo da Castiglionchio, and even Niccolò Niccoli.
Landino attempts to avoid charges of partiality by not naming eloquent
contemporaries who are still alive, but his real interest lies not with
matters of literary decorum but rather with the continued preoccupation
to promote present-day Florence. He goes on to fashion a mythologized
vision of the city as the cultural capital of Italy, as a new Athens which
is characterized by a marvellous admixture of doctrine and eloquence

combined with the present-day revival of Platonic studies and the desire
to imitate classical *ornate dicere*:

> Restono molti de' vivi, e quali per fuggire invidia non pongo. Ma certo
> è referta la nostra rep. d'huomini in ogni spetie di lectere illustrati. Né
> fu età alchuna dove più fussi congiunta la eloquentia colla doctrina.
> Habbiamo copia di peripatetici. Ma anchora possiamo gloriarci havere
> chi [sc. Marsilio Ficino] ha rivocato in luce la Platonica disciplina.
> Surgono poeti. Surgono historici [. . .] Ma credo veramente potere
> concludere nell'ornato del dire Fiorenza seguitare le vestigie della greca
> Athene. Conviensi nel nome, se è vero quello che non ignobili scriptori
> greci referiscono che Athene non sia decta da Athena, *i*. Minerva,
> ma da 'anthos', *i*. 'fiore'. Conviensi che chome quella [sc. Athens]
> vince tutti e greci idiomi, chosì questa tutti gl'italici. Et è connaturale
> in questa natione la eloquentia. Di che oltre alla experientia molti
> exempli posso indurre, che molti principi usono l'opera de' fiorentini
> nelle loro legationi.[33]

> There are many alive whom I do not name in order to avoid envy. But
> without doubt our republic is adorned with men endowed with every
> kind of literary learning. Nor was there any age in which eloquence was
> so coupled with doctrine. We have an abundance of Aristotelians, but
> we can also glory in having he who has brought to the light Platonic
> studies. Poets and historians abound [. . .] But I truly believe that I
> can conclude that in *ornate dicere* Florence follows the footsteps of
> Greek Athens. There is a similarity in the name if what worthy Greek
> writers state is true, namely, that Athens is not named after Athena,
> that is, Minerva but from 'anthos' which means 'flower'. The two
> cities are similar in that as Athens surpasses all Greek idioms, so too
> does Florence go beyond Italian ones. Eloquence comes naturally in
> this nation, and in this regard I can adduce many examples in addition
> to common experience, for many princes use the work of Florentines
> in their legations.

In the next three chapters of the *proemio*, this mythologizing of Florence
continues as Landino borrows from Villani by naming Florentines who
practised arts that occupied lowly positions in traditional hierarchies of
knowledge. In chapter v Landino deals with music, and modernizes his
source-text by making reference to the views of the Pythagorean and
Platonic school regarding the power of music, and by using examples

taken from Cicero and Pliny. The insertions show Landino's desire to weave a humanist texture for his commentary and to endow it with the authoritative teachings of Plato, the most recent ancient authority to be recovered in Florence. In chapter vi, Landino treats Florentine painters and sculptors in what is perhaps the best-known section of the *proemio*. Given Landino's connections with Alberti and his close acquaintance with Pliny's *Historia naturalis* – one of the most important classical sources for a more positive assessment of painting and sculpture – it is not surprising that the chapter offers an important revalorization of the visual arts. The chapter falls into three main parts. The opening section on ancient painters draws closely on Pliny; the next section concerns Giotto and some other fourteenth-century painters, and develops the idea – already present in Boccaccio's *Decameron* (VI. 5, 5) and especially Villani's *De origine* – that painting was reborn with Giotto. The final section is Landino's own updated account of fifteenth-century painters and sculptors, and shows his perspicacity as a commentator on art. Baxandall has discussed the frameworks from which Landino takes the terminology (often derived from classical literary theory) that he uses to describe the achievements of Masaccio, Filippo Lippi, Andrea del Castagno, and Fra Angelico.[34] The fact that, as Baxandall also shows, almost all of Landino's critical terminology corresponds to Alberti's, reveals again the composite nature of the *proemio*, its attempt to update Villani, and its critical sophistication in judging Florence's cultural achievements.

Chapter vii is the shortest in the entire prologue and takes its lead almost exclusively from Villani by mentioning several notable lawyers without adding any contemporaries. However, the final chapter in Landino's parade of illustrious Florentines treats the merchant class, and it has no precedent in Villani, even though earlier Florentine writers had often expressed pride in the city's thriving economy and mercantile activity.[35] The chapter reveals the extent of Landino's municipal patriotism, for he notes that Florentine merchants have obtained the highest rank in the maritime and mediterranean regions where mercantile activities thrive, and compares them to industrious bees which return to the hive with the wealth taken from each flower.[36] A strong patriotic spirit animates the remainder of the chapter as Landino outdoes earlier writings, and perhaps especially Bruni's *Laudatio florentine urbis*, by lavishing praise on the city's beauty and fame, the mental acuity of its inhabitants, its good air, cleanliness, agricultural land, villas, and nobility.[37] Florence is the centre of Italy and even her name has been changed to reflect the fact that intelligence and beauty flower in her:

> per ogni paese di tre titoli è insignita [sc. Florence], che sia famo-sissima, che sia bellissima, et che abbondi di sobtilissimi ingegni. Possiamo arrogere una exquisitissima monditia e puliteza nel victo, et veramente civile. Possiamo una somma solertia nella agricultura [...] Nessuna regione ci è pari nelle ville [...] arrogiamo se vi piace e doni naturali [...] È collocata nel mezo d'Italia. Il perché è facile al Fiorentino, aggiuntovi la sua industria, et congiungere et disiun-gere l'italiche potentie. È stata sempre copiosa di nobilità [...] Né solamente nelle chose grandi è sempre stata excellente questa rep., ma anchora nelle minori ha dimostro generosità; volle esser decta Floren-tia, in che certo appruovo la opinione di Plinio, el quale scrive la città esser stata da principio nomata Fluentia, perché era tra' due fiumi Arno et Mugnone collocata; ma dipoi fiorendo in epsa sì nobili in-gegni, fiorendo epsa d'ogni spetie di belleza, piacque a' suoi cittadini non più Fluentia, ma Florentia nominarla.[38]

In all lands, Florence is known by three titles, that she is most famous, most beautiful, and abounds in the keenest minds. We can observe a most exquisite pureness and truly civic cleanliness in its food, the most careful attention to agriculture [...] No region is our equal for its villas [...] we note, if you please, the natural qualities. She is placed in the middle of Italy, and for this reason it is easy for the Florentine, given the additional fact of his industriousness, to join and divide the Italian powers. She has always been abundant in nobility. Nor has this republic only ever been excellent in great matters, but has shown generosity in small ones; it wished to be called Florentia. In this regard, I endorse Pliny's view when he writes that the city had at first been named Fluentia, because she was situated between the rivers Arno and Mugnone, but that subsequently, as there flowered in the city such noble minds and every kind of beauty, it pleased the citizens no longer to call her Fluentia but rather Florentia.

In the final section of this chapter, Landino turns to the question of Dante's exile and his remains. Boccaccio and Manetti, in their lives of Dante, had viewed the city's failure either to erect a suitable monu-ment to Dante or to recover his body from Ravenna as a subject of utmost opprobrium for Florentines. Landino retains their passionate emphasis on Dante's unjust exile, but he does not relate this to any quality intrinsic to the Florentine people: Dante's banishment is rather explained away, as in chapter ii, as the wilful consequence of a few powerful and corrupt individuals from an earlier epoch. To show the support of the 'popolo' for Dante, Landino comments on their resolve in supporting a decree (which we have discussed in chapters 2 and 3) that provided for the erection of a marble tomb to the poet in the Florentine Cathedral. Landino attributes the failure of this initiative to the envy of a powerful minority, and, in rhetorically impassioned language, he calls for Dante to be returned to the city, and for the monument to be completed in his honour. In this way, Landino adds his voice to other contemporary efforts in the 1470s to recover Dante's remains from Ravenna and to house them in a setting worthy of the poet.[39]

3 Landino's 'Life of Dante' (chapter IX)

In chapter IX Landino gives a lengthy outline of the life and customs of Dante. The return to a more traditional format, one found widely in medieval and Renaissance commentaries, brings with it many common places that are familiar to us from the lives of Dante written by Boccaccio, Bruni, and Manetti. Cardini and Thompson have shown that Landino relies closely on Manetti's *Vita* (the biography which Landino in any case acknowledges as his most direct model at the close of chapter VIII, though characteristically he draws on details from more than one early biographer).[40] Thus, Landino begins his account with the dream of Dante's pregnant mother, and discusses the poet's love for Beatrice, his political career, participation at the Battle of Campaldino, exile, and post-exilic wanderings. He finds space to repeat Boccaccio's physiognomical description, the legend of the ladies of Verona, and several other anecdotes. Within the largely derivative account, there are nonetheless some elements of revision and innovation that can be related to Landino's own preferences and cultural context. For example, immediately after commenting upon Dante's exploits at Campaldino, Landino quotes eight lines from one of Horace's poems to illustrate the ennobling effects of the poet's love for Beatrice. The juxtaposition of a

Latin text extolling the force of love with the Campaldino incident suggests a subtle dissention, cast in a classicizing form, from Bruni's earlier account of Dante's military exploits in a life which had elided almost all reference to the poet's amatory pursuits.[41] Landino's use of Plato is, however, the most significant departure from earlier biographies. In his discussion of the dream of Dante's mother at the beginning of the life, Landino distinguishes himself from all earlier lives of Dante by interpolating a well-known legend, whereby bees were said to have brought honey to Plato's lips. The association between Dante and Plato is developed later in his life, when Landino discusses the poet's youthful love for Beatrice in a comment which reveals the influence of later fifteenth-century Florentine platonism:

> ardentissimamente fussi preso dall'amore d'una fanciulletta figliuola di Folco Portinari decta Bice, la quale lui dipoi sempre chiamò con più degno nome Beatrice [. . .] El quale amore benché degeneri da quel furore descripto da Platone et vero amore divino, nientedimeno qua giù in terra è questo amore della corporea belleza una effigie et imagine di quello. Né è, se si conserva casto et pudico, degno di vituperatione, ma di loda, perché per queste belleze terrene c'inalziamo alle divine.[42]

> he was seized most ardently by love for a young girl, the daughter of Folco Portinari, called Bice, whom he then always called with the more worthy name of Beatrice [. . .] This love, although it is of a lower species than that furor described by Plato and true divine love, nonetheless down here on earth this love of corporeal beauty is an effigy and image of that other love. If it be kept chaste and pure, this love deserves not condemnation, but rather praise because by means of these terrestrial beauties we rise up to divine ones.

The notion that corporeal beauty is a reflection of divine beauty is a theme most notably developed in Plato's *Symposium*, but this passage shows in particular Landino's close familiarity with Ficino's commentary on this dialogue, which makes beauty especially central to Plato's theory of love.[43] These departures from the lives of Boccaccio and Manetti indicate Landino's interests as a humanist, links with Ficino, and concern to interpret Dante through Platonic categories.

Landino's life goes on to mention most of Dante's writings, but our interest must focus upon his account *Comedy* in which he reiterates the

core concepts found in the *prolusione* to his course on Petrarch. The
relevant passage is worth quoting in full:

> Confessa ogni huomo che Danthe prima riduxe in luce gl'ornamenti
> rhetorici et poetici; et l'antica elegantia, compositione et dignità, già
> per molti secoli al tutto extincta, in gran parte riduxe in luce [...]
> *Interim* innumere et grandissime gratie gli renderemo, perché fu el
> primo che la lingua nostra patria insino a' suoi tempi roza inexercitata,
> et di copia et d'elegantia molto nobilitò, et fecela culta et ornata. Trovò
> Homero la lingua greca molto già abondante et exculta da Orpheo, et
> da Museo, et da altri poeti più vetusti di lui. Trovò la latina Virgilio
> già elimata et exornata, et da Ennio, et da Lucretio, da Plauto, et da
> Terentio, et altri poeti vetusti amplificata. Ma innanzi a Danthe in
> lingua toscana nessuno havea trovato alchuna leggiadria, né indocto
> elegantia o lume alchuno; et excepto le rime, benché anchora quelle
> sieno inepte e roze, niente hanno gl'antichi in che si vegga un minimo
> vestigio di poeta. Danthe fu il primo che conosciuto ne gli scriptori
> latini gl'ornamenti e quali sono comuni all'oratore et al poeta, et
> inteso quanto acuto ingegno è necessario nella inventione poetica,
> quanto giudicio nella dispositione, quanto varii colori et lumi nella
> elocutione, *preterea* di quanti figmenti debba essere velato el poema,
> et di quanta et quanto varia doctrina referto, tentò con felice auspicio
> indurre tutte queste cose nella nostra lingua. Il che ne' passati secoli
> nessuno havea tentato. Il perché lui decte principio, lui molto la riduxe
> inverso la perfectione. Il che rade volte tra' mortali è intervenuto. Lui
> primo dimostrò quanto fussi idoneo el fiorentino idioma, non solo ad
> exprimere ma ad amplificare, et exornare, tutte le chose che caggiono
> in disputatione.[44]

Everyone acknowledges that Dante first brought back to the light
the ornaments of rhetoric and poetry, and that in large measure he
brought back to the light the elegance, composition, and dignity of
the ancients which for many centuries had been completely extinct. In
the meantime, we will bestow upon him countless and great thanks,
because he was the first who greatly ennobled with abundance and
elegance the language of our homeland, which until then was coarse
and undeveloped; and he endowed our tongue with culture and ornament. Homer found the Greek language already very abundant and
cultivated by Orpheus and Musaeus and by other more ancient poets.
Virgil found the Latin language already polished and ornamented,
and amplified by Ennius and Lucretius, by Plautus and Terence,
and by many other ancient poets. But before Dante, in the Tuscan

language no-one had found any grace, or brought any elegance or light; and except for rhymes, although even they were still inept and coarse, earlier Italian poets have nothing in which one sees the least vestige of a poet. Dante was the first to have learnt from Latin writers the ornaments that are common to the orator and the poet, and to have understood how much incisive genius is necessary in poetic invention, how much judgment in disposition, how many figures and colours in elocution, and moreover with how many figments the poem must be veiled, and with how much and how varied learning it must be endowed – Dante was the first who tried with an auspicious beginning to bring all these things to our language. In the centuries past no-one had tried it. For this reason he gave it an origin, he brought it far towards perfection which has rarely happened amongst mortals. He first showed how much our Florentine idiom was a fitting medium not only to express but also to amplify and ornament all that which falls into disputation.

In comparison to both Homer and Virgil, who found their languages already polished, ornate, and abundant, Dante establishes an elegant and refined literary language almost *ex nihilo*, without suitable vernacular precedents to assist him. This judgement on Dante's extraordinary feat in basing his vernacular on the Latin classics goes far beyond all the favourable parallels between Dante and Homer and Virgil that we have met in Boccaccio, Salutati, Bruni, and Palmieri. Landino reverses the reservations of these writers concerning Dante's preference for the vernacular over Latin, as well as Poliziano's more recent criticism of Dante's 'antico rozzore'. For Landino, Dante played the foundational role in resurrecting poetry in the vernacular ('fu el primo [...] innanzi a Dante in lingua toscana nessuno [...] lui dette principio [...] Lui primo'), and in initiating literature in that language. This is the result of his close familiarity with the Latin tradition and his imitation of that tradition in Tuscan. It is precisely because Dante wrote in the vernacular in the way and at the time he did that he surpasses the classical writers.[45] The entire passage is given added charge when one recalls that Landino is in polemic with the impudent appropriation of Dante by non-Tuscans that we outlined in section I of this chapter. After discussing the poetry of Petrarch and Boccaccio, Landino concludes chapter IX by making general observations, that again echo his earlier *prolusione* on Dante, concerning the role of the *labor limae* in fashioning a literary language and the need for literature in the Florentine vernacular to imitate classical models, to have familiarity with ancient philosophy, and to practice 'transferimento'.[46]

4 Landino on poetry (chapters X–XIII)

Chapters X–XIII of the *proemio* all deal with questions related to the nature of poetry, its origin, and its divine qualities, by developing ideas that Landino had first formulated in his inaugural lectures to courses at the *Studio* and at the opening of Book III of his *Disputationes Camaldulenses*. In line with these earlier writings, Landino makes use of Ficino's account of poetic fury in a Latin epistle, *De divino furore* of 1 December 1457. This letter connects the *furor poeticus* to the Platonic concept of anamnesis or recollection and to the idea of the return of the soul.[47] Shut up in the shackles of the body and the corporeal realm, human beings forget the eternal realm of divine ideas in which they had once taken delight before descending into the prison of the body. It is only when the soul begins to contemplate again the divine ideas that it is able to fly back to heaven on two wings. The attempt to return to the heavens is, Ficino maintains, what Plato called divine frenzy and it has four parts – love, poetry, the mysteries, and prophecy. The first recollection of the divine occurs through the bodily senses, especially the eyes and ears, and when the poet is inspired by divine spirit, he imitates the echoes of the celestial harmony of the heavenly spheres, and often utters words that he does not later understand.

Landino draws on these Ficinian ideas (often repeating his authorities and arguments verbatim) in chapter X, and especially in chapter XI – chapters which are taken up with defending poetry as the supreme art which encompasses the realms of activity, knowledge, and contemplation. Poetry is, for Landino, an art more divine than liberal, because of its origins in the divine fury discussed by Plato:

> Ma che l'origine della poetica sia più excellente che l'origine dell'arti humane si manifesta, perché el divino furore onde ha origine la poesia è più excellente che la excellentia humana onde hanno origine l'arti. Et che dal furore divino proceda la facultà poetica efficacemente lo pruova Platone nel libro che lui intitola *Ion*, per tre segni [. . .] *Preterea* afferma nel *Phedro* che nessuno benché diligentissimo,

benché anchora eruditissimo sia, diviene poeta se non è concitato dal divino furore.[48]

But it is clear that poetry has a more excellent origin than that of the human arts, because divine fury from out of which poetry comes is more excellent than that human excellence which is the origin of the arts. And Plato in the book he calls *Ion* convincingly proves that poetic ability proceeds out of divine fury for three reasons [. . .] Moreover in his *Phaedrus* he asserts that no-one, no matter how diligent or erudite he may be, becomes a poet unless he is raised up by divine fury.

Armed with the authority of Plato and steeped in Ficinian borrowings, Landino develops a conception of poetry that is quite different from the views of many earlier and contemporary humanists. Poetry is not merely an important component in the ethical and political education of the individual, as it had been for Bruni and others. Poetry is rather that which embraces all intellectual activities and transforms all disciplines with which it enters into contact. Above all, poetry is understood to be a form of knowing based on the illumination of the mind by God and a means of representing divine truth under figments and metaphors:

> e poeti soli contro alla consuetudine de gl'altri scriptori invocono l'aiuto divino, perché intendono el poema essere divino, et non humano, et da divino furore procedente [. . .] Per la qual cosa non è maraviglia se e poeti sono antichissimi, conciosia che Dio volle che *ab initio* e suoi misterii fussino descripti a tutte le genti pe' poeti. Il che chome poco avanti dixi, induxe credo Aristotele a chiamare e poeti theologi.[49]

> poets alone, contrary to the custom of other writers, invoke divine assistance because they understand that poetry is divine and not human and that it proceeds from divine fury [. . .] For which reason it is no wonder that poets are most ancient, given that, *ab initio*, God willed poets to recount His mysteries to humankind. And as I said just now, this led Aristotle – I believe – to call poets theologians.

In such passages, it is clear that Landino enters into a critical dialogue with Bruni's *Vita di Dante*, which, as we saw in chapter 3, makes Dante a poet of study and discipline, not one of fury and mental abstraction.[50] Landino also differentiates himself from Bruni in his subsequent comments regarding the etymology of the word 'poet' and the daring use he makes of analogies between the work of the poet and that of God:

> e Greci dixono poeta da questo verbo 'poiein', el quale è in mezo tra 'creare', che è proprio di Dio quando di niente produce in essere alchuna chosa, et 'fare', che è de gl'huomini in ciaschuna arte quando di materia et di forma compongono. Imperoché benché el figmento del poeta non sia al tutto di niente, pure si parte dal fare et al creare molto s'appressa. Et è Idio sommo poeta, et è el mondo suo poema.[51]

> the Greeks use the word poet from this verb *poiein*, which is between the verb 'to create', which is proper to God when out of nothing he gives being to some thing, and the verb 'to make', which is said of men who compose things out of matter and form in all the productive arts. And thus although the poet's figment does not emerge wholly out of nothing, it nonetheless differs from making and comes quite close to creating. And God is the supreme poet and his poem is the world.

Landino's account of poetry also contains more distant connections with earlier Florentine discussion of poetry's status. In the final two books of the *Genealogie deorum gentilium* (a work well known to Landino and used directly by him at the beginning of chapter XII), Boccaccio had affirmed the divine origin and antiquity of poetry and the poet, as well as the close links between poetry and theology. Boccaccio had defined poetry in the *Genealogie* as a 'sort of fervid and exquisite invention, with fervid expression in speech or writing, of that which the mind has invented' which proceeds from God and is only found in the rarest of men.[52] Landino's interest in neoplatonic doctrine seems to have encouraged him to return to the concept of fervour and the poet-theologian that had not been extensively applied to Dante after Boccaccio. Boccaccio's view of poetry is not, of course, restricted solely to inspiration: craft, artistry, and learning are also important components (as they are in Salutati's *De laboribus Herculis*, too). And Landino will address such matters in his own portrait of Dante's encyclopaedic learning and crafted artistry in chapter XII. There is, however, a fundamental change in tone and emphasis between Landino's defence of poetry and the earlier Florentine defences of poetry by Boccaccio and Salutati. It is not a question either of defending poetry from the attacks of Dominicans regarding its truth-value or of stressing its links with biblical language and imagery. The Platonic concepts of participation and anamnesis enable Landino to present the *poeta-theologus* as an intermediary between the divine and the human, one who, by means of divine fury, communes directly with God and transmits His mysteries to humankind.

After discussing the ancient origins of poetry in chapter XII, Landino gives his own lengthy exposition of the characteristics of Dante's poetry (again following, often literally, his earlier treatment of this subject in the *prolusione* to his lectures on Dante at the *Studio*). The *Comedy* is supreme in invention, disposition, and elocution. It contains a marvellous variety which induces utmost jocundity in the ear, especially through its use of rhetorical colours and adaptation of similes of all kinds. After a lengthy discussion of Dante's use of figures of speech, the final section of the chapter returns to ideas elaborated in Landino's earlier works and it presents – with a *copia exemplorum* befitting an orator – Dante as a universalizing author whose *Comedy* encompasses theology, natural science, moral philosophy, and history in such a way that all sciences arise from and return to Dante:

> Ma che ingegno, o immortale Dio! Che profondità di mente! Abraccia el cielo. Abraccia la terra. Abraccia el tartareo regno. Et dal centro, havendo già expresse l'etherne pene de gli scellerati per spaventare gl'huomini da' peccati, pel purgatorio salendo con aquiline ale, vola alle superne sedie. Le quali chose benché sobto diversi velami nascondino somma scientia, nientedimeno dalla vera theologia in nessun luogo si dipartano. Et qual theologo con più ordine o con più manifeste demostrationi ha potuto ad noi mortali exprimere quello che gl'immortali spirti lassù nel lucidissimo fonte della natura contemplano? [. . .] In quale philosopho sono più aperte et manifeste o l'argumentationi le quali c'inducono al sommo bene et vera felicità, o regole et precepti e quali s'appartengono al bene et beato vivere? [. . .] Et chome dicono e Greci d'Homero, si può affermare lui essere simile all'occeano [. . .] chosì tutte le scientie da chostui [Dante] s'attingono, et in lui redondano. Arrogete a questo la cognitione delle historie, et quanto diligente investigatore è dell'antichità; et non solamente delle nostre chose, ma et delle greche et dell'hebraice et di tutte l'altre nationi sia stato [. . .] Hora essendo con sì incredibile copia di parole adornate; con sì admirabile gravità di sententie illustrate; con

tanta leggiadria di stilo composte; con tanta varietà di lumi et di colori distincte, chi non arrogerà bisognando *etiam* le nocturne vigilie, vedendo che in tale lectione ad somma utilità è congiunta somma iocondità?[53]

Oh immortal God what a genius! What a profound mind. He encompasses heaven, earth, and the Tartarean realm. And, leaving the centre, having already described the eternal punishments of the wicked in order to frighten men away from sin, and rising through Purgatory on eagle-like wings, he flies to the celestial seats. And though these things conceal the greatest wisdom beneath various veils, nonetheless they never depart at any point from true theology. And which theologian would be able to tell us mortals, with such order and lucid demonstrations, about that which the immortal spirits on high contemplate in the brightest fount of nature. In which philosopher does one find more clearly and manifestly the arguments that lead us to the highest good and true happiness, the rules and precepts which pertain to living a good and blessed life. And as the Greeks say of Homer, one can say that he too resembles the ocean [. . .] so likewise all knowledge has its origin in him and returns to him. Add to this his knowledge of histories and how much he is a diligent investigator of antiquity, not only pertaining to our things but also to the Greeks, the Hebrews, and all other nations. Now being adorned with such an incredible abundance of ornate words, illuminated by such admirably serious thoughts, composed with such a graceful style, marked out by such a variety of lights and colours, who will not dispense with it, even if nocturnal vigils are needed, seeing that in such a lesson to the utmost usefulness is joined the utmost jocundity?

Of course, the emphasis here upon Dante's great learning and his status as 'poet-theologian' is not new, and it reveals yet again how Landino consciously refashions earlier Florentine traditions that had praised such qualities. There are nonetheless several characteristic features to Landino's impassioned eulogy of Dante's learning, from his reference to Homer (which is borrowed from Quintilian) to the conviction about Dante's close knowledge of ancient history (far stronger than in Bruni), from the attempt to update Dante in relation to his knowledge of Greek and even Hebrew culture, to the desire to articulate a vision of Dante upon a Ciceronian framework which unites doctrine and eloquence.

5 Marsilio Ficino and Antonio Manetti (chapters XIII–XIV)

The final two chapters of the *proemio* show how fellow Florentines, who were closely involved with earlier efforts to promote Dante (see chapter 4, section 2), help Landino to 'return' Dante to Florence and associate his name with the city's newer initiatives.

Chapter XIII transcribes the full text of one of Ficino's Latin letters and appends an accompanying vernacular translation. This is not the first time that Ficino had offered one of his texts for insertion in another's work, but it is the only occasion when it is followed by a vernacular translation which may well be by Ficino himself.[54] The letter presents Florence as rejoicing in the return of Dante to his homeland after two centuries of exile, and it is modelled upon a series of echoes to Virgil's *Aeneid* that are suppressed in the vernacular version. Ficino makes reference to Dante's own 'prediction' that he would receive the laurel crown in the Florentine Baptistery (*Par.* XXV, 8–9), and he presents such a coronation as having come true through the agency of Landino himself. Ficino alludes to Landino's initiative in characteristically mythographic language:

> recently your [sc. Dante's] father Apollo, made pitiful from my long weeping and your eternal exile, sent Mercury to enter the devout mind of the divine poet Cristoforo Landino. Having assumed Landino's appearance, he used his wand to awake your sleeping soul, his wings to take you inside the walls of Florence, and finally he crowned your temples with Apollo's laurel.[55]

Ficino goes on to quote directly from the meeting of Aeneas and Anchises in Book VI of the *Aeneid* (687–91) in a parallel used by Dante himself (*Par.* XV, 25–27) but which in this context is designed to evoke how Dante, the now divine and immortal son of Florence, has been reunited with his *patria*. Ficino calls on Florentines to rejoice and exult, and he uses Dantean language (*Purg.* XVI, 107) in referring to two suns rising in one place – Dante and the first edition of Landino's *Comento*. Dante's return not only fulfils the poet's own 'prophecy', the commands of the gods, and the desire of Florence, but it also sets in motion a chain of miraculous events that herald a moment of spiritual renewal for the city and may well echo Dante's experiences as protagonist in the *Paradiso* (*Par.* I, 82: 'La novità del suono e 'l grande lume' ['the novelty of the sound and the great light']): the flames of the Empyrean, never seen fully, blaze in Dante's honour; and the unheard music of the heavenly spheres openly celebrates his coronation.

After the contrived mythological allegory of Ficino's letter, chapter XIV deals with questions concerning the site and size of Dante's Hell and the measurements of the Giants and Lucifer that the pilgrim encounters in *Inferno* XXXI and XXXIV. It provides further insight into Landino's intellectual eclecticism, and his desire both to make use of a wide range of Florentine traditions and to bring Dante into line with the city's more recent cultural initiatives. At the beginning of the chapter, Landino notes that Dante differs from Greek and Latin poets who describe Hell because of his exceptional interest in questions related to its site and measurement:

> non posso sanza sommo stupore considerare la sua nuova né mai da alchuno altro excogitata inventione. Ha posto lo 'nferno Homero. Hallo posto Eurypide. Hannolo posto più altri poeti greci. *Preterea* Virgilio, Ovidio et Claudiano [. . .] Ma che figura in quello fingono, che capacità gli danno? Che sito? [. . .] per alta sua fantasia illustrata da sobtilissima mente et da mathematicha disciplina innanzi a gl'occhi ci pone la forma, el quanto, et el quale.[56]

> I cannot think of his new and never previously thought of invention without the greatest wonder [. . .] There is an underworld in Homer and Euripides, and in other Greek poets. Moreover, it is found in Virgil, Ovid, and Claudian [. . .] But what shape, size, and site do they give to it? [. . .] through his high imagination illuminated by a most subtle mind and by mathematical study he places before our eyes the form, dimensions, and qualities [of Hell].

The interest in measuring Dante's Hell is peculiarly Florentine and had been developed by the city's technical writers and artists during the first half of the fifteenth century.[57] If we are to believe Vasari, Filippo Brunelleschi, who studied under Toscanelli, one of Landino's own mentors, 'devoted much effort at this time to matters related to Dante which he understood well with regard to sites and measures'.[58] In this respect, perhaps the most representative earlier figure is a merchant-reader of Dante and copyist of his works, Bonaccorso da Montemagno, who composed *c.* 1440 a topographical work entitled *Il cammino di Dante* and a short treatise on the poem's time-references.[59] This kind of approach to Dante's poem, when combined with a keen Florentine interest in cartography and the recovery of Greek mathematics and geography, form the general background to Landino's chapter. However, as Landino himself makes clear, his principal authority is Antonio Manetti, who, as we noted in the previous chapter, brought cosmographical enquiries to bear upon the *Comedy*.[60] Following Manetti's measurements, Landino establishes the circumference and diameter of the Earth, as well as the place and time of Dante's entry into Hell and its centre, and he uses these measures and parameters as fixed ratios by which to determine the size of Hell, Lucifer, and the Giants. Since Manetti left no definitive published version of his studies, it is difficult to know how faithfully Landino followed his teachings. The results of such investigations are not inaccurate in themselves, but the notion of applying the relevant measurements to Dante's Hell in its entirety is ill-conceived, since in the *Inferno* Dante does not provide enough consistent points of reference to make such calculations possible. In fact, Dante only refers to such distances in the final four cantos of the *Inferno*, and they are probably no more than a highly effective poetic device used to evoke the palpable reality and raw materiality of lower Hell. It is unfair, though, to judge Landino in this way, since to do so would be to lose sight of his own reasons for including this chapter at the end of the *proemio*. Considered in its own context, what underpins Landino's use of Manetti is once again a desire to engage with the most worthy components of contemporary Florentine culture, including non-humanist ones, in order to make a passionate case for Dante's universality and *novità*.

6

Tradition and innovation in Cristoforo Landino's *Comento*: platonism, natural science, and classicism

All the Dante commentaries that we have encountered in this book are characterized by their close relationship to the earlier commentary tradition on the *Comedy*, and Landino's extensive body of glosses or *chiosa* to his *Comento* is no exception. As Michele Barbi first illustrated, Landino's *chiosa* relies heavily upon the Trecento tradition of Dante exegesis, especially the commentaries by Pietro Alighieri, Giovanni Boccaccio, Benvenuto da Imola, and Francesco da Buti.[1] The nature and extent of Landino's borrowings are such that this section of the *Comento* is, as a whole, undoubtedly more traditional in its treatment of Dante than the *proemio*. And yet, despite his dependency on the earlier exegetical tradition, Landino brings a critical mentality to his use of earlier commentators, and – more importantly still – he introduces and expounds interests and preoccupations that are grounded in a contemporary Florentine context. The primary concern of this chapter is to explore Landino's tendency to amplify and modernize his commentary upon Dante in glosses that deal with Plato and Neoplatonic authorities, with scientific ideas, and with classical authors and related background material. Given the extensive body of annotations that Landino devotes to each of these subjects, and their importance in Medicean Florence, it is rather surprising that the topics have received very little critical attention. Much of the present chapter provides a critical assessment of these strands of the *chiosa*, by considering Landino's debts to earlier traditions (especially but not only Dante commentary) and examining the extent to which he was influenced by his contemporary Florentine context. This survey is presented in the form of three case-studies which will help us to appreciate the particular blend of tradition and innovation that is characteristic of the *chiosa* to the *Comento*. As in all earlier chapters of this book, then, a major preoccupation in what follows will be to study how Dante's text is read in relation to earlier traditions and in ways that acclimatize him to, and make him continuous with, Florentine concerns in the later fifteenth century.

1 Structure, modes of reading, and allegorical framework

Before we begin the case-studies, it may be helpful to outline the structure of Landino's *chiosa* and its hermeneutic strategies in general. The *chiosa* takes each canto of the poem and divides it into blocs of tercets for which it then provides either a general summary and/or a more specific, line-by-line commentary. No separation is made between the literal and the allegorical readings. This general approach, and the subdivisions themselves, owe much to Buti's *Commento* (c. 1385–95). As a commentator, Landino is particularly keen to provide his readers with a substantial body of literary instruction and encyclopaedic teaching. He makes extensive use of paraphrase to clarify elementary lexical and syntactical features of the poem. He repeatedly engages in linguistic and rhetorical commentary, especially when discussing Dante's use of various figures of speech.[2] He shows a strong interest in etymology.[3] And he develops lengthy digressions on matters of ancient and modern history, geography and natural lore, philosophy and theology, law, mythology, music, and many other topics. Similar annotations are, of course, found in varying degrees in almost all earlier Dante commentary texts, and Landino sometimes does no more than copy from them. But, as in the *proemio*, he also reorders and updates earlier discussions in order to fashion his own expanded syntheses. Landino is consciously backward-looking in electing this style of commentary, which often brings with it a sprawling mass of annotations, as opposed to the more exact reading of texts as artefacts whose authors belong to a specific age and context – the form of philological commentary that, in Florence, Landino's own former student, Poliziano, had begun to promote in his lectures at the *Studio*.[4]

Later in this chapter, we will consider several aspects of Landino's didacticism and encylopaedism, but here it is crucial to recognize two further features of the *chiosa* that are especially significant. The first is Landino's interest in providing commentary on Dante's use of language. In chapters 4 and 5, we studied the complex of patriotic, ideological, and linguistic motivations that lie behind Landino's advocacy of the Florentine language. This background helps to explain the seriousness and precision with which Dante's lexical choices are evaluated throughout the *chiosa*. In some two hundred passages, Landino provides a detailed linguistic commentary. He notes, for example, where the poet uses neologisms, Latinisms, regional dialects, and gallicisms, as well as Florentine words that have become dated; he repeatedly comments upon terms derived from Latin and Greek, and even those originally from Jewish and Hebrew. Landino is indebted for a number of etymologies and definitions to earlier writers on Dante, especially Boccaccio's *Esposizioni* which, despite its unfinished state, has a rich lexical commentary. However, Landino goes beyond Boccaccio, and indeed all earlier precedents, in providing a wide range of examples and constantly elucidating Latin and Greek etymologies.[5] Such critical practice probably owes much to materials accumulated during his years of teaching rhetoric and poetry at the *Studio*, and the close attention he pays to latinisms in the *Comedy* shows how he applies to Dante's language his own earlier propositions that 'whoever wants to be a good writer of Tuscan must be a good Latinist' and that 'if we want to enrich this language we must every day take Latin words and, without forcing the nature of Tuscan, bring them into our idiom'.[6] The following two passages, both without precedent in earlier Dante commentary, provide good examples of Landino's sensitivity in handling the linguistic texture of the *Comedy*. The first passage deals with Dante's reference to Geryon's movement towards him as a kind of swimming (*Inf.* XVI, 131) – an expression that he traces to Virgilian antecedents; the second comments on the opening tercet of *Purgatorio*, by offering a lengthy digression on Dante's use of metaphor. Both passages are also notable for the way Landino stresses Dante's intimate connections with Virgil's poetry:

> molti sono rimasi ingannati credendo, perché lui dice *venir notando*, quel luogho esser ripieno d'acqua; et non s'accorghono che lui imita Virgilio, el quale fa reciproca translatione dal mare all'aria. Onde dixe: 'mare velivolum', *i.* 'per quod velis volatur', et volare è solo nell'aria,

et chosì dall'aria al mare, onde in Mercurio dixe 'remigio alarum', benché e remi sieno solamente del mare. Similmente Danthe dixe *venir notando* benché el notatore sia proprio nell'acqua, et certo è mirabile fictione et al tutto degna della divinità di tanto ingegno [...] imperoché usando translatione et non proprii vocaboli accrescie degnità et auctorità alle chose come veggiamo in Virgilio et in molti altri poeti così greci come latini [...] Et accioché meglio dimostriamo questo ornamento rhetorico diciamo tutte le parole, le quali usiamo, sono o proprie o translate [...] Alchuna volta sono tanto antiche che quasi rimangono fuori d'ogni consuetudine come 'guari' et 'sovente', che l'una et l'altra è fiorentina ma non sono più in uso [...] Alcuna volta sono nuove et fabbricate da esso auctore chome quando Danthe dice 's'io m'intuassi chome tu t'inmii', imperoché innanzi a Danthe nessuno in lingua fiorentina dixe 'intuare' et 'inmiare'. Translate sono quando transferiamo le parole dalla propria significatione in un'altra significatione non dissimile alla propria, chome qui el poeta dice *la navicella del mio ingegno*.[7]

Many have been deceived in the belief that, because he (i.e. Dante) says *come swimming*, that place is full of water; and they do not realize that he is imitating Virgil, who makes metaphorical interchange between sea and air. And thus he writes 'sail-wing sea', that is, 'through which he flies with sails', and flying only takes place in the air and a transfer is made between air and water; hence, Mercury says 'the oars of his wings', even though oars only pertain to water. Similarly, Dante said *come swimming* although the word swimmer is strictly said of water and certainly this is a marvellous fiction and most worthy of the divinity of such a genius [...] using *translatio* and not the appropriate words confers dignity and authority on things, as we see in Virgil and in many other poets, both Greek and Latin [...] So that we better demonstrate this rhetorical ornament I say that all the words we use are either literal or figurative [...] Sometimes they are so old that they almost fall outside everyday usage like 'guari' and 'sovente', which are both Florentine, but are no longer in use [...] Sometimes they are new and fashioned by this author as when Dante says 'if I entered-into-you as you enter-into-me', for before Dante no-one in Tuscan said 'enter-into-you' and 'enter-into-me'. Words are metaphorical when we transfer them from their literal meaning to another one different from that sense, as here the poet says *the little ship of my wits*.

The attentiveness of Landino's linguistic commentary is more than matched by the subtlety of his allegoresis, which forms the second key feature of the *Comento* that is prominent throughout the *chiosa*. As several critics have shown, Landino's allegorical reading of the poem owes much to Buti, but he also develops his own emphases and concerns. Although allegorical readings are pervasive, Landino is not the inveterate allegorizer whom some have lambasted, and in several cases he refuses to provide an allegorical gloss where one is supplied by earlier commentators. What distinguishes Landino from his predecessors in the commentary tradition is the extent to which he uses allegorical readings to interpret the *Comedy* on a philosophical plane.[8] This is achieved primarily by evaluating the characters Dante and Virgil and their interrelationship with reference to psychological categories such as the appetites, sensuality, intellect, intelligence, and both inferior and superior reason. The following passage, from the *chiosa* to *Inferno* I, 61–66, illustrates this general interpretation and the range of psychologized categories he invokes:

> [...] acciochè nel processo del poema questo nome [sc. Virgil] non c'induca in alchuno errore o difficultà d'intendere el senso allegorico, già in questo principio ci sia noto che non *univoce* ma *equivoce* sarà posto Virgilio, et alchuna volta non sonerà altro che questo poeta. Alchuna volta significherà la ragione humana semplicemente, et Danthe sarà la sensualità. Altra volta lo interpreterremo per lo intellecto illustrato di varie et molte doctrine. Altra volta exprimerremo per quello la ragione superiore, et allora Danthe significherà non la sensualità sola, ma anchora la ragione inferiore.[9]

> in order that throughout the poem this name does not lead us into any error or difficulty in understanding the allegorical sense, already in this opening passage let it be known to us that Virgil is used both with a single and with many meanings. And sometimes his name will mean nothing other than this poet. Sometimes it will mean human reason alone, and Dante will be sensuality. At other times we will interpret his name as the intellect illuminated by many and various doctrines. At other times through his name we will express superior reason, and then Dante will not signify sensuality alone, but also inferior reason.

This kind of interpretative lens underpins a great many passages in Landino's *chiosa*, especially to the *Inferno*, where Dante-*personaggio*'s journey, and especially the actions, gestures, and dialogue of Dante-character and Virgil-character, are connected to psychological states. In

so doing, Landino re-uses ideas he had elaborated in his two earlier
Latin dialogues and adapts them to the *Comedy*. As a commentator
on Dante, he employs all the powers of the soul and mind discussed
in his *De anima*; and he constantly reworks the exegetical armature
of his own *Disputationes Camaldulenses*, whereby Aeneas' journey from
Troy to Italy represents the ascent of the mind from sensuality to the
contemplation of God through a series of interiorized mental processes
which have psychological, moral, and religious meanings. A passage
from the opening gloss to *Inferno* I illustrates how Landino adapts this
hermeneutic filter to the *Comedy*, as well as the close relationship he
thereby establishes between the finalities of Dante, Virgil, and Homer:

> È verisimile adunque, che Danthe si proponessi il medesimo fine
> el quale et apresso de' Greci Homero et apresso de' Latini Virgilio
> s'havevono proposto. Et chome quegli l'uno per Ulixe, l'altro per
> Enea dimostrano in che modo venendosi nella cognitione de' vitii
> et conosciutogli, purgandosi da quegli, s'arriva finalmente alla con-
> templatione delle chose divine, chosì Danthe sotto questo figmento
> per la peregrinatione finge haver facto con Virgilio, in persona di sé
> dimostra quel medesimo.[10]

It is likely therefore that Dante set himself the same end as that which
Homer and Virgil had set themselves amongst the Greeks and the
Latins respectively. And as the former uses Ulysses and the latter
Aeneas in order to show how, by acquiring knowledge of the vices
and having understood them, and by purging oneself from them,
one comes finally to contemplate divine things, so too does Dante
demonstrate the same by means of this fable regarding the pilgrimage
which as a character he pretends to have made with Virgil.

2 Plato and the *platonici*

Landino's use of Plato and the *platonici* or platonists, in both the *proemio*
and the *chiosa* of the *Comento*, is one of the most important features
of his engagement with his immediate Florentine context. It is also the
area of the commentary that most directly anticipates, and in some
cases influences, the estimates in contemporary Dante studies regarding
the strong Christian-neoplatonic orientation to Dante's thought and
poetry.[11] With over eighty references to Plato and neoplatonic writers

(the *platonici*), many of which make up detailed and extended glosses, Landino's interest is quite exceptional, especially when it is measured against the number and length of the comments made about Plato by Dante's earlier commentators. None of his references derive from Buti's *Commento*, his main source, as we have noted, for his general allegorical approach. Pietro Alighieri's *Comentum* may have informed, at least in part, two passages in the *Comento* where he deals with neoplatonic motifs. But Landino owes most to Benvenuto da Imola, whose own *Comentum* is used almost verbatim for four separate passages dealing with Plato.[12] All in all, though, the number of borrowings is extremely limited when it is compared to Landino's usual glossatorial tendency to draw closely on the work of earlier Dante commentaries. Landino's comments on Plato thus represent significant deviations from his normal practices as a commentator, and, as such, they reveal programmatic and personal emphases which may be closely linked to the recovery of Plato in the Florence of his time.

Throughout the *Comento*, Landino is quite explicit about the pre-eminence of Plato in matters of philosophy. He repeatedly refers to Plato as divine, as the most eloquent of philosophers, and as the prince of all philosophy. Landino mentions more Platonic dialogues than any earlier commentator on Dante, referring by name to six works: *Ion*, *Phaedrus*, *Crito*, *Symposium*, *Parmenides*, and *Timaeus*. Without being directly named, all these dialogues are widely employed elsewhere in the *Comento*. Landino also draws upon the *Phaedo* and makes some use of the *Gorgias*, *Letters*, *Republic*, and *Laws*.[13] Although several of Plato's works were available in Latin translations that had been completed by 1430, the range of dialogues used by Landino and the fact that he refers to a previously untranslated work such as the *Symposium* show his indebtedness to texts directly associated with Ficino's activities as a translator and interpreter of Plato in the 1460s and 1470s.[14] The majority of Landino's references and comments do not specify a dialogue, and, in these passages, Landino discusses Plato and the *platonici* within two principal contexts: doctrinal compilation on a wide range of subjects; and the use of Platonic and Neoplatonic images and concepts for exegetical purposes, usually as part of his own psychologized allegoresis of Dante's text (see also section 1). Let us examine each of these contexts more closely, using selected examples.

Like other humanists of the period, throughout the *chiosa*, Landino is keen to explain the background necessary to understand a particular doctrine, and this is often presented in the form of *sententiae*. Celebrated Platonic teachings such as transmigration, the theory of forms, and the doctrine of recollection are not neglected, and emphasis is also given to doctrines related to the administration of the state, providence, fate, and cosmology. But it is characteristic of Landino that moral teachings – on anger, the senses, the body, free will, sin, and other topics – form an especially important set of preoccupations. Landino's interest in Platonic doctrine is even more keenly felt in a cluster of ideas pertaining to the human soul, where he often draws upon his own earlier dialogue, the *De anima*. With reference to Plato and the *platonici*, he repeatedly discusses the nature of the soul, its creation by God, its simultaneous existence with all other souls, its descent into the body, and its return to the star allotted to it upon creation.[15] In almost all these passages, Landino uses Platonic teachings in a way which the Dantean text does not directly solicit. Indeed, it is significant that Landino is careful not to impose a Platonic reading upon the *Comedy* in the two principal passages where a Platonic doctrine is mentioned by Dante (*Purg.* IV, 1–6; *Par.* IV, 55–60). Landino also accepts Dante's own criticism of the limitations of Plato and Aristotle (*Purg.* III, 40–45). At such moments, Landino recognizes that Dante is in disagreement with Plato, and such solicitude with the letter of the *Comedy* contrasts markedly with the many other passages in his commentary, both doctrinal and exegetical, where Landino gives full rein to Plato and the *platonici*.

Amongst the doctrinal glosses, there are quite a number of passages that are of limited importance and involve stock references or conventional quotations. But this is not to deny either their cumulative effect or indeed their innovative quality, given the centrally important fact that, in a *chiosa* which is often closely dependent on earlier commentators, these references bear, as we have already noted, almost no relation to previous Dante exegesis. In addition to more conventional Platonic *topoi* and *sententiae*, there are many other doctrinal *chiose* in which Landino gives great prominence to Plato within a chain of authorities which often begins with Plato's viewpoint. An underlying preoccupation in several of these glosses is Landino's desire to reconcile Plato with Christianity.[16] One of the better examples of such tendencies is the discussion of fate, which arises from Dante's own reference to his journey as a 'fatale andare' ('preordained going') in *Inferno* v, 22. Here, Landino uses Plato, the prince of philosophers, as his principal authority because of the approval he received from Augustine, although his account bears strong traces of the views on fate and providence in later writers associated with the Platonic tradition such as Apuleius, Chalcidius, and Boethius.[17] In this way, the passage is representative of several other important doctrinal passages in the *Comento* where Landino stresses the centrality of Plato and his harmony with Christian teachings, but in so doing provides a formulation of Platonic teachings that is more in line with Neoplatonizing traditions. Further examples of such tendencies can be found in *chiose* that refer to Plato when discussing the relationship between free will and astral influence and the divine creation of the human soul.[18] There is, of course, a long-standing tradition concerned to harmonize Plato and Christianity, but Landino's own attempts are quite clearly shaped by issues specific to his cultural context. It is, for example, significant that his concern with the question of Plato's relationship with Christianity, as well as with the centrality of the human soul, of moral reform, and of questions related to free will and the power of the stars, lie at the heart of much of Ficino's work. And it is also significant that, like Landino in his exposition of fate and other topics, Ficino repeatedly uses Augustine as a key authority in supporting the view that Platonic texts foreshadow Christian teachings.[19]

Leaving aside the doctrinal glosses, Landino's use of Plato for more exegetical reasons takes us to the heart of his concerns as a critic of ancient and vernacular literature. In the *chiosa* as a whole, an important role is played by Platonizing concepts and images, such as the Phaedran chariot and the Two Venuses, as well as by more Neoplatonic motifs such as the *descensus ad inferos*, the wings of the soul and its flight back to God, and the hierarchy of moral and intellectual virtues. These concepts and images are used by Landino as the philosophical substratum for allegorized readings of many passages in the *Comedy*, and, as such, the relevant passages represent some of the most original aspects of Landino's use of Plato in the *Comento*.[20]

Landino's use of Plato and the *platonici* is not, however, simply a question of the *Comento* mediating contemporary historical realities and sources. If the Trecento commentators play a very limited role in transmitting Platonic teachings to Landino, other forms of literary mediation are more important and three classical authors are particularly significant: Cicero, Augustine, and Macrobius. Cicero provides Landino with the authority and vocabulary for praising Plato as a divine and the pre-eminent philosopher. And Ciceronian works such as the *Disputationes Tusculanae, De officiis*, and *De finibus*, furnish Landino with a variety of Platonic teachings for at least six passages where Plato is named directly but traces of Ciceronian influence can be detected. As for Augustine, in addition to the comment on *Inferno* v, 22, his authority is brought to bear on the fundamental question of Plato's relationship with Christianity in three further glosses. The presence of Macrobius, who is the most important source of all, is less easily detected, because he is not cited directly by Landino with reference to Plato. However, the *Commentarium in Somnium Scipionis* is nonetheless the most likely source for a variety of platonizing passages, both doctrinal and exegetical, in the *Comento*. That Landino is so heavily dependent on these three authors reveals the extent to which his relationship to Plato is secondary and highly mediated. Yet Landino's predilection for certain textual authorities is still deeply revealing of his cultural context, for, in addition to Augustine, both Cicero and Macrobius are important mediators of platonism in Ficino, especially the early Ficino.[21]

The most important intertexual relationship of all is precisely that between the *Comento* and Ficino's own earlier writings. These writings include his early letters, translations of the entire corpus of Platonic and pseudo-Platonic works, the *Theologia platonica*, and a number of important apologetic treatises. The Ficinian texts reveal a diverse set of intellectual interests and are marked not only by a Platonism inspired in part by Augustine, but also by close study of Hermetic, Platonic, and Neoplatonic sources, as well as by elements of scholastic Aristotelianism. Several close points of contact between Landino and Ficino are well known; and, as was noted in chapter 4, it is likely that Landino influenced Ficino's view, in the *proemio* to his vernacular version of *Monarchia*, that Dante 'adorned his books with many platonic thoughts'. In chapter 5, moreover, we explored Ficino's influence in the *proemio*, especially on Landino's conception of the *furor poeticus*. In the *chiosa* Landino makes five more direct references to Ficino as 'el nostro platonico', that is, as the pre-eminent figure in the platonic revival in Florence. Landino only quotes two Ficinian works directly in the *chiosa*. Commenting on 'splendor' ('splendours') in *Inferno* VII, 77, he refers his reader to one of Ficino's letters, later to be refashioned into the better-known *De lumine*, for further explanation about the nature and behaviour of light. And in the *prologo* to the *Paradiso* he mentions the *De raptu Pauli*, quoting a passage where Ficino is himself drawing on the Augustinian doctrine of the *pondus amoris*. Like Plato and Cicero, the historical Ficino is even deemed to be sufficiently important (and of course familiar to his Florentine audience) to be used as a homely example in order to elucidate a discussion of the internal senses in a *chiosa* that may well deliberately echo a related passage in Ficino's own *Theologia platonica*.[22]

Apart from these direct references, there are many other traces of Ficinian influence scattered throughout the *Comento*, in large measure through the transference of Platonic imagery, doctrines, quotations, and exegetical devices employed earlier in the *Disputationes Camaldulenses*.[23] Various passages from the most famous of Ficino's works, the *De amore*, the Latin version of his commentary on the *Symposium*, inform Landino's glosses on Plato that deal with the concept of beauty and the doctrine of the Two Venuses.[24] And more generally Ficino underpins Landino's attempts to unveil Christian teachings in the depths of Plato and to bring them to bear on his discussion of Dante's text. Such concerns correspond closely to Ficino's own central role in casting a mythologized genealogy or a *prisca theologia*, in which Plato occupies a prominent place.[25]

Despite these correspondences, some based on shared contextual factors, others of a more explicit and intertextual nature, Landino reveals his independence from Ficino in several respects. In the *Comento*, Landino names hardly any Neoplatonic writers, and although he often reads Plato in a Neoplatonizing vein, this is a general tendency shared by many writers, both late medieval and early Renaissance ones, because their understanding of Plato has been mediated by later representatives of the Platonic tradition. Landino does not share Ficino's interest in metaphysical principles, and, despite his firm desire to harmonize

Platonic philosophy with Christianity, he does not go as far as Ficino in viewing it as a way to union with God. At times, Landino emphasizes Plato's religious and intellectual orthodoxy, but this does not prevent him from openly criticizing Platonic teachings on delicate doctrinal questions such as the pre-existence of the soul and its descent into the body.[26] Such criticisms show that Landino's relationship to Platonic sources is more complicated than has often been suggested, especially in some recent interpretations of him as a committed exponent and unrestrained enthusiast of Plato.

In order to illustrate more closely the processes of textual and contextual mediation involved in Landino's use of Plato in the *chiosa*, let us conclude this case-study by examining two of the most important passages in the *Comento*, both from the *chiosa* to the *Inferno*: his opening comment on the first twenty-one lines of *Inferno* I; and his treatment, in *Inferno* IV, of the relative merits of Aristotle and Plato. In the first passage, Landino strategically brings Plato and a general Neoplatonic patina to bear upon Dante's text in a way that asserts his designs as a commentator, distinguishes him from all previous Dante commentators, and sheds light upon the cultural matrix which informs his view of Plato. The role of prologue sections in marking out ideological intent is a well-known feature of commentary literature and Landino's own opening comment to canto I, which in effect constitutes a sustained exposition of Dante *sub specie Platonis et Platonicis*, is very much part of this tradition.[27] With reference to the *crux* of 'nel mezo del camino' ('in the middle of the journey'), Landino declares his dissatisfaction with earlier solutions and outlines a markedly Platonic view of the opposition between body and soul, in which the descent of the soul into the body is described as a degrading lowering into the prison of materiality. It is this strong and explicit contrast between the divine soul and the material body that prompts Landino to make his first direct reference to Plato in order to support the view that there are two forms of death: the separation of the soul from the body; and its descent into the body:

> È l'huomo composto d'animo et di corpo. L'animo è divino, et semplice, immortale et incorruptibile. Et perché è prodocto da Dio a sua imagine, et similitudine, è divino, et pieno di luce, et è capace per la

contemplatione di venire alla cognitione delle chose divine, et fruire
Iddio; in che consiste el nostro sommo bene, chome in altro luogho più
absolutamente tracteremo. El corpo per l'opposito essendo composto
di materia de' quattro elementi, di sua natura è corruptibile, obscuro et
pieno di tenebre. L'animo adunque sommerso in questo obscuro
carcere perde quasi ogni suo celeste vigore, et per le tenebre del corpo
rimane quasi privato d'ogni luce di ragione, et puossi dire quello essere
sepulto sotto la corporea molle. Onde sapientemente el divino Platone
pone due spetie di morte, et l'una chiama morte d'animale, cosa nota a
tutti, la quale allhora viene, quando l'anima dal corpo si separa. L'altra
è morte d'anima, et questa è quando l'anima chome già habbiamo
decto sommersa dal pondo et obscurità del corpo, perde tanto di vigore, che nessuna delle sue excellenti potentie può adoperare. Il perché
veggiamo l'huomo non solamente ne' primi anni infantili et puerili,
ma in gran parte della adolescentia et gioventù vivere solamente secondo el senso. Et perché non conosce altro che quello, non crede sé
essere altro, et niente reputa bene, se non quelle chose che dilectano e
corporei sensi; né alchuna chosa male se non quella che gl'atrista. Et
chome ebbro et da profonda sonnolentia oppresso né sé conosce, né
ad che fine sia prodocto intende, né conosce la ignorantia sua né la
sua miseria in sino a tanto che, arrivato all'età già matura, parte per
la experientia di molte cose, parte per alchuna doctrina acquistata et
per precepti da' più savi di sé avuti, comincia a destare la ragione, et
allora finalmente conosce sé essere in obscura selva, cioè l'animo suo
essere oppreso da ignorantia et da vitii per la contagione del corpo.[28]

Man is made up of spirit and body. Spirit is divine, simple, immortal,
and incorruptible. And, because God makes him in His image and
likeness, it is divine and full of light and by means of contemplation is
able to gain knowledge of divine things and enjoy God, which is our
highest good as we will we show more definitively in another place.
On the other hand, by its nature, the body is corruptible, obscure,
and full of shadow, since it is composed out of the matter of the four
elements. Spirit, then, submerged in this dark prison, loses almost all
its celestial power, and because of the shadows of its body remains
almost deprived of the light of reason and one can say that it is buried
under its corporeal burden. Thus, divine Plato sagely puts forward
two kinds of death, one he calls animal death, something known to
all of us which comes about when the soul is separated from the body.
The other death is that of the soul, and this is when, as we have said,
the soul is submerged under the weight and darkness of the body, and

loses so much of its vigour that it cannot perform any of its higher powers. For this reason, we see that man lives according to his senses not only when he is an infant and a child but also for much of his adolescence and youth. And because he knows nothing other than this, and does not believe himself to be other than it, he only holds those things to be good which delight the bodily senses and those things to be bad which sadden them. And, like a drunk overcome by deep sleep, he neither knows himself or to what end he has been made. Nor does he know his own ignorance or his own misery until having reached an already mature age, in part through experience of many things, in part through acquired doctrine and the precepts of those wiser than him, reason begins to awaken. And then he finally knows himself to be in a dark wood, that is, he knows that his spirit is oppressed by ignorance and vice because of the contagion of the body.

This important passage, which is not simply a bringing together of Platonic *topoi*, bears many of the forms of intertextuality we have already outlined. In part it reformulates Landino's earlier treatment of related themes in the *Disputationes Camaldulenses*,[29] but it also incorporates new material, echoing several sections of the *Phaedo* and borrowing from other sources, including Neoplatonic ones. In the *Phaedo*, Plato does define the soul as divine, immortal, and incorruptible (80A–B) and he refers to death as the separation of the soul from the body (64C), as well as to contact with the body as a form of imprisonment and drunkenness (62B, 82E–83D, 79C). But nowhere in this dialogue or elsewhere does Plato refer to the soul's descent into the body as a kind of death. It is instead Macrobius' *Commentarium in Somnium Scipionis* to which Landino turns for the teaching on the two deaths; and the entire gloss seems to have been influenced by several other passages in Macrobius, as well by important Florentine authorities, especially Matteo Palmieri and Ficino.[30] The vision of man put forward by this comment, with its prominent emphasis on the divinity of mind and its capacity to awaken itself from the stultifying burden of corporeality, represents one of the most important interpretative keys in Landino's allegorical treatment of the poem. All in all, it is clear that his choice to place this lengthy *chiosa*, redolent with its Platonic and Neoplatonic reverberations, in such a textually marked position is highly strategic and programmatic.

The second passage, Landino's commentary on *Inferno* IV, 130–32, evaluates the relationship between Plato and Aristotle. For Dante, Aristotle is, of course, the 'maestro di color che sanno' ('master of those who know') (*Inf.* IV, 131), and, although Landino recognizes that Dante was himself a 'peripatetic', this does not prevent him from relaying Greek, Latin, and vernacular opinion about the interrelationship between the two thinkers so as to place Dante's assertion in a new dimension:

> Tra questi dà el primo luogo ad Aristotile, huomo sanza dubbio di mirabile ingegno, et di profonda doctrina, et el quale ha la palma per haver collocato in perfectissimo ordine tutta la philosophia, et con optima distinctione di tutte le sue parti haver tractato. Il perché el poeta lo prepose a Platone, non solo da questo mosso, ma forse anchora dalla sua professione, perché fu peripatetico. Né ardirei qui dare mio giudicio di due tanti huomini, né potrei volendo, prohibito dalla imbecillità del mio ingegno et dal defecto della doctrina, el quale è in me. Ma veggo appresso de' Greci Aristotile essere in somma admiratione nelle phisiche doctrine, et Platone essere giudichato superiore nelle metaphysice et divine. Onde Aristotile chiamano demonio, et Platone divino. E certo tutti gli antichi Latini, e quali non seperorono la eloquentia dalla doctrina, vogliono che 'l principe de' philosophi sia Platone. Né è in piccolo odio di questi incorso Aristotile per haverlo in molti luoghi dannato. Conciosia che *etiam* buona parte de' comentatori d'Aristotele difendono Platone dove Aristotele lo danna. Cicerone lo chiama Homero de' philosophi, et Augustino dice havere electo e platonici chome quegli che hanno inteso meglio la divinità. Et altrove scrive: 'taccia Aristotile, el quale contro a Platone è sempre fanciullo'. Et el nostro Petrarcha lo prepone dicendo: 'volsimi da man dextra et vidi Plato Che'n quella schiera andò più presso al segno Al quale aggiunge chi dal cielo è dato. Aristotele poi pien d'alto ingegno.'[31]

Amongst these he gives first place to Aristotle, a man undoubtedly of remarkable intelligence and profound learning, and who holds the prize for having arranged all philosophy in a most perfect order and for having handled each of its parts with utmost distinction. And for this reason the poet places him before Plato, being moved to do so not only by this but also by his profession, because he was a peripatetic. Nor would I dare to give my judgement here of two such great men, nor could I were I able to do so, impeded as I am by the imbecility of my intelligence and the lack of learning that is in me. But I see that amongst the Greeks Aristotle is held in profound admiration for his teachings on physics, and Plato is judged superior in matters that are metaphysical and divine. Thus, they call Aristotle demon and Plato divine. And without doubt all Latin writers of antiquity, who did not separate eloquence and doctrine, would have Plato as the prince of philosophers. Nor has Aristotle gained little scorn from these writers for having damned him in many places; and even a good section of Aristotelian commentators defend Plato where Aristotle damns him. Cicero calls him the Homer of philosophers, and Augustine says that he has chosen the Platonists as those who have best understood the deity. And elsewhere he writes: 'be silent Aristotle who is always childish towards Plato'. And our Petrarch places him first, saying: 'I turned to the left and saw Plato who in that rank went closest to the mark which one may reach by the grace of heaven. Then Aristotle full of high intellect.'

Apart from the modesty *topos*, which derives from Macrobius, the textual models for this passage are relatively easy to identify and they again serve to indicate the intertextual complexity of the *Comento*.[32] But to pursue sources in themselves is to neglect more important questions. For a start, it is instructive to compare this comment with the earlier tradition of Dante commentary. Even a commentator who is acquainted with Petrarch and humanistically inclined such as Benvenuto da Imola does not contradict Dante and accepts Aristotle's authority. *Mutatis mutandis* the same is true of all the Trecento commentators on this passage, as well as the fifteenth-century commentaries by Giovanni da Serravalle (*c.* 1416–17) and Guininforte Barzizza (*c.* 1438).[33] A further element of innovation is Landino's use of one of Petrarch's vernacular works, the *Trionfi*. Here, Landino displays considerable critical and literary acumen, for, not only did Petrarch act as a pioneer for the later development of Platonism, but in the very passage which Landino quotes from the *Trionfi* Petrarch inverts Dante's order by placing Plato before Aristotle. Landino's heightened sense of the value of the vernacular is also clear from the way he uses a quotation from Petrarch's vernacular text as an *auctoritas* on the same level as his Latin *auctores* in this matter of important contemporary philosophical debate.[34] The contrast here with Pietro Alighieri, who does not quote a single vernacular source in his *Comentum*, could not be more pronounced.

If we are to gain a still deeper sense of the significance of this gloss, it needs to be related to a fifteenth-century context in which Plato was a subject of much controversy. Bruni had been unsettled by Plato's views on the transmigration of the soul and marital communism in his *Vita Aristotelis* of 1429.[35] But the Aristotle–Plato controversy as such, which has its distant roots in Byzantine intellectual history, became more acute on Italian soil with the polemic that developed following Gemistus Pletho's provocative championing of Plato at the Council of Union in Florence in 1439, and his work in defence of Plato, the *De differentiis platonicae atque aristotelicae disciplinae*, of the same year. Although this treatise was composed in Greek and did not circulate widely, it helped to stimulate later tracts both for and against Plato. The most important and influential of these later writings were George of Trezibond's *Comparationes philosophorum Aristotelis et Platonis* (1455) and Cardinal Bessarion's *In calumniatorem Platonis* (Latin version, c. 1469).[36]

It is this context – before the popularizing of Platonism and its sixteenth-century courtly vogue – against which Landino's comment needs to be situated, a context that was still a time of antiplatonism and in which the *platonici* were often an 'embattled minority'.[37] Landino's passage raises the important general question of the extent to which Plato is consonant with Christian teachings. Like both Ficino and Bessarion, he sides with Plato as the supreme authority in divine matters, while still assigning an important role to Aristotle in natural philosophy.[38] Furthermore, the reason that Landino gives for Dante's own preference for Aristotle – his orderliness – is precisely that given by John Argyropoulos, a Byzantine scholar and rival of Landino who, as we noted in chapter 4, taught at the Florentine *Studio* from 1457 until 1471. Landino's view that Aristotle had 'collocato in perfectissimo ordine tutta la philosophia' can be connected with Argyropoulos' lectures c. 1460 on Aristotle's *De anima* in which he remarked that Aristotle gave supreme order to the sciences ('Aristoteles [...] dedit ordinem scientiarum summum').[39] At the *Studio* Argyropoulos taught the Greek Aristotle and also commented upon Plato, and it thus seems likely that, given Landino's own limited knowledge of Greek, he is one of the principal conduits for the emphasis upon Greek sources in this passage.

Elsewhere in the *Comento*, Landino's comments on both Aristotle and Plato are revealing. On occasion, Landino is in open conflict with Aristotle and the peripatetics, but, like his beloved Cicero and many contemporaries, including Ficino, he also presents Plato and Aristotle as having a complementary relationship to one another, with Plato being viewed as the philosopher of the divine.[40] It is also striking that, given the prevailing view of Landino as preeminently Platonic and/or Neoplatonic in his orientations, Aristotle is frequently used as an authority on ethical matters and topics of scientific and philosophical interest.[41] Although the majority of Landino's references to Aristotle derive from earlier commentators (see the next section), these passages nonetheless indicate that his philosophical interests in the *Comento* go beyond an exclusively Platonic outlook.

3 Landino's scientific glosses

Qual physico tutti e moti naturali o secondo el luogho o secondo la forma, o imperfecti, o perfecti, o animati, o inanimati con più lucide ragioni mai scripse? Qual corso di stella, qual congiunctione, qual revolutione di cielo è stata da llui pretermessa? Qual transformation d'uno in altro elemento, quale alteratione nell'aere o di grandine, piove, venti, saecte o d'altre simili, qual compositione di minere sobto la terra concreate hanno dimostro e physici che questo poeta non habbi almanco accennato? Ha l'anima quattro potentie; ha varii officii et varie proprietà, ma di tutte habbiamo vera cognitione apresso di Danthe. Et chi non sa con quanto vera cognitione et leggiadria hora l'universal sito della terra, hora alchuna particulare regione in epsa descrive?[42]

What natural philosopher ever wrote with greater lucidity about all natural motion, according to place or form, whether imperfect or perfect, animate or inanimate? Which planetary pathway, conjunction or heavenly orbit has been omitted by him? Which transformation of one element into another, which alteration in the atmosphere of hail, rain, wind, lightning and such like, which mineral composition formed under the earth – which of these things that natural philosophers have demonstrated has this poet failed at least to mention? The soul has four powers, and various offices and properties, yet we have true knowledge of them all in Dante. And who does not know with how much true learning and grace he describes now the universal site of the earth and now some particular region of it.

So writes Landino in his *proemio* to the *Comento*, confronting his reader with a series of rhetorical questions that serve to underline the variety and range of Dante's scientific ideas in the *Comedy*. To admire Dante's qualities as a natural philosopher with a keen interest in such disciplines as physics, astronomy and astrology, meteorology, mineralogy, and the human soul is not, of course, to break new ground. The *Comedy*, with its encyclopaedic qualities, multiple allusions and references to scientific lore, and lengthy doctrinal disquisitions, offered considerable scope for the Trecento commentators to clarify and explain relevant passages in Dante. Dante's poem also allowed them to satisfy didactic and encyclopaedic urges to indulge in lengthy digressions and *quaestiones* on diverse scientific topics, and to cite *auctoritates* from Aristotle, Ptolemy, Galen, Albumasar, Avicenna, and Albert the Great.[43] This kind of gloss is, in fact, one of the most pervasive in the Dante commentary tradition between Lana's commentary (*c.* 1324–28), in which it is first developed extensively, and Landino himself.[44] In several chapters of this book, moreover, we have seen that, outside the tradition of Dante exegesis, many earlier Florentine assessments of Dante emphasize his excellence in matters of natural philosophy.[45]

The most original aspect of Landino's praise of Dante's scientific poetry in the passage quoted above is his attention to the 'universal sito della terra', that is, to cosmographical matters. In comparison to the *proemio*, cosmographical concerns are not particularly prominent in the *chiosa*. However, Landino does make some use of the contemporary revival of interest in mathematics and geography in fifteenth-century Florence. Landino mentions Ptolemy's *Geographia* directly in one gloss, and he makes repeated reference to Pliny's *Historia naturalis* for geographical lore and much else.[46] Both these texts were widely perceived to be 'Florentine' because of the efforts made by humanists active in Florence to recover and study them.[47] Landino also refers to other Greek geographical lore through Diodorus Siculus and Strabo whose works had been rediscovered and translated into Latin after 1450.[48]

In general, though, the *chiosa* deals with scientific topics that had already become an established part of the earlier tradition of commentary upon the *Comedy*. Landino shows a particular interest in physics, astronomy and astrology, meteorology, medicine, and animal lore.[49] None of these subjects is in itself new to Dante commentary, and Landino makes close use of all his favoured Dante commentators. This is not the place for a full exposition of Landino's borrowings. But some select examples – which are not listed in the apparatus to Procaccioli's critical edition – will help to indicate his debts, which range from the almost verbatim transcription of doctrinal digressions in early commentators to the use of specific *auctores* and quotations. Landino's two references to the ninth-century Arab astrologer, Abû Ma'shar or Albumasar, both derive from the Pietro's *Comentum*, as do several references to astrological lore and to Aristotle.[50] Buti's *Commento* provides Landino with his account of alchemy in *Inferno* XXIX, as well as comments on meteorological phenomena and further references to Aristotle.[51] Benvenuto's *Comentum* furnishes Landino with information on astrology, meteorology, and medicine. Benvenuto also acts as a mediator for glosses in which Landino cites Aristotle, Galen, Avicenna, and Averroës; and Landino's dependence on the *Comentum* is especially notable in his re-use of Benvenuto's references to Albert the Great's scientific works.[52]

Despite these borrowings, not all the material is derivative and even where earlier commentators provide part of a gloss, Landino will often proffer his own additional information. The compiler's urge, so evident in Landino's *De anima*, remains strong in his *chiosa* to the *Comedy*, and it is undiminished in his later Latin commentaries on Horace and Virgil. Landino explicitly names his own *De anima* on eight occasions in the *Comento*,[53] and elsewhere he mines Book II of that dialogue, which deals at length with physiology and psychology, in glosses that either expand scientific subjects dealt with by the Trecento commentators or else digress upon topics that have no earlier precedent. In fact, one of the more prominent and original features of Landino's scientific *chiose* is his interest in medical doctrine.[54] A number of medical *chiose* in particular reveal his independence from the commentary tradition – some have no basis in the earlier tradition at all – and they also illustrate the varied, and at times critical, use to which Landino puts his own scientific learning.

Let us take two examples. The first is found in his commentary upon lines 65–66 of *Inferno* xv in response to Dante's semi-proverbial allusion to the difficulty of finding the 'dolce fico' ('sweet fig') amongst 'lazi sorbi' ('sour crab apples'). The passage does not call for the technical exposition which Landino provides, as he digresses at length upon the sense of taste, by relating the opposing viewpoints of Galen, Avicenna, and Averroës in a gloss that closely follows his own earlier treatment of this sense in Book II of the *De anima*,[55] which is itself dependent upon Argyropoulos' lectures on Aristotle's *De anima*. Once again, this passage shows how Landino reworks earlier writings in the *Comento* and uses scientific sources that are informed by writers active in contemporary Florence.[56]

My other example reveals how Landino's use of scientific information is motivated not only by reasons of didactic encyclopaedism, but also by the need to offer new critical readings of passages in the *Comedy*. In his commentary on lines 19–30 of *Inferno* xxiii, Landino deals with the internal senses, that is, the various psychological faculties responsible for imagining, sensing danger, thinking, and remembering. In so doing, Landino offers an accurate and detailed account of the scientific concepts that underpin the narrative moment in Dante, and at the same time he refines Buti's earlier and rather confused gloss on the same passage. The narrative context is one in which Dante the pilgrim's mental processes alert him to the threat posed by a group of demonic assailants and prompt him to seek immediate assistance from Virgil (*Inf.* xxiii, 21–24). In part, Landino offers an allegorical interpretation of these lines according to which Dante represents the sensitive part of the soul and Virgil, who responds to his urgent plea in the following three tercets, the intellect. However, the majority of his *chiosa* is taken up with a discussion of the five internal senses. Landino's account follows his earlier treatment of these faculties in his own *De anima*, which relies in turn on Albert the Great's paraphrase to Aristotle's *De anima*.[57] The details need not detain us here, but the key point to note is that Landino demonstrates how the protagonist's reactions are the result of the combined operations of his sense of sight and his imaginative and cogitative faculties:

> Ripetendo adunque quanto s'appartiene al presente luogo, vide
> Danthe la decina de' demonii. Il che fu officio dell'occhio et del

senso comune; et non solamente gli vide presenti, ma le imagini di quegli rimasono infixe nell'imaginativa el cui officio è serballe, *etiam* in absentia della cosa. Il perché la cogitativa sua voltandosi alla imaginativa vi trovò queste imagini non altrimenti che se le vedessi nello spechio e dalle imagini traxe le 'ntentioni [...] chosì la cogitativa di Danthe traxe dalle imagini de' demonii le 'ntentioni che erono crudeltà, perfidia, malivolentia, et simili. Il perché giudicò essere utile fuggirgli; et fu tanto potente la imaginatione, che gli parea sentirgli venire.[58]

Let us repeat, then, that which is relevant to the present passage: Dante saw the ten demons which was the office of the eye and the common sense; and not only did he see them before him, but the images of those demons remained imprinted in his imaginative faculty whose office is to retain them, even in the absence of the thing itself. For this reason, his cogitative faculty, on turning to the imaginative, found these images there as it would if it saw them in a mirror and drew out 'intentions' from them [...] likewise Dante's cogitative faculty elicited from the images of the demons 'intentions' which were cruelty, wickedness, malevolence, and the like. For this reason, he judged it worth fleeing from them; and the mental image of them was so powerful that he seemed to feel them coming after him.

This is in fact a highly pertinent analysis of the concepts that govern the narrative moment, and it provides an excellent example of how Landino's scientific interests do on occasion lead beyond digression towards a close and empathetic engagement with Dante's text.[59]

Apart from medicine, there are three other areas of scientific concern – meteorology, animal lore, and astrology – where Landino introduces comments that are in part independent from the Trecento commentators.[60] Of all the scientific subjects dealt with by Landino, astrology is the most important and the one which best illustrates how his reading of the poem is influenced both by earlier commentaries and by contemporary factors. In mid-fifteenth-century Florence astrology occupied an important place at a number of cultural levels, from popular traditions to matters of philosophical and theological debate. The *Signoria* employed astrologers to determine the time of day for *condottieri* to take up their batons, and the Medici used related concepts to emphasize their own pre-eminent role in the Republic. Astrology was taught at the Florentine *Studio*, where an astrologer and astrological poet as distinguished as Lorenzo Buonincontri occupied the post of Professor of Astrology from 1475–78. Astrological conceits and related language abound in the thought and letters of Ficino who also wrote a controversial work that deals with astral magic and the links between astrology and medicine. Moreover, in the fields of poetry (both in Latin and the vernacular) and the visual arts, one finds widespread recourse to astrological concepts and deities.[61]

Of course, Landino's dependence on earlier written sources, especially Dante commentary, means that one cannot read his discussions on astrology solely against this Florentine context.[62] Even when Landino may seem to have a technical knowledge of the discipline and of individual astrologers this is often not the case. For example, a gloss that mentions 'Alano astrologo' – not in fact an astrologer but the twelfth-century theologian and poet, Alain de Lille – is dependent upon Pietro Alighieri.[63] Similarly, Landino's unusual reference to Mishael, the eighth-century Jewish astrologer Masha'allah, in his gloss to *Paradiso* XXII, 118–20, seems to derive from an earlier medieval source, Bartholomew the Englishman's popular encyclopaedic work, *De proprietatibus rerum* (c. 1240–50).[64] And yet, a close analysis of Landino's astrological *chiose* also reveals that earlier sources are frequently recombined with more contemporary material in order to fashion a new point of view which is closely related to issues of contemporary resonance.

The most important astrological gloss in the entire *chiosa* is Landino's comment on the Dantean prophecy of the coming of a 'Greyhound' or 'Veltro' (*Inf.* I, 101). The 'Veltro' is, of course, one of the most notable *cruces* in Dante's poem and its precise meaning (if indeed it has one) remains a subject of dispute to this day. Following the lead of Lana, several early commentators of the *Comedy*, including Landino's most favoured authorities, had given an astrological interpretation to the passage in their commentaries.[65] Such a reading gains a particularly favourable reception in Pietro's first redaction of his *Comentum*. Pietro writes that Dante displays his astrological erudition to show himself to be learned in various fields and knowledgeable about judgements made relating to the stars. And although Pietro makes some allowance for the view that Dante is here speaking as a prophet, he goes on to favour an astrological reading by which the 'Veltro' alludes to an imminent conjunction of Saturn and Jupiter.[66] In his *chiosa* on *Inferno* I, 100–11,

Landino draws quite closely on Pietro's commentary, echoing the idea of a portentous future conjunction between Saturn and Jupiter, and he also follows Pietro (and perhaps also Benvenuto) in quoting from Virgil's Fourth Eclogue. But, despite being dependent upon Pietro for the general astrological framework and for some specific details, Landino also introduces several elements of innovation into his own astrological interpretation of the 'Veltro'. The most interesting and remarkable accretion he makes is to give what appears to be his own prophecy of an impending moral and religious reform in contemporary Florence. In so doing, Landino expresses his firm belief in Dante's own astrological abilities – he calls Dante an 'excellent astrologer' – and he gives precise details of the astrological configuration that will bring about an end to avarice through a change of religion, a 'mutatione di religione'. This 'mutation of religion' will be the result of a conjunction of Saturn with Jupiter in the sign of Scorpio and under the ascendant of the fifth degree of Libra, and it will occur on a precise date and at a precise time in the future:

> Io credo che el poeta chome optimo mathamatico havessi veduto per astrologia che per l'avenire havessino a essere certe revolutioni di cieli per la benignità delle quali habbi al tutto a cessare l'avaritia [...] Sarà adunque el veltro tale influentia la quale nascerà tra cielo et cielo. O veramente quel principe el quale da tale influentia sarà prodocto. Onde dirà disotto 'ch'io veggio certamente, et però el narro'. Et certo nell'anno.M.CCCC.LXXXXIIII., nel dì vigesimo quinto di novembre et a hore.xiii. et minuti.xli. di tale dì, sarà la coniunctione di Saturno et di Iove nello scorpione, nell'ascendente del quinto grado della libra, la quale dimostra mutatione di religione; et perché Iove prevale a Saturno, significa che tale mutatione sarà in meglio. Il perché non potendo essere religione alchuna più vera che la nostra, ho ferma speranza che la rep. christiana si ridurrà a optima vita et governo. In forma che poteremo veramente dire 'iam redit et virgo, redeunt Saturnia regna'.[67]

I believe that the poet, like an excellent astrologer, had seen by means of astrology that in the future there were to be certain revolutions of the heavens through whose beneficial influences avarice is to end once and for all [...] Thus, the 'veltro' will be such an influence which will originate between one heaven and another. Or rather that prince who will be produced under such an influence. And hence Dante later says 'for I see it for certain and thus I relate it'. And without doubt in the year 1484 on the twenty-fifth day of November and at the thirteenth hour and forty-first minute of that day there will be a conjunction of Saturn and Jupiter in the sign of Scorpio in the ascendant of the fifth degree of Libra which signifies a change of religion; and because Jupiter prevails over Saturn this means that this change will be for the better. For which reason, there being no religion truer than our own, I believe firmly that our Christian republic will return to most excellent life and government. In such a way that we can truly say: 'Now the Virgin returns, Saturn's reign returns.'

The ultimate source of Landino's astrological prophecy is a system of ideas which is now known as Arab conjunctionist astrology and was based principally upon the work of Albumasar. Albumasar's central doctrine concerned the conjunction of the two highest and slowest-moving planets, Saturn and Jupiter, which were believed to have more universal effects on the sublunary world, resulting in plagues, wars, and even religious events.[68] It is unlikely that Landino is directly dependent on Albumasar because, as we have already noted, references to him elsewhere in the *Comento* are derivative. But Landino shows greater precision than any earlier writer on Dante in providing a prediction to the minute and in his use of technical terms such as *mutatione*, the point at which conjunctions changed to another triplicity or set of three signs of the zodiac.[69]

In his application of the *scientia iudiciorum astrorum* to Dante's 'Veltro', Landino's prophecy bears the hallmarks of its general Renaissance and more immediate Florentine context.[70] Conjunctionist astrology was particularly important in Renaissance Italy, having gained significant momentum after the Great Plague of 1348. In Florence of the late 1470s and early 1480s there was an intense climate of astrological prophecy; celestial signs were repeatedly noted and commented upon, and numerous prophecies were made, with Ficino's own in his *Consiglio contro la pestilenza* of 1479 (first printed in 1481) being perhaps the best known.[71] As James Hankins has suggested, the publication of Ficino's *Platonis Opera Omnia* in 1484 may have been a direct response to the predictions associated with that year.[72] It may even be possible that Landino, like Ficino, was dependent upon Paul of Middelburg, Ficino's friend and correspondent, who had calculated that 1484 was a Great

Year.[73] Whatever the precise source of the prediction, the important point is that Landino's discussion of the 'Veltro' reveals a highly innovative blend of ideas that have been elaborated on the basis of both the early commentary tradition and more specific contextual factors.

Despite the seeming confidence in astrology that the 'Veltro' passage suggests, Landino shows some anxiety over its powers. An especially acute sense of unease emerges from his discussion of Dante's reference to every damned soul as being 'mal nata' ('ill-born') in line 7 of *Inferno* v. No earlier commentator had discussed the potential astrological implications of this line, yet Landino is clearly at pains to stress Dante's orthodoxy, by commenting on the soul's divine origin and translating into the vernacular the well-known Pseudo-Ptolemaic dictum that 'the wise man dominates the stars'.[74] This passage can also be related to a contemporary Florentine context which saw attacks by theologians against more extreme astrological teachings in the second half of the fifteenth century as a result of debates over determinism and freedom of will at the Council of Florence.[75]

Apart from commentary texts, Landino also accumulates late medieval astrological learning through the scientific works of Albert the Great, whose influence, transmitted by means of Benvenuto's commentary, has already been noted. The most notable example of Landino's independent use of Albert is his exposition to line 82 of *Paradiso* XVI ('Et chome el volgier del ciel della luna') which elicits a lengthy excursus amounting to twenty full lines of text in the 1481 edition (nearly 400 words) on the reasons for the greater efficacy of the powers of the sun and the moon. No previous commentator had digressed so extensively on this line, and although Landino does not mention any source, it can be shown that Landino's entire account is closely dependent upon several paragraphs of Albert's *De causis et proprietatibus elementorum* (c. 1250–52), a paraphrase of the eponymous Pseudo-Aristotelian treatise.[76]

Despite the fact that Landino's glosses to the *Paradiso* are less extensive than his commentary to the other two *cantiche*,[77] it is here that he gives greatest prominence to astrological doctrines. It is not perhaps surprising that Landino's commentary on the *Paradiso* has the most astrological material of all, given that Dante structures its first twenty-two cantos upon the expedient that souls descend to greet Dante the pilgrim in the heaven which exercised a strong astral influence over them in life.[78] Earlier commentators of the *Paradiso* had provided some discussion of the astrological properties of each heaven, and Landino shows some dependency on Buti, Pietro, and, to a lesser extent, Benvenuto, who all deliver digressions on astrological and astronomical matters.[79] But Landino goes far beyond all the earlier commentaries in both the length and detail of his observations.[80] The complexity of Landino's intertextual borrowings emerges in many of the passages he devotes to the planets and their astrological properties. Comparison of his comments with those of Lana, Pietro, Benvenuto, and Buti reveals that, while some of his astronomical data derive from Buti, the more strictly astrological material, despite being traditional in nature, bears relatively little correspondence to the generally brief comments of these commentators. Once again, it seems that medieval encyclopaedias, or later texts that condense their teachings, have played a part in providing Landino with doctrinal material for his *chiosa*. Such discussions amount to extensive catalogues of astrological data (with some concomitant astronomical details) and include information relating to malefics, benefics, exhaltations, nativities, conjunctions, aspects, domiciles, planetary qualities and colour, their mythological representations, and Greek names. The heterogeneous and often chaotic nature of this material can be related to Landino's likely sources which themselves combine mythological descriptions with scientific and astronomical information.

There is one further passage in Landino's commentary which is of particular interest for what it reveals about the intricate nature of the *Comento*'s relationship both to the earlier Dante commentary tradition and to more contemporary astrological concerns. The passage in question is the *chiosa* to lines 143–47 of canto XIII of the *Inferno* and it is especially interesting since it brings closely together astrology and magic. In these lines, Dante had problematically used the soul of a Florentine suicide to allude to the power of a broken statue of Mars over the fortunes of that city. Medieval chronicles and several Trecento commentators on this passage had explained that the statue was originally removed from the Temple of Mars and placed under an appropriate constellation according to the authority of certain prophets.[81] Landino's strategy for dealing with the question of the statue's powers initially conforms to that adopted by earlier commentators on the *Comedy* (especially Boccaccio and Benvenuto), who had argued that Dante is doing no more than relate the views of the suicide. But quite unexpectedly Landino changes tack with a characteristic statement of personal intervention in which he offers his own opinion about the possibility of astral power being received by statues. In so doing, he blends an interesting contemporary example of a statue erected by Paolo Toscanelli with a classical myth relating to the statue of Memnon:[82]

> Adunque in questo luogho Danthe pone l'oppinione che hebbono e nostri antichi di questa statua, la quale molti dicono essere heretica oppinione. Ma non sono queste sue parole, né sua oppinione, ma dello spirito che parla, el quale lui induce a dire questo per manifestare una vulgare oppinione di molti. Credo anchora, salvo sempre el più vero iudicio, che non sia contro a nostra religione che secondo astrologia si fabrichi una statua con tale constellatione che habbi qualche momento et forza in sé. Onde Paolo fiorentino mathematico ne' suoi tempi excellentissimo collocò la statua del leone in su la ringhiera che cigne el fiorentino palazo, la cui testa ragguarda Melano, che molti credono che non poco giovassi contro alla potentia de' Visconti in quegli tempi formidabile alla nostra republica. Leggesi anchora che Zoroastre persa fabbricò in Tebe Ecatompyle città d'Egypto la statua di Memnone chon la cythara, la quale sonava.[83]

Thus, in this place, Dante puts forward the view that our forefathers held regarding this statue, a view which many say to be heretical. But these are not his words, but those of the spirit who is speaking and whom Dante makes say this in order to show a vulgar opinion held by many. I nonetheless believe that, unless there is a truer judgement, it is not contrary to our religion to make, according to astrological teachings, a statue under such a constellation that it has some moment and power in it. Hence, the Florentine Paolo, a most excellent astrologer in his time, placed the statue of the lion with its head facing towards Milan on the *ringhiera* which surrounds the Florentine palazzo (i.e. Palazzo Vecchio); many believe that this greatly assisted our republic against the formidable power of the Visconti at that time. One also reads that the Persian Zoroaster made in Theban Hecatompylos, a city of Egypt, the statue of Memnon with the sitar which he used to play.

For Landino, then, it is not against the Christian religion to make a statue under a certain constellation and thereby to endow it with some power. This view is quite clearly a spirited and polemical response to the reservations of earlier Dante commentators, especially Boccaccio, who, as we noted in chapter 1, was very much concerned to argue that Mars does not possess any astrological potency over Florence and that such a belief is not only foolish and erroneous, but also pagan, sinful, and heretical.[84] Of course, Landino is not making claims for astrology that in any way might impinge on human free will, but he does endorse the view (vehemently countered by both Boccaccio and Benvenuto) that astral configuration is responsible for arousing the bellicose dispositions of the Florentine people, a view which we have already met in the *proemio*. More interestingly still, there is no foundation in earlier commentaries for his suggestion that astral power can be channelled into inanimate objects such as statues. In this context it is difficult not to think of Ficino, who emphasized the power of the stars to invest certain objects with special properties and in whose theory of magic the control of astral effluvia plays an especially important part.[85] Any such connections require considerable qualification. The *De vita coelitus comparanda*, the principal work in which Ficino developed his astral magic, was not printed until 1489, and it is vital to recognize that Landino makes no mention whatsoever of demons or the role of the *spiritus*, both of which are so essential to the statue and talismanic magic found in the *De vita*. All the same, Landino's originality with respect to other Dante commentators suggests quite strongly that the passage is marked by a contemporary context of revitalized interest in tapping and directing the powers of the heavens.

4 Classical references

In the *chiosa*, Landino's interest in relating the *Comedy* to classical culture is a preoccupation which, like scientific lore, runs through the Trecento commentary tradition, and is a notable feature in his preferred commentators. In fact, Landino makes frequent borrowings from Pietro, Benvenuto, and Buti in his many references to classical literature and philosophy, ancient history, and Graeco-Roman mythology.[86] However, a close comparison between all the classical material in the *chiosa* and that found in the earlier tradition of Dante exegesis reveals in Landino a greater command of the classical world, both Latin and Greek, and a stronger desire to reach out to its poets, prose-writers, historians, scientists, and philosophers. This tendency also brings with it an interest in patristic authors, Hellenistic authorities, and later Latin writers such as Boethius and Isidore. As well as his re-use of traditional *topoi*, stock quotations, and derivative references, one can identify several important glosses in the *Comento* which are without precedent in previous Dante commentators and owe much to the work of Italian humanists active in the fifteenth century. Given Landino's training, interests, connections, and historical milieu, such findings should perhaps come as no surprise. It is also notable that Landino provides new and more moderate responses to the critical reactions of both earlier and contemporary Florentine humanists who had emphasized the limitations in Dante's understanding of antiquity. This section surveys the range of classical *auctores* cited by Landino, examining the uses to which he puts them and outlines his principal debts and innovations. It then considers three representative sets of passages that cast further light on the balance between tradition and innovation in the *chiosa*.

It is impossible here to give a full conspectus of all the voluminous classical material used by Landino. However, as in previous sections, we will use several select examples – and further documentation in the notes to this section – in order to show that the debts to earlier commentators on Dante are often quite considerable. For instance, almost all Landino's references to Boethius derive from Buti's *Commento*, some quotations from Juvenal come from Pietro's *Comentum*, and several comments on Roman history derive from Benvenuto's *Comentum*.[87] These examples can be multiplied for almost all the Latin poets and prose-writers mentioned by Landino. A good number of *chiose* are mediated by the earlier commentary tradition even when Landino refers to Latin authors that he knew intimately such as Cicero, Virgil, Horace, and the Roman satirists, Persius and Juvenal – he lectured on all these *auctores* at the *Studio* between 1459 and 1465.[88] Similarly, glosses that make use of patristic writers, and which might be taken as evidence of a first-hand concern with such authorities, are often no more than Landino's own synthesis of the views and quotations found in earlier Dante commentators.[89] And in glosses that discuss etymologies and mythological figures Landino makes widespread use of other earlier sources, especially Boccaccio's *Genealogie* and Salutati's *De laboribus Herculis*.[90]

In spite of these borrowings, Landino nonetheless makes more extensive use of Latin literary culture – prose-writers, poets, and playwrights – than earlier Dante commentators, especially in his references to Cicero, Horace, Propertius, Juvenal, Persius, Plautus, and Terence.[91] What is more, he shows a familiarity with certain authors who had never previously been mentioned in the tradition of Dante commentary. In this respect, the most important area of innovation is the use of Greek material. An enthusiasm for Greek sources is not wholly absent in Pietro, Boccaccio (both as the author of the *Esposizioni* and the *Genealogie*), and Benvenuto.[92] However, Landino's *Comento* goes beyond their works by elucidating repeatedly Greek etymologies and offering comments on Greek poets, historians, and philosophers. This interest in Greek culture encompasses not only Homer (who was mentioned by Boccaccio and Benvenuto), but also authors as varied as the early Greek epic poet, Hesiod (fl. 800 BC), the historians, Herodotus (d. 432 BC) and Dion Chrysostomus (d. 112 AD), and the satirist, Lucian (d. 180 AD).[93] As we saw in the previous two sections of this chapter, this preoccupation also invests Plato's dialogues and some Greek scientific texts by Strabo and Diodorus Siculus. Another important Greek source which Landino uses extensively is Diogenes Laertius' *Vitae philosophorum* (*c.* AD 300) – a diffuse and compendious text which offered a wealth of material on Greek philosophy, and that had been translated into Latin by Traversari (*c.* 1425–33) and printed in 1472 by Nicolas Jenson.[94] All these examples of authorities that were little known in the first half of the fifteenth century show how Landino enriches his *chiosa* by drawing upon works that had been re-discovered, copied, studied, and translated by Italian humanists during this period.[95] In his use of Greek sources, Landino also conforms to the practices of the majority of humanists active in Italy at the time: he may elucidate Greek etymologies but his knowledge of the language is limited, and he only ever quotes Greek texts through Latin intermediaries. It may well be that, as we have seen with Argyropoulos, there is some overlap between Landino's classical interests and teachers of Greek philosophy and literature at the Florentine *Studio* such as Andronico Callisto who lectured there in 1473–74, reading Apollonius, Demosthenes, and Homer's *Iliad*.[96]

In the *Comento*, Landino uses Greek and Latin sources for a number of purposes and at varying levels of sophistication. Like earlier Dante

commentators, he employs such material for purely illustrative purposes, in digressions on moral, doctrinal, or linguistic matters, and in
comments that draw attention to Dante's imitation of classical models.
In all these glosses, Landino frequently goes beyond the range of observations and number of sources found in earlier Dante commentary.
The selection of three groups of passages that follows is intended to
give some sense of the variety of these *chiose* and to illustrate the uses to
which they are put. The passages have been chosen to exemplify further
Landino's tendency to compile his glosses in response both to the earlier
tradition of Dante commentary and to present-day humanist activity.

Our first set of passages all relate to Landino's interest in establishing
loci paralleli in classical literature for themes, images, and situations in
the *Comedy*. Landino often makes use of parallels put forward by earlier
commentators, but he also intervenes with suggestions of sources for
passages in Dante where earlier writers had made no such connections.
As we have seen in chapter 5, Virgil is the single most important authority in this respect. In the *chiosa*, Landino often makes parallels between
Dante's allegories and Virgil's *Aeneid*, but he also notes how Dante uses
Virgil for other reasons, commenting upon rhetorical figures, *sententiae*,
and the choice of individual words.[97] A closer study of the glosses on
Dante's verbal imitation of Latin poets may well provide some insight
into Dante's own intertexts, especially given that Landino is at times capable of refined literary judgements, as in his unprecedented statement
regarding Dante's use of Virgil in *Inf.* XVI, 131, or in his later suggestion
of Dante's affinities with Ovid where he compares the two poets for their
verisimilitude in handling the most difficult descriptive material.[98] Such
moments of critical sophistication are, however, relatively rare, and more
often one finds a strong element of display in Landino's desire to accu-
mulate references by using multiple citations from his favourite classical
auctores. Take, for example, the *chiosa* to *Inferno* VI, 85, where Landino
comments on Dante's reference to the souls of lower hell as being darker,
in a way that is representative of many other passages in the *Comento*:

> Risponde Ciaccho che questi sono di sobto *trall'anime più nere*: cioè
> dannati in luogho più obscuro. Et è imitatione di Virgilio, el quale
> volendo dire Daphnis essere anima celeste, dixe: 'candidus insuetum
> miratur limen Olim', *i.* se adunque quegli del cielo sono candidi,

quegli dello 'nferno sono neri. *Preterea* candido si pone per puro et immaculato, et nero per l'opposito. Onde Giovenale: 'qui nigra in candida vertunt'. Et Horatio: 'hic niger est, hunc tu Romane caveto'.[99]

Ciacco replies that these ones lower down are *amongst the blackest souls*: that is, damned in a darker place. And this is an imitation of Virgil, who, wishing to say that Daphnis is a celestial soul, said: 'brilliantly shining, she wonders at the unfamiliar threshold', that is, if those in heaven are white, those in hell are black. Moreover, by white one understands that which is pure and immaculate, and by black the opposite. Hence, Juvenal: 'those who turn black into white'. And Horace: 'that one is black, oh Roman, beware of him'.

At times, then, Landino seems more intent on displaying his own classical credentials than suggesting Dante's imitation of specific models, although the overall effect is to confer a humanistic patina upon the gloss itself (and by association upon Dante). Another notable example of this technique is provided by the gloss of Mount Parnassus (*Par.* 1, 16). Several earlier commentators had used this line in order to demonstrate their classical erudition, but none evinces the range of supporting texts advanced by Landino, who quotes from Virgil, Propertius, Servius, Ovid, Persius, and Lucan.[100] Our final example is, however, the best example of all. The passage in question concerns Ugolino's speech in *Inferno* XXXIII and it demonstrates the extent of Landino's interest in relating Dante to Virgil. After a lengthy medical gloss which refutes any reading of line 75 as a reference to Ugolino's cannibalism, Landino goes on to give a detailed exposition concerning the figures of speech and rhetorical force to be found in Ugolino's tale. In so doing, he quotes no fewer than thirteen separate passages from Virgil's *Aeneid* and *Georgics* to make the case – a legitimate one – for Dante's use of tragic, classicizing artifice in Ugolino's oration.[101]

Our second set of passages are all concerned with doctrinal compilation and take the form of digressions which illustrate Landino's passionate interest in all aspects of ancient life and literature, from classical mythology to the lives and writings of ancient authors, from moralizing *exempla* to observations on language, divinatory practices, and funeral rites.[102] In these glosses, Landino steers Dante in his own directions in order to make pedagogical insertions on all manner of topics. A good

example is Landino's excursus on chronography in his gloss to the astronomical periphrasis of *Inferno* XXIV, 1–3, where he reuses material from
one of his own earlier letters and devotes over a thousand words of commentary to an exposition of various forms of time-telling in antiquity.
This *chiosa* goes well beyond the immediate demands of Dante's reference to the 'giovinetto anno' ('youthful year'), even though Landino
does conclude his account with the pithy observation that Dante, in
calling January the youthful period of the year, does not speak in the
manner of the astrologers but follows the customs of the Romans.[103]
Landino digresses again on chronographical matters, and at even greater
length, in his *chiosa* to *Purgatorio* XVI, 25–27, where he notes the pleasure to be gained from this kind of annotation on the customs of the
ancients.[104] But the most frank admission of his own digressive tendencies is a comment on the dolphin (mentioned by Dante in the simile
of *Inferno* XXII, 19–21) where Landino uses over 400 words to relate the
teachings of Herodotus, Pliny, Theophrastus and Aristotle, yet ends up
by acknowledging that the gloss is of little assistance in understanding
Dante's text.[105]

Our final set of passages brings us back to Dante's critical reception
and illustrates how Landino not only draws upon recent humanist discoveries, but also tackles the potentially sensitive issue of deficiencies
in Dante's knowledge of antiquity. One important sub-set of glosses
makes use of recently discovered Greek and Latin texts in order to correct earlier Dante commentary. Landino gives prominence, for example,
to Diodorus Siculus in glosses on Greek mythology, and refers to Dion
Chrysostomos in order to argue that Hector killed Achilles.[106] But the
most interesting passages of all are those that deal with Dante's errors
regarding the ancient world. As we noted in the Introduction, Dante
wrongly believed that Statius was born in Tolosa (*Purg.* XXI, 89), because
he confused him with the Tolosan rhetorician, Lucius Statius Ursolo. In
1417, Poggio Bracciolini had discovered a manuscript of Statius' *Silvae*
and this previously unknown work revealed that Statius did in fact hail
from Naples. When Landino was drafting the *Comento*, Poliziano was
lecturing on the *Silvae* at the Florentine *Studio*; and his extant lecture
notes show that he was alert to Dante's error, and that he used his sophisticated tools of textual analysis in order to explain its causes.[107] In

the light of such discoveries, Landino cannot but accept that Dante is mistaken in his comment upon *Purgatorio* XXI, 89. However, his strategy for dealing with the passage reflects a quite different perspective from Poliziano's approach. Landino acknowledges Dante's error regarding Statius' place of birth, but he does not view this as evidence for any inadequacy in Dante himself: Dante was not concerned with such philological minutiae, and, in any case, the correction is of no value to our understanding of the passage itself:

> *Statio*: non è maraviglia, se questo poeta occupatissimo in chose sì excelse, sì varie, sì diverse, et sì numerose, seguitò l'oppinione, che occupò tutti gl'huomini de' suoi tempi, et non investigò la patria di Statio; il che niente gli serviva in questo luogho, perché tanto ingegno non stimava le chose minute [. . .] Ma Statio scrive nelle sue *Selve*, che el padre suo fu napoletano.[108]

> *Statius*: it is not a marvel if this poet, so preoccupied with such excellent, varied, diverse and numerous matters, followed the opinion held by all men in his time, and did not investigate the homeland of Statius; which was of no use to him in this place, because such genius did not consider minor matters [. . .] But Statius writes in his *Silvae* that his father was from Naples.

The remainder of this gloss deals with a further possible error identified by Petrarch and some Trecento commentators on the *Comedy* – Dante's allusion to the *Achilleid* as being an unfinished work (*Purg.* XXI, 93). In this instance, Landino exculpates Dante from any such charge by interpreting this line as meaning that the work was not incomplete but rather unperfected, and he upbraids Buti for criticizing Dante.[109]

At other points in the *chiosa*, Landino also deflects criticism from other possible shortcomings that might be identified in Dante's classical erudition. Unlike Benvenuto and Salutati, he does not justify *Inferno* I, 70, but instead postpones his commentary to a later passage where, rather than deal with the difficulty, he merely notes that Caesar is a name common to all Emperors.[110] Similarly, Landino's response to Dante's account of the origins of Mantua in *Inferno* XX avoids Bruni's well-known criticism (see above chapter 2, section 5). At first, Landino gives a resumé of ancient views, adding some new material from Diodorus Siculus, and he notes rather flatly that Dante varies considerably his own account of the founding of Mantua.[111] But later in the gloss to this canto, he takes a more vigorous stance and identifies a number of *loci paralleli* that link Dante's lexical choices with Virgil's *Georgics*:

> Inducendo Virgilio a porre l'origine di Mantova sua patria, era chosa conveniente che tanto poeta non sanza somma eloquentia et vari ornamenti d'oratione narrassi della sua patria. Il perché per questa chorographia, cioè descriptione del Mincio et della regione, dimostra la virgiliana eloquentia, et el sito dove è Mantova [. . .] *Italia bella*: che chosì la dimostra epso nella sua *Georgica* nella quale tracta delle sue lode [. . .] *ha nome Benaco*: questo è el suo nome antico, onde Virgilio: 'fluctibus et fremitu assurgens Benace marino'.[112]

> Prompting Virgil to deal with the origin of his homeland, Mantua, it was fitting that such a poet narrated the origin of his homeland with great eloquence and various ornaments of oratory. And thus by means of this chorography, that is description of the Mincio and the region, he reveals Virgilian eloquence [. . .] *beautiful Italy*: for so he shows it to be in his *Georgics* in which he sings its praises [. . .] *it has the name Benaco*: this is its ancient name; thus Virgil: 'you, Benacus, who swell with a sea's surge and roar'.

These references are not found in earlier commentators, and, as he had done with Ugolino's tale, Landino uses them in order to underline what he calls the 'virgiliana eloquentia' to be found in the account. Dante is, in short, a poet who textures his own work with allusions to ancient texts; and there is not the slightest suggestion of any impropriety or deficiency in his understanding of Latinity or his handling of Virgil's text.

5 Conclusion

The picture of Landino's *chiosa* that emerges from our three case-studies is one of borrowings from an intricate web of earlier authorities (especially the Trecento commentary tradition), of close connections with contemporary Florentine discussions and debates, and of distinctive adaptations. All the case-studies show that Landino's conservatism and his tendencies towards compilation are counterbalanced at least in part by passages in which a more personal blend of tradition and innovative accretion emerges. In this way, the *chiosa* provides a fascinating point of intersection between a popularizing and didactic concern to compile on the basis of the earlier tradition of Dante commentary and other texts, on the one hand, and a more individual response elicited by his own cultural and intellectual context, on the other. For these reasons, Landino's *chiosa*, though little-studied and often dismissed, provides much relevant material for all those interested in the interaction of texts and contexts. It emerges as a richly complex textual artefact in its own right, one which collapses the traditional boundaries between commentary and commented text.

Conclusion

As we noted in the Introduction, a significant strand of recent Dante scholarship has been devoted to considering Dante's own efforts to construct himself as an *auctor* and to pre-determine the shape of readerly responses.[1] And yet, in this book we have seen that such efforts have little influence on Dante's later readers in Florence and that his name, life, and his writings are never inviolate, but are constantly exploited by them. The urge to recreate and refashion takes many forms, yet almost always it involves attempts to adapt various aspects of Dante's earlier reception to new preoccupations and new contexts. Within Florence, Dante is a key site for both cultural contest and attempts to create cultural consensus, and his inherited prestige is repeatedly redefined through processes that involve what one might call readerly and writerly dialogue. The three parts of the book all support the general usefulness of an approach to Dante's reception that takes into account the activity of the reader and the reader's own background and context; and almost every chapter has shown the ways in which past interpretations are revised and recast in contemporary rewritings. The volume as a whole also reveals that, if one wishes to retain the notion of a horizon of expectation when approaching Dante's Florentine reception, one must do so with reference to several overlapping frames of reference and with a sense of the flexibility with which individuals may on occasion move between them.

Broadly speaking, two main lines of force have been traced, one that becomes deeply rooted in the city's civic traditions, the other that invests its humanist movement. Each of these lines is varied in its own right, as well as being intricately interwoven the one with the other. Initially, the civic tradition provides the most direct and positive evaluations of Dante, whom it promotes as a master of doctrinal and moral teaching, and as the founding father and supreme exponent of the vernacular. Florence's ruling groups transpose on to him their values and concerns and use him for the cause of self-assertion among the other Italian states. Within the city, the role that Dante plays in its civic life is most prominently displayed in the use of his visual type in civic spaces and in public readings of 'il Dante' during feast days – the very days that celebrate Florentine communal identity. The reactions of early Florentine humanists towards Dante are, by contrast, less fulsome. As the Florentine humanist movement gained greater sensitivity to Latin style and a heightened knowledge of Latin and Greek literature and civilization, it tended to dissociate itself from literary production in the vernacular. In this context, some early Florentine humanists express unease with Dante's cultural background and legacy, particularly in relation to his preference for the vernacular, his deficiencies in Latin, and the lacunae in his classical learning. Petrarch addresses a critique, veiled and subtle, against Dante for all these reasons, but it is Book 1 of Bruni's *Dialogi* that most directly exposes Dante's alterity from the tenets and values of Florentine humanism. Bruni delivers the strongest attack on a Dante who is seen to be without judgement in matters of classical literature and history, and who is rooted in a 'middle ages' replete with gothic barbarities. And Bruni also pinpoints another neuralgic point in Dante's Florentine reception – the poet's political views. For Dante either requires radical rewriting or necessitates highly partial interpretation if his attitude to Florence and to Empire is to be squared with the ardent municipal patriotism and zealous worship of the city's Republican traditions in the late fourteenth and early fifteenth centuries.

At times, the civic and the humanist traditions do compete with one another in open polemic (chapter 2), but more often the picture is not one of dichotomies but rather of a finely differentiated and many-layered reciprocity. The acclaim and interest of different readers, listeners, and viewers outside the mainstream of humanist culture made it almost impossible to ignore Dante. And he becomes an essential part of the patrimony and the identity that Florentine humanists are called upon to defend with their own culture. The variety of responses within each of our two force lines and their interactions allow considerable scope for nuance and independent thought. Indeed, many of the individuals and groupings that we have studied reveal an interesting confluence of civic and humanist motifs, and the examples of Boccaccio, Salutati, Bruni, and Landino are especially suggestive.

With some notable exceptions, almost all the humanists we have studied recognize Dante's merits as a vernacular poet, who, because of the 'onorabile fama' ('honourable fame')[2] he bestows on the city, can be used to assist the cause of its promotion among the other Italian states. In their own ways, Boccaccio, Villani, and Salutati view Dante as possessing the exceptional qualities of antiquity, but they do not escape the reservations about his linguistic choice that are put forward by Petrarch and Bruni. Bruni does, however, recognize Dante's value in the earlier phases of the Florentine literary revival, and, depending on audience and context, reads Dante in more than one key, from the perspective of classicizing writer who is keen to delimit his historical value to that of a servant of the Florentine state who is intent upon fashioning his own emblematic version of the poet as civic patriot. In spite of the hesitations in Boccaccio and Salutati, and more strident attempts to snuff out Dante's legacy because of his use of the vernacular, in the 1430s various efforts are made to rehabilitate the *volgare*, ranging from the hierarchy of value that is operative in Bruni to Alberti's attempts to integrate classical Latin with contemporary Tuscan. But the real breakthrough in the humanist acceptance of Dante and the vernacular comes in Laurentian Florence from the 1460s onwards, when a new literary climate helps to diminish the earlier humanistic polemic against Dante and vernacular literature, and attempts are made to enrich humanistically the Italian language, to re-evaluate the Duecento and Trecento vernacular heritage, and to erase the tensions between vernacular culture and Latinity. From the exchanges of Boccaccio and Petrarch onwards, Dante thus forms an important part of fourteenth- and fifteenth-century Florentine debates on the relationships between Latin and the vernacular. The most important single pattern of development within our chronological confines is an uneven movement towards the affirmation of Dante and the vernacular in relation to classical style, thought, and culture. The key step is made by Landino who stresses Dante's classical qualities and his foundational role in establishing Tuscan as a literary language. These are notions first put forward by Boccaccio, but Landino has none of his predecessor's hesitations, and he fashions a new conception of the vernacular's status as a language worthy of literary cultivation on the same level as Latin. Both Landino and Ficino also make a conscious attempt to re-evaluate Dante's cultural matrix by connecting him to the contemporary Florentine recovery of platonism; and, in so doing, they present the revival of platonism as the culmination of a Florentine cultural tradition which can trace its legacy back to Tuscan vernacular poetry of the late thirteenth and early fourteenth centuries.

As we have seen, the civic-humanist force lines have a strong ideological charge. Dante's texts and name are often used in order to bolster the interests of certain groups. Up to and beyond 1434, Dante is closely associated with the values and attitudes of the pre-Medici oligarchy, although the 1430s is a decade which provides a good example of the difficulties in assessing Dante's reception in terms of ideological divisions. Filelfo provides a clear-cut, if extreme, example of an ideologized reading of Dante, but Palmieri reveals how pro-Dante allegiances can coexist with pro-Medici tendencies. All the lives studied in this book, moreover, use Dante to put forward a vision of the traditions and ideals of Florence, and Bruni's is the most ideologically charged of all, even though it is not completely clear whether this is aimed at supporting or opposing the Medici. Later developments, especially from the 1460s, show how Dante comes to lose his earlier ideological polarity and to take on a new one, as he gradually becomes an integral part of Medici cultural politics through a variety of initiatives that help to rehabilitate him for political, linguistic, poetic, and epistemological reasons. Of all the texts we have studied, Ficino's *volgarizzamento* of *Monarchia* best illustrates how political and ideological factors that favour the Medici regime may even guide the selection of a Dantean text which was previously excluded on literary and humanistic grounds.

A similarly rich series of differentiations is observed when one turns to summarize the different styles of reading Dante, and especially the poem that took his own name. At times, Dante is interpreted in a doctrinal, scientific, and philosophical key; at others moments the dominant modes of reading are emulative, historicizing, and radically critical; and at still others he is refracted through lenses that are patriotic and propagandistic. Perhaps more interesting still is the fact that it is possible for several styles to be practised by individuals at one time, or by the same individual at different moments (the best examples of the latter tendency are provided by Boccaccio, Villani, and Bruni). Commentary brings all these forms of reading together and adds to them rhetorical and allegorical modes. Unlike Dante's own view of the commentary as having a servile role to the text, as being 'conoscente del bisogno del suo signore e a lui obediente' ('cognizant of the need of its lord and obedient to him': *Con.* I, v, 6), we have seen that commentary is in fact an important locus for renewing dialogue between reader and text, as well as between past and present. Indeed, as we have also seen, commentary often brings with it a set of complex external pressures that have relatively little to do with the text itself. And when fine discriminations are made for each commentator between glosses that draw heavily on earlier commentaries and more original interventions, the commentator has an important role to play in creating forms of authority for Dante (and for the commentator himself) and enabling his text to acquire new significance in new historical contexts. There has been a tendency within Dante studies to privilege those exegetes that are believed to best reflect Dante's *forma mentis*, yet this may lead us to neglect the important ways in which commentators such as Boccaccio, Villani, and Landino tailor Dante's text to their own Florentine readers. As well as offering valuable insights into how Dante is received in subsequent Florentine contexts, these commentaries provide some indication of the ideological and institutional factors which help to shape the way the poem is read in Florence. What is more, commentaries that are non-Florentine in origin also exercise a strong influence as hermeneutic filters within Florence. Guido da Pisa and Pietro Alighieri lend impetus to Boccaccio's attempt to classicize Dante; Benvenuto da Imola conditions a number of Salutati's views on Dante's poetry and is still active in Poliziano; Pietro, Benvenuto, and Francesco da Buti are all, *inter alia*, important 'sources' for Landino. Nor should one underestimate the influence that was exercised on later Florentine readings of Dante by Lana's commentary and the *Ottimo Commento* – the Trecento commentaries which most strongly present the poem as an encyclopaedic summa of scientific and theological learning in verse.[3]

As far as Dantean intertexuality is concerned, even the limited range of texts we have examined reveal a wide range of practices, from active and dynamic forms to more passive and static ones, from the reverential where Dante's language is appropriated almost as *obiter dicta* to the parodic in which the mood, tone, and intention are diametrically opposed to Dante's text. Burchiello and Lo Za are the best examples here and their reuse of Dante awaits fuller study, although we have commented upon such tendencies in Boccaccio and explored them in part in Lorenzo de' Medici's early poetry. Of course, even in the more reverential texts, echoes, images and phrases from Dante enter into the new poem's fabric in ways that admit its loyalty to him but also help to define its own identity. Texts that make use of structural features of the *Comedy* often do so in order to append their own digressions and disquisitions, and, in this sense, even the most plodding imitation is a partial and exploitative updating. More importantly, however, we have seen how it is possible for an individual writer – perhaps the best examples are Boccaccio, Alberti, and Lorenzo – to use a range of Dantean intertextual modes and to do so for a variety of purposes. Echoes of Dante may also be used agonistically so as to overturn his own messages and to update or even criticize his cultural and classical background (this preoccupation is found in the vernacular works of Boccaccio, Petrarch, Palmieri, Poliziano, and others).

In assessing the wider cultural and ideological issues raised in relation to Dante, this book has shown that these are carried out by means of dialogue between a number of key figures writing on Dante. The textual dialectics (if one may call it that) of Dante's Florentine reception is especially prominent in the responses of Boccaccio and Petrarch, in the relationship between Salutati and his students, and in the competing judgements of Landino and Poliziano. But dialogicity *sub specie Dantis* is also apparent in the Florentine lives of Dante, all of which engage in a lively internal debate with one another, throughout the tradition of Dante commentary (and not merely Florentine commentary), and in more submerged forms in Florentine works of poetics and historiography. Part III has presented Landino's *Comento* from the point of view of a recovery of Dante that harmonizes, often through a form of syncretic dialogue, the civic and humanist responses, making Dante into an emblem both of modern Florence and of the ancient world. The *Comento* is concerned with presenting Dante, his language and thought, as a deeply Florentine phenomenon, and the commentary as a whole may be taken as the culminating moment of many of the themes in the book. But the history of Dante's Florentine reception does not, of course, end here. Landino's commentary, with its Platonic vision of the poet, its encyclopaedism, and summative qualities, exercised an enduring fascination over later readers in Florence, Italy, and sixteenth-century Europe. The *Comento* went through six reprints even before the end of the fifteenth century, was used by all educated readers and commentators in the sixteenth century, and its own textual fortune was only to decline towards the end of that century.[4]

And yet, for all its influence, the conditions that helped to bring about Landino's commentary were short-lived. In Florence the rise of a Dominican friar and firebrand, Girolamo Savonarola, to a position of power in the city in the mid-1490s, brought an agenda of civic promotion fired not by the hegemonizing preoccupations of the Medici, but rather by a zealous programme of religious reform. Alongside the various modes of reading we have already mentioned, Dante is now viewed – and long after Savonarola's execution continues to be read – in a prophetic key (a mode not without some precedent in Landino) in the work of a number of poets closely identified with the Savonarolan movement in Florence.[5] Outside Florence, the 1490s see the invasion of Italy by foreign armies and the collapse of the system of Italian states. Landino's vision of linguistic unification based upon a reformed Tuscan and concentrated on Florence itself is impossible to achieve in such conditions. Attempts are made instead to create a suprapolitical Italian language and it is the Venetian humanist and courtier, Pietro Bembo, who is most closely associated with them. In 1502 Bembo publishes an edition of the *Comedy* in Venice at the presses of Aldus Manutius, and presents Dante in what Chaucer would have called a naked text, that is, one without commentary.[6] In Bembo's edition, Dante's text differs considerably from Landino's, and it owes its greater accuracy to a delightful historical accident: the fact that it is based closely on the manuscript of the *Comedy* (Vatican Latin 3199) which Boccaccio had earlier owned and presented to Petrarch. Bembo's edition with the title *Terze rime di Dante* represented a more serious provocation than that which Nidobeato had posed Landino. It was not merely a question of a 'foreigner' teaching Florentines about their own vernacular classic. By not providing a commentary and using a new title that stressed its vernacular status, Bembo subtly devalued the content and status of Dante's poem. No longer do we have, as in Landino, a divine poem whose classical qualities and great learning necessitates erudite commentary and whose author's (and the commentator's) *fiorentinità* was promoted in the title.[7] Like many other readings that we have met, Bembo's vision of the value of Dante's language and thought is partial and restrictive, and it was to elicit its own series of Florentine responses throughout the sixteenth century. In a book that has been concerned to show how reception constantly re-orders, shifts, and distorts, these later developments, which encompass Landino and yet take us beyond our chronological end-point, seem a fitting way to close.

Notes

1. Some of the territory has been mapped before in essay form and often expertly; see Bigi, 'Dante e la cultura fiorentina'; Dionisotti, 'Dante nel Quattrocento'; Garin, 'Dante nel Rinascimento'; Grayson, 'Dante and the Renaissance'; Resta, 'Dante nel Quattrocento'. For useful anthologies, see Caesar (ed.), *Dante: The Critical Heritage*; Thompson and Nagel (eds.), *The Three Crowns*. This is, however, the first time that Dante and Florence have received exclusive emphasis within a broad chronological framework which explores how his name and writings acquire cultural authority and how that authority is appropriated for a variety of purposes, primarily political, epistemological, and literary.

2. Guido da Pisa, *Expositiones*, ed. Cioffari, p. 4: 'Ipse enim mortuam poesiam de tenebris reduxit ad lucem' ('But he brought back dead poetry from the darkness to the light'); cf. *Purg.* I, 7–8: 'Ma qui la morta poesì resurga, | o sante Muse, poi che vostro sono' ('But here let dead poetry rise up again, Oh holy Muses, since I am yours').

3. See e.g. Montano, *Dante e il Rinascimento*; Renaudet, *Dante humaniste*. For important qualifications, see Billanovich, 'Tra Dante e Petrarca', pp. 8, 16, 22, 39; Padoan, 'Dante di fronte all'umanesimo'; Weiss, 'Dante e l'umanesimo'. On early Italian humanism, see now Witt, *In the Footsteps*.

4. References in order: *Inf.* I, 70 (Virgil's birth); *Purg.* XXI, 89 (Statius as Tolosan); *Purg.* X, 80 (anachronism regarding e.g. Roman insignia). For Dante's knowledge of classical authors, see Pastore Stocchi, 'Classica, Cultura', in *ED* II, 30–6.

5. See e.g. Benvenuto, I, 45, 46–47, 509–11; IV, 36.

6. References in order: *Inf.* XXV, 94–99 (competition with Lucan and Ovid); *Inf.* XX, 58–99; *Purg.* VI, 28–48; *Purg.* XXII, 37–45 (rewriting of *Aeneid*); *Purg.* XXII, 64–93 (Statius' Christianity). On Dante's transformative critique of classical literature, see esp. Barolini, *Dante's Poets*; *Dante e la 'bella scola'*, ed. Iannucci.

7. On the possible influence of northern Italian humanism on Dante, see most recently Witt, *In the Footsteps*, pp. 218–23. Despite valuable general considerations, Witt pays little attention to the limitations, as well as the highly personal and innovative qualities, of Dante's approach to classical literature. One passage that may illustrate an evolution in Dante's interests is *Purg.* XXII, 94–114 (cf. *Inf.* IV, 86–90); however, for the

view that the later passage represents an experimental critique of classical authors, see Picone, 'Dante e il canone', pp. 19–23. See also Richard Kay, 'La mentalità', who remarks on Dante's scholastic humanism and how elements of the *Monarchia* are directed to the Paduan humanists.

8. See esp. *Eg.* ii, 52–54 in reply to *Eg.* i, 6–7. On this correspondence, see Martellotti, 'Giovanni del Virgilio', 'Egloghe', in *ED* ii, 193–94, 644–46.

9. See esp. *Par.* xvii, 40–154. See too Davis, 'Il buon tempo antico'; Keen, 'Signs'.

10. On universal empire, the Dantean *loci classici* are: *Con.* iv, iv–v; *Par.* vi; *Mon.* iii.

11. On Dante's admiration for Aristotle, see esp. *Con.* i, ix, 9; iv, ii, 16; *Inf.* iv, 132.

12. *Ep.* xiii, x, 31: 'ad modum loquendi, remissus est modus et humilis, quia locutio vulgaris in qua et mulierculae comunicant' ('the style is unstudied and humble, since it is in vernacular speech in which even women talk'). On Dante's preference for the vernacular it is best to compare the theoretical strictures of *De vulgari eloquentia* with the poetic experimentalism of the *Comedy*, but see also *Con.* i, x, 6; *Dve*, i, i, 4.

13. *Con.* i, ii, 13; i, iii, 3–6; *Par.* xxv, 1–9; cf. *Par.* i, 25–27; *Eg.* ii, 42–44.

14. The Neoplatonic axiom was known to Dante through the *Liber de causis* (prop. 20) and it forms the philosophical basis for his views on causality; see e.g. *Con.* iii, vii, 2–3.

15. *Con.* i, x, 10: 'temendo che 'l volgare non fosse stato posto per alcuno che l'avesse laido fatto parere [...] providi a ponere lui, fidandomi di me più che d'un altro' ('fearing that the vernacular version might be done by someone who would make it appear ungainly [...] I had the foresight to do it myself, trusting in myself more than in someone else'); iii, xiv, 7: 'lo errore de li translatori' ('the error of the translators').

16. The dangers of a partial reading of romance literature are made clear in *Inf.* v, 127–38. In *Purg.* xxii, 67–73, Dante provides an eschatological reading of Virgil's Fourth Eclogue. The limitations of classical literature are dealt with widely in the poem but perhaps the single most important canto is *Inferno* xx. The Bible is, of course, the Book, and it remains the ultimate spiritual guide, see *Par.* v, 76–77, and Barański, *Dante e i segni*, esp. pp. 37–38, 88–89, 121–25, 147–98, 208–12.

17. On the role of the reader, see Beall, 'Dante and His Reader'; Carruthers, *The Book of Memory*, pp. 185–88; Cornish, 'I miti biblici'. On interpolation and *terza rima*, see Barański, 'The Poetics of Meter', pp. 15–16. This still did not prevent later attempts at interpolation; for examples, see Cavallari, *La fortuna*, pp. 86–87; Folena, 'La tradizione', p. 48. On auto-exegesis, see Ascoli, 'Access to Authority'; Barański, 'Sole nuovo, luce nuova', pp. 30–32; Iannucci, 'Autoesegesi dantesca'.

18. Jauss, *Toward an Aesthetic of Reception*, esp. pp. 3–45, 76–109. For a useful overview, see Holub, *Reception Theory*. An elegant application of some of its insights to classical scholarship is Martindale, *Redeeming the Text*, passim, but esp. pp. 3–5.

19. The limitations of reception theory in this respect are well known, and it is the history of reading which has done most to show how diverse factors from typographical layout to physical circumstances have a powerful effect on the reader's experience

of a text; see esp. Cavallo and Chartier (eds.), *Storia della lettura*; Chartier, *The Order of Books*.

20. For recent critiques of Jauss that develop some of these points in different contexts, see Hume, *Reconstructing Contexts*, pp. 20–25; Martindale, *Redeeming the Text*, pp. 9–10.

21. On the textual *fortuna* of Dante's works, see Bologna, 'Tradizione testuale', pp. 538–99; Folena, 'La tradizione', pp. 1–78. For *recensiones* of manuscripts of the *Comedy*, see Petrocchi, *La 'Commedia'*, I, 481–563; Roddewig, *Dante Alighieri. Die 'Göttliche Komödie'*. Some critical commentary is found in Miglio, 'Lettori della *Commedia*'.

22. On the 'Gruppo del Cento', see Folena, 'La tradizione', pp. 54–56; Petrocchi, *La 'Commedia'*, I, 66–67, 78, 85–86, 289–313.

23. On the Latin translations by Giovanni Bertoldi da Serravalle (1416–17) and Matteo Ronto (*c.* 1427–31), see respectively Dionisotti, 'Dante', pp. 335–44, and Tagliabue, 'Contributo' (with a list of other partial Latin translations). In the 1390s, Serravalle taught theology at the Franciscan *studium* in Florence; see Piana, *La facoltà*, p. 86. Ronto's translation is re-used in Latin poetry in Florence of the 1460s, see below ch. 4, note 48. The Latin commentaries on the *Comedy* by Graziolo de' Bambaglioli, Guido da Pisa, Benvenuto da Imola, and Filippo Villani all provide a *deductio de vulgari in latinum*. For Salutati's Latin translations, see below ch. 2, pp. 60 and 66.

24. Petrucci, 'Storia e geografia', p. 1229: 'l'unico grande testo volgare [sc. the *Comedy*] che nel corso del Trecento sia stato riprodotto e diffuso secondo tutta la gamma dei modelli grafico-librari correnti' ('the only major vernacular text which in the course of the fourteenth century was reproduced and circulated in the full range of available graphic and book forms').

25. Bec, *Cultura e società*, esp. pp. 160–69; idem, *Les livres*; idem, *Les marchands*; idem, 'I mercanti scrittori'; Miglio, 'Lettori della *Commedia*', pp. 298–300. On the very limited group of codices of the *Comedy* transcribed in humanist script *c.* 1425–50, see Miglio, 'Dante Alighieri. Manoscritti miniati'.

26. Much work remains to be done to explore the mercantile reading of Dante; for example, no one has yet made a detailed study of merchant readings of the *Comedy* through an analysis of marginal annotations and the material form of relevant manuscripts. For isolated commentary and examples, see Miglio, 'Lettori della *Commedia*', pp. 295, 303–09; McCormick, 'Goro Dati's Transcription'.

27. Amongst the Trecento commentaries the most important are: (Bologna) Graziolo de' Bambaglioli (1324: Latin, *Inferno* only); Jacopo della Lana (1324–28: vernacular, entire poem); Benvenuto da Imola (1379–87: Latin, entire poem in three redactions); (Florence) Jacopo Alighieri (1322: vernacular, *Inferno* only); Ottimo Commento (i.e. Andrea Lancia) (1329–33: vernacular, entire poem in three redactions); Giovanni Boccaccio (1374: vernacular until *Inferno* XVII); Anonimo Fiorentino (?1400: vernacular, entire poem); (Pisa) Guido da Pisa (?1327–28: Latin, *Inferno* only); Francesco da Buti (1385–95: vernacular, entire poem); (Verona) Pietro Alighieri (1339–64: Latin, entire poem in three redactions). The commentaries that had the widest diffusion in Florence are those by Lana, Pietro (especially the first redaction), Benvenuto, and Buti; Lana's is the most widely diffused of all, see

Roddewig, *Dante Alighieri. Die 'Göttliche Komödie'*, pp. 393–95. On the Trecento commentary tradition, see Barański, *'Chiosar con altro testo'*; Jenaro-MacLennan, *The Trecento Commentaries*; *Medieval Literary Theory* (eds.), Wallace and Scott, pp. 440–58; Nasti, 'Autorità'; Sandkühler, *Die frühen Dantekommentare*; Mazzoni, *ED* I, 143–45, 147–49, 291–92, 506–07; III, 325–28, 563–65; IV, 220–22. For Renaissance Dante commentary, see esp. Parker, *Commentary*. For an on-line database listing 500 Dante manuscripts and accompanying commentaries, see www.centropiorajna.it.

28. Many codices from the late fourteenth and fifteenth century include: the *Credo di Dante* (a *terza rima* poem by Antonio da Ferrara defending Dante against charges of heresy); the *Credo* of Jacopo Alighieri; the *capitoli* of Jacopo Alighieri and Bosone da Gubbio; Boccaccio's *Trattatello in laude di Dante* (esp. the first redaction, often known as the *Vita di Dante*); and a sonnet (sometimes attributed to Boccaccio), 'Dante Alighieri son, minerva oscura'. This material is also found in printed editions, see e.g. Vindelino da Spira's 1477 Venetian printing of the *Comedy* edited by Cristoforo Berardi da Pesaro which contains all the above, as well as Lana's commentary (which is erroneously attributed to Benvenuto).

29. On the first printed edition(s) of Dante, see Casamassima, *La prima edizione*; Coglievina, 'Lettori della *Commedia*'; Dionisotti, 'Dante nel Quattrocento', pp. 366–67; Richardson, 'Editing Dante's *Commedia*'. The Trecento commentary tradition continued to be popular with the advent of printing. In addition to the da Spira Venetian edition (see previous note), Lana's commentary was also published in the Milanese edition of March 1478 edited by Martino Paolo Nibbia of Novara (Nidobeato) and printed by Ludovico and Alberto Piemontesi (see below ch. 5, p. 167). The vernacular works of Petrarch and Boccaccio were both printed for the first time in 1470 in Venice and Naples respectively.

30. On the reception of 'Così nel mio parlar', see Gorni, *Metrica*, pp. 44–45. The *canzoni* receive comment throughout the fifteenth century. An inventory of Cosimo de' Medici's library from 1418 includes reference to a 'Chanzone di Dante in banbagia', see Pintor, 'Per la storia', n. 60, p. 199. For a later Florentine commentary on a moral *canzone* (but interpreted theologically), see Coglievina, 'Un commento'. The first printed edition of the *canzoni* is found in a Venetian reprinting of the *Comedy* (with Landino's *Comento*) by Piero de' Piasi and Pietro Cremonese in 1491. On the continued popularity of the *canzoni* in sixteenth-century Florence, see Barbi, *Dante nel Cinquecento*, pp. 88–89.

31. On the manuscript diffusion of the *Convivio*, see Vasoli (ed.), *Il Convivio*, pp. lxxxi–iii. For heightened interest in the 1460s, see Gorni, 'Appunti', pp. 7–12. The first printed edition is *Convivio di Dante Alighieri fiorentino* by ser Francesco Bonaccorsi (20 September 1490), see Bianchi, 'Le prime'.

32. The first printed edition of the *Vita nuova* is 1576, but all its verse compositions are reproduced earlier in the 1527 Giuntine edition of the *Comedy*.

33. The *De vulgari eloquentia* was rediscovered by Giovan Giorgio Trissino, who in 1529 published a vernacular translation in Vicenza at the press of Bartolomeo Zanetti; see Pistolesi, 'Con Dante'.

34. The *princeps* of the *Questio* is the Venetian edition published by Manfred of Monferrato in 1508.

35. The tradition begins with Dino Compagni's *Cronaca*, where Dante only receives a passing mention, but he is a common point of reference in Giovanni Villani's *Nuova cronica* which offers a detailed commentary on his character, the *Comedy*, and his civic commitment, see below ch. 1, note 25; Giovanni Aquilecchia, 'Villani, Giovanni', in *ED* v, 1013–16. For commentary on the Dantean appropriations in *cronisti* and *storie di Firenze*, see Varese, *Storia e politica*, esp. pp. 126–27.

36. Dante is an important presence in the poetics and defences of poetry written by Boccaccio, Salutati, and Bartolomeo Fonzio.

37. This is especially true for the epistolography of Petrarch and Salutati, see below ch. 1, note 56; ch. 2, pp. 58–63.

38. This includes *libri di casa*, *libri della ragione*, *ricordanze*, *zibaldoni*, *ricordi*, and *memorie*. On Dante and merchant readers/writers, see also notes 25–26 above.

39. Dante was closely studied by Filippo Brunelleschi (see below ch. 5, note 58) and Dantean concepts and echoes are found in the treatises on art by Lorenzo Ghiberti and Leonardo da Vinci. Dante's place in artistic theory is a topic still largely to be investigated, but for some suggestive remarks, see Kemp, 'From "Mimesis"', pp. 362–63, 396; Parronchi, 'Come gli artisti'.

40. See Papanti, *Dante*; Papini, *La leggenda di Dante*. The most celebrated *novelle* concern the oral 'performances' of 'il Dante' by a blacksmith and a donkey-herder, see Sacchetti, *Il Trecentonovelle*, nos. 114–15, ed. Marucci, pp. 345–50; but see also nos. 4 (on Hell), 8 (on love), 121 (on religious reverence for Dante), pp. 12–17, 26–28, 368–70. For later Latin collections of stories, see below ch. 1, note 47; ch. 4, note 3.

41. See Orvieto, *La poesia comico-realistica*, part 1. With reference to Dante, see Guerri, *La corrente popolare*, pp. 41–43; Lanza, *Polemiche*, pp. 273–79, 280, 357, 367, 373. On Lo Za (Stefano Finiguerri, fl. 1380–1445) and Burchiello (Domenico di Giovanni), see Lanza, *Polemiche*, pp. 267–320, 337–430.

42. For example, chronicles and histories of Florence draw especially on Dante's invectives; see Varese, *Storia e politica*, p. 126.

43. The following individuals were appointed and paid to lecture on Dante in Florence: Boccaccio (1373–74); Antonio Pievano da Vado (1381; possibly the author of the commentary known as the Anonimo Fiorentino); Filippo Villani (various appointments, 1391–1404); Giovanni Malpaghini (1412–17, 1417–22); Giovanni Gherardi da Prato (various appointments, 1417–26); Antonino di Cipriano Neri d'Arezzo (various appointments, 1425–33); Francesco Filelfo (1431–32); Antonio da Castello (1432); Lorenzo di Giovanni da Pisa (various appointments, 1431–46); the Dominicans, Girolamo di Giovanni da Firenze (1439–40, 1445–46) and Domenico di Giovanni da Corella (1469–70). For much relevant documentation (and an important re-evaluation of the role of the *Studio*), see Davies, *Florence and the University*, esp. pp. 14–16. See also Park, 'The Readers', pp. 265, 276–90, 292–95, 297, 300–01, 303.

44. *Eg.*, 1, 12–13: 'que tamen in triviis nunquam digesta coaxtat | comicomus nebulo, qui Flaccum pelleret orbe' ('but without ever having understood them a well-dressed

wretch, who would even like to expel Horace, goes mangling these things in the marketplace').

45. See note 40 above. Dante is also presented in a popularizing vein in histories of Florence, commentary texts, and other sources, see below ch. 1, notes 25 and 47.

46. On the poem's oral reception, see Ahern, 'Singing'; Armour, 'Comedy'. On the popularity of public lectures on Dante, see Bec, *Les marchands*, p. 395; Bryce, 'The Oral World', p. 87. For the role of preachers, see Rheinfelder, 'Dante, il suo pensiero'; cf. Lorenzo de' Medici, *Comento de' miei sonetti*, proemio, § 66, in *Tutte le opere*, ed. Orvieto, 1, 369: 'le frequenti allegazioni [sc. of the *Comedy*] che da santi e eccellenti uomini ogni dì si sentono nelle loro pubbliche predicazioni' ('the frequent citations that we hear holy and learned men make every day in their public preaching').

47. On Dante's portrait, see Chastel, 'Dante au Quattrocento'; Freedman, 'A Note'; Gombrich, 'Dante's Portrait?'; Holbrook, *Portraits of Dante*. On Michelino, see Altrocchi, 'Michelino's Dante'; Casini Wanrooij, 'Domenico di Michelino'; Marchisio, *Il monumento pittorico*, esp. pp. 23–47, 175–77. See also *Dante and the Art of the Italian Renaissance*, ed. Parker.

48. *Il Duomo di Firenze*, ed. Poggi, II, 132. For Dante's visual type in public buildings, see Donato, 'Gli eroi romani'; idem, ' "Famosi cives" '; idem, 'Per la fortuna monumentale' (with relevant plates).

49. On manuscript illuminations, see Brieger, Meiss, and Singleton (eds.), *Illuminated Manuscripts*. See also Battaglia Ricci, 'Il commento illustrato'; idem, 'Testo e immagini'; Miglio, 'Dante Alighieri. Manoscritti miniati'; Owen, 'Dante's Reception'.

50. On Botticelli's illustrations (with further bibliography), see Gizzi (ed.), *Botticelli e Dante*; *Sandro Botticelli: The Drawings*; Gentile (ed.), *Sandro Botticelli pittore*.

51. Pietro Bembo, *Prose della volgar lingua*, in *Prose e rime*, ed. Dionisotti, p. 178: 'quanto sarebbe stato più lodevole che egli [sc. Dante] di meno alta e di meno ampia materia posto si fosse a scrivere, e quella sempre nel suo mediocre stato avesse, scrivendo, contenuta, che non è stato, così larga e così magnifica pigliandola, lasciarsi cadere molto spesso a scrivere le bassissime e le vilissime cose; e quanto ancora sarebbe egli miglior poeta che non è, se altro che poeta parere agli uomini voluto non avesse nelle sue rime. Che mentre che egli di ciascuna delle sette arti e della filosofia e, oltre acciò, di tutte le cristiane cose maestro ha voluto mostrar d'essere nel suo poema, egli men sommo e meno perfetto è stato nella poesia. Con ciò sia cosa che affine di poter di qualunque cosa scrivere, che ad animo gli veniva, quantunque poco acconcia e malagevole a caper nel verso, egli molto spesso ora le latine voci, ora le straniere, che non sono state dalla Toscana ricevute, ora le vecchie del tutto e tralasciate, ora le non usate e rozze, ora le immonde e brutte, ora le durissime usando [. . .] e talora, senza alcuna scielta o regola, da sé formandone e fingendone, ha in maniera operato che si può la sua Comedia giustamente rassomigliare ad un bello e spazioso campo di grano, che sia tutto d'avene e di logli e d'erbe sterili e dannose mescolato' ('how much more praiseworthy it would have been, had he set himself material to write on of a

less noble and ample nature, and if he had, in his writing, always kept it in its mediocre state, as was not the case; for, having taken such broad and magnificent material, he let himself fall into writing the lowest and basest things. And how much better a poet he would be than he already is, if he had not wished, in his verses, to appear other than a poet in men's eyes. For while he wanted to appear in his poem to be a master of each of the seven arts, philosophy and, besides, all Christian matters, he excelled less and was less perfect in his poetry. So that in order to be able to write on anything which came into his mind, however unsuitable for verse, and however uneasily it sat in this form, he would very often use now Latin words, now foreign ones which have not been accepted in Tuscan, now really old, abandoned ones, at times the out of the ordinary and the coarse, at others, the filthy and the ugly, or the very harsh [...] and, at other times, without any discrimination or rule, created and invented words by himself. He has thus acted in such a way that his *Comedy* may justifiably be compared to a beautiful spacious field of wheat which is interspersed all over with oats, tares, and sterile, harmful grasses', trans. in Caesar, *Dante: The Critical Heritage*, pp. 236–37).

I BOCCACCIO AND PETRARCH

1. On Dante's Trecento reception, see esp. Alessio, 'La *Comedia* nel margine'; Barański, *'Chiosar con altro testo'*; Jenaro-MacLennan, *The Trecento Commentaries*; Paparelli, 'Dante e il Trecento'; Vittorio Rossi, 'Dante nel Trecento'; Sandkühler, *Die frühen Dantekommentare*. With emphasis upon negative estimates, see di Pino, 'L'antidantismo'; Nardi, *Nel mondo*, pp. 174–91.

2. See Billanovich, 'Dalla *Commedia*'; idem, 'La leggenda dantesca'; Grahber, 'Il culto'; Padoan, 'Boccaccio, Giovanni', in *ED* I, 645–50; idem, 'Il Boccaccio "fedele" di Dante'; Aldo Rossi, 'Dante nella prospettiva del Boccaccio'. For prominent emphasis on differences in their cultural and ideological strategies, see Cazalé Bérard, 'Dante e Boccaccio'; Picone, 'Tipologie culturali'.

3. See Folena, 'La tradizione', pp. 4, 11, 15–16, 34, 37, 57–59; Petrocchi, *La 'Commedia'*, I, 17–47.

4. The three main sets of manuscripts are now known as Toledano 104.6 (*c.* 1355), Riccardiano 1035 (before 1360), and Vatican Chigiano L.V.176 and L.VI.213 (part of the same manuscript, *c.* 1363–66). In the Toledano and Chigiano manuscripts, the *Trattatello* and verse compositions from the *Vita nuova* are placed before the *Comedy* and fifteen *canzoni* are included. The Riccardiano contains the *Comedy* and fifteen *canzoni*. See also note 19 below. On the *Argomenti* (placed before each *cantica* in the Toledano) and *Rubriche* (in the Chigiano only), see Boccaccio, *Tutte le opere*, v(i), pp. 147–60.

5. Ciardi Dupré dal Poggetto, 'Boccaccio "visualizzato"', pp. 205–06.

6. *Gli zibaldoni di Boccaccio* (eds.), Picone and Cazalé Bérard, pp. 315–25, 425–53.

7. For isolated commentary on Boccaccio's imitation of Dante in his first vernacular fiction, the *terza rima Caccia di Diana* (1333–34), see Mercuri, 'Genesi', p. 381. On

the *Filoloco*, see also Mercuri, 'Genesi', pp. 382–83. The *ottave* poems, *Il Filostrato* (1335–1338/40) and the *Teseida* (1339–41) contain repeated echoes of Dante's works, see the notes to the critical editions by Branca and Limentani in *Tutte le opere*, ii. The *Teseida* may itself have been conceived in part as a response (see lib. xii, § 84) to Dante's comment that no work on arms existed in the Italian tradition (cf. *Dve*, ii, ii, 9). References to Dantean allusions in the *Comedia delle ninfe fiorentine* (1341–42) and the *Amorosa visione* are found in the notes to the critical editions in *Tutte le opere*, ii and iii. On the *Elegia di Madonna Fiammetta* (1343–44), see Delcorno, 'Note sui dantismi', who notes the emphasis given to the *Vita nuova* (pp. 253–60). The *Decameron* (?1348–52) has received most attention, see Bettinzoli, 'Per una definizione delle presenze dantesche nel *Decameron*. I.'; idem, 'Per una definizione delle presenze dantesche nel *Decameron*. II.'; Bruni, *Boccaccio, l'invenzione*, pp. 289–301; Fido, 'Dante personaggio mancato'; Hollander, *Boccaccio's Dante*. Most *dantismi* are found in the *proemio*, *introduzione*, and 'cornice', but there are also parallels which are structural (100 cantos-*novelle*; a comedic progression from an 'orrido cominciamento') and thematic (a *summa* of human vices and virtues; an exploration of contemporary moral decadence), and even the age of the authors at the fictional date of each work is the same. For the extensive *dantismo* in the *Corbaccio*, see Armstrong, *Boccaccio*; Hollander, *Boccaccio's Last Fiction*.

8. Metrical organization ranges from the use of *terza rima* and division into cantos in his poetry (e.g. *Caccia di Diana*, *Amorosa visione*) to the prominent use of Dantean hendecasyllables in his prose (*Decameron*). Thematic fields include: the quest for spiritual enlightenment; the relationship between literature and love; the significance of the lady. Boccaccio is particularly drawn towards Dantean *topoi* in representations of the guide, the *locus amoenus*, the infernal hunt, and Marian adoration (see also note 10 below).

9. *Filocolo*, v, 97, 6, in *Tutte le opere*, ed. Quaglio, i, 674: 'i misurati versi del fiorentino Dante [. . .] il quale tu [Boccaccio's 'libretto'] sì come piccolo servidore molto dei reverente seguire' ('the measured verses of the Florentine Dante [. . .] who you like a small servant must follow most reverently'); *Amorosa visione*, esp. vi, 2–3, in *Tutte le opere*, ed. Branca, iii, 39: '[. . .] il maestro dal qual io | tengo ogni ben [. . .]' ('the master from whom I take every good thing'). For the *Decameron*, see notes 7 and 11.

10. In the *Filocolo*, *Amorosa visione*, *Comedia delle ninfe fiorentine*, *Decameron*, and *Corbaccio*, Boccaccio re-uses all the following: the Paolo and Francesca episode (*Inf.* v, 73–142); the infernal hunt (*Inf.* xiii, 109–29); the cantos dealing with Terrestrial Paradise (*Purg.* xxvii–xxxiii), esp. the presentation of Lia; and the hymn to Mary (*Par.* xxiii, 1–22). On the centrality of the Francesca episode, see Cazalé Bérard, 'Dante e Boccaccio', pp. 29–33 (see also notes 11 and 66 below). On his likely knowledge of the *Convivio*, see Ferreri, 'Appunti'.

11. Use of Dante for ironic or parodic effect occurs in some individual *novelle* of the *Decameron* (iii, 8, v, 8; vi, 9), but it is especially marked in the subtitle to the book, *Prencipe Galeotto*. Here, Boccaccio alludes to the book which led Paolo and Francesca into lustful dalliance (*Inf.* v, 137: 'Galeotto fu 'l libro e chi lo scrisse'

['Galeotto was the book and he who wrote it']), but there is an evident disjunction between his vision of literature as mediating between lovers and Dante's moralizing view of its erotic pitfalls. On parodic rewriting, see Bettinzoli, 'Per una definizione delle presenze dantesche nel *Decameron*. II'; Hollander, *Boccaccio's Last Fiction*; Mercuri, 'Genesi', pp. 381–428.

12. *De casibus virorum illustrium*, lib. IX, c. 23, §§ 6–7, in *Tutte le opere*, IX, 834–36: 'clarissimum virum et amplissimis laudibus extollendum Dantem Aligherii, poetam insignem [. . .] civitatis nostre decus eximium' ('Dante Alighieri, most excellent man, worthy of the greatest praise and highest poet [. . .] the exceptional glory of our city'). On Boccaccio's references to Dante in his Latin works, see Zaccaria, 'Presenze'. However, Boccaccio constantly renders the vernacular Dante into Latin, and these echoes remain largely unexplored; see e.g. quotations of *Par*. XII, 141 and X, 114 in the *De mulieribus claris*, c. 104, in *Tutte le opere*, X, 426, 430 (for Dante in Petrarch's Latin works, see below note 56).

13. References in order: *Genealogie deorum gentilium libri*, lib. III, c. 5 and c. 17, ed. Romano, I, 124–27, 136 (Dante as authority); lib. XIV, cc. 10 and 22; lib. XV, c. 6, ed. Romano, II, 710, 748, 760–61 (Dante as poet-theologian; see below ch. 2, note 94). For poetic theory, compare lib. XIV, c. 7, ed. Romano, II, 699–701 with the commentary in both the *Trattatello* and the *Esposizioni*.

14. On Petrarch's attitude towards Dante and its effect upon Boccaccio, see Bernardo, 'Petrarch's Attitude'; Lerner, 'Petrarch's Coolness'; McLaughlin, *Literary Imitation*, pp. 50–59; Padoan, 'Boccaccio, Giovanni'; Paparelli, 'Due modi opposti'; Vallone, *Storia*, I, 133–47; Veglia, 'Sul nodo'.

15. On this important manuscript, see Pulsoni, 'Il Dante'. See also below Conclusion, p. 237.

16. 'Ytalie iam', in *Tutte le opere*, V(i), pp. 430–33.

17. 'Theologus Dantes nullius dogmatis expers, | quod foveat claro philosophia sinu: | gloria musarum, vulgo gratissimus auctor, | hic iacet et fama pulsat utrumque polum' lines 1–4 ('Here lies Dante, a theologian who lacked no doctrine which philosophy nurtures in her illustrious breast: glory of the Muses, the most beloved author of the common people, whose fame reverberates throughout the world'). For Boccaccio's use of this epitaph, see Paolazzi, *Dante e la 'Comedia'*, pp. III–30, and section 2 of this chapter.

18. 'Ytalie iam', lines 8–9, 10–12, p. 430: '[. . .] voluisse futuris | quid metrum vulgare queat monstrare modernum, | [. . .] quod persepe frementes | invidia dixere truces, quod nescius olim | egerit hoc auctor [. . .]' ('he wanted to show to posterity what modern vernacular verse could do [. . .] not because the author did so from ignorance as is said by his enemies who quiver with envy').

19. For the datings, see Ricci, 'Le tre redazioni'. The first redaction is found in the Toledano autograph, the longer second redaction is found in the Chigiano manuscript. The first redaction only has the Latin title *De origine, vita, studiis et moribus viri clarissimi Dantis Aligerii poete illustris, et de operibus compositis ab eodem, incipit feliciter*, but it circulated, in manuscript and print, under the title *Vita di Dante*. To avoid confusion with Leonardo Bruni's biography, I adopt Boccaccio's

own designation of the work as a 'trattatello in laude di Dante Alighieri' (*accessus*, § 36).

20. For the inclusion of the *Trattatello* – and Dante's *canzoni* on the basis of the tradition established by Boccaccio – in the *Raccolta Aragonese*, see below ch. 4, p. 139. The first Florentine printed edition is dated 26 March 1576 by Bartolomeo Sermartelli, but it is included in Vindelino da Spira's 1477 Venetian edition of the *Comedy*.

21. Bruni, *Boccaccio, l'invenzione*, p. 33.

22. Boli, 'Boccaccio's *Trattatello*', p. 410.

23. See e.g. *Trattatello in laude di Dante*, §§ 21, 24, 28, 51, 75, in *Tutte le opere*, ed. Ricci, III, 442–43, 444, 449, 455.

24. See Kirkham, 'The Parallel Lives'.

25. The principal Boccaccian legends and stories are told in relation to his character (§§ 121–23, 165–66) and the *Comedy* (§§ 179–82, 184–89; 'divina *Comedia*' at § 185, p. 485). On Dante's scornful attitude, see also § 163 (p. 477): 'd'animo alto e disdegnoso molto' ('of a very proud and disdainful spirit') (cf. *Purg.* VI, 62). This kind of presentation is prominent in *novelle* involving Dante and in other sources, see e.g. Giovanni Villani, *Nuova cronica*, lib. X, c. 136, ed. Porta, I, 337: 'Questo Dante per lo suo savere fue alquanto presuntuoso e schifo e isdegnoso, e quasi a guisa di filosofo mal grazioso non bene sapea conversare co' laici' ('This Dante, because of his learning was somewhat haughty and sniffy and disdainful, and almost like a philosopher he was lacking in social graces and did not know well how to converse with laymen'). For Dante's lust, see §§ 172–74; cf. *Decameron*, IV, introd, § 33. Dante's erotic mastery is also mentioned in the novelistic tradition, see Sacchetti, *Trecentonovelle*, 8, § 2, ed. Marucci, p. 26.

26. See Ricci's notes to his edition, but his references can be multiplied; see e.g. note 36 and *Trattatello*, § 40 (*VN*, XXII).

27. Aristotle, *Metaphysics* 1.3.82b17–22; for its application to Dante, see Boyde, *Dante Philomythes*. See also Battaglia, *Esemplarità*, I, 271–301; Curtius, *European Literature*, pp. 217–22; Greenfield, *Humanist and Scholastic Poetics*, ch. 1; Kallendorf, 'From Virgil to Vida'; Mésoniat, *Poetica theologia*.

28. For del Virgilio's epitaph, see above note 17. For earlier commentators, see Guido da Pisa, *Expositiones*, pp. 6, 31; Pietro, ed. Nannucci, p. 3: 'gloriosus theologus, philosophus et poeta'; Benvenuto, I, 9–10. For Boccaccio, see *Esposizioni sopra la Comedia di Dante*, I, i, § 75, in *Tutte le opere*, ed. Padoan, VI, 35.

29. On poetry and theology in Boccaccio and Petrarch, see Billanovich, 'La leggenda dantesca'; Martelloti, 'La difesa della poesia'; the studies listed in note 27.

30. See lines 9–10 of del Virgilio's epitaph: 'Huic ingrata tulit tristem Florentia fructum | Exilium, vati patria cruda suo' ('Ungrateful Florence, a cruel homeland to its poet, bestowed upon him the painful fruit of exile'). On Florence's cruelty, see also Cino da Pistoia's *canzone* 'Su per la costa', lines 27–34, in *Poeti del Duecento*, II, 690; Antonio Pucci, *Centiloquio*, lines 289–94, ed. Solerti, in *Le vite*, p. 7; idem, sonnet on Dante's portrait, lines 12–14 in Corsi (ed.), *Rimatori del Trecento*, p. 822. The tradition continues well into the Cinquecento, see Martelli, *Una giarda fiorentina*,

pp. 9–93; Michelangelo, *Rime*, 248 and 250 (*c.* 1545–46), in *Rime e lettere*, ed. Mastrocola, pp. 256–58.

31. Boccaccio, *Trattatello*, §§ 92–109, with classical analogies in §§ 95–99; see also §§ 68–69. This concern is not completely absent in the second redaction (see §§ 66–67), but it is heavily abbreviated. See also *Amorosa visione*, VI, 14–15, in *Tutte le opere*, III, 39: 'gloria de' Fiorentin, da' quali ingrati | fu la tua vita assai mal conosciuta!' ('the glory of the ungrateful Florentines, by whom your life was so badly judged'); *De casibus*, lib. IX, c. 23, § 7, p. 836: 'ingrate patrie'.

32. On attempts to recover Dante's remains and to erect a suitable monument to his memory, see Bellomo, 'Prime vicende'; Ricci, *L'ultimo rifugio*.

33. Trans. Bernardo, p. 203. Latin text in Petrarch, *Familiares*, XXI, 15, §§ 7–8, ed. Rossi, IV, 95–96: 'ut quibus esset preter similem fortunam, studiorum et ingenii multa similitudo, nisi quod exilio, cui pater in alias curas versus et familie solicitus cessit, ille [sc. Dante] obstitit, et tum vehementius cepto incubuit, omnium negligens soliusque fame cupidus. In quo illum satis mirari et laudare vix valeam, quem non civium iniuria, non exilium, non paupertas, non simultatum aculei, non amor coniugis, non natorum pietas ab arrepto semel calle distraheret, cum multi magni tam delicati ingenii sint, ut ab intentione animi leve illos murmur avertat; quod his familiarius evenit, qui numeris stilum stringunt, quibus preter sententias preter verba iuncture etiam intentis, et quiete ante alios et silentio opus est'.

34. See McLaughlin, 'Humanist Concepts'.

35. Trans. Durling, in *The Divine Comedy*, I, 403.

36. *Trattatello*, § 82, p. 457: 'Non poterono gli amorosi disiri, né le dolenti lagrime, né la sollecitudine casalinga, né la lusinghevole gloria de' publici ofici, né il miserabile esilio, né la intollerabile povertà giammai con le lor forze rimuovere il nostro Dante dal principale intento, cioè da' sacri studi' ('Neither amorous desires, nor painful tears, nor domestic cares, nor the seductive glory of public office, nor the misery of exile, nor intolerable poverty could ever with all their power distract our Dante from his principal aim, namely, his holy studies'). On echoes of Dante's Ulysses elsewhere in Boccaccio and Petrarch, see Mercuri, 'Genesi', pp. 312, 408–11; Pulsoni, 'Il Dante', pp. 187–89; Aldo Rossi, 'Dante nella prospettiva del Boccaccio', pp. 81–83. Boccaccio and Petrarch are the first to establish the affinities between Dante and his Ulysses, a linkage that is now a critical commonplace in contemporary Dante studies.

37. On *otium* in Petrarch as a non- or even anti-Dantean concern, see Mercuri, 'Genesi', pp. 309–11.

38. Trans. Bernardo, p. 203; *Familiares*, XV, 21, § 9, p. 96: 'cum ut vides, odii materia nulla sit, amoris autem plurime, et patria scilicet et paterna amicitia et ingenium et stilus in suo genere optimus, qui illum a contemptu late prestat immunem'.

39. Trans. Bernardo, p. 204; ibid., § 13, p. 97: 'Hodie enim ab his curis longe sum; et postquam totus inde abii sublatusque quo tenebar metus est, et alios omnes et hunc ante alios tota mente suscipio. Iam qui me aliis iudicandum dabam, nunc de aliis in silentio iudicans, varie quidem in reliquis, in hoc ita, ut facile sibi vulgaris eloquentie palmam dem'. See too *Seniles*, V, 2 (to Boccaccio, *c.* 1365–66), where

Dante is also referred to as 'nostri eloquii dux vulgaris' ('the leader of our eloquent vernacular').

40. *Familiares*, XXI, 15, § 15, p. 97.

41. See above Introduction, note 40.

42. *Trattatello*, §§ 113, 218, ed. Ricci, pp. 465, 492. See also 'Ytalie iam', lines 2–4, p. 430.

43. Trans. Bernardo, pp. 204–05; *Familiares*, XXI, 15, §§ 16–17, p. 97: 'Et id forte meo iure dixerim, si ad hanc etatem pervenire illi datum esset, paucos habiturum quibus esset amicior, quam michi – ita dico si quantum delectat ingenio, tantum moribus delectaret –; sicut ex diverso nullos quibus esset infestior, quam hos ineptissimos laudatores, qui omnino quid laudent quid ve improbent ex equo nesciunt, et qua nulla poete presertim gravior iniuria, scripta eius pronuntiando lacerant atque corrumpunt; que ego forsitan, nisi me meorum cura vocaret alio, pro virili parte ab hoc ludibrio vendicarem. Nunc quod unum restat, queror et stomacor illius egregiam stili frontem inertibus horum linguis conspui fedarique; ubi unum, quod locus exigit, non silebo, fuisse michi non ultimam causam hanc stili eius deserendi.'

44. Trans. Bernardo, pp. 205–06; ibid., § 22, p. 99: 'aut cui tandem invideat qui Virgilio non invidet, nisi forte sibi fullonum et cauponum et lanistarum ceterorum ve, qui quos volunt laudare vituperant, plausum et raucum murmur invideam, quibus cum ipso Virgilio cumque Homero carere me gratulor?'. For classical precedents that invoke such categories in order to denigrate poetry performed in public, see e.g. Martial, *Epigrammata*, III, 16 and 59, ed. Ker, I, 172, 200. Martial also mentions a character called Fidentinus several times in the context of faulty recitation. For classical *topoi* that belittle comic poets, see below ch. 2, note 102.

45. On 'delectability', see *Esposizioni*, I, ii, 24, p. 59: 'in esso [sc. Dante's 'libro'] si possono i rozi dilettare [. . .]' ('in it the coarse may find enjoyment'); Buti, I, 12: 'alle sue allegorie o vero moralità, è da premettere la narrazione litterale [. . .] per satisfare a più comuni ingegni, che forse pur di quello prenderanno diletto' ('we must place an account of the literal sense before his allegories or moral senses [. . .] in order to satisfy the more common intelligences who will perhaps take delight in that alone'). Cf. Quintilian, *Institutio oratoria*, X.1.43, ed. Butler, IV, 26.

46. Trans. Bernardo, p. 206; *Familiares*, XXI, 15, § 24, p. 99: 'Iurato michi fidem dabis, delectari me hominis ingenio et stilo, neque de hoc unquam me nisi magnifice loqui solitum. Unum est quod scrupulosius inquirentibus aliquando respondi, fuisse illum sibi imparem, quod in vulgari eloquio quam carminibus aut prosa clarior atque altior assurgit.'

47. *Rerum memorandarum libri*, lib. II, c. 83, ed. Billanovich, I, 98: 'Dantes Allegherius, et ipse concivis nuper meus, vir vulgari eloquio clarissimus fuit, sed moribus parumper contumacior et oratione liberior quam delicatis ac fastidiosis etatis nostre principum auribus atque oculis acceptum foret' ('Dante Alighieri, who, not long ago was my fellow-citizen, was most excellent in vernacular eloquence, but through his obstinacy in deeds and words was freer than was pleasing to the delicate and studious eyes and ears of our princes'). For Boccaccio, see above note 25.

48. *Canzoniere*, 287, ed. Santagata, p. 1132.

49. *Trionfi* (*Triumphus Cupidinis*), IV, 28–34, ed. Pacca, pp. 188–90.

50. See Ahern, 'Singing', p. 227; Feo, 'Petrarca, Francesco', in *ED* IV, 450.

51. For *dantismo* in the *Canzoniere*, see esp. De Robertis, 'Petrarca petroso'; Picone, 'Riscritture'; Santagata, *Per moderne carte*, pp. 25–78; Trovato, *Dante in Petrarca*. See also Luca Carlo Rossi, 'Petrarca dantista involontario'.

52. Mercuri, 'Genesi', pp. 305–76, argues that Petrarch uses Dante in order to present a critique of his ideology and poetry, often inverting Dantean values with reference to his own conception of poetry, his attitude towards Rome, interest in the individual, and polemical exclusion of the woman as guide. On Petrarch's systematic opposition, in the *Rerum vulgarium fragmenta*, to the *Comedy*'s ideological and narrative structures, see Picone, 'Riscritture'.

53. On the *Trionfi* and the *Comedy*, see Bernardo, 'Petrarch's Attitude', pp. 506–10; idem, 'Triumphal Poetry'; Giunta, 'Memoria'; Riccucci, 'L'esordio'; *I Triumphi*, ed. Berra, *ad indicem*.

54. *Trionfi* (*Triumphus Pudicitie*), I, 10–12 and 155–59, ed. Pacca, pp. 228, 254–56: '[...] Dido | ch'amor pio del suo sposo a morte spinse, | non quel d'Enea, com'è 'l publico grido [...] quella che per lo suo diletto e fido | sposo, non per Enea, volse ire al fine: | taccia il vulgo ignorante! io dico Dido, | cui studio d'onestate a morte spinse | non vano amor, com'è 'l publico grido' ('Dido who was driven to death by her pious love for her spouse rather than by love for Aeneas as the common cry would have it [...] she who for her beloved and faithful spouse, not for Aeneas, wished to end her life: let the ignorant common herd be silent! I speak of Dido who was driven to death by the pursuit of honesty not for vain love as the common cry would have it'); cf. *Inf.* v, 61–62: 'L'altra è colei che s'ancise amorosa | e ruppe fede al cener di Sicheo' ('The next is she who killed herself for love and broke faith with the ashes of Sichaeus'). The concern is shared by Boccaccio, Benvenuto, and Buti in their commentaries *ad loc.*, and by Salutati in his *De laboribus Herculis*, lib. II, c. 2, § 12, ed. Ullman, I, 86 (see also ch. 4, note 54). In the *Triumphus Fame*, III, 4–7, ed. Pacca, pp. 433–34, Petrarch inverts Dante's order by placing Plato before Aristotle; cf. *Inf.* IV, 130–35 where Socrates and Plato gaze with admiration upon Aristotle. For Landino's later treatment of this passage, see below ch. 6, p. 208. For Ulysses, see *Triumphus cupidinis*, III, 22, ed. Pacca, p. 138: 'Quel sì pensoso è Ulixe, affabile ombra' ('That is Ulysses, the affable shade, who is so pensive').

55. Compare *Trionfi* (*Triumphus Cupidinis*), I, 1–15, ed. Pacca, pp. 47–53 with *Inf.* I, 37–43 for resemanticization of time, the place of love, and sleep.

56. For incontrovertible evidence of Dante's Latin and vernacular works in Petrarch's Latin writings, see Baglio, 'Presenze dantesche'; Mercuri, 'Genesi', esp. p. 232; Velli, 'Il Dante'.

57. For the *Achilleid* as complete, see Petrarch, *Seniles*, XI, 17. For the 'Petrarchan' critique of Dante's view that the *Achilleid* was incomplete (*Purg.* XXI, 93), see De Angelis, ' "Magna questio" ', pp. 170–71: '[...] questio fuit preposita coram Dante et domino Francisco Petrarca et Virgiliano qui eglogas fecit. Dominus Franciscus et Virgilianus erant unius opinionis, videlicet quod esset completus; sed Dantes erat oppositus' ('a topic for debate was posed to Dante, master Francis Petrarch and Virgil who wrote the eclogues. Master Francis and Virgil were of one opinion,

namely that it was complete, but Dante held the opposing view'). See also Luca Carlo Rossi, 'Prospezioni filologiche', pp. 211–14. On the title, see Buti, I, 543: 'Messer Francesco Petrarca in una sua epistola che comincia: *Ne te laudasse poeniteat* ec., muove questa questione e dice: *Nec cur comoediam vocet video*' ('Francesco Petrarca in one of his epistles which begins "Ne te laudasse poeniteat", etc., puts forward this topic of discussion and says: "Nor do I understand why it is called comedy" ').

58. On this point, see esp. Hainsworth, 'Rhetorics'.

59. Paolazzi, *Dante e la 'Comedia'*, pp. 131–221.

60. See e.g. *Trattatello*, § 226, p. 494: 'a rispetto dell'alto e maestrevole stilo letterale [i.e. Latin] che usa ciascun altro poeta, è sozzo [. . .]' ('it is foul in comparison to the high and masterful literary style which all other poets use'); cf. §§ 190–92.

61. Compare the two redactions §§ 195–201 with §§ 133–38.

62. The first redaction (§ 38) rejects the view that Dante's lyric compositions show Beatrice to be an intellectual and poetic stimulus; by contrast the second redaction states (§ 30, p. 503): 'Dal viso di questa giovane donna [. . .] fu primieramente nel petto suo desto lo 'ngegno al dovere parole rimate dire' ('The ability to write poetry was first awoken in his breast by the sight of this young woman').

63. Latin provisions in Gherardi (ed.), *Statuti*, pp. 161–62.

64. *Rime*, 122–26, in *Tutte le opere*, v(i), pp. 95–96.

65. See also Buti as quoted in note 57.

66. On narrativity in the *Esposizioni*, see Cazalé Bérard, 'Dante e Boccaccio'; Russo, *Con le muse*, pp. 109–65. Boccaccio's most celebrated narrative insertion is his embellished account of the circumstances surrounding Francesca's ill-fated marriage, see Russo, ibid., pp. 154–65. A novelistic concern (but of a very different literary order) is also evident in Lana's commentary (see e.g. *Commento*, III, 444–45).

67. See e.g. *Esposizioni*, IV, i, § 20 where he prefers 'aere eterno' to 'aura eterno' (*Inf.* IV, 27) on the basis of the peremptory judgement that 'alcuna soavità non ha in inferno'.

68. See e.g. *Esposizioni*, I, i, §§ 13–14, 26–29; II, i, § 5; XI, §§ 77–81; XV, §§ 30–32 (astronomy/astrology); I, i, §§ 16 and 37; XV, §§ 14, 79–80 (medicine); *accessus*, § 65; IX, i, § 83; XIV, i, §§ 14–19; XVI, §§ 66–74 (geographical annotations); III, i, §§ 19, 89; IV, i, § 7; XII, ii, § 23 (meteorology); I, i, §§ 152–53; III, i, §§ 27–28 (theology). On compilation, see Minnis, *Medieval Theory of Authorship*, pp. 192–97. For doctrinal and encyclopaedic *compilatio* in earlier Dante commentary, see Caglio, 'Materiali'; Caricato, 'Il *Commentarium*'; De Medici, 'Le fonti'.

69. See the apparatus to Padoan's edition, and Kallendorf, *In Praise of Aeneas*, pp. 150–52.

70. On the polemic with Guido, see Mazzoni, 'Guido da Pisa interprete di Dante'. For Pietro's attempt to connect Dante with the classical world, see Chiamenti, introd. to *Comentum*, pp. 69–76 and his critical apparatus; Mazzoni, 'Pietro Alighieri interprete di Dante'.

71. *Esposizioni*, *accessus*, §§ 61–65; I, ii, § 96; IV, i, §§ 4–6.

72. Ibid., II, i, § 45; III, i, §§ 9, 64, 76; XII, ii, § 22 (use of *Aeneid*); XIII, i, § 71 (justification).

73. Ibid., IV, i, §§ 91–III; II, i, §§ 13, 35; I, ii, § 30; XV, § 93 (Homer); III, i, § 26; X, § 23; XII, ii, § 29 (Greek etymologies).

74. For Cecco, see below ch. 2, note 37. On theological controversies, see Venchi, 'Domenicani', in *ED* II, 544–46. For unease in Dante commentary, see e.g. Guido da Pisa, *Expositiones*, ed. Cioffari, pp. 30–31; Buti, I, 120. The rapid diffusion of the *Comedy* amongst the Dominican order is well known, as is the episode in which the Florentine Chapter of the Order prohibited (8 September 1335) the reading of Dante's vernacular works to younger friars. For later criticism of Dante's Limbo by Antonino Pierozzi, the Dominican Bishop of Florence (1446–59), see ed. Solerti, in *Le vite*, p. 152. By the early Quattrocento, however, Dominican friars were teaching Dante in the Florentine *Studio*, see Piana, *La facoltà*, pp. 34–35, 136–37.

75. For Petrarch's acute sense of the potential for violations of textual integrity, see e.g. *Familiares*, XVIII, 5, §§ 5–7, ed. Rossi, III, 283.

76. For these examples, see Paolazzi, *Dante e la 'Comedia'*, pp. 279–80; Cavallari, *La fortuna*, pp. 231–32 respectively. The most interesting example of Petrarch's authority being used to support Dante is Benvenuto, I, 79; here, Benvenuto quotes *Familiares* XXI, 15 in bolstering his view (the opposite of that expressed by Petrarch himself) that Dante's Latin was able to deal with the most arduous matter. See also Luca Carlo Rossi, 'Presenze di Petrarca'.

77. Uberti, 'Benvenuto da Imola dantista allievo del Boccaccio'; Barański, *'Chiosar con altro testo'*, pp. 99–116, who illustrates Benvenuto's emulative strategies towards the *Trattatello*.

78. For the *Esposizioni* in later commentators, see e.g. Buti, I, 357; Anonimo Fiorentino (see Rocco, 'Presenze boccacciane'); Filippo Villani (see below ch. 2, pp. 73 and 75); Cristoforo Landino (see below ch. 6, pp. 194 and 196 and ch. 6, notes 5, 7, and 84).

79. *Esposizioni*, XV, § 34, ed. Padoan, p. 672: 'non solamente nella nostra città, ma per gran parte del mondo, e nel conspetto di molti eccellenti uomini e grandissimi prencipi, per questo suo libro egli è in maravigliosa grazia e in fama quasi inestinguibile' ('he is held in marvellous grace and has almost inextinguishable celebrity because of this book of his, not only in our city, but thoughout most of the world, and in the judgement of many excellent men and very great princes').

2 FLORENTINE HUMANISM AND VERNACULAR CULTURE: PERSPECTIVES ON DANTE, 1375–1430

1. On Florentine humanism in the late fourteenth and fifteenth centuries, see Baron, *The Crisis*; Black, 'Florence'; Fryde, *Studies in Humanism*; Gombrich, *The Heritage*, pp. 93–110; Holmes, *The Florentine Enlightenment*; Stinger, 'Humanism in Florence'. For specific developments, see Cammelli, *I dotti Bizantini*, I; Cochrane, *Historians*, pp. 3–33; de la Mare, *The Handwriting*; Stinger, *Humanism and the Church Fathers*; Ullman, *The Humanism*; idem, *The Origin*; idem and Philip A.

Stadter, *The Public Library*; Vasoli, *Tra 'Maestri'*, pp. 58–92; Weiss, 'Gli inizi'; idem, *The Renaissance Discovery*; Wilcox, *The Development*, pp. 1–129.

2. See Introduction, note 48 and this chapter, note 54 below.

3. See esp. Lanza, *Firenze*; idem, *Letteratura tardogotica*; idem, *Polemiche*; Wesselofsky, *Il Paradiso*, esp. 1/1, 77, 93.

4. This account is indebted to Witt, *Hercules*. See also De Rosa, *Coluccio Salutati: il cancelliere*; Petrucci, *Coluccio Salutati*; Ullman, *The Humanism*; Witt, *Coluccio Salutati and His Public Letters*. For Salutati and Dante, see Aguzzi-Barbagli, 'Dante e la poetica'; Dionisotti, 'Salutati, Coluccio', in *ED* II, 708–09; Vallone, *Storia*, I, 193–99.

5. References in order: *Epistolario*, ed. Novati, III, 373 ('divinissimum Dantis nostri'); III, 189 (embryology); III, 645–6 (nobility; see too note 11 below). See also III, 504 (cf. *Inf.* IV, 145–7).

6. Ibid., I, 183: '[. . .] [Petrarcha] omnium consensu et compatriotam suum Aldegherium Dantem, divinum prorsus virum, et ceteros antecessit'.

7. See Benvenuto, IV, 309: 'quanto Petrarcha fuit maior orator Dante, tanto Dantes fuit maior poeta ipso Petrarcha, ut facile patet ex isto sacro poemate'. For passages where Benvenuto draws attention to Dante's vernacular excellence as being either equal or superior to the ancients, see ibid., I, 8–9, 12–13, 16, 51–52, 88, 155, 295; II, 249; IV, 336–37.

8. *Epistolario*, II, 77.

9. Benvenuto, I, 45: '[. . .] Virgilius potius vult denominare originem suam a Caesare privato, quam ab aliis consulibus'. On this line in Dante and later interpretations, see further De Angelis and Alessio, ' "Nacqui sub Julio" '; Wigodsky, ' "Nacqui *sub Iulio*" '.

10. *Epistolario*, I, 79. The same point is made, but in a different context, by Benvenuto, IV, 435.

11. See *Epistolario*, II, 98–104 on *Inf.* V, 60 where Dante appears to confuse two Babylons, the Egyptian and the Mesapotamian; only the latter was ruled over by Semiramis. Following Benvenuto (I, 198), Salutati relies on ancient sources to argue that Semiramis extended her dominion to occupy Egypt, and that consequently Dante is not guilty of historical error. For links between Seneca and Dante's views on nobility in the *canzone* 'Le dolci rime' and the *Convivio*, see *Epistolario*, III, 644–48.

12. Witt, *Hercules*, esp. pp. 314–15, 428. For Salutati's heightened interest in Dante *c.* 1395–1406, see also Vallone, *Storia*, I, 198.

13. See esp. Dionisotti, 'Salutati'.

14. *Epistolario*, III, 141: 'Sum summi factura Dei; merces sua talis, | Quod miserum vestre me non contingit erumne, | Meque nec invadunt huiusce incendia flamme' ('I am made by highest God in His mercy such that your misery does not touch me, nor do the flames of this fire harm me'). For the later translations, see below note 35.

15. Ibid., III, 84: 'summum vulgaris eloquentie decus et nulla scientia vel ingenio comparandum qui nostris temporibus floruit, aut etiam cuipiam antiquorum, Dantem Alligherium, pretermittam'.

16. Ibid., III, 491: 'sentio tamen alium recte, nisi fallor, tam latiali quam preco preferendum Homero, si latine potuisset, sicut materni sermonis elegantia, cecinisse'.

17. Ibid., I, 77. On Salutati's attitude to the vernacular, see Dionisotti, 'Salutati'; Witt, *Hercules*, pp. 421, 432–33. For his vernacular verse, see *LTQ*, II, 459–64.

18. The earliest attested use of the term *dantista* is found in a sonnet *c.* 1346–47 by Menghino Mezzani, see Paparelli, 'Dante e il Trecento', pp. 32, 34. For other early attestations, see Guglielmo Maramauro (*c.* 1369–73), *Expositione* (eds.), Pisoni and Bellomo, p. 167; Benvenuto (*c.* 1378), I, 473; III, 371.

19. Latin text in *Epistolario*, III, 371–73. On the term 'correctus', see Rizzo, *Il lessico filologico*, p. 215. A later letter to Tuderano reiterates the petition in the most ardent terms; see *Epistolario*, III, 383, 388: 'quem summe desidero reperire [. . .] iterum atque iterum de Dante rogo' ('which I greatly desire to find [. . .] again and again I ask about Dante'). On Mezzani and his glosses to the *Comedy*, see Campana, 'Mezzani, Menghino', in *ED* III, 937–39; Petrocchi, *Itinerari danteschi*, pp. 174–75, 220–21 (who identifies the glosses with a manuscript dated 1363 and housed as HRC 35 in the Library Chronicle of Austin University, Texas).

20. For the use of 'divine' in relation to the *Comedy*, see above ch. 1, note 25. On Dante as 'poeta divinus', see also Benvenuto, IV, 315. By contrast, Petrarch reserves the adjective 'divinus' for Virgil's *Aeneid*, see *Seniles*, IV, 5 (cf. Statius, *Thebaid*, XII, 816–19).

21. For the same categories applied earlier to Dante, see Benvenuto, I, introd., 7, 8, 9, 12–13, 19; V, 515.

22. See Witt, *Hercules*, pp. 229–31. Benvenuto makes several observations about textual variants and corruption but without suggesting remedies, see I, 25, 77, 171, 177, 287–88; II, 543.

23. *Epistolario*, III, 374: 'cum communis calamitas sit, in hoc libro [sc. *Comedy*] latius obrepsit et copiosius, quoniam vulgares et imperiti perite non possunt que periti fecerint exemplare' ('though it is a common misfortune in this book it has crept in more extensively since ignorant and common men cannot copy skillfully an original by a learned man'). His most extensive treatment of this subject is *De fato et fortuna*, tr. II, c. 6, ed. Bianca, pp. 47–50.

24. Florence, Biblioteca Medicea Laurenziana, Ashb. 942. On these annotations, see Ullman, *Studies*, pp. 239–45.

25. For Bracciolini's attitude towards the vernacular, see *Opera omnia*, ed. Fubini, I, 52ff. On his reservations over Dante's choice of the vernacular, see also ibid., I, 409.

26. *Epistolario*, IV, 161: 'crede michi, preter Dantem et eum ipsum rythmis vulgaribus, non habuit inclyta nostra Florentia clariorem divino eloquentissimoque Petrarca, ut non debeas tu vel alius, qui Florentinus sit, fame nostri civis vel leviter derogare'.

27. *Invectiva in Antonium Luschum Vicentinum*, in *PLQ*, p. 34: 'Ubi Dantes? Ubi Petrarcha? Ubi Boccaccius?'. On this work, see Lanza, *Firenze*, pp. 58–65.

28. For Salutati's defences of poetry, see Cinquino, 'Coluccio Salutati Defender'; Craven, 'Coluccio Salutati's Defence'; D'Episcopo, 'Retorica'; O'Donnel, 'Coluccio Salutati and the Poet-Teacher'; Trinkaus, *In Our Image*, II, 697–704; Witt, 'Coluccio Salutati and the Conception of the *Poeta Theologus*'.

29. *Epistolario*, I, 298–307; III, 285–308, 539–43; IV, 170–203. Salutati does not mention Dante here, but he does receive comment in other contemporary humanist defences of poetry; see e.g. Robey (ed.), 'Virgil's Statue', p. 194, referring to Dante's 'singulares meditationes [. . .] quamvis ore materno compactas' ('singular conceptions [. . .] although they are expressed in his mother tongue'); Marrone (ed.), 'Domenico Silvestri's Defence', p. 126.

30. *De laboribus Herculis*, lib. II, c. 9, § 2, ed. Ullman, I, 112: 'sicut inquit admirabilis Dantes noster', with reference to *Purg.* xxv, 37–45, 49–51; see also *Epistolario*, III, 189. This Dantean passage exercised a strong appeal on its Tuscan readership, see below note 72.

31. *De laboribus Herculis*, lib. I, c. 2, §§ 1–3, 16, ed. Ullman, I, 10 and 14.

32. Ibid., §§ 12–15, ed. Ullman, I, 20.

33. Aristotle, *De arte poetica*, §§ 4, 6, ed. Valgimigli, pp. 6, 8–9.

34. Benvenuto, introd. I, 7–10, 12, 17.

35. See *De fato et fortuna*, tr. III, cc. II, 12; tr. I, c. 3, ed. Bianca, pp. 192, 199–200, 19 (translating *Inf.* VII, 73–96; *Purg.* XVI, 56–83, 70–72 respectively).

36. Witt, *Hercules*, p. 329. For the Dantean material, see esp. *De fato et fortuna*, tr. I, c. 3 and tr. III, cc. II–12, ed. Bianca, pp. 18–19, 185–206. On the equivalence between poetic and philosophical sources, see also tr. II, c. 5, p. 33.

37. See Bianca, introd., pp. xlv–xlvi and *ad indicem*. For possible links with Pietro Alighieri's commentary, see also Peterson, 'Some Remarks', p. 12. On Cecco and Dante, see Frasca, ' "I' voglio" '; Camuffo, 'Presenze dantesche'.

38. Latin text in *De fato et fortuna*, tr. III, c. II, ed. Bianca, pp. 191–93.

39. On the *De tyranno*, see Baron, *The Crisis*, pp. 146–66; Coturri, 'Coluccio Salutati e la sua concezione'; De Rosa, *Coluccio Salutati: il cancelliere*, pp. 135–68; Witt, 'The *De tyranno*'; idem, *Hercules*, pp. 368–87. For broader overviews, see Parker, *Commentary*, pp. 53–88; Ruini, 'Bruto e Cassio'.

40. *Epistolario*, I, 191–92; III, 116. For classical, medieval, and Renaissance evaluations of Brutus, see Clarke, *The Noblest Roman*, pp. 85–91. The issue is not straightforward in Dante who uses Brutus as an example of *libertas* in *Mon.* II, v, 13, and displays some ambivalence to Caesar in *Purg.* XXVI, 76–78.

41. On Dante's exaltation of Caesar, see esp. *Con.* IV, v, 12; *Mon.* III, xv; *Ep.* V, 3–9; VII, 1–3; *Inf.* IV, 123; *Par.* VI, 55–72.

42. Latin text in *Il trattato 'De tyranno'*, c. 5, §§ 1, 4, 6, ed. Ercole, pp. 35, 37–38.

43. *Expositio*, pref., §§ 32, 47, ed. Bellomo, pp. 38, 41. Villani also quotes from the *canzone* 'Io son venuto' and makes use of the *Convivio*, see Bellomo's edition *ad indicem*.

44. Marchesini, 'Filippo Villani pubblico lettore'. The 1391 appointment reiterates the motivation of moral teaching, see *Utiliter edoceri*, ed. Spagnesi, p. 145: 'Considerantes quantum lectura Dantis est proficua populo florentino, cum ipso homines erudiantur et ad capescendas virtutes et vitia detestenda' ('Considering how much the reading of Dante is profitable for the Florentine people, since it educates men to seek after virtue and detest vice').

45. On Villani as *dantista*, see Aurigemma, *Studi*, pp. 49–59; Basile, 'Il *Comentum*'; idem, 'Villani, Filippo', in *ED* v, 1011–13; Bellomo, 'Luigi Marsili tra Dante e Petrarca'; idem, introd. to *Expositio*.
46. On Villani's skills in textual reconstruction, see Folena, 'La tradizione', pp. 59–60; Petrocchi, *La 'Commedia'*, i, 11–14.
47. See Maissen, 'Attila, Totila e Carlo Magno'; Rubinstein, 'The Beginnings'; Weinstein, 'The Myth'. For Dante's views, see Davis, *Dante and the Idea of Rome*.
48. On Claudian as Florentine, see Boccaccio, 'Ytalie iam', lines 20–21, 29–30, ed. Velli, p. 430; *Trattatello*, § 99, ed. Ricci, p. 462; Matteo Palmieri (*c.* 1448), *De temporibus*, ed. Scaramella, p. 43; Landino (below ch. 5, pp. 177–78); Cino Rinuccini, *Risponsiva*, § 38, ed. Lanza, p. 193. The first Dante commentator to identify him as a Florentine is Benvenuto, ii, 197 and 222. Claudian is also included as a Florentine in painted cycles of *Uomini famosi*.
49. Latin text in *De origine civitatis Florentie et de eiusdem famosis civibus*, c. 22, §§ 4–7, ed. Tanturli (1st redaction) pp. 72–73; (2nd redaction), p. 348.
50. See also ibid., c. 20, §§ 17–18, pp. 67–68.
51. Ibid., c. 22, §§ 12, 28–30, pp. 73–74, 76.
52. Ibid., c. 22, § 38, p. 78: 'offitiosus civis glorie patrie et exalationi toto studeret animo'. See also Lanza, *Polemiche*, pp. 180–81.
53. For Villani's later influence, see Tanturli, 'La Firenze', pp. 3, 9–10, who notes that there is a *volgarizzamento* by 1478. For Bruni's response, see this chapter, p. 85. For Landino's widespread use of the *De origine*, see below ch. 5, section 2.
54. See Bernacchioni, 'Alcune precisazioni'; Donato, 'Gli eroi romani', p. 136; Hankey, 'Salutati's Epigrams'.
55. Bellomo, introd. to *Expositio*, pp. 13–17.
56. *Expositio*, *exp.*, § 145, ed. Bellomo, p. 113. On Villani's use of *auctoritates* and earlier commentators, see Bellomo, introd., pp. 21–25 and notes.
57. See e.g. ibid., *exp.*, §§ 21, 32, 167, 202, 217–18, 247–51, 353–54, 368–69, 435 (grammar/rhetoric); §§ 79, 401, 448 (linguistic commentary).
58. See esp. ibid., *exp.*, §§ 81, 176, 230–31, 475, 483; cf. Benvenuto, i, 182; iii, 93.
59. See ibid., *exp.*, §§ 62–70, pp. 44–46 and Bellomo's notes *ad locum*. See also *exp.*, § 379, p. 167: 'in materia, in integumentis et eloquentie dignitate Maronem imitatus est' ('in subject-matter, and in its worthy use of *integumenta* and eloquence, he imitated Virgil').
60. See e.g. ibid., *exp.*, §§ 35, 76, 82, 160, 208, 229, 357, 395, 403, 466.
61. Ibid., *pref.*, § 196; *exp.*, § 378.
62. Ibid., *exp.*, §§ 170 and 246.
63. Latin text in ibid., *exp.*, §§ 270–71, p. 142.
64. Ibid., *pref.*, §§ 225–26, p. 77: 'Audivi, patruo meo Iohanne Villani hystorico referente, qui Danti fuit amicus et sotius, poetam aliquando dixisse quod, collatis versibus suis cum metris Maronis, Statii, Oratii, Ovidii et Lucani, visum ei fore iuxta purpuram cilicium collocasse. Cumque se potentissimum in rithmis vulgaribus intellexisset, ipsis suum accommodavit ingenium. Amplius aiebat vir prudens

id egisse ut suum idioma nobilitaret et longius veheret, addebatque sic se facere ut ostenderet etiam elocutione vulgari ardua queque scientiarum posse tractari'.

65. Gherardi's principal poetic works are: the *Trattato d'una angelica cosa mostrata per una divotissima visione*, ed. Wesselofsky, *Il Paradiso*, 1/2, 385–435; and the *Philomena* (*c.* 1430) in ibid., 1/2, 109–92. Both works develop the dream-vision form and make extensive use of Dantean doctrine, themes, and language; in the *Philomena* Dante even appears as one of Gherardi's guides; see also Lanza, *Letteratura tardogotica*, pp. 702–12.

66. *Il Paradiso degli Alberti*, lib. 1, § 2, ed. Lanza, p. 4. Most critics now tend to date it from the late 1420s though they accept that it reflects in part discussions and events of the late 1380s. On *Il Paradiso*, see Garilli, 'Cultura'; Lanza, *Letteratura tardogotica*, pp. 839–65; idem, *Polemiche*, pp. 167–82; Marietti, 'Le marchand'; Ricci, 'Gherardi, Giovanni', in *ED* III, 138–39.

67. Lanza, *Polemiche*, pp. 174–75.

68. Rubinstein, 'The Beginnings', pp. 224–25.

69. See e.g. *Il Paradiso*, lib. 1, § 81, ed. Lanza, p. 32: 'il dotto Policreto e gli altri che più valore ebbon dell'arte ne sarieno e rimarieno iscornati' ('wise Policretus and the others who were worthier in the art will be and will remain outdone'); cf. *Purg.* X, 32–33. The repetitions of 'Vedea' in lib. 1, pp. 40–41, 43–44 echo *Purg.* XII, 25–31. There are strong reminiscences of *Purg.* XXVIII in *Il Paradiso*, lib. 1, §§ 70–75, pp. 28–30 (on Boccaccio's own predilection for Dante's Terrestrial Paradise, see above ch. 1, note 10).

70. *Il Paradiso*, lib. 1, § 158–59, pp. 51–52.

71. See Martelli, *Letteratura fiorentina*, pp. 156–59.

72. *Il Paradiso*, lib. IV, § 24, p. 216. For Tuscan interest in *Purg.* XXV, see Villani, *Expositio, exp.*, § 315, p. 152; Agnolo Torini, in Hijmans-Tromp (ed.), *Vita*, pp. 236, 253, 271, 279; Gherardi, *Trattato d'una angelica cosa*, pp. 412–14.

73. *Il Paradiso*, lib. IV, §§ 27–28, p. 217.

74. On Rinuccini, see Baron, *The Crisis*, pp. 94–97, 98–99, 286–90; Lanza, *Letteratura tardogotica*, pp. 453–63; idem, *Polemiche*, pp. 129–58; Martines, *The Social World*, pp. 110–12; Ricci, 'Rinuccini, Cino', in *ED* IV, 967–68; Tanturli, 'Cino Rinuccini'.

75. Witt, 'Cino Rinuccini's *Responsiva*'; Lanza, *Firenze*, pp. 39–45, 50–58.

76. *Responsiva*, § 32, ed. Lanza, p. 193.

77. For Virgil as 'ragione' and Dante as 'sensualità', see e.g. Buti, 1, 51.

78. Quoted from Wesselofksy, 1/2, 310–13 punctuation slightly amended (bracketed references to the *Comedy* are mine).

79. On brevity as common to Dante and Virgil, see instead Benvenuto, 1, 335; Tasso, *Discorsi*, ed. Poma, p. 248.

80. The seminal study of Niccoli is by Zippel (1890), reprinted in his *Storia e cultura*, pp. 68–157. For important recent contributions, see Martin C. Davies, 'An Emperor'; Lanza, *Polemiche*, esp. pp. 155–58; Stadter, 'Niccolò Niccoli'. See also the mythologized presentation of his classicizing dress and table-manners in Vespasiano da Bisticci, *Le vite*, ed. Greco, II, 229–30, 234–35, 239–40.

81. Holmes, *The Florentine Enlightenment*, pp. 10–11: 'perhaps the most important figure of the early Renaissance'; Davies, 'An Emperor', p. 128: 'the inspirer and arbiter of the emergent philology'. On Niccoli's collection of classical texts which became the core of the library established by Cosimo de' Medici in the rebuilt San Marco, see Ullman and Stadter, *The Public Library*.

82. On Bruni, see Griffiths, Hankins, and Thompson, *The Humanism of Leonardo Bruni*; Luiso, *Studi*; Tanturli, 'Dante, Firenze, Leonardo Bruni'; Viti (ed.), *Leonardo Bruni, cancelliere*; idem, *Leonardo Bruni e Firenze*; idem (ed.), *Opere*, introd. pp. 9–66. For Bruni's vernacular verse, see *LTQ*, I, 330–35. On Bruni's life, see Vasoli, 'Leonardo Bruni', in *DBI* 14, 618–33.

83. *Dialogi ad Petrum Histrum*, lib. I, § 40, ed. Baldassarri, p. 253: 'Dantem vero, si alio genere scribendi usus esset, non eo contentus forem ut illum cum antiquis nostris compararem, sed et ipsis et Graecis etiam anteponerem'.

84. *Laudatio Florentine urbis*, §§ 33–42, ed. Baldassarri, pp. 15–19. For the dating, see Hankins, *Plato*, II, 367–78.

85. *Dialogi*, lib. I, § 44, ed. Baldassarri, pp. 255–56: 'Dante quodlibeta fratum atque eiusmodi molestias lectitasse, librorum autem gentilium, unde maxime ars sua dependebat, nec eos quidem qui nobis reliqui sunt, attigisse. Denique, ut alia omnia sibi affuissent, certe latinitas defuit. Nos vero non pudebit eum appellare, et Vergilio etiam anteponere, qui latine loqui non possit? Legi nuper quasdam eius litteras, quas ille videbatur peraccurate scripsisse; erant enim propria manu atque eius sigillo obsignatae. At, mehercule, nemo est tam rudis quem tam inepte scripsisse non puderet! Quamobrem, Coluci, ego istum poetam tuum a concilio litteratorum seiungam, atque eum zonariis, pistoribus atque eiusmodi turbae relinquam. Sic enim locutus est ut videatur voluisse huic generi hominum esse familiaris' (Eng. trans adapted from Thompson, in *The Three Crowns*, p. 36). For the link with Petrarch, see Tanturli, 'Il disprezzo', p. 214. Compare Boccaccio's positive judgement of Dante's use of quodlibeta in *Trattatello*, § 123 (1st redaction), ed. Ricci, pp. 467–68.

86. *Dialogi*, lib. II, § 85, ed. Baldassarri, pp. 271–72: 'hic vir studia humanitatis, quae iam extincta erant, repararit, et nobis, quemadmodum discere possemus, viam aperuerit'.

87. Bruni, *Oratio in Nebulonem Maledicum*, in Viti (ed.), *Opere*, p. 342.

88. Baron, *The Crisis*, esp. pp. 225–44.

89. For these points, see Baldassarri, *Dialogi*, introd. pp. 20–21, 61–64; Hankins, 'The Baron Thesis'.

90. Siegel, '"Civic humanism"'.

91. See esp. Mortensen, 'Leonardo Bruni's *Dialogus*'. See also Bausi, 'Note sul procedimento'; Marsh, *The Quattrocento Dialogue*, pp. 24–37.

92. Lanza, *Polemiche*, pp. 152–55. See also Dionisotti, 'Bruni, Leonardo', in *ED* II, 708–09; Gualdo Rosa, 'Leonardo Bruni e le sue vite "parallele"', p. 388; Santini, 'La produzione volgare', p. 293.

93. Lanza, *Polemiche*, pp. 47–49, 140.

94. See Baldassarri, *Dialogi*, introd., pp. 59–61. See also Giovanni Villani, *Nuova Cronica*, lib. x, c. 136, ed. Porta, I, 337: 'fece la Commedia, ove in rima pulita, e con grandi e sottili questioni morali, naturali, strolaghe, filosofiche, e teologhe [. . .]' ('he composed the *Comedy* where in polished rhyme and treating grandiose and subtle themes that cover moral, natural, astrological, philosophical and theological matters'); Boccaccio, *De genealogie deorum*, lib. xiv, c. 10, ed. Romano, II, 710: 'Quis tam sui inscius nostrum Dantem sacre theologie implicitos persepe nexus mira demonstratione solventem, non sentiat eum non solum phylosophum, sed theologum insignem fuisse?' ('is anyone so insensible not to perceive that Dante was a great theologian as well as a philosopher when he often unties with amazingly skilful demonstration the hard knots of theology'); *Trattatello*, § 24, ed. Ricci, p. 443: 'nella profondità altissime della teologia con acuto ingegno si mise' ('with sharp intelligence he ventured into the highest depths of theology').

95. For similar emphases, see esp. Fubini, *L'umanesimo italiano*, pp. 75–103. For the polemic between Salutati and Bruni, see Quint, 'Humanism and Modernity'; Trovato, 'Dai *Dialogi*'. For the codicological and intertextual reasons outlined by Baldassarri in his edition, I nonetheless disagree with Fubini and Trovato who date the *Dialogi* after Salutati's death.

96. Bruni, *Historiarum Florentini populi libri XII*, lib. I (eds.), Santini and di Pierro, p. 24: 'medium illud tempus'. See also McLaughlin, 'Humanist Concepts'.

97. On Domenico, see Baron, *The Crisis*, pp. 279–86; Lanza, *Firenze*, pp. 503–21, 589–607, 641–48; idem, *Polemiche*, pp. 189–207 (dating on p. 196).

98. Bruni, Letter, x, 25 (26 April 1418) to Gianfrancesco Gonzaga, in *Leonardi Bruni Arretini epistolarum*, ed. Mehus, II, 226–28: '[. . .] Nec ullus est auctor, qui contra sentiat [sc. that Mantua was founded by Tuscans] praeter unum Dantem, de quo valde admirari compellor, quod cum Tuscus ipse fuerit, et Virgilii, ut asserit, sectator, ea, quae de Tuscorum potentia a tot et tam claris auctoribus scripta sunt, neque legisse unquam, neque notasse videtur, et usque adeo a Virgilio discedit, ut cum ille de Tusco sanguine ortos Mantuanos asserat, et Ocnum nominet conditorem, iste, quasi ignarus omnium, aliam quendam originem assignet. Sed neque auctorem ullum opinionis suae, neque argumentum aliquod ad confirmandum inducit [. . .] Haec igitur divinandi ars Tiresiae filia, idest inventio fuit, quam Dantes quidem virginem dixit, Virgilius autem doctius et verius matrem appellavit. Vanum igitur et puerile est credere, Manto fuisse hominem [sic? <virginem>], in Italiam venisse cum servis intra paludem remotam ab omni humano commercio constitisse, nisi hoc totum poëtice accipitur'. The letter circulated widely in vernacular versions; on its use in later Florentine writers, see Bessi, 'Appunti', pp. 165–66; Tanturli, 'Dante, Firenze, Leonardo Bruni', pp. 190–91; and below ch. 6, p. 228.

99. Hollander, *Studies in Dante*, pp. 131–218.

100. On the Etruscan legacy of Florence, see Bruni, *Historiae*, ed. Santini, p. 7; *Oratio in funere Nannis Strozae*, in Viti (ed.), *Opere*, p. 714. See also Cipriani, *Il mito etrusco*, pp. 1–36.

101. Quoted from *LTQ*, I, 511–12.

102. For examples from Catullus, Martial, and Horace, see Feo, 'Tradizione latina', n. 12, p. 363.
103. *LTQ*, I, 513.

3 DANTE AS A CIVIC AND LINGUISTIC MODEL, 1430–1441

1. Filelfo, ed. Benaducci, 'Prose', p. 23 (oration, 26 December 1431).
2. On Filelfo, see *Francesco Filelfo nel quinto centenario*, ed. Avesani *et al.*; Robin, *Filelfo in Milan*; Viti, 'Filelfo, Francesco', *DBI* 47, 613–26; Zippel, *Storia e cultura*, pp. 215–41. With reference to Dante, see Bottari, 'Francesco Filelfo e Dante'; D'Episcopo, 'Orazioni'; Garin, 'Dante nel Rinascimento', pp. 125–27; Ricci, 'Filelfo, Francesco', in *ED* II, 871–72.
3. Documents in Gherardi (ed.), *Statuti*, pp. 245–46, 415–19, 423–24, 435. See also Park, 'The Readers', pp. 284–85, 287, 290.
4. Vespasiano, *Le vite*, ed. Greco, II, 54.
5. Bec, 'I mercanti', p. 109; see also Garin, 'Dante nel Rinascimento', p. 127; Parker, *Commentary*, pp. 53–55. On factional rivalries in this period, see Kent, *The Rise*.
6. Filelfo, ed. Benaducci, 'Prose', p. 3.
7. Ibid., p. 3: '[. . .] io non ardirei alcun altro degli antichi per mio giudicio preporgli. Una cosa non dubito da niuno mi fia negata, non essere già mai alcun altro stato nell'italico eloquio, da cui, oltre l'armonica melodia del suo divino Poema, più universalmente ognuno utilità prendere possa' ('In my judgement I would not dare to place any of the ancients above him. I doubt whether anyone can deny me one thing: never has there been any other in the Italian tongue from whom, beyond the melodious harmony of his divine poem, all may draw utility in the most universal way').
8. Ibid., pp. 21 and 23.
9. Ibid., pp. 25–27. For echoes of the *Trattatello*, cf. the passage quoted above in ch. 1, p. 32.
10. Ibid., p. 27.
11. See Zippel, *Storia e cultura*, pp. 215–44.
12. On Palmieri, see Carpetto, *The Humanism of Matteo Palmieri*; Finzi, *Matteo Palmieri dalla 'Vita civile'*; Holmes, *The Florentine Enlightenment*, pp. 150–52; Martelli, 'Palmeriana'; Martines, *The Social World*, pp. 138–42, 191–98; Messeri, 'Matteo Palmieri cittadino'; Messina, 'Palmieri, Matteo', in *ED* IV, 263–64.
13. On the dating, see Tanturli, 'Sulla data', pp. 5–11.
14. *Vita civile*, lib. I, proemio, §§ 8–10, ed. Belloni, pp. 5–6.
15. Ibid., lib. I, §§ 148–49, pp. 44–45: 'Oggi veggiano per padre et ornamento delle lettere essere mandato nel mondo el nostro Leonardo aretino come splendido lume della eleganzia latina, per rendere agl'huomini la dolcezza della latina lingua' ('Today we see that our Leonardo Aretino – the father and ornament of literature – has been sent to the world, as the bright light of Latin elegance, in order to restore to men the sweetness of the Latin language'). See also lib. IV, § 3, p. 149, where Palmieri observes that his dialogue has been criticized not for its content

but because 'così publicamente m'era dato a comporre libri volgari' ('I had so publicly devoted myself to writing books in the vernacular').

16. Quintilian, *Institutio oratoria*, x.1.46, ed. Butler, IV, 28: 'Hunc [sc. Homer] nemo in magnis rebus sublimitate, in parvis proprietate superaverit. Idem laetus ac pressus, iucundus et gravis, tum copia tum brevitate mirabilis, nec poetica modo sed oratoria virtute eminentissimus' ('No-one has ever surpassed him in the sublimity with which he deals with great themes or in propriety that he shows for little ones. He is both luxuriant and concise, lively and serious, admirable for his abundance and his brevity, and supreme not only for poetic, but also for oratorical power').

17. *Vita civile*, proemio, § 12, p. 7.

18. Ibid., lib. I, §§ 94–97, pp. 32–33; cf. Dante, *Con.* IV, xxiv, 12.

19. See *L'Ottimo commento*, ed. Torri, I, 3; Boccaccio, *Esposizioni*, ed. Padoan, pp. 19–20; Benvenuto, I, 23; Buti, I, 24; Anonimo Fiorentino, ed. Fanfani, I, 12.

20. Buti, I, 24–25; Villani, *Expositio, pref.* §§ 183–89 and *exp.* § 14, pp. 66–67, 82; Pietro, ed. Nannucci, pp. 11–17 and 26.

21. *Vita civile*, lib. IV, §§ 241–44, pp. 200–01.

22. See Tanturli, 'Sulla data', pp. 11–13.

23. *Vita civile*, lib. IV, §§ 247–49, 252–53, pp. 201–03.

24. For further background, see Maissen, 'Attila, Totila e Carlo Magno', pp. 586, 610–16; Jordan, *Pulci's 'Morgante'*, pp. 20–23.

25. For echoes of the *Comedy*, see e.g. *Vita civile*, lib. IV, §§ 253–55, 262, 272–73, pp. 203, 205, 207: 'Et ecco, sanza sapere come, mi ritrovai [...] Questa mi parea (*Inf.* I, 2, 10, 46) [...] Et ecco un vechio di riverente auctorità m'aparve (*Purg.* I, 31–32) [...] come servo infedele et della sua legge ribello, gli chiude questi porti per le quali io venni a te, né vuole che per lui in sua città si ritorni (*Inf.* I, 124–26) [...] sancte luci (*Par.* VII, 141; XX, 69) [...] de' razi del sole s'accende et orna (*Par.* XX, 4) [...] Venere [...] al sol si vagheggia (*Par.* VIII, 12) [...] più rosseggia [...] Marte' (*Purg.* II, 14). References to the *Comedy* are mine.

26. E.g. *Vita civile*, lib. IV, §§ 261, 263, pp. 204–05 (see also ch. 4, note 53). Although such emphases are not absent in Dante (cf. *Par.* XXXIII, 31–32), Palmieri leaves no room for his preoccupation with the body and its resurrection (*Inf.* VI, 94–111; XIII, 103–08; *Par.* XIV, 13–66; XXX, 43–45).

27. *Vita civile*, lib. IV, § 278, p. 208.

28. The key passages are: *Inf.* VI, 49–90; *Inf.* XVI, 28–63 (cf. *Inf.* VI, 79–87); *Purg.* VI, 127–151. For criticisms of Florence and Florentines, see *Inf.* X, 46–51, 74–87; XIII, 143–50; XV, 61–78; XXVI, 1–3; *Purg.* VI, 127–51; XIV, 49–51; XXIII, 98–108; *Par.* IX, 127–32. Of course, Dante also identifies with Florentine causes and reversals (*Inf.* XXVII, 103–11), does not damn all Florentines (Forese and Piccarda Donati are notable exceptions), and his attitude towards the city is also tinged by nostalgic longing and fraternal feeling (*Inf.* X, 26; XIV, 1–3; XIX, 17; *Par.* XVI, 25; XV, 5; cf. *Inf.* XVI, 67–68 and *Par.* XV, 130–33).

29. On Bruni's translation of Aristotle, see Fubini, *L'umanesimo italiano*, pp. 108–29.

30. See Viti, *Leonardo Bruni e Firenze*, p. 49.

31. *Historiae*, lib. IV, ed. Santini, pp. 77, 90, 92, 95, 105–06.

32. Provision of the *Signoria* (23 December 1396) in Fubini, *L'umanesimo italiano*, p. 102: 'Et quod pro quolibet ipsorum facere et fieri fecisse in Maiori Ecclesia Florentina unam eminentem et honorabilem sepulturam ornatam sculturis marmoreis et aliis ornamentis de quibus et prout honori civitatis Florentie et fame ac virtuti talium et tantorum virorum viderint convenire; et ossa cuiuslibet predictorum facere in sua sepultura recondi ad perpetuam famam et celebrem memoriam omnium predictorum et civitatis ac reipublice Florentine'.

33. Viti, *Leonardo Bruni e Firenze*, pp. 78–79: 'Si nos universusque populus noster singulari ac precipua affectione dilectioneque existit erga inclitam indeficibilemque memoriam Dantis Alagherii, poete optimi atque famosissimi, nec vos necque alium quequem decet admirari. Gloria quippe huius viri talis est ut etiam civitati nostre splendorem et laudem procul dubio afferat et illustret patriam illius ingenii lumen. Quis enim tanta celebritate tantaque immortalitate nominis hactenus fuit quanta hic poeta in presenti est et, ut coniectare quimus, erit in posterum sempiternum? Cuius libri tanta elegantia scripti sunt ut nichil excogitari queat prestantius; tanta sapientia et doctrina tantaque varietate et copia ut et indoctos delectare et doctissimos prestantissimosque homines docere et universos dirigere ac instruere possint? [. . .] Cum itaque illorum cineres atque ossa in patriam reportanda et monumentis eisdem condenda decreto patriae existant, sintque in civitate Vestra ravennati cineres atque ossa Dantis ipsius, Magnificentiam Vestram affectuosissime rogamus ut non difficilem sese velit exhibere circa illorum reductionem.'

34. *Oratio in funere Iohannis Strozae*, ed. Viti, p. 720: 'Quis enim vel nostra vel superiori etate poetam aliquem nominare potest nisi florentinum?' ('Who can name a poet from our age or from an earlier one who was not Florentine?'); cf. Bruni, *Laudatio florentine urbis*, § 91, ed. Baldassarri, p. 34.

35. See Lanza, *Firenze*, pp. 147–52; idem, *Polemiche*, p. 181; Viti, *Opere*, p. 534. Note also that in 1434 Bruni had begun to recirculate his *Laudatio*.

36. *Vita di Dante*, ed. Viti, p. 538; English translations here and subsequently are taken from Nagel, in *The Three Crowns*, pp. 57–73.

37. On the *Vita*, see Gualdo Rosa, 'Leonardo Bruni e le sue vite "parallele" '; Madrignani, 'Di alcune biografie'; Mansi, 'La *Vita di Dante*'; Thompson, *The Humanism of Leonardo Bruni*, pp. 59–62; Trovato, 'Dai *Dialogi*'. See also Dionisotti, 'Dante nel Quattrocento', p. 350, who, perhaps undervaluing Landino's *Comento*, describes the work as 'il capolavoro della critica dantesca del Quattrocento' ('the masterpiece of Dantean criticism in the fifteenth century').

38. *Vita di Dante*, ed. Viti, pp. 537–38; see e.g. Boccaccio, *Trattatello*, § 28, 2nd redaction, ed. Ricci, p. 502: 'gli [sc. effect of Beatrice on Dante] fu in più provetta età di cocentissimi sospiri e d'amare lagrime assai spesso dolorosa cagione' ('she was very often the painful cause of burning sighs and bitter tears in his earliest years').

39. *Vita di Dante*, ed. Viti, pp. 540–41. For Filippo Villani, see above ch. 1, note 25.

40. The preface to the life of Cicero is echoed in the *proemio* to the life of Dante, where Bruni also mentions a moment of leisure and the re-reading of a familiar text as prompting his work; see *Opere*, ed. Viti, p. 416. Bruni's life of Aristotle, the *Vita Aristotelis* (1429), is also important for its comparison between Aristotle

and Plato, which anticipates the one between Dante and Petrarch. On these two lives, see Ianzitti, 'A Life'; idem, 'Leonardo Bruni and Biography'. On the committed citizen and intellectual, see also Bruni's *Isagogicon moralis disciplinae* (1423).

41. *Vita di Dante*, p. 542; cf. Dante, *Con.* IV,iv, 2. See also Bruni, *De militia*, ed. Bayley, p. 370.

42. *Vita di Dante*, p. 542. See also Trovato, 'Dai *Dialogi*', pp. 280–81, who argues pertinently that Niccoli lies antithetically behind the image of Dante as husband, father, politician, and cultural figure.

43. *Historiae*, ed. Santini, pp. 88–141 for *Vita di Dante*, ed. Viti, pp. 543–46.

44. *Vita di Dante*, p. 547. For Dante's 'reverenza', see also the passage from Boccaccio's *Trattatello* quoted in ch. 1, p. 32.

45. Ibid., p. 548: 'non per libidine, ma gentilezza di cuore' ('not out of lustfulness, but because of nobility of heart'); cf. Boccaccio, *Trattatello*, §§ 171–74 (1st redaction). Villani had earlier excised all mention of Dante's lustfulness in his life, see *De origine*, c. 22, § 34, ed. Tanturli, p. 77.

46. On *furor poeticus*, see also Bruni's letter to Giovanni Marrasio (7 October 1429) *Epistolarium*, lib. VI, 1, ed. Mehus, II, 36–40. For an echo of *Purg.* XXIV, 54 in this letter, see Gualdo Rosa, 'Una prolusione', n. 31, p. 285.

47. *Vita di Dante*, pp. 548–49.

48. See Petrarch, *Familiares*, X, 4, § 4; Boccaccio, *Genealogie*, lib. XIV, c. 7, ed. Romano, II, 700; Salutati, *De laboribus Herculis*, lib. I, c. 2, § 21, ed. Ullman, I, 16.

49. *Vita di Dante*, pp. 549–50.

50. Ibid., pp. 550–51; cf. *VN*, XXV, 3: 'ché dire per rima in volgare tanto è quanto dire per versi in latino, secondo alcuna proporzione' ('for writing in vernacular verse is like writing in Latin verse, according to a certain proportion').

51. Mazzocco, *Linguistic Theories*, part 1; Tavoni, *Latino*, pp. 3–72.

52. Baron, *The Crisis*, pp. 338, 341–44. For Tavoni's critique, see *Latino*, p. 49.

53. *Vita di Dante*, p. 552.

54. Field, 'Leonardo Bruni, Florentine Traitor?', p. 1127. Bruni is presented as a supporter of the pre-Medicean oligarchy in a dialogue by Filelfo, see Ferraù, 'Le *Commentationes*', p. 374. Also of note is Bruni's *De militia* (1422), dedicated to Rinaldo degli Albizzi, which stresses the oligarchic values of moral integrity, lack of self interest, and service for public good; see Bayley (ed.), *War and Society*.

55. For Bruni's letter against Filelfo and Florence's candidature for the Council in 1436, see Viti, *Leonardo Bruni e Firenze*, pp. 133–35 and n. 34, p. 146. On Bruni and Cosimo, see Hankins, 'Cosimo'.

56. *Opere volgari*, ed. Grayson, III, 154.

57. Ibid., III, 155–56. See also *Teogenio*, ed. Grayson, II, 55: 'e parsemi da scrivere in modo ch'io fussi inteso da' miei non litteratissimi cittadini' ('and it seemed to me that I should write so as to be understood by my fellow citizens who were not highly literate').

58. For Alberti's vernacular prose, see Maraschio, 'Aspetti'; idem, 'Interferenze'. On Alberti's linguistic theories, see further Patota, *Lingua e linguistica*, pp. 99–125; Tavoni, *Latino*, pp. 42–72; idem, *Il Quattrocento*, pp. 63–65.
59. See Grayson (ed.), *La prima grammatica*; Patota (ed.), *'Grammatichetta'*. I follow the dating proposed by Gorni and Patota. On debts to classical grammars, see Vineis, 'La tradizione grammaticale'.
60. For important commentary, see Pasquini, 'Tradizione e fermenti'. On the vernacular eclogue, see Grayson, *Studi*, pp. 103–18.
61. Pasquini, 'Tradizione e fermenti', esp. pp. 343–48, 354–56, 364–66, n. 153, p. 368, and n. 81, p. 383, referring to the *Comedy* as Alberti's *livre de chevet*. See also *Rime e versioni poetiche*, ed. Gorni, n. 2, pp. 226–27: 'richissimo il catalogo delle fonti dantesche nelle poesie dell'Alberti' ('there is a very rich list of Dantean sources in Alberti's poetry').
62. *Rime*, IV, lines 12–14, ed. Gorni, p. 15. Line 12 echoes *Par.* XII, 121, while line 14 quotes *Par.* XXII, 16. For other Dantean echoes in this sonnet, see Gorni's notes.
63. On the *Certame coronario*, see Altamura, *Il Certame*; Bertolini (ed.), *De vera amicitia*; Gorni, 'Storia'; Grafton, *Leon Battista Alberti*, pp. 170–74.
64. Bertolini (ed.), p. 285 (lines 14–17). For other Dantean echoes, see Bertolini's commentary *ad locum*. On the Dantean metre, see Gorni, 'Storia', p. 162.
65. Bertolini (ed.), pp. 251–52 (lines 12 and 14).
66. For Ciriaco's sonnet (Bertolini, pp. 337–38), the rhyme words for lines 1, 4–5 follow *Purg.* VIII, 80–84; the 'etterne | ninfe' of lines 3–4 follow *Par.* XXIII, 26; and lines 10–12 echo *Par.* XXIX, 22–36 and XXXIII, 88. In his *capitolo* 'Nel tempo che riduce il carro d'oro' (associated with the *Certame* but not read at it; see Bertolini, pp. 481–87), Francesco Malecarni elaborates a dream-vision landscape reminiscent of *Decameron*, V, 8, but with various Dantean echoes and a direct mention of Francesca da Rimini (lines 160–62, text in Altamura, *Il Certame*, p. 63).
67. Gorni, 'Storia', p. 177.

4 DANTE AND FLORENTINE VERNACULAR HUMANISM: CRITICAL JUDGEMENTS AND LITERARY EXPERIMENTS

1. *Vitae*, ed. Solerti, in *Le vite*, p. 110: 'apud eruditos et doctos cuncta passim vulgaria scripta [...] floccipendentes et pro nihilo habentes parvi existimantur et fiunt. Ita evenit ut plerumque ab ignaris et indoctis hominibus laudentur, eruditorum vero nullus vel poemata, vel fabulas, aliave eorum scripta, nisi forte vel ridendi, vel iocandi gratia, aliquando in manus sumit'.
2. Ibid., p. 144: 'quippe poeticam, diu antea per noningentos circiter annos vel demortuam vel sopitam, summus hic poeta primum in lucem excitavit'.
3. Bracciolini, *Facetiae* (completed 1452), nos. 57–58, 121, ed. Pittaluga, pp. 64–66, 134.

4. On the *Studio* in this period, see Davies, *Florence and the University*, pp. 106–24. On Argyropoulos, see Bigi, 'Argiropulo, Giovanni', in *DBI* 4, 129–31; Cammelli, *I dotti Bizantini*, II, 92–119; Field, *The Origins*, pp. 119ff.

5. On Argyropoulos' lecture-notes, see Bianchi, 'Un commento'. On Aristotle's reception in Quattrocento Florence, see esp. Lines, *Aristotle's Ethics*, pp. 174–220; Staico, 'Esegesi aristotelica'.

6. The seminal work on Ficino and Florentine Platonism is by Michael J. B. Allen, Eugenio Garin, James Hankins, Paul Oskar Kristeller, and Raymond Marcel. See also *Ficino and Renaissance Platonism* (eds.), Eisenbichler and Zorzi Pugliese; *Marsilio Ficino: His Theology* (eds.), Allen and Rees; *Marsilio Ficino e il ritorno di Platone* (ed.), Garfagnini. For biographical details, see Vasoli, 'Ficino, Marsilio', in *DBI* 47, 378–95.

7. On the 1460s, see Martelli, *Letteratura fiorentina*. On Florentine vernacular humanism, see Bigi, *Poesia latina e volgare*; Cardini, *La critica*, pp. 113–232; Tanturli, 'I Benci'; idem, 'La cultura'; Tavoni, *Il Quattrocento*.

8. On the *prolusione*, see Tanturli, 'Proposta'.

9. *SCT*, I, 33.

10. Ibid., I, 37–38.

11. Ibid., I, 38.

12. Ibid., I, 32; see too Cardini, *La critica*, esp. p. 217.

13. *SCT*, I, 36.

14. The most important critical evaluations of the the *Raccolta* are: Barbi, *Studi sul Canzoniere*, pp. 217–326; Cardini, *La critica*, pp. 200–04; Delcorno Branca, 'Percorsi', pp. 363–67; De Robertis, 'Lorenzo aragonese'; Tanturli, 'La Firenze', pp. 27–34.

15. On Poliziano's authorship, see Santoro, 'Poliziano o il Magnifico?'.

16. Delcorno Branca, 'Percorsi', pp. 364–65; Tanturli, 'La Firenze', p. 30.

17. *Epistola*, in Garin (ed.), *PLQ*, pp. 986–87.

18. For these points, see Cardini, *La critica*, pp. 124–25, 200–06, 212–22; idem, *SCT*, I, 137.

19. On the inclusion of the *Convivio*, see De Robertis, *Editi*, pp. 50–65 (on an earlier version of the *Raccolta c.* 1470); Cherchi, 'Un nuovo'.

20. On Dante in the *Raccolta*, see esp. Barbi, *Studi sul Canzoniere*, pp. 302–08; De Robertis, 'Lorenzo aragonese', p. 6.

21. See above ch. 1, section 4, esp. note 62.

22. *Epistola*, p. 989.

23. Delcorno Branca, 'Percorsi', pp. 365–66.

24. *Epistola*, p. 989; cf. Petrarch, *Trionfi* (*Triumphus Cupidinis*), IV, 35–36, ed. Pacca, p. 190. The idea of Dante's 'coarseness' is taken up in Pico della Mirandola's celebrated 1484 letter which compares Lorenzo de' Medici to both Petrarch and Dante (in *PLQ*, p. 800). On Pico's letter, see Bausi, 'Giovanni'; Thompson, 'Pico'. For Bembo on Dante's 'voci rozze' ('coarse words'), see above Introduction, note 51.

25. Aside from Salutati, Villani, and Bruni, see Benedetto Accolti's *Dialogus de praestantia virorum sui aevi* (*c.* 1459), ed. Galletti, p. 122: 'Quid enim dulcius, quid ornatius, quid sententiis clarius, quid varietate rerum illustrius, quam eorum [sc.

Dante and Petrarch] versus excogitari potest?' ('Can one think of anything that is sweeter, more ornate, more lucid in its thoughts, more illustrated with varied things than their poetry?'). On Accolti (1415–66), a participant in the *Certame* who taught law at the *Studio* and was Chancellor of Florence from 1458, see Black, *Benedetto Accolti*; Fubini, *L'umanesimo italiano*, pp. 121–27.

26. On Manetti and his role in the *Raccolta*, see De Robertis, *Editi*, pp. 50–64, 183–230. See also Ricci, 'Manetti, Antonio', in *ED* III, 801.

27. Florence, Biblioteca Nazionale, II, i, 33.

28. For Manetti's cosmography in Landino, see below ch. 5, section 4.

29. *Notizia*, ed. Milanesi, pp. 169–80. Manetti also petitioned Lorenzo de' Medici *c.* 1476 to make efforts in order to recover Dante's remains, see the letter in del Lungo, *Florentia*, pp. 451–57.

30. On 'transferimento' in the *volgarizzamento* (*c.* 1472–74) of Pliny's *Historia naturalis* (printed by Nicolas Jenson, Venice 1476), see *SCT*, I, 83: 'hai voluto [. . .] che Plinio di latino diventi toscano e di romano fiorentino, acciò che essendo scritto in lingua commune a tutta Italia e a molte esterne nazioni assai familiare, l'opera sua giovi a molti' ('you wished that Pliny from being Latin and Roman becomes Tuscan and Florentine, so that being written in a language common to all Italy and known to many foreign nations, his work is of use to many'); on the difficulties of translating technical terms, see esp. pp. 91–92. On this work, see Camillo, 'Voci quotidiane', pp. 126–32; Cardini, *La critica*, pp. 155–86; Tavoni, *Il Quattrocento*, pp. 70–79.

31. For these three *volgarizzamenti*, see respectively Martelli, 'La cultura letteraria', p. 43; Bessi, 'Un traduttore'; Tanturli, 'La Firenze', p. 3.

32. See esp. Tanturli, 'I Benci'; idem, 'Codici'.

33. For Ficino's vernacular interests, see Kristeller, 'Marsilio Ficino as a Man of Letters'. On Dante and Ficino, see also Aldo Rossi, 'Un autografo ficiniano'; Vasoli, 'Interpretazione'.

34. *Notizia*, ed. Milanesi, p. 170.

35. Tanturli, 'I Benci', pp. 212–31.

36. On the *prisca theologia*, see Walker, *The Ancient Theology*, pp. 1–21; Vasoli, 'Da Giorgio Gemisto'.

37. On the earlier movement, see Maggini, *I primi volgarizzamenti*; Segre (ed.), *Volgarizzamenti*.

38. Florence, Biblioteca Nazionale, II, iii, 210; Biblioteca Riccardiana, 1043; both manuscripts contain *inter alia* Bernardo's transcriptions of the *Convivio* which were completed by 20 September 1456 and 21 May 1461. For Bernardo's transcription of the vernacular *Monarchia*, see Shaw, 'Il volgarizzamento'.

39. Vasoli, 'Note'. For stylistic analysis of the *volgarizzamento*, see Bigi, *Poesia latina*, pp. 51–61; Shaw, 'La versione ficiniana', pp. 308–24.

40. See esp. Fubini, *Quattrocento Fiorentino*, pp. 233–301.

41. Shaw, 'La versione ficiniana', p. 327.

42. On the Platonized Virgil, see e.g. Augustine, *De civitate Dei*, lib. X, c. 30; lib. XIII, c. 19; lib. XIV, c. 3, in *CCSL* 47:307; 48:401–2, 417; Benvenuto, III, 96. Macrobius

repeatedly applies Platonic and Neoplatonic teachings to the *Aeneid* in his *Commentarium in Somnium Scipionis*, lib. I, c. 3, §§ 17–20; lib. I, c. 9, §§ 8–9, ed. Willis, pp. 12, 41.

43. See Field, 'A Manuscript', referring to *recollecta* of Landino's lectures on *Aeneid* I–VI and the connections it records between Virgil and Dante.

44. On Dantean echoes in Ficino's *Liber de christiana religione*, see Vasoli, *Filosofia*, pp. 50–51, 68–69.

45. *De raptu Pauli/Il rapimento di Paolo*, in *PLQ*, esp. pp. 933–45. For commentary, see Vasoli, *Quasi sit Deus*, pp. 241–61. On the *De raptu* and Dante, see Vasoli, 'Interpretazione', pp. 138–40.

46. *El Libro dell'Amore*, ed. Niccoli, p. 3.

47. See Ciavolella, 'Eros/Ereos'.

48. On Luigi Pulci and Dante, see Martelli, *Letteratura fiorentina*, p. 28; Messina, 'Pulci, Luigi', in *ED* III, 738–39 (with further bibliography). For Luca, see Martelli, *Letteratura fiorentina*, pp. 170–75. For Verino's use of Dante in Latin epic (interestingly mediated through Ronto's Latin translation of the *Comedy*, above Introduction, note 23), see Bausi, 'L'epica'.

49. For the dating, see Tanturli, 'I Benci', n. 5, pp. 229–30. The only modern edition (an unsatisfactory text based on Laurenziano XL 53) is *Città di Dio*, ed. Rooke. For Dati's commentary, see Flamini, 'Leonardo di Piero Dati'. The best discussion to date is Martelli, *Letteratura fiorentina*, pp. 63, 254–69.

50. On Palmieri's use of Origen and the poem's heterodox teachings, see Boffito, 'L'eresia'; Wind, 'The Revival', pp. 48–52; cf. Vespasiano, *Le vite*, ed. Greco, I, 566.

51. See e.g. the following (very select) examples: *Città di Dio*, I, 7, 1: 'Oppresso di stupor con gran dilecto' (*Par.* XXII, 1); I, 9, 40: 'Qualunque se del sommo ben spoglia | per dilectarsi in cosa che non dura' (*Par.* XV, 11–13); I, 13, 1: 'Soleva al tempo del gentile errore | creder el mondo aver nocivi idij' (*Par.* VIII, 1–2); I, 18, 20: 'el sol montava con le prime stelle' (*Inf.* I, 38); I, 18, 25: '[. . .] el male | del universo tutto quivi insacca' (*Inf.* VII, 18); I, 28, 1: 'Io dico seguitando che poi vidi' (*Inf.* VIII, 1); II, 1, 18: 'Non sien di dyte qui le leggi ropte' (*Purg.* I, 46); II, 2, 1: 'Perdete ogni speranza voi ch entrate' (*Inf.* III, 9); III, 2, 9: 'sommo bene' (*Par.* XIV, 47); II, 12, 35: 'O dura terra ben fu maraviglia | se non ti aprisiti [. . .]' (*Inf.* XXXIII, 66); II, 18, 10: 'Lor vanita qui par sia persona' (*Inf.* VI, 36); III, 23, 37: 'Et vo che sappi' (*Inf.* IV, 33); III, 24, 1: 'Fiso guardando' (*Par.* XXIII, 9); III, 24, 22: 'Quale e colui che si rivolge & guata' (*Inf.* I, 23–24).

52. On astrology, see esp. ibid., I, 7, 8–50 (general premises); I, 12 (Saturn); I, 13 ('male impressioni'); I, 15 (Jupiter); I, 17 (Mars); I, 19–20 (Sun); I, 22 (Venus); I, 26 (Mercury); I, 28 (Moon).

53. *Città di Dio*, ed. Rooke, pp. 23–24. For the stultifying effects of body, see also I, 7, 6; I, 9, 15; I, 11, 42–44; I, 18, 27–28; I, 23, 21; I, 29, 16–20.

54. For contemporary themes, see ibid., I, 18 (number symbolism); I, 21 (judgement of Paris); I, 23 (religion and wisdom); I, 27 (ancient names for the moon); II, 21 (classical tyrants); II, 23 (glory); II, 24, 32–49 (Virgil's ahistorical treatment of Dido); III, 4 (ancient teachings on the ultimate good); III, 5, 39–46 (classical

examples of prudence); III, 6, 46–49 and III, 18, 37–49 (civic temperance); III, 8, 38–50 (fortitude); III, 14, 23–48 (legislators); III, 20, 26–50 (Hercules); III, 27 (prophetic powers of pagans).

55. On Berlinghieri's *Geographia*, see below ch. 6, note 46. Sardi's *De anima peregrina* (1493–1509), ed. Rooke is in three books and 100 *capitoli*.

56. See Bessi, 'Per un nuovo commento'; idem, 'Le *Stanze*'. See also Branca, *Poliziano e l'umanesimo*, pp. 44–55; Ghinassi, *Il volgare letterario*; McLaughlin, 'Poliziano's *Stanze*'; Orvieto, 'Boccaccio mediatore'; Storey, 'The Philosopher'. For a survey of recent interpretations, see Bigi, 'Impegno'. On Neoplatonism, see esp. Martelli, *Angelo Poliziano*, pp. 101–37.

57. Delcorno Branca, 'Percorsi', pp. 367–69; Curti, 'Dantismi'. See also Lo Cascio, 'Il Poliziano'.

58. Delcorno Branca, 'Percorsi', pp. 364, 367–69; Curti, 'Dantismi', p. 555. Neither critic notes that Dante's Earthly Paradise is also mediated to Poliziano through Boccaccio's romance fiction and perhaps even Gherardi (see above ch. 1, note 10 and ch. 2, note 69). See also Lanza, *Letteratura tardogotica*, pp. 168, 675, 707, 845.

59. *Stanze*, ed. Carrai, pp. 90–91; *Purg.* XXVIII trans. Durling, in *The Divine Comedy*, II, 475.

60. De Robertis, 'Interpretazione', pp. 144–45. On Poliziano's theory of imitation, see McLaughlin, *Literary Imitation*, pp. 187–216.

61. *Sylva in Scabiem*, ed. Orvieto, p. 78. For other echoes of Dante's Malebolge, see Bigi, *La cultura*, pp. 149–63; Delcorno Branca, 'Percorsi', pp. 369–71.

62. Benvenuto, I, 570. For Poliziano's familiarity with Benvenuto's *Comentum*, see Delcorno Branca, 'Percorsi', pp. 380–81.

63. *Sylva*, ed. Orvieto, pp. 76–78. For classical analogues, see the notes to Orvieto's edition.

64. On Lorenzo's influences and poetic output, see Bigi, 'Lorenzo de' Medici e la letteratura'; Martelli, 'La cultura letteraria'; idem, *Letteratura fiorentina, ad indicem*; idem, *Studi laurenziani*; Rochon, *La jeunesse*, pp. 139–91; Tanturli, 'La Firenze'. On Dante and Lorenzo, see Greco, 'Dante nella poesia di Lorenzo', but Orvieto's notes to *Tutte le opere* are the most valuable resource.

65. *Tutte le opere*, ed. Orvieto, II, 629.

66. For examples (with parodic intent) not noted in Orvieto's notes to the *Simposio*, see e.g. II, 73, 76, 79: 'Colui chi è [. . .] Quel ch'è più grasso [. . .] L'altro' (cf. *Purg.* VII, 91, 97, 112); III, 16–19: 'Questo, come da' suoi primi anni crebbe, | dette presagio ver della sua vita, | che beitor e goditor sarebbe' (cf. *Purg.* XXX, 115–17); III, 43–45: 'Conosco, innanzi dica, el tuo disio' (cf. *Par.* XV, 68–69; XIX, 15).

67. *Tutte le opere*, ed. Orvieto, II, 613–14.

68. On this point, see Cardini, *La critica*, p. 197.

69. See esp. *Canzoniere*, LXXV, LXXIX, XCV, and CXXXVIII, ed. Orvieto, I, 160–68, 174–76, 199–202, 244–45.

70. *Comento*, proemio, § 68, ed. Orvieto, I, 369–70.

71. See the notes in the edition by Orvieto.

72. Ibid., § 58, ed. Orvieto, I, 367.
73. On the importance of the 1470s, see Tanturli, 'I Benci', p. 241.

5 CRISTOFORO LANDINO ON DANTE AND FLORENCE:
THE PROLOGUE TO THE *COMENTO*

1. There is no definitive biography, but see the outline in Field, *The Origins*, pp. 232–39. For Landino's teaching and inaugural lectures, see Field, 'Cristoforo Landino's First Lectures'; La Brasca, '*Scriptor*'.
2. On the print run, see Landino's letter in *Comento*, I, 113–14. However, for the view that 1200 copies is the combined number of the 1481 edition and the 1484 Venetian edition, see Scapecchi, 'Cristoforo Landino', p. 45. For known exemplars and the *editio princeps*, see *Comento*, I, 127–47, 169–73.
3. Text in *Comento*, I, 108–12.
4. On the *intagli* (all nineteen are reproduced in a very limited number of exemplars), see the plates in *Comento*, I; see also fig. 3. For further discussion, see Donati Barcellona, 'Baldini, Baccio', in *ED* I, 498; Dreyer, 'Botticelli's Series'. Despite their unfinished state, the engravings made the *Comento* one of the more prestigious illustrated printed books produced in Italy before Francesco Colonna's *Hypnerotomachia Poliphili* of 1499.
5. See Cardini, *La critica*; idem, 'Landino e Dante'; La Brasca, 'L'humanisme vulgaire'; idem, 'Du prototype'; idem, 'Tradition exégétique'; Lentzen, *Studien*; Parker, *Commentary*, pp. 76–85; Procaccioli, *Filologia*; idem, introd. to *Comento*, I, 9–105. General overviews are: Dionisotti, 'Landino, Cristoforo', in *ED* III, 566–68; Field, *The Origins*, pp. 240–72. In this chapter, I am especially indebted to Cardini's valuable notes to his edition of the *proemio*, see *SCT*, II, 102–224.
6. See Ganda, 'L'edizione nidobeatina'; Luca Carlo Rossi, 'Per il commento'.
7. Rossi (ed.), 'Per il commento', p. 1714: 'sed Iacobus Lanaeus materna eadem et Bononiensi lingua superare est visus, cum sit illa urbs ita in umbilico Italiae posita ut assiduo commertio non tersa solum vocabula, sed provintiis omnibus etiam communia habeat, nec minore gratia dignitateque sit in Italia bononiensis sermo quam laconicus olim in Graecia fuit'.
8. *Comento*, I, 221, 64–73. For Nidobeato's provocation, see Cardini, *La critica*, pp. 206–12; Dionisotti, 'Dante nel Quattrocento', pp. 369–72. For later direct criticism, see *Comento*, II, 102, 13–15.
9. On the dating, see Cardini, *SCT*, II, 102–03; Procaccioli, *Filologia*, pp. 146, 168–69.
10. See e.g. Cardini, *La critica*, n. 31, p. 18; Procaccioli, *Comento*, notes to II, 836–39. For other material re-used in the *Comento*, see Cardini, *SCT*, II, 102–224; Procaccioli, *Filologia*, pp. 146, 168–69.
11. *Comento*, I, 110: 'Ma perché le parole non commesse alle lettere presto volano de' pecti humani, et spesso nessuno vestigio di sé lasciano, tentai quelle medesime sententie mandare alle letere, le quali havevo molti anni nel vostro celeberrimo gymnasio [sc. the Florentine *Studio*] a voce viva expresso' ('But because words which are not committed to the page soon depart from the memory of humankind,

and often leave no trace of themselves, I attempted to set those very thoughts down on paper, which I had expressed orally for many years in our celebrated university'). The oration also reiterates the importance of his earlier allegorical reading of the *Aeneid*, and his desire to free the poem from external idioms (pp. 110–11).

12. See e.g. *Comento*, I, 265, 128: 'Ma udiamo e versi [. . .]' ('But let us listen to the lines'); II, 483, 57: 'chosa certamente degna d'essere udita' ('a thing which is certainly worthy of being heard').

13. On the dating, see now Fubini, *Quattrocento Fiorentino*, pp. 328–29.

14. On the *Disputationes Camaldulenses*, see Kallendorf, *In Praise of Aeneas*, pp. 129–65; McNair, *Cristoforo Landino on the Human Soul*; idem, 'Cristoforo Landino'. For its relationship to the *Comento*, see Cardini, *La critica*, pp. 152–54; Kallendorf, *In Praise of Aeneas*, pp. 138, 155–61; Lentzen, *Studien*, pp. 137–57; Procaccioli, *Filologia*, pp. 156–57, 173. The *DC* was printed in Florence *c.* 1480 by Niccolò Tedesco. Landino refers to a vernacular version by Andrea Cambini (which is no longer extant) in *Comento*, I, 311, 68–69.

15. *DC*, lib. IV, ed. Lohe, pp. 190, 253–54: 'Nonne e nostris Danthem virum omni doctrina excultum gravissimum auctorem habemus, qui eius itineris, quo mundum omnem ab imis Tartaris ad supremum usque caelum peragrat, in eo sibi illum ducem fingit, in quo summum hominis bonum perquirens miro quodam ingenio unicam Aeneida imitandam proponit, ut, cum pauca omnino inde excerpere videatur, nunquam tamen, si diligentius inspiciemus, ab ea discedat? Nam nonne statim a principio ea, quae de medio aetatis tempore, quae de silva, quae de tribus feris, quae de montis sublimi iugo iam solis radiis illustrato conscripsit, hinc omnia sunt? Mitto cetera, quae ita abdita in Danthis poemate sunt, ut non nisi a paucis iisdemque doctissimis deprehendi possint. Praeponit igitur sibi ducem Maronem in ea rem, quae ad summum bonum, non autem ad physicen spectet [. . .] Dum enim mihi planum reddere Maronem tentas idque efficis, eodem tempore in nostris civis divinum poema inducis. Nunc enim demum perspicio, quid sibi velit Danthes, qui primum ad inferos descendat atque inde emergens nullam aliam viam nisi per purgatoria loca ad caelum inveniat [. . .] Nunc autem, cum universum rei argumentum mente percurro, summa admiratione eius viri ingenium prosequor. Nam cum in opere suo texendo pauca omnino fila de Virgiliana tela mutuari videatur, tamen inde omnia paene sint. Quam ob rem nunc id demum intelligo, quod nos ex Ciceronis praecepto saepenumero Landinus admonere solet esse in aliquo imitando diligentem omnino rationem adhibendam; neque enim id agendum, ut idem simus, qui sunt ii, quos imitatur, sed eorum ita similes, ut ipsa similitudo vix illa quidem neque nisi doctis intelligatur.'

16. *Comento*, I, 219–20, 22–28.

17. The most important precedent for Landino's reading (not noted in earlier studies) is Filippo Villani's *Expositio*, see *pref.* § 62, ed. Bellomo, p. 49. For links and divergences with Boccaccio, see Kallendorf, *In Praise of Aeneas*, pp. 154–56.

18. The *accessus* is found in the Florentine commentaries by Boccaccio and Villani, as well as in other Trecento commentaries that had wide circulation in Florence (see Introduction, note 27).

19. For the *Comento*'s links with humanist commentary, see Dionisotti, 'Dante nel Quattrocento', pp. 369–70. More generally, see Grafton, 'Renaissance Readers'; Lo Monaco, 'Alcune osservazioni'.

20. *Comento*, I, 219, 10–17 (quotation at lines 10–11).

21. References in order: Jacopo, *Chiose all' 'Inferno'*, ed. Bellomo, pp. 111–12; Boccaccio, *Trattatello*, § 103, ed. Ricci, p. 462; Giovanni Villani, *Nuova cronica*, lib. XIII, c. 20 and c. 97, ed. Porta, I, 349, 509–10; Filippo Villani (see ch. 2, note 52); Bruni, *Historiae*, ed. Santini, p. 105: 'Quod equidem nec levitate, nec malignitati praestantis ingenio et doctrina viri tribuendum puto, sed tempori' ('I think this [sc. Dante's anti-Florentine outburst in *Epistole* VI] should not be set down to frivolity or malignity, since we are dealing with a man of exceptional intellect and learning, but rather to the times').

22. *Comento*, I, 223, 43–47, 52–53, 59–61. This kind of justification is found earlier in Bruni's *Laudatio florentine urbis*, § 51, ed. Baldassarri, p. 21: 'Quare non, si unus atque alter in hac urbe minus probatis moribus fuere, id communiter ad calumniam civitatis referri par est [. . .] perversitas ac malitia paucorum universam rem publicam recte factorum laudibus privare non debet' ('if one citizen or another in this city has been shown to lack morals, this is no good reason to condemn the entire city [. . .] the wickedness and evil of a few should not deprive the entire nation of being praised for its good deeds').

23. See *Comento*, IV, 1706, 17–23; III, 1259, 10–13 (paraphrase); II, 881, 1–11; III, 1148, 1–7 (rhetorical comment); II, 476, 22–30; IV, 1781, 25–30; IV, 1908, 19–21 (justification). For the two critical passages, see ibid., II, 692, 22–29 (on *Inf.* XV, 61–63): 'è d'havere per excusato el poeta nostro se in vituperare la patria trapassa e termini di quella modestia, la quale debba essere in huomo philosopho et theologo; et dimentica la reverentia et pietà la quale debba havere ogni cittadino alla sua rep., perché essendo stato a grandissimo torto poco avanti privato degl'honori, delle dignità, del patrimonio, et della patria, et finalmente relegato in duro exilio, non pote por freno a sì fresca ingiuria. Ma invero era più officio della sua sapientia parlare più modestamente' ('our poet is to be excused if in condemning the homeland he exceeds the bounds of that modesty which is fitting in a philosopher and theologian; and he forgets the reverence and piety which every citizen must have towards his republic. Having only recently been deprived most wrongly of honours, dignities, patrimony, and his homeland and finally having been sent into harsh exile, he was not able to remain silent over such a recent offence. But in truth it was more fitting of his wisdom to speak with greater modesty'); III, 1225, 24–27 (on *Purg.* XI, 112–14): 'Non posso fare, che in questo luogho, o in alchuno altro, non mi dolghi, perché vorrei, che tanto poeta, et di sì mirabil ingegno et doctrina, non s'havessi lasciato traportare dalla perturbatione dell'animo inverso la sua patria' ('I cannot fail to be pained in this passage and in others, because I wish that such a poet with such marvellous genius and learning had not allowed himself to be transported by animus against his homeland'). For Bruni on Dante's reverence, see *Vita di Dante*, ed. Viti, p. 547; cf. Manetti, *Vitae*, ed. Solerti, in *Le vite*, pp. 135–36. These examples lessen the charge of Procaccioli's view (*Filologia*, p. 253) that the 'problematica civile'

of the *proemio* is lost in the *chiosa*. Note also that Landino endorses (and adapts to his own age) Dante's outburst against Florentine women, see *Comento*, III, 1397, 1–6. For other passages that reveal a mysognist and/or patriarchal strain in Landino, see ibid., II, 739, 27–28; III, 1171–72, 26–31; III, 1245, 7–9 (cf. Benvenuto, III, 354); III, 1395, 3–8.

24. *Comento*, I, 224–25, 92–102.
25. See Bruni, *Historiae*, ed. Santini, pp. 162–65, noted by Cardini, *SCT*, II, 114–15. See also *Laudatio florentine urbis*, §§ 68–77, ed. Baldassarri, pp. 27–30.
26. See e.g. Compagni, *La cronaca*, lib. I, c. I, ed. del Lungo, p. 6.
27. See e.g. Cicero, *De inventione*, I.1.1, ed. Hubbell, pp. 2–4. See also Landino's preface to his commentary on Horace (1482), in *SCT*, I, 198–99. The theme is evoked in Landino's *prolusioni* to courses on Cicero, Virgil, and Petrarch (it has some basis in Dante who brings together pagan philosophers and poets in *Inf.* IV).
28. Cardini, *SCT*, II, 127–28.
29. See Gadol, *Leon Battista Alberti: Universal Man*, pp. 178–95; Garin, 'La cultura filosofica', pp. 88–90; Larner, 'The Church'; Rose, *The Italian Renaissance*, pp. 9–13, 26–36.
30. See e.g. Cicero, *De oratore*, I.8.30–34, ed. Rackham, pp. 22–6; idem, *Pro Archia*, VIII.19, ed. Watts, p. 26; Horace, *Ars poetica*, 391–6. The theme is a leitmotif in Landino's *oeuvre*.
31. Bruni, *Historiae*, ed. Santini, pp. 14–15.
32. *Comento*, I, 236, 17–22, 28–31.
33. Ibid., I, 238–39, 94–106. The parallel with Athens is implicit to Bruni's *Laudatio florentine urbis* which is modelled closely on the celebration of Athenian cultural and political pre-eminence in Aelius Aristides' *Panathenaicus* (see Baldassarri's introd., pp. xviii–xx).
34. Baxandall, *Painting and Experience*, pp. 114–51; idem, 'Alberti and Cristoforo Landino'.
35. See e.g. Salutati, *Invectiva in Antonium Luschum Vicentinum*, in *PLQ*, p. 34; Alberti, *Libri della famiglia*, ed. Grayson, III, 140–42; Palmieri, *Vita civile*, lib. IV, §§ 183–85, pp. 187–88. For the 'industria' and wealth of Florence, see also Bruni, *Laudatio*, §§ 53, 90, 92, ed. Baldassarri, pp. 22, 34–35.
36. *Comento*, I, 243, 4–6, 22–25.
37. For Florentine precedents, see the texts anthologized in *Images of Quattrocento Florence* (eds.), Baldassarri and Saiber, pp. 39–60, 72–76, 83–87. For non-Florentine documents, see also ibid., pp. 299–324.
38. *Comento*, I, 243–45, 26–29, 31, 40–43, 75–81.
39. See also *Comento*, II, 908, 13–16: 'El corpo del poeta giace honoratamente in Ravenna; et è giudicio d'ogni savio et licterato huomo che el popolo fiorentino doverrebbe ridurlo nella patria, et honorarlo di sepultura degna di tal poeta' ('The body of the poet lies with honour in Ravenna; and it is the judgement of all learned and literate men that the Florentine people should bring it back to his homeland and honour it will a burial place worthy of such a poet'), and Landino's 1481 letter

to Bernardo Bembo in *SCT*, ii, 167–69. See further ch. 4, note 29; Bellomo, 'Prime vicende', pp. 56–57; Ricci, *L'ultimo rifugio*, pp. 396–97.

40. *Comento*, i, 246, 128–29: 'da molti altri docti huomini, et *maxime* da Giannoctio Manetti, è stata absolutamente, et con molta elegantia, narrata' ('it has been recounted by many other learned men, and above all by Gianozzo Manetti has it been supremely and most elegantly told'). On Landino's re-use of Manetti and Boccaccio, see Cardini, *SCT*, ii, 170–206; Thompson, 'Landino's Life'.

41. Thompson, 'Landino's Life', p. 123.

42. *Comento*, i, 248–49, 47–49, 52–56.

43. Plato, *Symposium* 210A–211E. For Ficino's influence on this passage, see Gilson, 'Plato, the *platonici*', p. 27.

44. *Comento*, i, 252–53, 178–81 and 197–216.

45. See Cardini, *La critica*, pp. 124–25.

46. *Comento*, i, 255, 268–70, 278–79, 281–83: 'non sia alchuno che creda non solamente essere eloquente, ma pure tollerabile dicitore nella nostra lingua, se prima non harà vera et perfecta cognitione delle latine lettere [...] Né mai potrà lo scriptore havere o sucho o nervi nello stilo, quando non fia se non al tutto docto, almancho alquanto introdocto in philosophia [...] è necessario che la nostra [sc. lingua] di riccha vengha ricchissima, se ogni dì più transferiremo in quella nuovi vocabli tolti da' Romani' ('let no-one believe that any writer can be not only eloquent but merely tolerable in our tongue unless he first has a true and perfect knowledge of Latin literature. Nor will a writer ever have energy or robustness in his style unless he has at least some training in philosophy, even if he is not fully schooled [...] it is necessary that ours will become richer and richer if every day we transfer into it new words taken from the Romans').

47. For Landino's earlier works re-used in this chapter, see Cardini, *SCT*, ii, 206–09. On Ficino's *De divino furore*, see Gentile, 'In margine'. There are close connections between Landino's account and other Ficinian works, see Ficino, *Opera omnia*, i, 287 and 634–35. On poetic fury, see Scott, 'Perotti'; Coppini, 'L'ispirazione', pp. 134–44.

48. *Comento*, i, 257–58, 25–29, 41–43; cf. Plato, *Ion*, 533D–534E; *Phaedrus*, 244A–245A (see also ch. 3, note 46).

49. *Comento*, i, 258, 45–51.

50. See Cardini, *La critica*, pp. 85–112.

51. *Comento*, i, 258, 55–60.

52. *Genealogie deorum*, lib. xiv, c. 7, ed. Romano, ii, 699: '[...] fervor quidam exquisite inveniendi atque dicendi, seu scribendi quod inveneris'. See also Salutati, *De laboribus Herculis*, lib. i, c. 3, § 1, ed. Ullman, i, 17. These accounts echo Cicero, *Pro Archia*, viii.18, ed. Watts, p. 26.

53. *Comento*, i, 266–67, 169–213 (see also above ch. 4, p. 138); cf. Quintilian, *Institutio oratoria*, x.1.46, ed. Butler, iv, 28. See also Dante, *VN*, ii, 8.

54. On Ficino's letter, see Gentile, in *Comento*, i, 114–18; Vasoli, 'Dante e la cultura fiorentina', pp. 18–19.

55. *Comento*, I, 268, 6–11: 'nuper tuus pater Apollo, et longum fletum meum, et diuturnum tuum exilium miseratus, mandavit Mercurio, ut pie Christophori Landini divini vatis menti prorsus illaberetur; Landineosque vultus indutus, alma primum virga dormientem te suscitaret, deinde alarum remigio te sublatum menibus Florentinis inferret; denique Phebea tibi lauro tempora redimeret'; cf. Virgil, *Aeneid* 1.300–02.

56. *Comento*, I, 270–71, 2–3, 7–9.

57. Toussaint, *De l'enfer*, esp. pp. 23–82.

58. Vasari, *Le vite* (eds.), Bettarini and Barocchi, III, 144: 'diede ancora molta opera in questo tempo alle cose di Dante, le quali furono da lui bene intese circa i siti e le misure'.

59. *Cammino di Dante*, in Bruschi (ed.), 'Ser Piero Bonaccorsi'. See further Ciociola, 'Lo scrittoio'.

60. On Manetti's Dantean cosmography, see Barbi, *Dante nel Cinquecento*, pp. 131–35; Foà, 'Il *Dialogo*'. See also Kleiner, *Mismapping*, pp. 23–56.

6 TRADITION AND INNOVATION IN CRISTOFORO LANDINO'S *COMENTO*: PLATONISM, NATURAL SCIENCE, AND CLASSICISM

1. Barbi, *Dante nel Cinquecento*, pp. 146–79; see also Lentzen, *Studien*, pp. 171–78. On the *chiosa* and the Trecento commentators, see now Procaccioli, *Filologia*, esp. pp. 41–42, 143, 148, 152–53. Procaccioli has provided an important survey for the *Inferno*, see ibid., pp. 143–254 and a valuable apparatus for the entire *Comento* in his critical edition.

2. For rhetorical commentary, see e.g. the following passages from the *Comento*: I, 287, 172–73 (interjection); I, 287, 168–73 (exclamation); II, 490, 104–06 (hyperbole); I, 462, 63–67 (repetition); III, 378, 188–90 (interpretation); I, 461–62, 57–59 (*sententia*); II, 560, 38–42 (onomatopeia); II, 830, 1–4 (*precisio*); II, 862, 11–12 (congemination); II, 881, 6–11 (apostrophe/irony); II, 887, 7–11 (circumlocution); III, 1038–39, 33–62; IV, 1933, 14–15 (metaphor); III, 1037, 1–30 (*propositio* and *invocatio*); III, 1161, 2 (*translatio*); III, 1547, 27–29 (enigma).

3. On Landino's interest in etymology, see the index in *Comento*, IV, 2033–39, and note 5 below.

4. On Poliziano's initiatives, see Grafton, 'Renaissance Readers', pp, 618–19; idem, 'On the Scholarship'; Branca, *Poliziano e l'umanesimo*, pp. 16–19, 73–90.

5. For Landino's linguistic commentary, see the passages anthologized in *SCT*, II, 212–20. Landino uses Boccaccio's *Esposizioni* for the following (not noted in Procaccioli's apparatus): 'bieco', 'bizzarro', 'broda', 'buffa', 'burli', 'calle', 'ceraste', 'cherici', 'cionco', 'Clio', 'Cocito', 'cola', 'Euterpe', 'gora', 'himno', and 'poza'. For updating, see e.g. 'cuna' (*Inf.* XIV, 100 in *Comento*, III, 678, 65–68), where Landino follows Boccaccio's general definition but also adds Latin and Greek etymologies.

6. See above ch. 4, p. 136.

7. *Comento*, II, 717, 21–29; III, 1037–39, 16–18, 34–35, 39–43, 45–50. The first passage is in polemic with Boccaccio, cf. *Esposizioni*, XVI, § 87, ed. Padoan, pp. 705–06.

8. On allegory, see esp. Cardini, *La critica*, pp. 31–32; idem, *SCT*, II, 106–07 (with examples of Landino's refusal to allegorize).

9. *Comento*, I, 310, 38–45. For psychological categories in the *DC*, see ed. Lohe, pp. 158, 160–70, 196–97; McNair, *Cristoforo Landino on the Human Soul*, pp. 147, 191. For Landino's keen interest in psychological structures related to Dante-*personaggio*, see Cardini, *SCT*, II, p. xxxi; Field, *The Origins*, pp. 263–64; La Brasca, 'Tradition exégétique', p. 118; Procaccioli, *Filologia*, p. 155. The concern is developed in some earlier Dante commentators, see esp. Buti, I, 45; Villani, *Expositio, pref.* §§ 92–109, ed. Bellomo, pp. 51–54.

10. *Comento*, I, 284, 84–91.

11. Landino makes especially pertinent comments regarding the Platonic background to Dante's use of symbols, the divine creation of the soul, and *Par.* IV, 49–63. On Dante's Neoplatonic orientations, see now Barański, *Dante e i segni*, pp. 1–2, 28–30, 54–56, with extensive earlier bibliography (esp. the works by Bruno Nardi, and the American Dantists, John Freccero, Robert Durling and Ronald Martinez, and Joseph Anthony Mazzeo) at n. 24, p. 55.

12. For these commentators, see Gilson, 'Plato, the *platonici*', pp. 9–10 and nn. 22–24.

13. Ibid., pp. 6–7 and appendices for a full list of references to Plato and his dialogues.

14. On translations of Plato before Ficino, see Hankins, *Plato*, I, parts 1 and 2. On Ficino's early translations of Plato, see Kristeller, 'Marsilio Ficino as a Beginning Student'. By 1468–69 Ficino had prepared translations for all Plato's dialogues, even though he was not to publish them until the printed edition, the *Platonis Opera Omnia* of 1484. That Landino had knowledge of several of these translations by the mid-1470s is clear from references in the *Disputationes Camaldulenses*, see Lohe's edition *ad indicem* (pp. 271–72).

15. See Gilson, 'Plato, the *platonici*', nn. 11–16, p. 42.

16. *Comento*, I, 373, 29–31 and 434, 20–31; II, 482–83, 16–30; III, 1034, 48–51; IV, 1923, 10–12.

17. Fuller discussion in Gilson, 'Plato, the *platonici*', pp. 8–9.

18. *Comento*, II, 446–47, 81–91 and 505–06, 65–74; III, 1294, 32–42.

19. Augustine, *De civitate Dei*, lib. VIII, cc. 4–12, in *CCSL* 47:219–29. On Augustine in Ficino, see Kristeller, *Studies*, esp. pp. 367–71; Vasoli, *Quasi sit Deus*, pp. 91–112.

20. See Gilson, 'Plato, the *platonici*', pp. 18–19.

21. Ibid., pp. 10–11 and nn. 26–29.

22. *Comento*, II, 817, 35–39, following Ficino, *Theologia platonica*, lib. VIII, c. 1, in *Opera omnia*, I, 182. In an identical context (a discussion of the imagination), Landino uses Ficino as his example where Ficino had earlier used Plato. For another homely example involving Ficino, see *Comento*, II, 1004, 71–76. For the other direct borrowings, see Gilson, 'Plato, the *platonici*', pp. 39–40.

23. Insufficient attention has been paid to points of dependence and subtle shifts in emphasis between the *Disputationes* and the *Comento*. Landino never refers to Dante as a 'platonico' in the *Comento*, but he is quite explicit about Virgil's dependence on Plato, see *DC*, lib. III, pp. 118–19; lib. IV, pp. 202, 221–22, 237, 253, 256, 258–59.

24. See Gilson, 'Plato, the *platonici*', p. 13.

25. *Comento*, I, 341, 107–10 and 373, 19–11; II, 482–83, 16–30. On *prisca theologia*, see above ch. 4, note 36.

26. *Comento*, I, 374, 62–66; I, 392, 27–32; II, 580, 55–57. Hankins, *Plato*, I, 257–59, notes that pre-existence was a major problem for Renaissance writers.

27. On the exceptionality of Landino's *chiosa* on *Inferno* I, see Procaccioli, *Filologia*, pp. 167, 172. For prologue section(s) as marking ideological allegiances, see Barański, *Dante e i segni*, pp. 109–11, 130–32, 159–62.

28. *Comento*, I, 284–85, 91–116.

29. *DC*, lib. I, p. 17; lib. III, pp. 141, 143; lib. IV, p. 216.

30. See Gilson, 'Plato, the *platonici*', nn. 56–59, pp. 47–49. For Palmieri, see above ch. 3, p. 107.

31. *Comento*, I, 434–45, 5–25.

32. Gilson, 'Plato, the *platonici*', n. 70, p. 50.

33. Ibid., n. 71, p. 50.

34. For the vernacular Petrarch in the *Comento*, see the anthology in Cardini, *SCT*, II, 192–203. On this passage, see also above ch. 1, note 54.

35. Bruni, *Opere*, ed. Viti, pp. 518–20.

36. For Trezibond and Bessarion, see Hankins, *Plato*, I, 217–37, 245–63. On the Plato–Aristotle controversy, see Hankins, *Plato*, I, 193–263; Kristeller, *Renaissance Concepts*, pp. 85–109; Monfasani, 'Marsilio Ficino'; Moreau, 'De la concordance'; Woodhouse, *George Gemistos Plethon*, pp. 365–69. For Landino's familiarity with Bessarion's apology, see McNair, 'Cristoforo Landino's *De anima*'.

37. Hankins, *Plato*, I, 347.

38. On Plato's authority in divine matters, see Hankins, *Plato*, I, 95. See also Ficino, *Theologia platonica*, lib. VI, c. 1, in *Opera omnia*, I, 770; Palmieri, *Vita civile*, lib. I, § 132, ed. Belloni, p. 40.

39. Quoted in Field, 'John Argyropoulos', p. 316. For Argyropoulos' likely influence on Landino's presentation of the Platonic doctrine of Ideas, see Gilson, 'Plato, the *platonici*', p. 38.

40. Gilson, 'Plato, the *platonici*', n. 79, p. 51.

41. For references to Aristotle, see *Comento*, IV, 2077–78 (see also notes 50–52 below).

42. *Comento*, I, 266–67, 178–88; the passage is modelled on Landino's *prolusione* to his lectures on Dante, see Cardini, *SCT*, I, 53.

43. For an overview, see Gilson, 'Medieval Science'.

44. For compilation in earlier Dante commentators, see above ch. 1, note 68. On later 'scientific' readings of Dante in the Florentine Academy, see Barbi, *Dante nel Cinquecento*, pp. 180–235.

45. See above ch. 2, notes 5 and 72, and ch. 3, p. 118. For Bruni's comments, see *Dialogi*, lib. I, § 44, ed. Baldassarri, pp. 255–56; *Vita di Dante*, ed. Viti, pp. 549, 551.

46. For Landino and geography, see *Comento*, II, 670, 196–97 (citing Ptolemy's *Geographia*); III, 1139, 19–24; III, 1594, 4–7. See also Gentile, 'Dante', pp. 34–39. More generally, see Larner, 'The Church'; Bessi, 'Appunti'. Francesco Berlinghieri's *terza rima* adaptation of Ptolemy's *Geographia*, printed in 1482 by Niccolò Tedesco,

bristles with echoes of Dante. For studies of scientific interests in Quattrocento Florence, see above ch. 5, note 29.

47. The first translation of Ptolemy's *Geographia* from the Greek was made by Jacopo Angeli da Scarperia between 1406 and 1410 from a text brought to Florence by Manuel Chrysoloras. Petrarch, Boccaccio, Salutati and Niccoli all show interest in Pliny's *Historia naturalis* and its popularity amongst humanists increased markedly (for doctrinal, antiquarian, and philological reasons) during the Quattrocento.

48. Strabo's *Geographia* was translated by Guarino Veronese, a pupil of Chrysoloras, *c.* 1453–58 and printed in 1469; see Fryde, *Studies in Humanism*, pp. 72–82. The works of Diodorus Siculus were brought to Italy by Giovanni Aurispa in the 1450s; on their translation, see Fryde, *Studies in Humanism*, pp. 27–28. For Landino's references, see Procaccioli, IV, *ad indicem*.

49. See e.g. *Comento*, II, 677, 38–47; II, 684, 8–12; II, 783, 18–21; II, 847, 78–80; III, 1076, 19–27; III, 1090, 11–15 (physics); I, 301, 37–39, 43–64; II, 782–83, 1–26; II, 838, 57–77; III, 1067, 30–46; III, 1107, 13–24, 1110–11, 5–44; III, 1179, 23–53 (astronomy). On meteorology and medicine, see notes 52, 54, and 60. For other subjects, see III, 1044, 15–17; III, 156–57, 16–46; III, 1190, 17–20 (mineralogy); III, 1272, 16–17 (perspective); II, 839, 86–88 (chronography).

50. For Albumasar, see *Comento*, II, 871, 23–24 (Pietro, *Inf.* XXV, 80 *ad loc.*); IV, 1589, 3–5 (Pietro, *Par.* II, 58–63 *ad loc.*). Further Aristotelian references and/or quotations in Landino taken from the first redaction of Pietro's commentary *ad locum* include: *Inf.* III, 16–18 (I, 381, 29–30); *Purg.* XVI, 73–75, 88–90 (III, 1294, 32–42 and 1296, 27–28); *Purg.* XXVII, 97–105 (III, 1448, 42–45).

51. On alchemy, see *Comento*, II, 949, 21–46, which reproduces almost verbatim Buti, I, 751–52, including reference to a Pseudo-Aristotelian work, *De mineralibus* (Buti is himself dependent on Lana, *Commento*, I, 452). Further Aristotelian references derived from Buti *ad locum* include: *Comento*, II, 514, 4–6 (Buti, I, 216); II, 612, 1–3 (Buti, I, 312); II, 816–18, 17–76 (Buti, I, 592–93; this gloss is greatly expanded by Landino); III, 1120, 13–20 (Buti, II, 107); III, 1296, 14–16 (Buti, II, 377); IV, 1684, 20–23 (Buti, III, 257); IV, 1617, 5 (Buti, III, 110); IV, 1692, 5–6 (Buti, III, 271).

52. See (a) astrology: *Comento*, I, 320–21, 54–68 (Benvenuto, I, 55–56, 58); II, 781, 18–20 (Benvenuto, II, 90–91); III, 1349, 29–31 (Benvenuto, III, 520); (b) meteorology: III, 1128, 1–12 (Benvenuto, III, 161); (c) medicine: I, 441, 237–41 (Benvenuto, I, 181); II, 559, 12–14 (Benvenuto, I, 319); IV, 2023, 40–41 (Benvenuto, V, 521); (d) astronomical instruments: III, 1104–05, 55–64 (Benvenuto, III, 122). For references to Aristotle and Aristotelian doctrine derived from Benvenuto, see *Comento*, I, 282, 21 (Benvenuto, I, 22); I, 354, 57–58 (Benvenuto, I, 91); II, 491, 4–5 (Benvenuto, I, 245–46); II, 610, 32–36 (Benvenuto, I, 374); II, 632, 10–12 (Benvenuto, I, 406); II, 687, 20–21 (Benvenuto, I, 502); II, 821, 33–36 (Benvenuto, II, 163); III, 1079, 26–27 (Benvenuto, III, 77); III, 1211, 17–19 (Benvenuto, III, 276); III, 1547, 27–29 (Benvenuto, IV, 275); IV, 1710–11, 28–33 (Benvenuto, V, 28); IV, 1756, 8–10 (Benvenuto, III, 104); IV, 1973, 15 (Benvenuto, V, 436). For Albert the Great, see *Comento*, II, 663, 12–16 (Benvenuto, I, 473–74); II, 685–86, 27–50 (Benvenuto, I,

566); II, 722–23, 1–21 (Benvenuto, I, 566); II, 851, 37–39 (Benvenuto, II, 206); III, 1272, 8–14 (Benvenuto, III, 405–06); III, 1549, 29–31 (Benvenuto, IV, 278). There is no precedent for Landino's reference to Albert on breathing in III, 1074, 3–9.

53. On Landino's *De anima*, see Field, *The Origins*, pp. 256–59; McNair, *Cristoforo Landino on the Human Soul*. Its purpose is to gather Platonic, Aristotelian, and Stoic views in an encyclopaedic and elegant form, see *De anima*, proem (eds.), Paoli and Gentile, p. 2, and *Comento*, II, 580–81, 82–89. For direct use of this dialogue in the *Comento*, see *Comento*, IV, 2100–01.

54. For medical glosses, see esp. *Comento*, I, 317, 101–06 (veins); II, 559, 12–14 (nerves, following Benvenuto, I, 319); II, 843–44, 22–31; III, 1074, 3–9 (lungs/breathing); II, 598, 43–55 (smell); II, 693, 50–64 (smell; cf. *De anima*, II, 93–94); II, 816–18, 17–89 (internal senses; cf. *De anima*, II, 98–111); III, 1305–06, 2–22 (cf. *De anima*, II, 98–101, 105–06 and III, 37–38); IV, 1927, 8–11 (eye membranes; cf. *De anima*, II, 61–62). On the coction of food, see *Comento*, III, 1414, 22–50; cf. Albert, *De anima*, II.2.8, ed. Stroick, pp. 92–94. Other medical glosses include: I, 406, 41–44 (sleep); II, 543, 24–25 (pallor); II, 769, 9–14 (paralysis); II, 873, 83–87 (yawning); II, 882–83, 30–56 (dreams, cf. Buti, I, 669–70); II, 959, 1–14 (dropsy); II, 1003, 18–76 (fasting); II, 959, 5–7; III, 1162, 11–17 (complexion); III, 1202, 6–7 (purging); III, 1502, 32–35 (fear); III, 1388, 10–13 (drunkenness); IV, 2023, 40–41 (*letargo*). The discussion of *letargo* is wholly derived from Benvenuto (V, 521), that of paralysis in part (II, 66); the other passages provide a more technical physiological analysis than earlier Dante commentators.

55. See *Comento*, II, 693, 50–64; cf. Landino, *De anima*, II, 93–94.

56. McNair, *Cristoforo Landino on the Human Soul*, n. 130, p. 166; and see further ibid., pp. 165–78. The Albertine source is *De anima*, II.3.29, ed. Stroick, pp. 140–41.

57. Landino, *De anima*, II, 111–13. For the likely source, see Albert, *De anima*, II.4.7 and III.1.1–3, ed. Stroick, pp. 156–58, 166–69.

58. *Comento*, II, 818, 64–70, 74–77. On the episode in Dante, see Boyde, *Perception and Passion*, pp. 234–40. On the internal senses, see also *Comento*, III, 1305–06, 2–22; III, 1321, 10–17.

59. See note 101 below for another original medical gloss.

60. On meteorology, see *Comento*, II, 558, 29–36 (wind; following in part Boccaccio, *Esposizioni*, ed. Padoan, p. 481; Buti, I, 262, but with supplementary references); II, 667–68, 87–165 (on lightning); II, 839–40, 110–18 (frost); III, 1129, 17–19 (air; cf. Benvenuto, III, 161–62); III, 1366–67, 8–16 (rain, hail, snow, dew, and frost; cf. Benvenuto, IV, 8). On animal lore, see *Comento*, I, 298, 41, 51; I, 459, 2–3; II, 802–03, 14–56; II, 815, 65–72; II, 855, 1–20; III, 1304, 10–15; III, 1403, 1–4. All these glosses are based upon Pliny (see Procaccioli's apparatus *ad locum*), as are several of Landino's references to minerals and metals.

61. See Gilson 'Tradition', pp. 49–51.

62. Almost all the Trecento commentators mention the importance of Dante's astrological learning and its place in the *Comedy*. For astrological material in miniatures to the *Comedy*, see *Illuminated Manuscripts*, I, 98, 104 and plates at II, 446a, 456c, 477a.

63. *Comento*, III, 1335, 19–20; cf. Pietro, ed. Nannucci, p. 429.
64. *Comento*, IV, 1882, 9–13; cf. Bartholomew the Englishman, *De proprietatibus rerum*, VIII.II, ed. Richter, p. 390.
65. See Gilson, 'Tradition', pp. 53–54.
66. Pietro, ed. Nannucci, p. 42: 'ut ostendat se poetam instructum in diversis, vult nunc se ostendere in judiciis astrorum scientificatum'; see also ibid., pp. 43, 532.
67. *Comento*, I, 320–21, 54–68.
68. On conjunctionist theory, see Garin, *Lo zodiaco*, ch. 1.
69. See Albert, *De causis et proprietatibus elementorum*, I.2.9, ed. Hossfeld, p. 78. On Landino's familiarity with this Albertine work, see below note 76. Landino mentions triplicities via Albert in *Comento*, II, 838, 81.
70. On prophecy in later fifteenth-century Florence, see Chastel, *Art et humanisme*, pp. 344–46; Garin, *Lo zodiaco*, p. 86; Hankins, *Plato*, I, 173–74.
71. Ficino, *Contra la pestilenza*, c. 23, p .4. See also c. 2, p. 3 where pestilence is said to be caused by 'constellationi maligne, massime dalle coniuntioni di Marte con Saturno ne i segni humani' ('malignant constellations, above all by the conjunctions of Mars with Saturn in the human signs').
72. Hankins, *Plato*, I, 278, 302–04.
73. On Paul of Middelburg, see Ficino, *Le Lettere*, ed. Gentile, introd., pp. xli–xlii.
74. *Comento*, I, 446–47, 81–91.
75. See esp. Ficino, *Disputatio contra iudicium astrologorum* (*c.* 1477), in *Supplementum Ficinianum*, ed. Kristeller, II, 29: 'celum non est causa proxima peccatum' ('the heavens are not the proximate cause of sin'). For the concern with free will, see *Disputatio*, pp. 12, 23, 71–74.
76. There are direct correspondences in phrasing, argumentation, and examples between *Comento*, IV, 1796, 22–46 and Albert, *De causis et proprietatibus elementorum*, I.2.4, pp. 67–68; see also *Comento*, II, 839, 86–88 and Albert, I.2.9, p. 78.
77. Landino's abbreviated commentary to the *Paradiso* is in part related to the fact that he discusses at length key exegetical devices and doctrinal matters on the first occasion that comment is required (see Buti, III, 79 and 822 for a similar approach).
78. Dante, *Par.* III, 50–57; IV, 34–48; VI, 112–13; IX, 32–33; XVII, 31–33; XXI, 13–15.
79. See esp. Buti, III, 82: 'E perchè qui si fa menzione delle influenzie dei pianeti, dirò in ciascun pianeto le influenzie sue, secondo che pone Abbumasar [sic], trattato VII del suo introduttorio' ('And because here he mentions the influences of the planets, I will state the influences of each, following what Albumasar writes in tractate VII of his *Introductorium*').
80. The principal *chiose* are: *Comento*, IV, 1603, 15–25 (Moon); IV, 1638–39, 55–76; IV, 1681–82, 50–71 (Mercury); IV, 1711–13, 1–62 (Sun); IV, 1767–68, 15–33 (Mars); IV, 1826–27, 27–49 (Jupiter); IV, 1863–64, 45–80 (Saturn).
81. See Gatti, 'Il mito'.
82. On Landino and Toscanelli, see Cardini, *SCT*, II, 135–37. Memnon, a King of the Ethiopians and son of Tithonus and Aurora, was killed by Achilles at Troy; he later became associated with the Colossus of Amenophis near the Egyptian city

of Thebes. The musical qualities of the Colossus are mentioned in some classical sources (e.g. Tacitus, *Annales*, II.61, ed. Jackson, p. 490).

83. *Comento*, II, 657–58, 57–70.

84. Boccaccio, *Esposizioni*, XIII, i, §§ 103–04, 106, ed. Padoan, pp. 627–28; Benvenuto, I, 462–63.

85. See Gilson, 'Tradition', pp. 71–72.

86. Pietro and Benvenuto sometimes provide more extensive classicizing glosses than Landino; see e.g. Pietro, *Par.* XVII, 55–57 *ad loc.* and Benvenuto, *Purg.* XXVIII, 139–48 *ad loc.* On the classical material in Pietro, see Sabbadini, *Le scoperte*, II, 97–105 and the studies by Chiamenti and Mazzoni in ch. 1, note 70.

87. For Boethius mediated via Buti, see *Comento*, III, 1262, 37–38 (Buti, II, 232); IV, 1575, 9–10 (Buti, III, 24); IV, 1597, 15–16 (Buti, III, 68); IV, 1599, 15–18 (Buti, III, 70); IV, 1752, 34–35 (Buti, III, 395); IV, 1884, 4 (Buti, III, 622–23); IV, 1905, 11–12 (Buti, III, 663); IV, 1942, 27–28 (Buti, III, 723); IV, 1964, 10–12 (Buti, III, 761). For three Boethian references derived from Pietro, see *Comento*, II, 504, 21–22 and 507–08, 130 (Pietro, *Inf.* VII, 67–96 *ad loc.*); IV, 1564, 26–27 (Pietro, *Par.* I, 1–3 *ad loc.*). For Juvenal via Pietro *ad locum*, see *Par.* XI, 70–72 (IV, 1729–30, 36–39); *Par.* XXIV, 1–3 (IV, 1907, 14–15); *Par.* XXXIII, 34–36 (IV, 2017–18, 25–30). For historical material mediated by Benvenuto, compare the respective commentaries on *Par.* VI, and *Comento*, III, 663, 11–15 (Benvenuto, I, 473–74). These examples are not found in Proccaccioli's apparatus.

88. For (select) examples, see (a) Virgil: *Comento*, II, 512, 26–27 (Buti, I, 216–17); II, 921, 11–14 (Pietro, *Inf.* XXVIII, 1–3 *ad loc.*); III, 1076, 7–9 (Buti, II, 46); III, 1108, 53–54 (Buti, II, 86); III, 1151, 15 (Benvenuto, III, 194; Buti, II, 251); (b) Cicero: III, 1103, 5–6 (Pietro, *Purg.* IV, 31–33 *ad loc.*); (c) Horace: II, 338, 4–5 (Benvenuto, I, 79); IV, 1932, 2–4; (Benvenuto, V, 384). See also (a) Lucan: II, 471, 22–24 (Pietro, *Inf.* VI, 25–27 *ad loc.*); II, 770, 16–17 (Pietro, *Inf.* XX, 22–24 *ad loc.*); II, 891, 21–23 (Pietro, *Inf.* XXVI, 52–54 *ad loc.*); III, 1370, 15–18 (Buti, II, 509); IV, 1729–30, 34–36 (Pietro, *Par.* XI, 70–72 *ad loc.*); IV, 1790, 18–20 (Pietro, *Par.* XVI, 10–12 *ad loc.*; Buti, III, 468); IV, 1883, 13–17 (Pietro, *Par.* XXII, 133–35 *ad loc.*, but Landino also refers to Cicero); (b) Ovid: II, 883, 57–58 (Pietro, *Inf.* XXVI, 7–9 *ad loc.*); II, 905, 25–29 (Pietro, *Inf.* XXVII, 7–12 *ad loc.*; Landino also quotes Juvenal and Propertius); III, 247–48, 18–19, 30–35 (Pietro, *Purg.* XIII, 46–48 *ad loc.* for all three quotations); (c) Claudian: II, 510, 228–30 (Pietro, *Inf.* VII, 88–90 *ad loc.*); (d) Sallust: II, 863, 16–17 (Buti, I, 642); (e) Seneca: II, 814, 22–26 (Buti, I, 589, but with the 'Florentine' addition of Bruni); II, 963, 33–35 (Pietro, *Inf.* XXX, 97–99 *ad loc.*). These examples are not found in Procaccioli's apparatus.

89. On humanist interest in patristic writers, see Fubini, *L'umanesimo italiano*, pp. 137–81; Kristeller, *Renaissance Thought*, pp. 66–81; Trinkaus, *In Our Image*. But for examples that derive from early commentators, see (a) John Chrysostom: *Comento*, III, 1194, 67–69 (Benvenuto, III, 270); IV, 1566, 83–86 (Pietro, *Par.* I, 4–6 *ad loc.*); (b) Jerome: I, 343, 175–77 (Benvenuto, I, 84); III, 1248, 41–42 (Pietro, *Purg.* XIII, 46–48 *ad loc.*); IV, 1611, 13–16 (Pietro, *Par.* III, 118–20 *ad loc.*); (c) Gregory the Great: III, 1218, 83–85 (Benvenuto, III, 30). For multiple patristic authorities

mediated through Pietro and Benvenuto, see e.g. III, 1079, 16–35 (Benvenuto, II, 76–77) and III, 1145, 39–43 (Pietro, *Purg.* VI, 115–17 *ad loc.* for biblical, patristic, and classical quotations). The majority of Landino's biblical quotations in the *Comento* come from Pietro. These examples are not found in Procaccioli's apparatus.

90. See *Comento*, IV, 2050 and 2066 for references to Boccaccio and Salutati; see further Procaccioli, introd., p. 33. The *Genealogie* is mentioned favourably by Bruni and Poggio; the full extent of its influence, on Landino and other Italian humanists, is yet to be investigated, but see Tomè Marcassa, 'Giovanni Tortelli e la sua fortuna umanistica'.

91. Landino shows independence from the Dante commentary tradition in his use of quotations from Horace, Persius, Juvenal, Plautus, and Terence.

92. For Homer, see e.g. *Comento*, II, 773, 30–33 (Benvenuto, II, 74); III, 1338, 18–22 (Benvenuto, III, 591). See also II, 978 and 979, 10–11, 9–10 (Boccaccio, *Genealogie*, lib. IV,c. 18 and lib. x, c. 47, ed. Romano, I, 177, 518); III, 1231, 19–20 and 24–27 (*Genealogia*, lib. IV,c. 18, loc. cit).

93. References in order: *Comento*, IV, 2091 (Hesiod: ten direct references); II, 834, 9–21 (Lucian). For Diodorus and Dion, see notes 48 and 106.

94. On Traversari's translation, see Gigante, 'Ambrogio Traversari interprete'; Sottili, 'Il laerzio'. Landino mentions Diogenes by name only once in *Comento*, II, 482, 17–19 (see Gilson, 'Plato, the *platonici*', p. 14 and n. 44), but Procaccioli (*Comento*, IV, 2054) suggests over thirty parallels in his apparatus.

95. In addition to the studies listed above in ch. 2 note 1, see Sabbadini, *Le scoperte*; Franceschini, *Giovanni Aurispa e la sua biblioteca*.

96. On Andronico Callisto, see *DBI* 3, 162–63.

97. On the use of Virgil, see e.g. *Comento*, II, 763, 25–26; II, 830, 3–4 (rhetorical illustration); III, 1165, 20–25 (*sententia*); II, 780, 22–23; II, 878, 79–82 (word choice).

98. Ibid., IV, 1850, 25–29: 'È certamente maravigliosa phantasia in questo poeta el quale in forma narra la sua fictione, che fa quasi che lo impossibile paia credibile; et molto è simile allo ingegno del poeta Ovidio, el quale nelle sue monstruose transformationi, fa le chose quasi verisimili' ('There is certainly marvellous imagination in this poet who narrates his fiction in a form that makes even the impossible seem credible; and he is very similar in genius to the poet Ovid, who, in his monstrous transformations makes things almost believable'). Dante's strong affinities with Ovid have been the focus of much recent Dante scholarship, see esp. Picone, 'L'Ovidio di Dante'.

99. Ibid., II, 481, 38–44 (classical references noted in Procaccioli, II, 481).

100. Ibid., IV, 1569, 51–66.

101. For scientific reasons against Ugolino's cannibalism, see *Comento*, II, 1002–04, 13–75 (the passage is without precedent in Dante commentary literature and it shows the full extent of Landino's familiarity with medical doctrine). On the Virgilian parallels, see II, 1004–05, 79–114.

102. See e.g. *Comento*, II, 746, 46–64 (adulation, citing Juvenal, Diogenes, Plato, and Cicero); II, 822–23, 29–43 (hypocrisy, quoting Plautus, with four separate passages

from Terence and Cicero); II, 985, 47–53 (language); II, 767–78, 1–41 (divination); II, 890, 4–8 (funeral rites). See also III, 1140–41, 21–36 (slavery); III, 1104, 38–52 (quadrant); III, 1297–98, 4–6 (law). In such passages, Pliny is often the principal source.

103. Ibid., II, 836–38, 1–77: 'chiamando Danthe gennaio la gioventù dell'anno non parla secondo gl'astrologi, ma secondo la consuetudine de' Romani' (at lines 76–77); see further III, 1104, 38–52. Landino's earlier letter is in Lentzen, *Studien*, pp. 213–22.

104. Ibid., III, 1287–90, 9–107: 'Et perché mi pare chosa non inutile, et assai gioconda, intendere apuncto e dì del mese notati dagl'antichi, ripeteremo alquanto più di lontano con che ordine et numero di dì gl'antichi segnassino e loro anni' (at lines 13–15).

105. Ibid., II, 802–03, 21–56: 'Ho scripto queste poche chose di molte più tosto invitato da sì nobile natura d'animale, che perché giudicassi esser necessario in questo luogo' ('I have written these few things out of many, being drawn to do so by the very noble nature of the animal rather than because I judged it to be necessary in this place') (lines 54–55).

106. Ibid., I, 429, 21–24: 'Ma Dione Chrisostomo, sommo philosopho et diligente investighatore dell'antichità, dimostra et per le historie de gli Egyptii, et per molti segni, che non Acchille Hectorre, ma Hectorre Achille uccidessi' ('But Dion Chrysostomos, the great philosopher and diligent investigator of antiquity shows from the histories of the Egyptians and for many other reasons that Achilles did not kill Hector but rather Hector killed Achilles'). For Dion in similar contexts, see I, 456–57, 82, and 106–07; II, 955, 61–64. For a further example of classical updating not found in earlier commentators, see IV, 2023, 44–49.

107. Poliziano, *Commento inedito alle Selve*, ed. Cesarini Martinelli, p. 8: 'Sed et Florentinus Dantes, poeta alioqui excellentissimus, et Tolosanum falso hunc prodidit' ('But the Florentine Dante, a poet most excellent in other respects, wrongly wrote that he was Tolosan'). See further Delcorno Branca, 'Percorsi', pp. 377–80. Dante's 'errore' is also noted by Bartolomeo Fonzio, see Trinkaus (ed.), 'A Humanist's Image', pp. 143–44. For Landino's responsiveness (at least in part) to Poliziano's philology, see the modification of the medieval spelling Virgilius to Vergilius in his 1488 edition and commentary on the *Aeneid* (noted by Cardini, *La critica*, n. 1, p. 312).

108. *Comento*, III, 1371, 28–34.

109. Ibid., III, 1371, 38–48: '*ma caddi in via con la seconda soma*: *i.* non decti perfectione al secondo libro, che fu l'Acchilleide' ('*but I fell along the way with the second burden*: that is, I did not bring to perfection the second book which was the *Achilleid*'). For Petrarch's critique, see above ch. 1, p. 40 and note 57. See also Luca Carlo Rossi, 'Prospezioni filologiche', pp. 215–16; Sabbadini, *Le scoperte*, II, 186–88, 252–53.

110. *Comento*, II, 650, 65–82.

111. Ibid., II, 775, 33–34: 'Edificò adunque Mantua Ochno, et da Mantho sua madre gli decte el nome. Benché Danthe alquanto varii la historia chome leggerai ne' sequenti versi' ('Thus, Ocnus founded Mantua, and named it after Manto his

mother, although Dante somewhat varies the story, as you will read in the following lines').

112. Ibid., 11, 776, 1–8, 10–12.

CONCLUSION

1. See esp. the works by Ascoli, Barański, and Iannucci cited in Introduction, note 17. See also Taylor, 'A Text'; however, I disagree with Taylor's view that Dante necessarily bends the reader to his will.

2. Villani, *Nuova Cronica*, lib. x, c. 136, ed. Porta, 1, 338. See also ch. 1, notes 12, 17, 31, 79; ch. 2, note 26; ch. 3, notes 32–33.

3. For examples of later Florentine interest in the *Ottimo Commento*, see Bruschi, 'Ser Piero Bonaccorsi', pp. 23, 30; McCormick, 'Goro Dati's Transcription'. On Lana's popularity, see above Introduction, notes 27–29.

4. For reprintings, see Richardson, 'Editing Dante's *Commedia*', pp. 255–57. Landino's *Comento* was one of the most reprinted fifteenth- and sixteenth-century humanist books. Landino's own reception merits further study; for discussion and further bibliography, see Procaccioli, introd., pp. 92–104.

5. The topic merits further exploration in relation to individuals such as Giovanni Nesi, Benedetto Luschino, Paolo Orlandini, Francesco Gerini, Tommaso Sardi (see ch. 4, note 55), and Zanobi Ceffini. Another Savonarolan with strong Dantean interests was Girolamo Benivieni, who edited the 1506 Giuntine edition of the poem; see Roush, 'Dante'. For general background, see Polizzotto, *The Elect Nation*.

6. Chaucer, *Legend of Good Women*, prologue, l. 86. I take Chaucer to mean the original form and order of words as distinct from its commentary. For other resonances and further discussion, see Delany, *The Naked Text*, esp. pp. 118–23.

7. For Bembo's celebrated broadside against Dante's style and content, see above Introduction, note 51. By contrast, one notes how Landino avoids using 'rime' with regard to Dante's *Comedy* (ch. 5, p. 184) and his very different comments on Dante's varied lexicon (ch. 6, p. 197).

Select bibliography

PRIMARY SOURCES

Accolti, Benedetto, *Dialogus de praestantia virorum sui aevi*, ed. Gustavo Camillo Galletti, in *Philippi Villani liber de origine civitatis Florentiae et eiusdem famosis civibus* (Florence: Mazzoni, 1847), pp. 105–28

Albert the Great, *De anima*, ed. Clemens Stroick (Münster: Aschendorff, 1968)
  De causis et proprietatibus elementorum, ed. Paul Hossfeld (Münster: Aschendorff, 1980)

Alberti, Leon Battista, *'Grammatichetta' e altri scritti sul volgare*, ed. Giuseppe Patota (Rome: Salerno, 1996)
  Opere volgari, ed. Cecil Grayson, 3 vols. (Bari: Laterza, 1960)
  La prima grammatica della lingua volgare. La Grammatichetta Vaticana Cod. Vat. Reg. Lat. 1370, ed. Cecil Grayson (Bologna: Commissione per i testi di lingua, 1964)
  Rime e versioni poetiche, ed. Guglielmo Gorni (Naples: Ricciardi, 1975)

Anonimo Fiorentino, *Commento alla Divina Commedia d'Anonimo Fiorentino del secolo XIV*, ed. Pietro Fanfani, 3 vols. (Bologna: Romagnoli, 1866–74)

Anonymous, Latin defence of poetry, ed. David Robey, 'Virgil's Statue at Mantua and the Defence of Poetry. An Unpublished Letter of 1397', *Rinascimento* II ser./9 (1969), 183–203

Aristotle, *De arte poetica*, ed. Erse Valgimigli (Bruges–Paris: Desclée de Brouwer, 1953)

Augustine, *De civitate Dei*, in *CCSL*, vols. 47–48 (Turnhout: Brepols, 1955)

Bartholomew the Englishman, *De proprietatibus rerum*, ed. Wolfgang Richter (Frankfurt, 1601; facsimile repr., Frankfurt: Minerva, 1964)

Bembo, Pietro, *Prose e rime*, ed. Carlo Dionisotti (Turin: UTET, 1960)

Benvenuto da Imola, *Comentum super Dantis Aldigherij Comoediam*, ed. J. P. Lacaita, 5 vols. (Florence: Barbèra, 1887)

Boccaccio, Giovanni, *Tutte le opere di Giovanni Boccaccio*, ed. Vittore Branca *et al.* 12 vols. (Milan: Mondadori, 1964–)
  Genealogie deorum gentilium libri, ed. Vincenzo Romano, 2 vols. (Bari: Laterza, 1951)

Bonaccorsi, Piero, *Cammino di Dante*, ed. G. Bruschi, 'Ser Piero Bonaccorsi e il suo *Cammino di Dante*', *Il Propugnatore*, 4 (1891), I, 5–38; II, 308–48

Bracciolini, Poggio, *Opera omnia*, ed. Riccardo Fubini, 4 vols. (Basel, 1538; facsimile repr., Turin: Bottega d'Erasmo, 1964–69)

Select bibliography

Bruni, Leonardo, *Dialogi ad Petrum Histrum*, ed. Stefano Ugo Baldassarri (Florence: SISMEL, 1995)

Epistolae, in *Leonardi Bruni Aretini epistolarum libri VIII*, ed. Lorenzo Mehus, 2 vols. (Florence, 1741)

Historiaa Florentini populi libri XII, eds., Emilio Santini and Carmine di Pierro (Città di Castello: Lapi, 1914)

Laudatio Florentine urbis, ed. Stefano Ugo Baldassarri (Florence: SISMEL, 2000)

De militia, ed. Charles Calvert Bayley, in *War and Society in Renaissance Florence: The 'De militia' of Leonardo Bruni* (Toronto: University of Toronto Press, 1961)

Opere letterarie e politiche di Leonardo Bruni, ed. Paolo Viti (Turin: UTET, 1996)

Cicero, Marcus Tullius, *De inventione*, ed. H. M. Hubbell (London: Heinemann, 1968; 1st edn 1949)

De oratore, ed. E. W. Sutton and H. Rackham, 2 vols. (London: Heinemann, 1942)

Oratio pro Archia poeta, ed. N. H. Watts (London: Heinemann, 1923)

Compagni, Dino, *La cronica di Dino Compagni delle cose occorrenti ne' tempi suoi*, ed. Isidoro del Lungo (Città di Castello: Lapi, 1907–16)

Dante Alighieri, *La 'Commedia' secondo l'antica vulgata*, ed. Giorgio Petrocchi, 4 vols. (Milan: Mondadori, 1966–67)

Convivio, eds. Cesare Vasoli and Domenico De Robertis, in *Opere minori* (Milan–Naples: Ricciardi, 1988), I/ii

De vulgari eloquentia, ed. Pier Vincenzo Mengaldo, in *Opere minori* (Milan–Naples: Ricciardi, 1979), II, 1–237

The Divine Comedy of Dante Alighieri, volume 1 Inferno/volume 2 Purgatorio, ed. and trans. Robert M. Durling (New York–Oxford, 1996 and 2003)

Egloge, ed. Enzo Cecchini, in *Opere minori*, II, 647–89

Epistole, eds. Arsenio Frugoni and Giorgio Brugnoli, in *Opere minori*, II, 505–643

Monarchia, ed. Bruno Nardi, in *Opere minori*, II, 241–503

Rime, ed. Gianfranco Contini, in *Opere minori* (Milan–Naples: Ricciardi, 1984), I/i, 249–552

Vita nuova, ed. Domenico De Robertis, in *Opere minori*, I/i, 1–247

Dante: The Critical Heritage, ed. Michael Caesar (London and New York: Routledge, 1989)

del Nero, Bernardo, *Monarchia (volgarizzamento)*, ed. Prue Shaw, 'Il volgarizzamento inedito della *Monarchia*', *SD* 47 (1970), 59–224

Domenico da Prato, 'Prefazione', in *LTQ*, I, 511–14

Il Duomo di Firenze: Documenti sulla decorazione della chiesa e del campanile tratti dall'archivio dell'opera, ed. Giovanni Poggi, 2 vols. (Florence: Edizioni Medicea, 1988; 1st edn 1909)

Ficino, Marsilio, *Contra la pestilenza* (Florence, 1576)

Le Lettere I. Epistolarum familiarum liber I, ed. Sebastiano Gentile (Florence: Olschki, 1990)

El Libro dell'Amore, ed. Sandra Niccoli (Florence: Olschki, 1987)

Monarchia (volgarizzamento), ed. Prue Shaw, 'La versione ficiniana della *Monarchia*', *SD* 51 (1978), 298–408

Opera omnia, 2 vols. (Basel, 1576; facsimile repr., Turin: Bottega d'Erasmo, 1959, 1983)

De raptu Pauli/Il rapimento di Paolo, in *PLQ*, ed. Eugenio Garin, pp. 933–1009

Supplementum Ficinianum, ed. Paul Oskar Kristeller, 2 vols. reprint (Florence: Olschki, 1973; 1st edn, 1938)

Filelfo, Francesco, vernacular writings, ed. Giovanni Benaducci, 'Prose e poesie volgari di Francesco Filelfo', *Atti e memorie della Reale Deputazione di storia patria per le provincie delle Marche* 5 (1901), xli–262

Fonzio, Bartolomeo, orations, ed. Charles Trinkaus, 'A Humanist's Image of Humanism: The Inaugural Orations of Bartolommeo della Fonte', *Studies in the Renaissance* 7 (1960), 90–147

Francesco da Buti, *Commento di Francesco da Buti sopra la 'Divina Comedia' di Dante Allighieri*, ed. Crescentino Giannini, 3 vols. reprint (Pisa: Nistri–Lischi, 1989; 1st edn 1858–62)

Giovanni Gherardi da Prato, *Il Paradiso degli Alberti*, ed. Antonio Lanza (Rome: Salerno, 1975)

Trattato d'una angelica cosa mostrata per una divotissima visione, ed. Wesselofsky, I/2, 385–435

Philomena (partial edn), ed. Wesselofsky, I/2, 109–92

Guido da Pisa, *Expositiones et Glose super Comediam Dantis*, ed. Vincent Cioffari (Albany: University of New York Press, 1974)

Horace, Flaccus Quintus, *Ars poetica*, ed. H. Rushton Fairclough (London: Heinemann, 1929)

Illuminated Manuscripts of the Divine Comedy, eds. Peter Brieger, Millard Meiss, and Charles S. Singleton, 2 vols. (New York–Princeton: Princeton University Press, 1969)

Jacopo Alighieri, *Chiose all' 'Inferno'*, ed. Saverio Bellomo (Padua: Antenore, 1990)

Jacopo della Lana, *Comedia di Dante degli Allagherii col commento di Jacopo di Giovanni della Lana bolognese*, ed. L. Scarabelli, 3 vols. (Milan: Civelli, 1864–65)

Landino, Cristoforo, *De anima*, eds. A. Paoli and G. Gentile, in *Annali delle università toscane* 34 (1915), 1–50 and n.s. 1 (1916), 1–138 and n.s. 2 (1917), 1–96

Comento sopra la Comedia, ed. Paolo Procaccioli, 4 vols. (Rome: Salerno, 2001)

Disputationes Camaldulenses, ed. Peter Lohe (Florence: Sansoni, 1980)

Scritti critici e teorici, ed. Roberto Cardini, 2 vols. (Rome: Bulzoni, 1974)

Lirici toscani del Quattrocento, ed. Antonio Lanza (Rome: Bulzoni, 1973)

Macrobius, *Commentarium in Somnium Scipionis*, ed. J. Willis (Leipzig: Teubner, 1963)

Manetti, Antonio, *Notizia di Antonio Manetti a Giovanni Niccolò Cavalcanti di Guido di messer Cavalcante suo consorte sotto forma di visione*, in *Operette istoriche inedite e edite di Antonio Manetti matematico ed architetto fiorentino*, ed. Gaetano Milanesi (Florence, 1887), pp. 171–80

Manetti, Gianozzo, *Vita Dantis poetae florentini*, in *Le vite di Dante*, ed. Solerti, pp. 113–51

Maramauro, Guglielmo, *Expositione sopra l'Inferno di Dante Alighieri*, eds. Pier Giacomo Pisoni and Saverio Bellomo (Padua: Antenore, 1996)

Select bibliography

Martial, Marcus Valerius, *Epigrammata*, ed. Walter C. A. Ker, 2 vols. rev. edn (London: Heinemann, 1968; 1st edn 1920)

Medici, Lorenzo de', *Tutte le opere*, ed. Paolo Orvieto, 2 vols. (Rome: Salerno, 1992)

Michelangelo Buonarroti, *Rime e lettere*, ed. Paola Mastrocola (Turin: UTET, 1992)

Ottimo Commento (Andrea Lancia), *L'Ottimo commento della Divina Commedia. Testo inedito d'un contemporaneo di Dante*, ed. A. Torri, 3 vols. (Pisa: Capurro, 1829)

Palmieri, Matteo, *Città di Dio*, ed. Margaret Rooke, *Smith College Studies in Modern Languages* 8 (1926–27) and 9 (1928)

    Vita civile, ed. Gino Belloni (Florence: Sansoni, 1985)

    De temporibus, ed. Gino Scaramella (Città di Castello: Lapi, 1906–15)

Petrarca, Francesco, *Canzoniere*, ed. Marco Santagata, 3rd edn (Milan: Mondadori, 1999)

    Letters on Familiar Matters. Rerum familiarium libri XVII–XXIV, trans. Aldo S. Bernardo (Baltimore–London: Johns Hopkins University Press, 1985)

    Rerum familiares libri XXIV, ed. Vittorio Rossi, 4 vols. (Florence: Sansoni, 1933–42)

    Rerum memorandarum libri, ed. Giuseppe Billanovich, 2 vols. (Florence: Sansoni, 1943)

    Trionfi, Rime estravaganti, Codici degli abbozzi, eds. Vinicio Pacca, Laura Paolino, introd. Marco Santagata (Milan: Mondadori, 1996)

Pico della Mirandola, 'Ioannes Picus Mirandula Laurentio Medico s.p.d.' [Epistle to Lorenzo de' Medici, 15 July 1484], in *PLQ*, ed. Eugenio Garin, pp. 796–804

Pietro Alighieri, *Comentum super poema Comedie Dantis*, in *Super Dantis ipsius genitoris Comoediam Commentarium*, ed. Vincenzo Nannucci (Florence: Angelum Garinei, 1845)

Poeti del Duecento, ed. Gianfranco Contini, 2 vols. (Milan–Naples: Ricciardi, 1960)

Poliziano, Angelo, *Commento inedito alle Selve di Stazio*, ed. Lucia Cesarini Martinelli (Florence: Sansoni, 1978)

    Epistola to the *Raccolta Aragonese*, in *PLQ*, ed. Eugenio Garin, pp. 985–90

    Stanze, Fabula di Orfeo, ed. Stefano Carrai (Milan: Mursia, 1988)

    Sylva in Scabiem, ed. Paolo Orvieto (Rome: Salerno, 1989)

Prosatori latini del Quattrocento (Milan–Naples: Ricciardi, 1952)

Pucci, Antonio, *Centiloquio* (selection on Dante's life), in *Le vite di Dante*, ed. Solerti, pp. 5–7

Quintilian, *Institutio oratoria*, ed. H. E. Butler, 4 vols. (London: Heinemann, 1922)

Rimatori del Trecento, ed. Giuseppe Corsi (Turin: UTET, 1969)

Rinuccini, Cino, *Responsiva alla Invettiva di messer Antonio Lusco*, ed. Antonio Lanza, *Firenze contro Milano. Gli intellettuali fiorentini nelle guerre con i Visconti, 1390–1440* (Anzio: De Rubeis, 1991), pp. 187–97

    Invectiva contra a certi caluniatori di Dante, del Petrarca e del Boccaccio, ed. Wesselofsky, I/2, 303–16

Sacchetti, Francesco, *Il Trecentonovelle*, ed. Valerio Marucci (Rome: Salerno, 1996)

Salutati, Coluccio, *Epistolario di Coluccio Salutati*, ed. Francesco Novati, 5 vols. (Rome: Istituto Storico Italiano, 1891–1911)

Select bibliography

De fato et fortuna, ed. Concetta Bianca (Florence: Olschki, 1985)

Invectiva in Antonium Luschum Vicentinum, in *PLQ*, ed. Eugenio Garin, pp. 8–37

De laboribus Herculis, ed. B. L. Ullman, 2 vols. (Zurich: Thesauri Mundi, 1951)

De tyranno, ed. Francesco Ercole, in *Il trattato 'De tyranno' e lettere scelte* (Bologna: Zanichelli, 1942)

Sardi, Tommaso, *De anima peregrina*, ed. Margaret Rooke, *Smith College Studies in Modern Languages* 10 (1929), 1–69

Silvestri, Domenico, defence of poetry, ed. Steven P. Marrone, 'Domenico Silvestri's Defence of Poetry', *Rinascimento* II ser./13 (1973), 115–32

Statuti dell'Università e Studio fiorentino dell'anno MCCCLXXXVII seguiti da un'appendice di documenti dal MCCCXX al MCCCCLXXII, ed. Alessandro Gherardi (Florence: Cellini, 1881)

Tacitus, *Annales*, ed. John Jackson, reprint (London: Heinemann, 1943)

Tasso, Torquato, *Discorsi dell'arte poetica e del poema eroico*, ed. Luigi Poma (Bari: Laterza, 1964)

The Three Crowns of Florence. Humanist Assessments of Dante, Petrarca, and Boccaccio, eds. and trans. David Thompson and Alan F. Nagel (New York: Harper & Row, 1972)

Torini, Agnolo, *Vita e opere di Agnolo Torini*, ed. Irene Hijmans–Tromp (Leiden: Universitaire Pers Leiden, 1957)

Utiliter edoceri. Atti inediti degli ufficiali dello Studio fiorentino (1391–96), ed. Enrico Spagnesi (Milan: Giuffré, 1979)

Vasari, Giorgio, *Le vite de' più eccellenti pittori, scultori e architettori nelle redazioni del 1550 e 1568*, eds. Rosanna Bettarini and Paola Barocchi, 7 vols. (Florence: Sansoni, 1966–)

De vera amicitia. I testi del primo Certame coronario, ed. Lucia Bertolini (Modena: Panini, 1993)

Vespasiano da Bisticci, *Le vite*, ed. Aulo Greco, 2 vols. (Florence: Istituto Nazionale di Studi sul Rinascimento, 1970–76)

Villani, Filippo, *Expositio seu Comentum super 'Comedia' Dantis Allegherii*, ed. Saverio Bellomo (Florence: Le Lettere, 1989)

De origine civitatis Florentie et de eiusdem famosis civibus, ed. Giuliano Tanturli (Padua: Antenore, 1997)

Villani, Giovanni, *Nuova cronica*, ed. Giuseppe Porta, 3 vols. (Parma: Fondazione Pietro Bembo, 1991)

Le vite di Dante, Petrarca e Boccaccio scritte fino al secolo decimosesto, ed. Angelo Solerti (Milan: Villardi, 1904)

Volgarizzamenti del Due e Trecento, ed. Cesare Segre (Turin: UTET, 1953)

SECONDARY SOURCES

Agnolo Poliziano, poeta, scrittore, filologo. Atti del Convegno Internazionale di Studi, Montepulciano, 3–6 novembre 1994, eds. Vincenzo Fera and Mario Martelli (Florence: Le Lettere, 1998)

Select bibliography

Aguzzi-Barbagli, Danilo, 'Dante e la poetica di Coluccio Salutati', *Italica* 42 (1965), 108–31

Ahern, John, 'Singing the Book: Orality in the Reception of Dante's *Comedy*', *Annals of Scholarship* 2:4 (1981), 17–40

Alessio, Gian Carlo, 'La *Comedia* nel margine dei classici', in *Studi di filologia medievale offerti a d'Arco Silvio Avalle* (Milan–Naples: Ricciardi, 1996), pp. 1–25

Altamura, Antonio, *Il Certame Coronario*, reprint (Naples: Società Editrice Napoletana, 1974; 1st edn 1952)

Altrocchi, Rudolph, 'Michelino's Dante', *Speculum* 6 (1931), 15–59

Aquilecchia, Giovanni, *s.v.* 'Villani, Giovanni', in *ED* v, 1013–16

Armour, Peter, 'Comedy and the Origins of Italian Theatre around the Time of Dante', in *Writers and Performers in Italian Drama from the Time of Dante to Pirandello: Essays in Honour of G. H. McWilliam*, eds. J. R. Dashwood and J. E. Everson (Lewiston–Queenston–Lampeter: Edwin Mellen Press, 1991), pp. 1–31

Armstrong, Guyda, *Boccaccio, Dante, and the Corbaccio: A Literary Relationship*, unpublished PhD dissertation, University of Leeds, 2000

Ascoli, Albert Russell, 'Access to Authority: Dante in the Epistle to Cangrande', in *Seminario Dantesco Internazionale/International Dante Seminar I*, ed. Zygmunt G. Barański (Florence: Le Lettere, 1997), pp. 309–52

Atti del Congresso Internazionale di Studi Danteschi (20–27 aprile 1965), 2 vols. (Florence: Sansoni, 1965–66)

Aurigemma, Marcello, *Studi sulla cultura letteraria fra Tre e Quattrocento (Filippo Villani, Vergerio, Bruni)* (Rome: Bulzoni, 1976)

Baglio, Marco, 'Presenze dantesche nel Petrarca latino', *SP* n.s. 9 (1992), 77–136

Baldassarri, Stefano Ugo and Arielle Saiber, eds., *Images of Quattrocento Florence: Selected Writings in Literature, History, and Art* (New Haven–London: Yale University Press, 2000)

Barański, Zygmunt G., *'Chiosar con altro testo'. Leggere Dante nel Trecento* (Florence: Cadmo, 2001)

    Dante e i segni. Saggi per una storia intellettuale di Dante Alighieri (Naples: Liguori, 2000)

    'The Poetics of Meter: *Terza rima*, "canto", "canzon", "cantica"', in *Dante Now*, ed. Cachey, pp. 3–41

    'Sole nuovo, luce nuova'. Saggi sul rinnovamento culturale in Dante (Turin: Scriptorium, 1996)

Barbi, Michele, *Dante nel Cinquecento* (Rome: Polla, 1975, 1st edn 1890)

    Studi sul Canzoniere di Dante con nuove indagini sulle raccolte manoscritte e a stampa di antiche rime italiane (Florence: Sansoni, 1915)

Barolini, Teodolinda, *Dante's Poets: Textuality and Truth in the 'Comedy'* (Princeton: Princeton University Press, 1984)

Baron, Hans, *The Crisis of the Early Italian Renaissance: Civic Humanism and Republican Liberty*, 2nd edn (Princeton: Princeton University Press, 1966)

Basile, Bruno, 'Il *Comentum* di Filippo Villani al canto I della *Commedia*', *LI* 23 (1971), 197–224

    s.v. 'Villani, Filippo', in *ED* v, 1011–13

Select bibliography

Battaglia, Salvatore, *Esemplarità e antagonismo nel pensiero di Dante*, 2 vols. (Naples: Liguori, 1967)

Battaglia Ricci, Lucia, 'Il commento illustrato alla *Commedia*: schede di iconografia trecentesca', in *Per correr*, 1, 601–40

'Testo e immagini in alcuni manoscritti illustrati della *Commedia*: le pagine di apertura', in *Studi offerti a Luigi Blasucci dai colleghi e dagli allievi pisani*, eds. Lucio Lugnani, Marco Santagata, and Alfredo Stussi (Lucca: Pacini Fazzi, 1996), pp. 23–49

Bausi, Francesco, 'L'epica tra latino e volgare', in *La Toscana*, II, 357–73

'Giovanni Pico della Mirandola a Lorenzo de' Medici. Testo, traduzione e commento', *Interpres* 17 (1998), 7–57

'Note sul procedimento antilogico nei *Dialogi* di Leonardo Bruni', *Interpres* 12 (1992), 275–83

Baxandall, Michael, 'Alberti and Cristoforo Landino: The Practical Criticism of Painting', in *Convegno internazionale indetto*, pp. 143–54

Painting and Experience in Fifteenth-Century Italy: A Primer in the Social History of Pictorial Style, 2nd edn (Oxford: Clarendon Press, 1988; 1st edn 1972)

Beall, Chandler B., 'Dante and His Reader', *Forum Italicum* 13 (1979), 299–343

Bec, Christian, *Cultura e società a Firenze nell'età della Rinascenza* (Rome: Salerno, 1981)

Les livres des florentins (1413–1608) (Florence: Olsckhi, 1984)

Les marchands écrivains, affaires et humanisme à Florence (1375–1434) (Paris–La Haye: Mouton, 1967)

'I mercanti scrittori, lettori e giudici di Dante', *Letture Classensi* 12 (1983), 99–111

Bellomo, Saverio, 'Luigi Marsili tra Dante e Petrarca: un'ipotesi', *SP* n.s. 5 (1988), 293–300

'Prime vicende del sepolcro di Dante', *Letture Classensi* 28 (1999), 55–71

Bernacchioni, Anna Maria, 'Alcune precisazioni su un perduto ciclo di Uomini illustri in Palazzo Vecchio', *Paragone* n.s. 44–46 (1994), 17–22

Bernardo, Aldo S., 'Petrarch's Attitude towards Dante', *PMLA* 70 (1955), 488–517

'Triumphal Poetry: Dante, Petrarch, and Boccaccio', in *Petrarch's Triumphs. Allegory and Spectacle*, eds. Konrad Eisenblicher and Amilcare A. Iannucci (Toronto: University of Toronto Press, 1990), pp. 33–45

Bessi, Rossella, 'Appunti sulla *Geographia* di Francesco Berlinghieri', *Rivista geografica italiana* 100 (1993), 159–75

'Per un nuovo commento alle *Stanze* del Poliziano', *LI* 31 (1979), 309–41

'Le *Stanze* del Poliziano e la lirica del primo Quattrocento', *LI* 48 (1996), 3–24

'Un traduttore al lavoro: Donato Acciaiuoli e l'elaborazione del volgarizzamento delle *Historiae*', in *Leonardo Bruni, cancelliere*, ed. Viti, pp. 321–38

Bettinzoli, Attilio, 'Per una definizione delle presenze dantesche nel *Decameron*. I. I registri "ideologici", lirici, drammatici', *SBoc* 13 (1981–82), 267–326

'Per una definizione delle presenze dantesche nel *Decameron*. II. Ironizzazione e espressivismo antifrastico-deformatorio', *SBoc* 14 (1983–84), 209–40

Bianchi, Luca, 'Un commento "umanistico" ad Aristotele. L'*Expositio super libros ethicorum* di Donato Acciaiuoli', *Rinascimento* II ser./30 (1990), 29–55

Select bibliography

Bianchi, Natascia, 'Le prime quattro edizioni del *Convivio* di Dante. Appunti per una ricerca', *Medioevo e Rinascimento* n.s. 11 (2000), 233–41

Bigi, Emilio, 'Argiropulo, Giovanni', in *DBI* 4 (1962), 129–31

    La cultura del Poliziano e altri studi umanistici (Pisa: Nistri–Lischi, 1967)

    'Dante e la cultura fiorentina del Quattrocento', in his *Forme e significati nella Divina Commedia* (Bologna: Cappelli 1981), pp. 145–72

    'Impegno civile e allegorie neoplatoniche nelle *Stanze*', in *Agnolo Poliziano*, eds. Fera and Martelli, pp. 45–54

    'Lorenzo de' Medici e la letteratura', in *La Toscana*, II, 341–56

    Poesia latina e volgare nel Rinascimento italiano (Naples: Morano, 1989)

Billanovich, Giuseppe, 'Dalla *Commedia* e dall'*Amorosa visione* ai *Trionfi*', *GSLI* 123 (1945–46), 1–52

    'La leggenda dantesca del Boccaccio. Dalla *lettera di Ilaro* al *Trattatello in laude di Dante*', *SD* 28 (1949), 45–144

    'Tra Dante e Petrarca', *IMU* 8 (1965), 1–43

Black, Robert, *Benedetto Accolti and the Florentine Renaissance* (Cambridge: Cambridge University Press, 1985)

    'Florence', in *The Renaissance in National Context*, eds. Roy Porter and Mikulas Teich (Cambridge: Cambridge University Press, 1992), pp. 21–41

Boffito, Giuseppe, 'L'eresia di Matteo Palmieri', *GSLI* 37 (1901), 1–69

Boli, Todd, 'Boccaccio's *Trattatello in laude di Dante* or Dante Resartus', *RQ* 41:3 (1988), 379–412

Bologna, Corrado, 'Tradizione testuale e fortuna dei classici italiani', in *Letteratura italiana. Teatro, musica, tradizione dei classici*, ed. Alberto Asor Rosa (Turin: Einaudi, 1986), pp. 445–928

Bottari, Guglielmo, 'Francesco Filelfo e Dante', in *Dante nel pensiero*, pp. 385–94

Botticelli e Dante, ed. Corrado Gizzi (Milan: Electa, 1990)

Boyde, Patrick, *Dante Philomythes and Philosopher: Man in the Cosmos* (Cambridge: Cambridge University Press, 1981)

    Perception and Passion in Dante's 'Comedy' (Cambridge: Cambridge University Press, 1993)

Branca, Vittore, *Poliziano e l'umanesimo della parola* (Turin: Einaudi, 1993)

Bruni, Francesco, *Boccaccio, l'invenzione della letteratura mezzana* (Bologna: Il Mulino, 1990)

Bryce, Judith, 'The Oral World of the early Accademia Fiorentina', *RS* 9:1 (1995), 77–103

Caglio, A. M., 'Materiali enciclopedici nelle *Expositiones* di Guido da Pisa', *IMU* 24 (1981), 213–56

Camillo, Elena, 'Voci quotidiane, voci tecniche e toscano nei volgarizzamenti di Plinio e Pietro de' Crescenzi', *Studi di lessicografia italiana* 11 (1991), 125–50

Cammelli, Giuseppe, *I dotti Bizantini e le origini dell'Umanesimo*, 3 vols. (Florence: Le Monnier, 1941, 1954)

Campana, Augusto, *s.v.* 'Mezzani, Menghino', in *ED* III, 937–39

Camuffo, Maria Luisa, 'Presenze dantesche nell'*Acerba* di Cecco d'Ascoli', *Rivista di letteratura italiana* 5 (1987), 91–100

Cardini, Roberto, *La critica del Landino* (Florence: Sansoni, 1973)
'Landino e Dante', *Rinascimento* II ser./30 (1990), 175–90

Caricato, Luigi, 'Il *Commentarium* all'*Inferno* di Pietro Alighieri: Indagine sulle fonti', *IMU* 26 (1983), 125–50

Carpetto, George M., *The Humanism of Matteo Palmieri* (Rome: Bulzoni, 1984)

Carruthers, Mary J., *The Book of Memory* (Cambridge: Cambridge University Press, 1992)

Casamassima, Emanuele, *La prima edizione della 'Divina Commedia'. Foligno 1472* (Milan: Il Polifilo, 1972)

Casini Wanrooij, Marzia, 'Domenico di Michelino, illustratore della *Commedia*', *Antichità viva* 24: 5–6 (1985), 12–17

Cavallari, Elisabetta, *La fortuna di Dante nel Trecento* (Florence: Perrella, 1921)

Cavallo, Guglielmo and Roger Chartier, eds., *Storia della lettura* (Rome–Bari: Laterza, 1998)

Cazalé Bérard, Claude, 'Dante e Boccaccio: Due strategie del narrare d'amore', *RELI* 4 (1994), 11–34

Chartier, Roger, *The Order of Books: Readers, Authors, and Libraries in Europe between the Fourteenth and Eighteenth Centuries*, trans. Lydia G. Cochrane (Cambridge: Polity Press, 1994)

Chastel, André, *Art et humanisme à Florence au temps de Laurent le Magnifique* (Paris: Presses Universitaires, 1959)
'Dante au Quattrocento', *Revue des études italiennes* n.s. 5 (1958), 247–61

Cherchi, Paolo, 'Un nuovo (vecchio?) inventario della Biblioteca Aragonese', *SFI* 47 (1989), 255–59

Chiamenti, Massimiliano, introd. to *Comentum super poema Comedie Dantis. A Critical Edition of the Third and Final Draft of Pietro Alighieri's Commentary on Dante's Divine Comedy* (Tempe: Arizona Center for Medieval and Renaissance Studies, 2002), pp. 1–78

Ciardi Dupré dal Poggetto, Maria Grazia, 'Boccaccio "visualizzato" dal Boccaccio, I. Corpus dei disegni e cod. Parigino It. 482', *SBoc* 22 (1994), 197–225

Ciavolella, Massimo, 'Eros/Ereos: Marsilio Ficino's Interpretation of "Donna me Prega"', in *Ficino and Renaissance Platonism*, eds. Eisenbichler and Pugliese, pp. 39–48

Cinquino, Joseph, 'Coluccio Salutati Defender of Poetry', *Italica* 26 (1949), 131–35

Ciociola, Claudio, 'Lo scrittoio di un "acerbista" fiorentino del Quattrocento: ser Piero di ser Bonaccorso Bonaccorsi', in *Studi offerti a Gianfranco Contini dagli allievi pisani* (Florence: Le Lettere, 1984), pp. 67–111

Cipriani, Giovanni, *Il mito etrusco nel Rinascimento fiorentino* (Florence: Olschki, 1980)

Clarke, M. L., *The Noblest Roman: Marcus Brutus and His Reputation* (Ithaca: Cornell University Press, 1981)

Cochrane, Eric, *Historians and Historiography in the Italian Renaissance* (Chicago: University of Chicago Press, 1980)

Coglievina, Leonella, 'Un commento quattrocentesco a "Tre donne intorno al cor"', *Interpres* 4 (1981–82), 152–246
'Lettori della *Commedia*: le stampe', in *Per correr*, I, 325–70

Select bibliography

Convegno internazionale indetto nel V Centenario di Leon Battista Alberti, Roma–Mantova–Firenze, 25–29 aprile 1972 (Rome: Accademia Nazionale dei Lincei, 1974)

Coppini, Donatella, 'L'ispirazione per contagio: "furor" e "remota lectio" nella poesia latina del Poliziano', in *Agnolo Poliziano*, eds. Fera and Martelli, pp. 127–64

Cornish, Alison, 'I miti biblici. La sapienza di Salomone e le arti magiche', in *Dante. Mito e Poesia*, eds. Michelangelo Picone and Tatiana Crivelli (Florence: Cesati, 1999), pp. 391–403

Coturri, Enrico, 'Coluccio Salutati e la sua concezione della "Civitatis Libertas" e il *De tyranno*', in *Homo sapiens*, ed. Tarugi, I, 157–65

Craven, W. G., 'Coluccio Salutati's Defence of Poetry', *RS* 10:1 (1996), 1–30

Curti, Elisa, 'Dantismi e memoria della *Commedia* nelle *Stanze* del Poliziano', *LI* 52:4 (2000), 530–68

Curtius, E. R., *European Literature and the Latin Middle Ages* (London: Routledge & Kegan Paul, 1953)

Dante and the Art of the Italian Renaissance, ed. Deborah Parker, special edition of *Lectura Dantis*, 22–23 (1998)

Dante e la 'bella scola' della poesia: autorità e sfida poetica, ed. Amilcare A. Iannucci (Ravenna: Longo, 1993)

Dante e il locus inferni. Creazione letteraria e tradizione interpretativa, eds. Simona Foà and Sonia Gentili (Rome: Bulzoni, 2000)

Dante nel pensiero e nell'esegesi dei secoli XIV e XV. Atti del III Congresso Nazionale di Studi Danteschi, Melfi, 27 settembre–2 ottobre 1970 (Florence: Olschki, 1975)

Dante Now: Current Trends in Dante Studies, ed. Theodore J. Cachey Jr (Notre Dame: University of Notre Dame Press, 1995)

Davies, Jonathan, *Florence and the University during the Early Renaissance* (Leiden: Brill, 1998)

Davies, Martin C., 'An Emperor without Clothes? Niccolò Niccoli under Attack', *IMU* 30 (1987), 95–148

Davis, Charles T., 'Il buon tempo antico', in *Florentine Studies*, ed. Rubinstein, pp. 45–69

  Dante and the Idea of Rome (Oxford: Clarendon Press, 1957)

D'Episcopo, Francesco, 'Orazioni di Francesco Filelfo e di suoi discepoli su Dante Alighieri', *Res Publica Litterarum* 10 (1987), 77–83

  'Retorica ciceroniana e poetica umanistica nella difesa della poesia di Coluccio Salutati', *Esperienze Letterarie* 1 (1976), 47–61

De Angelis, Violetta, ' "Magna questio preposita coram Dante et domino Francisco Petrarca et Virgiliano" ', *SP* n.s. 1 (1984), 103–209

  and Gian Carlo Alessio, ' "Nacqui sub Julio, ancora che fossi tardi" (*Inferno*, 1, 70)', in *Studi vari di lingua e letteratura offerti a Giuseppe Velli*, 2 vols. (Milan: Cisalpino, 2000), I, 127–46

de la Mare, A., *The Handwriting of Italian Humanists* (Oxford: Oxford University Press, 1973)

Delany, Sheila, *The Naked Text: Chaucer's Legend of Good Women* (Berkeley: University of California Press, 1994)

Delcorno, Carlo, 'Note sui dantismi nell'*Elegia di Madonna Fiammetta*', *SBoc* 11 (1979), 251–94

Delcorno Branca, Daniela, 'Percorsi danteschi del Poliziano', *LI* 51:3 (1999), 360–82

della Torre, Arnaldo, *Storia dell'Accademia Platonica di Firenze* (Florence: Carnesecchi, 1902)

del Lungo, Isidoro, *Florentia. Uomini e cose del Quattrocento* (Florence: Barbèra, 1897)

De Medici, Giuliana, 'Le fonti dell'*Ottimo Commento* alla *Divina Commedia*', *IMU* 26 (1983), 71–123

De Robertis, Domenico, *Editi e rari. Studi sulla tradizione letteraria tra Tre e Cinquecento* (Milan: Feltrinelli, 1978)

   'Interpretazione della "Sylva in Scabiem" ', *Rinascimento* II ser./7 (1967), 139–56

   'Lorenzo aragonese', *Rinascimento* II ser./34 (1994), 3–14

   'Petrarca petroso', *Revue des études italiennes* 29 (1983), 13–37

De Rosa, Daniela, *Coluccio Salutati: il cancelliere e il pensatore politico* (Florence: La Nuova Italia, 1980)

Dionisotti, Carlo, *s.v.* 'Bruni, Leonardo', 'Salutati, Coluccio' in *ED* II, 708–09; IV, 1086–87

   'Dante nel Quattrocento', in *Atti del Congresso Internazionale di Studi Danteschi*, I, 333–78

di Pino, Guido, 'L'antidantismo dal Trecento al Quattrocento', *Letture Classensi* 5 (1976), 125–48

Dizionario biografico degli italiani (Rome: Istituto della Enciclopedia Italiana, 1960–)

Donati Barcellona, Maria, *s.v.* 'Baldini, Baccio', in *ED* I, 498

Donato, Maria Monica, 'Gli eroi romani tra storia ed "exemplum". I primi cicli umanistici di "Uomini Famosi" ', in *Memoria dell'antico nell'arte italiana. I generi e i temi ritrovati*, ed. Salvatore Settis, 2 vols. (Turin: Einaudi, 1985), II, 97–152

   '"Famosi cives": testi, frammenti e cicli perduti a Firenze fra Tre e Quattrocento', *Ricerche di storia dell'arte* 30 (1986), 27–42

   'Per la fortuna monumentale di Giovanni Boccaccio fra i grandi Fiorentini: notizie e problemi', *SBoc* 17 (1988), 287–342

Dreyer, Peter, 'Botticelli's Series of Engravings "of 1481" ', *Print Quarterly* I (1984), 111–15

Enciclopedia Dantesca, ed. Giorgio Petrocchi *et al.*, 6 vols. (Rome: Istituto della Enciclopedia Italiana, 1970–78)

Feo, Michele, *s.v.* 'Petrarca, Francesco', in *ED* IV, 454–58

   'Tradizione latina', in *Letteratura italiana. V. Le questioni*, ed. Alberto Asor Rosa (Turin: Einaudi, 1986), pp. 311–78

Ferraù, Giacomo, 'Le *Commentationes Florentiae de exilio*', in *Francesco Filelfo*, eds., Avesani *et al.*, pp. 369–88

Select bibliography

Ferreri, Rosario, 'Appunti sulla presenza del *Convivio* nel *Decameron*. I. Il proemio del *Decameron*; II. La novella VI, 6 e la *quaestio* della nobiltà', *SBoc* 19 (1990), 63–77

Ficino and Renaissance Platonism, eds. Konrad Eisenbichler and Olga Zorzi Pugliese (Ottawa: Dovehouse Editions, 1986)

Fido, Franco, 'Dante personaggio mancato del Decameron', in his *Il regime delle simmetrie imperfette* (Milan: FrancoAngeli, 1988), pp. 111–23

Field, Arthur, 'Cristoforo Landino's First Lectures on Dante', *RQ* 39 (1986), 16–48

'An Inaugural Oration by Cristoforo Landino in Praise of Virgil (From Codex '2', Casa Cavalli, Ravenna)', *Rinascimento* 11 ser./21 (1981), 235–45

'John Argyropoulos and the "Secret Teachings" of Plato', in *Supplementum Festivum: Studies in Honor of Paul Oskar Kristeller*, eds. James Hankins *et al.* (Binghamton: Medieval and Renaissance Texts and Studies, 1987), pp. 299–326

'Leonardo Bruni, Florentine Traitor? Bruni, the Medici, and an Aretine Conspiracy of 1437', *RQ* 51 (1998), 1109–50

'A Manuscript of Cristoforo Landino's First Lectures on Virgil, 1462–63 (Codex 1368, Biblioteca Casanatense, Rome)', *RQ* 31 (1978), 17–20

The Origins of the Platonic Academy of Florence (Princeton: Princeton University Press, 1988)

Finzi, Claudio, *Matteo Palmieri dalla 'Vita civile' alla 'Città di vita'* (Rome: Giuffrè, 1984)

Flamini, Francesco, 'Leonardo di Piero Dati', *GSLI* 16 (1890), 1–107

Florentine Studies. Politics and Society in Renaissance Florence, ed. Nicolai Rubinstein (London: Faber & Faber, 1968)

Foà, Simona, 'Il Dialogo sul sito, forma e misura dell'inferno di Girolamo Benivieni e un particolare aspetto dell'esegesi dantesca tra XV e XVI secolo', in *Dante e il locus inferni*, eds., Foà and Gentili, pp. 179–90

Folena, Gianfranco, 'La tradizione delle opere di Dante Alighieri', in *Atti del Congresso Internazionale di Studi Danteschi*, 1, 1–78

Franceschini, Adriano, *Giovanni Aurispa e la sua biblioteca. Notizie e documenti* (Padua: Antenore, 1976)

Francesco Filelfo nel quinto centenario della morte. Atti del XVII convegno di studi maceratesi (Tolentino, 27–30 settembre 1981), eds. Rino Avesani *et al.* (Padua: Antenore, 1986)

Frasca, Gabriele, '"I' voglio qui che 'l quare covi il quia": Cecco d'Ascoli "avversario" di Dante', in *Dante e la scienza*, eds. Patrick Boyde and Vittorio Russo (Ravenna: Longo, 1995), pp. 243–63

Freedman, Luba, 'A Note on Dante's Portrait in Boccaccio's "Vita"', *SBoc* 15 (1985–86), 253–63

Fryde, Edmund B., *Studies in Humanism and Renaissance Historiography* (London: Hambledon Press, 1983)

Fubini, Riccardo, *Quattrocento fiorentino. Politica, diplomazia, cultura* (Pisa: Pacini Fazzi, 1997)

L'umanesimo italiano e i suoi storici. Origini rinascimentali, critica moderna (Milan: FrancoAngeli, 2001)

Select bibliography

Gadol, Joan, *Leon Battista Alberti: Universal Man of the Early Renaissance* (Chicago–London: Chicago University Press, 1973)

Ganda, Arnaldo, 'L'edizione nidobeatina della *Commedia*. Considerazioni e documenti', in *Bibliologia e critica dantesca. Saggi dedicati a Enzo Esposito*, ed. Vincenzo De Gregorio, 2 vols. (Ravenna: Longo, 1997), II, 271–97

Garilli, Francesco, 'Cultura e pubblico nel *Paradiso degli Alberti*', *GSLI* 149 (1972), 1–47

Garin, Eugenio, 'La cultura filosofica fiorentina nell'età medicea', in *Idee, istituzioni, scienza ed arti nella Firenze dei Medici*, ed. Cesare Vasoli (Florence: Giunti–Martello, 1980), pp. 83–112

'Dante nel Rinascimento', *Rinascimento* II ser./7 (1967), 3–28

Lo zodiaco della vita: La polemica sull'astrologia dal Trecento al Cinquecento (Bari: Laterza, 1976)

Gatti, Luca, 'Il mito di Marte a Firenze e la "pietra scema". Memorie, riti e ascendenze', *Rinascimento* II ser./35 (1997), 203–11

Gentile, Sebastiano, 'Dante, Botticelli e gli umanisti fiorentini: tra manoscritti e studi geografici', in *Sandro Botticelli*, ed. Gentile, I, 34–39

'In margine all'Epistola "De divino furore" di Marsilio Ficino', *Rinascimento* II ser./23 (1983), 33–77

Ghinassi, Ghino, *Il volgare letterario nel Quattrocento e le 'Stanze' del Poliziano* (Florence: Le Monnier, 1957)

Gigante, Marcello, 'Ambrogio Traversari interprete di Diogene Laerzio', in *Ambrogio Traversari nel VI centenario della nascita. Convegno internazionale di studi (Camaldoli–Firenze, 15–18 settembre, 1986)*, ed. Gian Carlo Garfagnini (Florence: Olschki, 1988), pp. 367–459

Gilson, Simon A., 'Medieval Science in Dante's *Commedia*: Past Approaches and Future Directions', *Reading Medieval Studies* 27 (2001), 39–77

'Plato, the *platonici*, and Marsilio Ficino in Cristoforo Landino's *Comento sopra la Comedia*', *The Italianist* 23 (2003.i), 5–53

'Tradition and Innovation in Cristoforo Landino's Glosses on Astrology in his *Comento sopra la Comedia* (1481)', *Italian Studies* 58 (2003), 48–74

Giunta, Claudio, 'Memoria di Dante nei *Trionfi*', *Rivista di letteratura italiana* 11 (1993), 411–52

Gombrich, E. H., 'Dante's Portrait?', *The Burlington Magazine* 121 (1979), 471–83

The Heritage of Apelles: Studies in the Art of the Renaissance (London: Phaidon, 1976)

Gorni, Guglielmo, 'Appunti sulla tradizione del *Convivio*', *SFI* 55 (1997), 5–22

Metrica e analisi letteraria (Bologna: Il Mulino, 1993)

'Storia del certame coronario', *Rinascimento* II ser./12 (1972), 135–81

Grafton, Anthony, *Leon Battista Alberti: Master Builder of the Italian Renaissance* (London: Allen Lane, 2001)

'Renaissance Readers and Ancient Texts: Comments on Some Commentaries', *RQ* 38 (1988), 615–49

'On the Scholarship of Politian and its Context', *JWCI* 40 (1977), 150–88

Grahber, Carlo, 'Il culto del Boccaccio per Dante e alcuni aspetti delle sue opere dantesche', *SD* 30 (1951), 129–56

Grayson, Cecil, 'Dante and the Renaissance', in *Italian Studies Presented to E. R. Vincent*, eds., C. P. Brand, Kenelm Foster, and Uberto Limentani (Cambridge: Heffer, 1962), pp. 57–75

Studi su Leon Battista Alberti, ed. Paola Claut (Florence: Olschki, 1998)

Greco, Aulo, 'Dante nella poesia di Lorenzo de' Medici', in *Dante nel pensiero*, pp. 117–25

Greenfield, Concetta Carestia, *Humanist and Scholastic Poetics, 1250–1500* (London–Toronto: Associated University Presses, 1981)

Griffiths, Gordon, James Hankins, and David Thompson, *The Humanism of Leonardo Bruni. Selected Texts* (Binghamton: Medieval and Renaissance Texts and Studies, 1987)

Gualdo Rosa, Lucia, 'Leonardo Bruni e le sue "vite parallele" di Dante e del Petrarca', *LI* 47:3 (1995), 386–401

'Una prolusione inedita di Francesco Filelfo del 1429, rielaborata dal figlio Gian Mario nel 1467', in *Francesco Filelfo*, eds. Avesani *et al.*, pp. 275–323

Guerri, Domenico, *La corrente popolare nel Rinascimento. Berte, burle e baie nella Firenze del Brunellesco e del Burchiello* (Florence: Sansoni, 1931)

Hainsworth, Peter, 'Rhetorics of Autobiography in Dante, Petrarch, and Boccaccio', *Journal of the Institute of Romance Studies* 3 (1994–95), 53–63

Hankey, Teresa, 'Salutati's Epigrams for the Palazzo Vecchio at Florence', *JWCI* 22 (1959), 363–65

Hankins, James, 'The Baron Thesis after Forty Years and Some Recent Studies of Leonardo Bruni', *JHI* 56 (1995), 309–38

'Cosimo de' Medici as a Patron of Humanistic Literature', in *Cosimo 'Il Vecchio' de' Medici 1389–1464: Essays in Commemoration of the 600th Anniversary of Cosimo de' Medici's Birthday*, ed. Frances Ames-Lewis (Oxford: Clarendon Press, 1992), pp. 69–94

'Lorenzo de' Medici as a Patron of Philosophy', *Rinascimento* II ser./34 (1994), 15–35

Plato in the Italian Renaissance, 2 vols. (Leiden–New York: Brill, 1990)

Holbrook, Richard Thayer, *Portraits of Dante from Giotto to Raffael: A Critical Study, With A Concise Iconography* (London: Warner, 1896)

Hollander, Robert, *Boccaccio's Dante and the Shaping Force of Satire* (Ann Arbor: University of Michigan Press, 1997)

Boccaccio's Last Fiction: Il Corbaccio (Philadelphia: University of Pennsylvania Press, 1988)

Studies in Dante (Ravenna: Longo, 1980)

Holmes, George, *The Florentine Enlightenment, 1400–1500* (London: Weidenfeld and Nicolson, 1969)

Holub, Robert C., *Reception Theory: A Critical Introduction* (London–New York: Methuen, 1984)

Homo sapiens, homo humanus, ed. Giovannangiola Tarugi, 2 vols. (Florence: Olschki, 1990)

Hume, Robert D., *Reconstructing Contexts: The Aims and Principles of Archaeo-Historicism* (Oxford: Oxford University Press, 1999)

Select bibliography

Iannucci, Amilcare, 'Autoesegesi dantesca: la tecnica dell' "episodio" parallelo', *LI* 33:3 (1981), 305–28

Ianzitti, Gary, 'Leonardo Bruni and Biography: The *Vita Aristotelis*', *RQ* 55:3 (2002), 805–32

'A Life in Politics: Leonardo Bruni's Cicero', *JHI* 61 (2000), 39–58

Jauss, Hans Robert, *Towards an Aesthetic of Reception*, trans. Timothy Bahti (Minneapolis: University of Minnesota Press, 1982)

Jenaro-MacLennan, L., *The Trecento Commentators on the Divina Commedia and the Epistle to Cangrande* (Oxford: Clarendon Press, 1974)

Jordan, Constance, *Pulci's 'Morgante': Poetry and History in Fifteenth-Century Florence* (Washington–London–Toronto: Folger, 1986)

Kallendorf, Craig, *In Praise of Aeneas: Virgil and Epideictic Rhetoric in the Early Italian Renaissance* (Hanover: University Press of New England, 1989)

'From Virgil to Vida: The *Poeta Theologus* in Italian Renaissance Commentary', *JHI* 56:1 (1995), 41–62

Kay, Richard, 'La mentalità della *Monarchia* di Dante', in *Homo sapiens*, ed. Tarugi, I, 79–88

Keen, Catherine, 'Signs of *Fiorentinità*: The Baptistery and its Meanings in Dante's Florence', in *Sguardi sull'Italia. Miscellanea dedicata a Francesco Villari* (Leeds: SIS, 1999), pp. 29–42

Kemp, Martin, 'From "Mimesis" to "Fantasia": The Quattrocento Vocabulary of Creation, Inspiration and Genius in the Visual Arts', *Viator* 8 (1977), 347–98

Kent, Dale, *The Rise of the Medici: Faction in Florence, 1426–1434* (Oxford: Clarendon Press, 1978)

Kirkham, Victoria, 'The Parallel Lives of Dante and Virgil', *DS* 110 (1992), 233–53

Kleiner, John, *Mismapping the Underworld: Daring and Error in Dante's 'Comedy'* (Stanford: Stanford University Press, 1994)

Kristeller, Paul Oskar, 'Marsilio Ficino as a Beginning Student of Plato', *Scriptorium* 20 (1966), 41–54

'Marsilio Ficino as a Man of Letters and the Glosses Attributed to Him in the Caetani Codex of Dante', *RQ* 36 (1983), 1–47

Renaissance Concepts of Man (New York–London: Harper & Row, 1972)

Renaissance Thought and its Sources, ed. Michael Mooney (New York: Columbia University Press, 1979)

Studies in Renaissance Thought and Letters (Rome: Edizioni di Storia e Letteratura, 1956)

La Brasca, Francesco, 'L'humanisme vulgaire et la genèse de la critique littéraire: Étude descriptive du commentaire dantesque de Cristoforo Landino', *Chroniques italiennes* 6 (1986), 3–96

'Du prototype à l'archétype: lecture allégorique et réécriture de Dante dans et par le commentaire de Cristoforo Landino', in *Scritture di scritture: Testi, generi, modelli nel Rinascimento*, eds., Giancarlo Mazzacurati and Michel Plaisance (Rome: Bulzoni, 1987), pp. 69–107

'*Scriptor in cathedra*: Les cours inauguraux de Cristoforo Landino au *Studio* de Florence (1458–74)', in *L'écrivain face à son public en France et en Italie à la Renaissance. Actes du colloque international de Tours, 4–6 decembre 1986*, eds. Charles Adelin Fiorato and Jean-Claude Margolin (Paris: Vrin, 1989), pp. 107–25

'Tradition exégétique et vulgarisation néoplatonicienne dans la partie doctrinale du commentaire dantesque de C. Landino', in *Culture et société en Italie du moyen-âge à la Renaissance. Hommage à André Rochon* (Paris: Université de la Sorbonne Nouvelle, 1985), pp. 117–29

Lanza, Antonio, *Firenze contro Milano. Gli intellettuali fiorentini nelle guerre con i Visconti, 1390–1440* (Anzio: De Rubeis, 1991)

Letteratura tardogotica: arte e poesia a Firenze e Siena nell'autunno del Medioevo (Anzio: De Rubeis, 1994)

Polemiche e berte letterarie nella Firenze del primo Rinascimento (1375–1449), 2nd edn (Rome: Bulzoni, 1989; 1st edn 1971)

Larner, John, 'The Church and the Quattrocento Renaissance in Geography', *RS* 12:1 (1998), 26–39

Lentzen, Manfred, 'Le lodi di Firenze di Cristoforo Landino', *Romanische Forschungen* 97 (1985), 42–46

Studien zur Dante-exegese Cristoforo Landinos. Mit einem Anhang bisher unveröffentlicher Briefe und Reden (Cologne–Wein: Böhlau, 1971)

Leonardo Bruni, cancelliere della Repubblica di Firenze. Convegno di Studi, Firenze, 27–29 ottobre 1987, ed. Paolo Viti (Florence: Olschki, 1990)

Lerner, Robert E., 'Petrarch's Coolness Toward Dante: A Conflict of "Humanism"', in *Intellectuals and Writers in Fourteenth-Century Europe*, eds. Piero Boitani and Anna Torti (Tübingen: Narr, 1986), pp. 204–25

Lines, David A., *Aristotle's Ethics in the Italian Renaissance (ca. 1300–1650)* (Leiden: Brill, 2002)

Lo Cascio, Renzo, 'Il Poliziano e Dante', in *Dante nel pensiero*, pp. 395–402

Lo Monaco, Francesco, 'Alcune osservazioni sui commenti umanistici ai classici nel secondo Quattrocento', in *Il commento ai testi. Atti del Seminario di Ascona, 2–9 ottobre 1989*, eds., Ottavio Besomi and Carlo Caruso (Basel–Boston–Berlin: Verlag, 1992), pp. 103–39

Lorenzo il Magnifico e il suo tempo, ed. Gian Carlo Garfagnini (Florence: Olschki, 1992)

Luiso, Francesco Paolo, *Studi su l'epistolario di Leonardo Bruni*, ed. Lucia Gualdo Rosa (Rome: Istituto Storico per il Medio Evo, 1980)

Madrignani, Carlo Alberto, 'Di alcune biografie umanistiche di Dante e Petrarca', *Belfagor* 18 (1963), 29–48

Maggini, Francesco, *I primi volgarizzamenti dai classici latini* (Florence: Le Monnier, 1952)

Maissen, Thomas, 'Attila, Totila e Carlo Magno fra Dante, Villani, Boccaccio e Malispini. Per la genesi di due leggende erudite', *ASI* 152 (1994), 561–640

Mansi, Maria Luisa, 'La *Vita di Dante e del Petrarca* di Leonardo Bruni', in *Dante nel pensiero*, pp. 403–15

Maraschio, Nicoletta, 'Aspetti del bilinguismo albertiano nel *De pictura*', *Rinascimento* II ser./12 (1972), 183–228

'Interferenze tra verbo latino e verbo volgare nel bilingue *De pictura* albertiano', *Studi di grammatica italiana* 4 (1974–75), 51–69

Marchesini, Umberto, 'Filippo Villani pubblico lettore della *Divina Commedia* in Firenze', *ASI* Vser./16 (1895), 273–79

Marchisio, Cesare, *Il monumento pittorico a Dante in Santa Maria del Fiore* (Rome: Palombi, 1956)

Marietti, Martina, 'Le marchand seigneur dans *Il Paradiso degli Alberti* de Giovanni Gherardi', in *L'après Boccace. La nouvelle italienne au XVe et XVIe siècles* (Paris: Université de la Sorbonne Nouvelle, 1994), pp. 43–78

Marsh, David, *The Quattrocento Dialogue. Classical Tradition and Humanist Innovation* (Cambridge–London: Harvard University Press, 1980)

Marsilio Ficino e il ritorno di Platone. Studi e documenti, ed. Gian Carlo Garfagnini, 2 vols. (Florence: Olschki, 1986)

Marsilio Ficino: His Theology, His Philosophy, His Legacy, eds., Michael J. B. Allen and Valery Rees with Martin Davies (Leiden: Brill, 2002)

Martelli, Mario, *Angelo Poliziano: Storia e metastoria* (Lecce: Conte, 1995)

'La cultura letteraria nell'età di Lorenzo', in *Lorenzo il Magnifico*, ed. Garfagnini, pp. 39–84

Una giarda fiorentina: Il dialogo della lingua attribuito a Niccolò Machiavelli (Rome: Salerno, 1978)

Letteratura fiorentina del Quattrocento. Il filtro degli anni Sessanta (Florence: Le Lettere, 1996)

'Palmeriana', *Interpres* 5 (1983–84), 277–90

Studi laurenziani (Florence: Olschki, 1965)

Martellotti, Guido, 'La difesa della poesia nel Boccaccio e un giudizio su Lucano', *SBoc* 4 (1967), 265–79

s.v. 'Giovanni del Virgilio', 'Egloghe', in *ED* II, 193–94, 644–46

Martindale, Charles, *Redeeming the Text: Latin Poetry and the Hermeneutics of Reception* (Cambridge: Cambridge University Press, 1993)

Martines, Lauro, *The Social World of the Florentine Humanists, 1390–1460* (Princeton: Princeton University Press, 1963)

Mazzocco, Angelo, *Linguistic Theories in Dante and the Humanists: Studies in Language and Intellectual History in Late Medieval and Early Renaissance Italy* (Leiden: Brill, 1993)

Mazzoni, Francesco, 'Guido da Pisa interprete di Dante e la sua fortuna presso il Boccaccio', *SD* 35 (1958), 29–128

'Pietro Alighieri interprete di Dante', *SD* 40 (1963), 279–360

s.v. 'Alighieri, Iacopo', 'Alighieri, Pietro', 'Anonimo Fiorentino', 'Bambaglioli, Graziolo de'', 'Guido da Pisa', 'Lana, Iacopo della', 'Ottimo commento', in *ED* I, 143–45; I, 147–49; I, 291–92; I, 506–07; III, 325–28; III, 563–65; IV, 220–22

McCormick, Andrew P., 'Goro Dati's Transcription of the *Ottimo Commento* on Dante', *Rinascimento* II ser./22 (1982), 251–55

Select bibliography

McLaughlin, Martin L., 'Humanist Concepts of Renaissance and Middle Age in the Tre- and Quattrocento', *RS* 2:2 (1988), 131–42

Literary Imitation in the Italian Renaissance: The Theory and Practice of Literary Imitation from Dante to Bembo (Oxford: Clarendon Press, 1995)

'Poliziano's *Stanze per la giostra*: Postmodern Poetics in a Proto-Renaissance Poem', in *Culture in Crisis: Italy in the 1490s*, eds. Jane Everson and Diego Zancani (Oxford: Legenda, 2000), pp. 129–51

McNair, Bruce G., 'Cristoforo Landino and Coluccio Salutati on the Best Life', *RQ* 47 (1994), 747–69

'Cristoforo Landino's *De anima* and his Platonic Sources', *Rinascimento* II ser./32 (1992), 227–45

Cristoforo Landino on the Human Soul: The 'Disputationes Camaldulenses' and 'De anima', unpublished PhD dissertation, Duke University, 1991

Medieval Literary Theory and Criticism c. 1100–1375, eds. A. J. Minnis and A. B. Scott with David Wallace (Oxford: Clarendon Press, 1988)

Mercuri, Roberto, 'Genesi della tradizione letteraria italiana in Dante, Petrarca e Boccaccio', in *La letteratura italiana. Storia e geografia*, ed. Alberto Asor Rosa (Turin: Einaudi, 1987), I, 229–455

Mésoniat, Claudio, *Poetica theologia. La 'Lucula Noctis' di Giovanni Dominici e le dispute letterarie tra '300 e '400* (Rome: Edizioni di Storia e Letteratura, 1984)

Messeri, Antonio, 'Matteo Palmieri cittadino di Firenze secolo XV', *ASI* V ser./13 (1894), 257–340

Messina, Michele, *s.v.* 'Pulci, Luigi', 'Palmieri, Matteo', in *ED* III, 738–39; IV, 263–64

Miglio, Luisa, 'Lettori della *Commedia*: i manoscritti', in *Per correr*, I, 295–323

'Dante Alighieri. Manoscritti miniati', in *Enciclopedia dell'arte medievale*, 12 vols. (Rome: Istituto della Enciclopedia Italiana, 1991–2002), V, 627–35

Minnis, Alistair J., *Medieval Theory of Authorship: Scholastic Literary Attitudes in the Later Middle Ages*, 2nd edn (Aldershot: Scolar Press, 1988)

Monfasani, John, 'Marsilio Ficino and the Plato–Aristotle Controversy', in *Marsilio Ficino: His Theology*, ed. Allen, pp. 137–58

Montano, Rocco, *Dante e il Rinascimento* (Naples: Guida, 1942)

Moreau, Joseph, 'De la concordance d'Aristote avec Platon', in *Platon et Aristote à la Renaissance* (Paris: Vrin, 1976), pp. 45–58

Mortensen, Lars B., 'Leonardo Bruni's *Dialogus*: A Ciceronian Debate on the Literary Culture of Florence', *Classica et mediaevalia* 37 (1986), 259–302

Nardi, Bruno, *Nel mondo di Dante* (Rome: Edizioni di Storia e Letteratura, 1944)

Nasti, Paola, 'Autorità, topos e modello. Salomone nei commenti trecenteschi alla *Commedia*', *The Italianist* 19 (1999), 5–49

O'Donnel, J. Reginald, 'Coluccio Salutati and the Poet-Teacher', *Mediaeval Studies* 22 (1960), 240–56

Orvieto, Paolo, 'Boccaccio mediatore di generi e dell'allegoria d'amore', *Interpres* 2 (1979), 7–104

La poesia comico-realistica: Dalle origini al Cinquecento (Rome: Carocci, 2000)

Select bibliography

Owen, Rachel, 'Dante's Reception by Fourteenth- and Fifteenth-Century Illustrators of the *Commedia*', *Reading Medieval Studies* 27 (2001), 163–225

Padoan, Giorgio, *s.v.* 'Boccaccio, Giovanni', in *ED* I, 645–50

  'Il Boccaccio "fedele" di Dante', in his *Il Boccaccio, le Muse, il Parnaso e l'Arno* (Florence: Olschki, 1978), pp. 229–46

  'Dante di fronte all'umanesimo letterario', *LI* 17:3 (1965), 237–57

Paolazzi, Carlo, *Dante e la 'Comedia' nel Trecento* (Milan: Pubblicazioni della Università Cattolica, 1989)

Papanti, Filippo, *Dante secondo la tradizione e i novellatori* (Livorno: Vigo, 1873)

Paparelli, Gioacchino, 'Dante e il Trecento', in *Dante nel pensiero*, pp. 31–70

  'Due modi opposti di leggere Dante: Petrarca e Boccaccio', in *Giovanni Boccaccio editore e interprete di Dante* (Florence: Olschki, 1979), pp. 73–90

Papini, Giovanni, *La leggenda di Dante. Motti, facezie e tradizioni dei secoli XIV–XIX* (Lanciano: Carabba, 1911)

Park, Katherine, 'The Readers at the Florentine Studio According to Comunal Fiscal Records (1357–1380, 1413–1446)', *Rinascimento* II ser./20 (1980), 249–310

Parker, Deborah, *Commentary and Ideology: Dante in the Renaissance* (Durham–London: Duke University Press, 1993)

Parronchi, Alessandro, 'Come gli artisti leggevano Dante', *SD* 43 (1966), 97–134

Pasquini, Emilio, 'Tradizione e fermenti nuovi nella poesia dell'Alberti', in *Convegno internazionale indetto*, pp. 305–68

Pastore Stocchi, Manlio, *s.v.* 'Classica, Cultura', in *ED* II, 30–36

Patota, Giuseppe, *Lingua e linguistica in Leon Battista Alberti* (Rome: Bulzoni, 1999)

'Per correr miglior acque . . .'. Bilanci e prospettive degli studi danteschi alle soglie del nuovo millenio. Atti del convegno di Verona–Ravenna, 25–29 ottobre 1999, 2 vols. (Rome: Salerno, 2001)

Peterson, Erik, 'Some Remarks on Coluccio Salutati's *De fato et fortuna*', *Cahiers de l'institut du moyen-âge grec et latin* 18 (1976), 5–17

Petrocchi, Giorgio, *La 'Commedia' secondo l'antica vulgata*, 4 vols. (Milan: Mondadori, 1966–67)

  Itinerari danteschi, ed. Carlo Ossola (Milan: FrancoAngeli, 1994)

Petrucci, Armando, *Coluccio Salutati* (Rome: Istituto della Enciclopedia Italiana, 1972)

  'Storia e geografia delle culture scritte (dal secolo XI al secolo XVIII)', in *Letteratura italiana. Storia e geografia*, ed. Alberto Asor Rosa (Turin: Einaudi, 1988), pp. 1195–1292

Piana, Celestino, *La facoltà teologica dell'università di Firenze nel Quattro e Cinquecento* (Grottaferrata: Collegium S. Bonaventure, 1977)

Picone, Michelangelo, 'Dante e il canone degli *Auctores*', *RELI* 1 (1992), 9–26

  'L'Ovidio di Dante', in *Dante e la 'bella scola'*, ed. Iannucci, pp. 107–44

  'Riscritture dantesche nel *Canzoniere* di Petrarca', *RELI* 2 (1993), 115–26

  'Tipologie culturali: da Dante a Boccaccio', *Strumenti critici* 30 (1976), 263–74

  and Claude Cazalé Bérard, eds., *Gli zibaldoni di Boccaccio: Memoria, scrittura, riscrittura. Atti del seminario internazionale di Firenze–Certaldo (26–28 aprile 1996)* (Florence: Cesati, 1998)

Pintor, Fortunato, 'Per la storia della libreria Medicea nel Rinascimento', *IMU* 3 (1960), 189–210

Pistolesi, Elena, 'Con Dante attraverso il Cinquecento: Il *De vulgari eloquentia* e la questione della lingua', *Rinascimento* II ser./40 (2000), 269–90

Polizzotto, Lorenzo, *The Elect Nation: The Savonarolan Movement in Florence, 1494–1545* (Oxford: Clarendon Press, 1994)

Procaccioli, Paolo, *Filologia ed esegesi dantesca nel Quattrocento: L'Inferno' nel 'Comento sopra la Comedia' di Cristoforo Landino* (Florence: Olschki, 1989)

Introd. to *Comento sopra la Comedia*, ed. Paolo Procaccioli, 4 vols. (Rome: Salerno, 2001), pp. 9–105

Pulsoni, Carlo, 'Il Dante di Francesco Petrarca: Vaticano latino 3199', *SP* 10 (1993), 156–208

Quint, David, 'Humanism and Modernity: A Reconsideration of Bruni's *Dialogus*', *RQ* 38 (1985), 423–45

Renaudet, Augustin, *Dante humaniste* (Paris: Les Belles Lettres, 1952)

Resta, Gianvito, 'Dante nel Quattrocento', in *Dante nel pensiero*, pp. 71–91

Rheinfelder, Hans, 'Dante, il suo pensiero, il suo tempo nella predicazione di San Bernardino da Siena', in *Dante nel pensiero*, pp. 93–114

Rocco, Flavia, 'Presenze boccacciane nel commento dantesco dell'Anonimo Fiorentino', *SBoc* II (1979), 403–11

Rochon, André, *La jeunesse de Laurent de Medicis (1449–1478)* (Paris: Les Belles Lettres, 1963)

Ricci, Corrado, *L'ultimo rifugio di Dante Alighieri*, reprint, ed. Eugenio Chiarini (Ravenna: Longo, 1965; 1st edn 1921)

Ricci, Pier Giorgio, *s.v.* 'Filelfo, Francesco', 'Gherardi, Giovanni', 'Manetti, Antonio', 'Rinuccini, Cino', in *ED* II, 871–72; III, 138–39; III, 801; IV, 967–68

'Le tre redazioni del *Trattatello in laude di Dante*', *SBoc* 8 (1974), 197–214

Riccucci, Maria, 'L'esordio dei *Triumphi*: tra *Eneide* e *Commedia*', *Rivista di letteratura italiana* 12 (1994), 313–49

Richardson, Brian, 'Editing Dante's *Commedia*, 1472–1629', in *Dante Now*, ed. Cachey, pp. 237–62

Rizzo, Silvia, *Il lessico filologico degli umanisti* (Rome: Edizioni di Storia e Letteratura, 1973)

Robin, Diana, *Filelfo in Milan: Writings 1451–1477* (Princeton: Princeton University Press, 1991)

Roddewig, Marcella, *Dante Alighieri. Die 'Göttliche Komödie'. Vergleichende Bestandsaufnahme der 'Commedia'-Handschriften* (Stuttgart: Hiersemann, 1984)

Rose, Paul Lawrence, *The Italian Renaissance of Mathematics* (Geneva: Droz, 1975)

Rossi, Aldo, 'Un autografo ficiniano delle *Egloghe* alla Nazionale di Parigi', *SD* 37 (1960), 291–8

'Dante nella prospettiva del Boccaccio', *SD* 37 (1960), 63–139

Rossi, Luca Carlo, 'Per il commento di Martino Paolo Nibia alla *Commedia*', in *Filologia umanistica. Per Gianvito Resta*, eds., Vincenzo Fera and Giacomo Ferraù, 3 vols. (Padua: Antenore, 1996), III, 1677–1716

'Petrarca dantista involontario', *SP* n.s. 5 (1988), 301–16

Select bibliography

'Presenze di Petrarca in commenti danteschi fra Tre e Quattrocento', *Aevum* 70 (1996), 441–76

'Prospezioni filologiche per lo Stazio di Dante', in *Dante e la 'bella scola'*, ed. Iannucci, pp. 205–24

Rossi, Vittorio, 'Dante nel Trecento e nel Quattrocento', in his *Scritti di critica letteraria. Saggi e discorsi su Dante*, 3 vols. (Florence: Sansoni, 1930), I, 293–332

Roush, Sherry, 'Dante as Piagnone Prophet: Girolamo Benivieni's "Cantico in laude di Dante"', *RQ* 55 (2002), 49–80

Rubinstein, Nicolai, 'The Beginnings of Political Thought in Florence. A Study of Mediaeval Historiography', *JWCI* 5 (1942), 198–227

Ruini, Roberto, 'Bruto e Cassio in *Inf.* XXXIV 55–69 e la riflessione politica fiorentina quattrocentesca', in *Dante e il locus inferni*, eds. Foà and Gentili, pp. 145–78

Russo, Vittorio, *Con le Muse in Parnaso. Tre studi su Boccaccio* (Naples: Bibliopolis, 1983)

Sabbadini, Remigio, *Le scoperte dei codici latini e greci ne' secoli XIV e XV*, 2 vols. (Florence: Sansoni, 1967; 1st edn 1914)

Sandkühler, B., *Die frühen Dantekommentare und ihr Verhältnis zur mittelalterlichen Kommentartradition* (München: Verlag, 1967)

Sandro Botticelli: The Drawings for Dante's Divine Comedy (London: Royal Academy of Arts, 2000)

Sandro Botticelli pittore della 'Divina Commedia', ed. Sebastiano Gentile, 2 vols. (Milan: Skira, 2000)

Santagata, Marco, *Per moderne carte. La biblioteca volgare di Petrarca* (Bologna: Il Mulino, 1990)

Santini, Emilio, 'La produzione volgare di Leonardo Bruni Aretino e il suo culto per le tre corone fiorentine', *GSLI* 60 (1912), 289–339

Santoro, Mario, 'Poliziano o il Magnifico?', *Giornale italiano di filologia* 1 (1948), 139–49

Scapecchi, Piero, 'Cristoforo Landino, Niccolò di Lorenzo e la *Commedia*', in *Sandro Botticelli pittore*, ed. Gentile, I, 44–47

Scott, William O., 'Perotti, Ficino and *Furor poeticus*', *Res Publica Litterarum* 4 (1981), 273–84

Siegel, Jerrold, '"Civic humanism" or "Ciceronian Rhetoric"? The Culture of Petrarch and Bruni', *Past & Present* 34 (1966), 3–48

Sottili, Agostino, 'Il laerzio latino e greco e altri autografi di Ambrogio Traversari', in *Vestigia*, eds., Avesani *et al.*, II, 699–745

Stadter, Philip A., 'Niccolò Niccoli: Winning Back the Knowledge of the Ancients', in *Vestigia*, eds., Avesani *et al.*, II, 747–64

Staico, Ubaldo, 'Esegesi aristotelica in età medicea', in *La Toscana*, III, 1275–1321

Stinger, Charles L., *Humanism and the Church Fathers: Ambrogio Traversari (1386–1439) and Christian Antiquity in the Italian Renaissance* (Albany: University of New York Press, 1977)

'Humanism in Florence', in *Renaissance Humanism. Foundations, Forms, and Legacy*, ed. Albert Rabil, Jr, 2 vols. (Philadelphia: University of Pennsylvania Press, 1988), I, 175–208

Select bibliography

Storey, Christina, 'The Philosopher, the Poet, and the Fragment: Ficino, Poliziano, and *Le Stanze per la Giostra*', *Modern Language Review* 98:3 (2003), 602–19

Tagliabue, Mauro, 'Contributo alla biografia di Matteo Ronto traduttore di Dante', *IMU* 26 (1983), 151–88

Tanturli, Giuliano, 'I Benci copisti. Vicende di cultura fiorentina volgare fra Antonio Pucci e il Ficino', *SFI* 36 (1978), 197–313

'Cino Rinuccini e la scuola di Santa Maria in Campo', *Studi Medievali* III ser./17 (1976), 625–74

'Codici di Antonio Manetti e ricette del Ficino', *Rinascimento* II ser./20 (1980), 313–26

'La cultura fiorentina volgare del Quattrocento davanti ai nuovi testi greci', *Medioevo e Rinascimento* 2 (1988), 217–43

'Dante, Firenze, Leonardo Bruni', *SD* 76 (2001), 179–203

'Il disprezzo per Dante dal Petrarca al Bruni', *Rinascimento* II ser./25 (1985), 194–215

'La Firenze laurenziana davanti alla propria storia letteraria', in *Lorenzo il Magnifico*, ed. Garfagnini, pp. 1–38

'Proposta e riproposta. La prolusione petrarchesca del Landino e il codice cavalcantiano di Antonio Manetti', *Rinascimento* II ser./32 (1992), 213–25

'Sulla data e la genesi della *Vita civile* di Matteo Palmieri', *Rinascimento* II ser./36 (1996), 3–48

Tavoni, Mirko, *Latino, grammatica, volgare. Storia di una questione umanistica* (Padua: Antenore, 1984)

Il Quattrocento (Bologna: Il Mulino, 1992)

Taylor, Karla, 'A Text and Its Afterlife: Dante and Chaucer', *Comparative Literature* 35:1 (1983), 1–20

Thompson, David, 'Landino's Life of Dante', *DS* 88 (1970), 119–27

'Pico della Mirandola's Praise of Lorenzo (and Critique of Dante and Petrarch)', *Neophilologus* 54 (1970), 123–26

Tomè Marcassa, Paola, 'Giovanni Tortelli e la fortuna umanistica del Boccaccio', *SBoc* 29 (2001), 229–59

La Toscana al tempo di Lorenzo il Magnifico. Politica, economia, cultura e arte, 3 vols. (Pisa: Pacini Fazzi, 1996)

Toussaint, Stéphane, *De l'enfer à la coupole. Dante, Brunelleschi et Ficin. À propos des 'codici Caetani di Dante'* (Rome: L'Erma di Bretschneider, 1997)

Trinkaus, Charles, *In Our Image and Likeness: Humanity and Divinity in Italian Humanist Thought*, 2 vols. (London: Constable, 1970)

I Triumphi di Francesco Petrarca, ed. Claudia Berra (Milan: Cisalpino, 1999)

Trovato, Paolo, *Dante in Petrarca. Per un inventario dei dantismi nei 'Rerum Vulgarium Fragmenta'* (Florence: Olschki, 1979)

'Dai *Dialogi ad Petrum Histrum* alle *Vite di Dante e del Petrarca*. Appunti su Leonardo Bruni e la tradizione trecentesca', *SP* n.s. 2 (1985), 263–84

Uberti, Maria Luisa, 'Benvenuto da Imola dantista allievo del Boccaccio', *SBoc* 12 (1980), 275–319

Ullman, B. L., *The Humanism of Coluccio Salutati* (Padua: Antenore, 1963)

The Origin and Development of Humanistic Script (Rome: Edizioni di Storia e Letteratura, 1963)

Studies in the Italian Renaissance (Rome: Edizioni di Storia e Letteratura, 1972; 1st edn 1955)

and Philip A. Stadter, *The Public Library of Renaissance Florence: Niccolò Niccoli, Cosimo de' Medici and the Library of San Marco* (Padua: Antenore, 1972)

Vallone, Aldo, *Storia della critica dantesca dal XIV al XX secolo* (Milan–Padua: Vallardi, 1981)

Varese, Claudio, *Storia e politica nella prosa del Quattrocento* (Turin: Einaudi, 1961)

Vasoli, Cesare, 'Bruni, Leonardo', in *DBI* 14 (1972), 618–33

'La cultura laurenziana: tendenze e ambienti intellettuali', in *Lorenzo il Magnifico*, ed. Garfagnini, pp. 153–75

'Da Giorgio Gemisto a Ficino: nascita e metamorfosi della Prisca theologia', in *Miscellanea di studi in onore di Claudio Varese* (Rome: Vecchiarelli, 2001), pp. 787–800

'Dante e la cultura fiorentina del maturo Quattrocento', in *Sandro Botticelli pittore*, ed. Gentile, 1, 12–25

'Ficino, Marsilio', in *DBI* 47 (1997), 378–95

Filosofia e religione nella cultura del Rinascimento (Naples: Guida, 1988)

'Interpretazione ficiniana di Dante', *RELI* 2 (1993), 127–40

'Note sul volgarizzamento ficiniano della *Monarchia*', in *Miscellanea di studi in onore di Vittore Branca*, 5 vols. (Florence: Olschki, 1983), III, 451–74

Quasi sit Deus. Studi su Marsilio Ficino (Lecce: Conte, 1999)

Tra 'Maestri' umanisti e teologi. Studi quattrocenteschi (Florence: Le Lettere, 1991)

Veglia, Marco, 'Sul nodo culturale del *Corbaccio*', *Studi e problemi di critica testuale* 52 (1996), 79–100

Velli, Giuseppe, 'Il Dante di Francesco Petrarca', *SP* n.s. 2 (1985), 185–200

Venchi, Innocenzo, *s.v.* 'Domenicani', in *ED* II, 542–44

Vestigia. Studi in onore di Giuseppe Billanovich, eds. Rino Avesani *et al.*, 2 vols. (Rome: Edizioni di Storia e Letteratura, 1984)

Vineis, Edoardo, 'La tradizione grammaticale latina e la grammatica di Leon Battista Alberti', in *Convegno internazionale indetto*, pp. 289–303

Viti, Paolo, 'Filelfo, Francesco', in *DBI* 47 (1997), 613–26

Leonardo Bruni e Firenze. Studi sulle lettere pubbliche e private (Rome: Bulzoni, 1992)

Introd. to his *Opere letterarie e politiche di Leonardo Bruni* (Turin: UTET, 1996), pp. 9–66

Walker, D. P., *The Ancient Theology: Studies in Christian Platonism from the Fifteenth to the Eighteenth Centuries* (London: The Warburg Institute, 1972)

Weinstein, Donald, 'The Myth of Florence', in *Florentine Studies*, ed. Rubinstein, pp. 15–44

Weiss, Roberto, 'Dante e l'umanesimo del suo tempo', *Letture Classensi* 2 (1969), 11–27

'Gli inizi dello studio del greco a Firenze', in *Medieval and Humanist Greek. Collected Essays by Roberto Weiss*, ed. Rino Avesani *et al.* (Padua: Antenore, 1977), pp. 227–54

The Renaissance Discovery of Classical Antiquity (Oxford: Blackwell, 1969)

Wigodsky, Michael, '"Nacqui *sub Iulio*" (*Inf.* 1, 70)', *DS* 93 (1975), 177–83

Wilcox, Donald L., *The Development of Florentine Humanist Historiography in the Fifteenth Century* (Cambridge: Harvard University Press, 1969)

Select bibliography

Wind, Edgar, 'The Revival of Origen', in his *The Eloquence of Symbols: Studies in Humanist Art* (Oxford: Clarendon Press, 1983), pp. 42–55

Witt, Ronald G., 'Cino Rinuccini's *Responsiva alla Invectiva di Messer Antonio Lusco*', *RQ* 23 (1970), 133–49

'Coluccio Salutati and the Conception of the *Poeta Theologus* in the Fourteenth Century', *RQ* 30 (1977), 539–42

Coluccio Salutati and His Public Letters (Geneva: Droz, 1976)

'The *De tyranno* and Coluccio Salutati's View of Politics and Roman History', *Nuova rivista storica* 53 (1969), 434–74

In the Footsteps of the Ancients: The Origins of Humanism from Lovato to Bruni (Leiden: Brill, 2000)

Hercules at the Crossroads: The Life, Works and Thought of Coluccio Salutati (Durham: Duke University Press, 1983)

Woodhouse, C. M., *George Gemistos Plethon. The Last of the Hellenes* (Oxford, Clarendon Press, 1986)

Zaccaria, Vittorio, 'Presenze di Dante nelle opere latine del Boccaccio', in *Miscellanea di Studi Danteschi in memoria di Silvio Pasquazi*, eds. Alfonso Paolella, Vincenzo Placella, and Giovanni Turca, 2 vols. (Naples: Federico & Ardia, 1993), II, 893–903

Zippel, Giuseppe, *Storia e cultura del Rinascimento italiano*, ed. Gianni Zippel (Padua: Antenore, 1979)

Index

Index

Index

Index

Index

poetry 135–38, 139, 141, 178, 184, 272; *De anima* 169, 199, 201, 213, 214, 278; *Disputationes Camaldulenses* (*DC*): 169–72, 186, 199, 204, 207, 271, 276; (printed edition) 270; (vernacular version) 271; vernacular version of Pliny's *Historia Naturalis* 141, 267; *Xandra* (Latin poetry) 163

see also Alberti, Leon Battista; *Comento sopra la Comedia*; Dante Alighieri: surpasses ancient writers; Greek: etymology of 'poet'; Manetti, Antonio Tuccio; Platonism; Poliziano, Angelo

Lanza, Antonio 87, 243, 254, 255, 257, 258, 259, 260, 263, 269

Lapo da Castiglionchio 178

Larner, John 273, 277

Latin
  decline of eloquence in 177
  humanist debate on 98, 121–22, 125
  prose style in 3, 56

Latini, Brunetto 115

Lentzen, Manfred 166, 270, 275, 282

Leonardo da Vinci 243

Lerner, Robert C., 247

Liber de causis 240

Limbo (in Dante) 2, 48, 253

Lines, David A., 265

Lippi, Filippo 180

Livy 2

Lo Cascio, Renzo 268

Lombard, Peter 78, 81

Lo Monaco, Francesco 271

Lorenzo di Giovanni da Pisa 243

Loschi, Antonio 57, 63, 78

Lovati, Lovato dei 2

Lucan 75, 226, 281

Lucian 224, 282

Lucretius 2, 184

Luiso, Francesco Paolo 258

Luschino, Benedetto 284

Macrobius 30, 111, 203, 207, 209, 267
  Commentarium in Somnium Scipionis 203, 207, 267

Madrignani, Carlo Alberto 263

Maggini, Francesco 267

Maissen, Thomas 257, 262

Malecarni, Francesco 265

Malpaghini, Giovanni 99, 243

Manetti, Antonio Tuccio 135, 141, 176
  and Ficino 142, 143, 145
  copyist of Dante (*Comedy/Convivio*) 141, 143
  cosmographical studies of *Inferno* 141, 193

edition of *Comedy* 141
  works: letter to Lorenzo de' Medici on Dante's remains 266; *Notizia* 141, 142, 266, 267

Manetti, Gianozzo 132–33, 175
  biographer of Dante 132–33, 182, 183
  on Dante's participation at Battle of Campaldino 133
  on Dante's remains 181
  on Dante's treatment by Florence 133
  work: *Vitae* 132, 265, 272

Manfred of Monferrato 243

Mansi, Maria Luisa 263

Manutius, Aldus 237

Maramauro, Guglielmo
  Dante commentary: *Expositione* 255

Maraschio, Nicoletta 264

Marcel, Raymond 265

Marchesini, Umberto 256

Marchisio, Cesare 244

Marietti, Martina 258

Marrasio, Giovanni 264

Marsh, David 259

Marsili, Luigi 76

Marsilio da Santa Sofia 77

Marsuppini, Carlo 99, 103, 126

Martelli, Mario 248, 258, 261, 266, 267, 268, 269

Martellotti, Guido 240, 248

Martial 2, 250
  work: *Epigrammata* 250

Martindale, Charles 240, 241

Martines, Lauro 258, 261

Martinez, Ronald L., 276

Masaccio 180

Masha'allah (Mishael) 216

Mazzeo, Joseph Anthony 276

Mazzocco, Angelo 122, 264

Mazzoni, Francesco 242, 252

McCormick, Andrew P., 241, 283

McLaughlin, Martin L., 247, 249, 260, 268, 269

McNair, Bruce G., 270, 275, 277, 278, 279

Medici, Cosimo de' 97, 98, 123, 134, 142, 176
  his library 242, 258

Medici, Giuliano de' 151, 167

Medici, Giuliana de' 252

Medici, Lorenzo de' 131, 134, 138, 156–60, 163, 167
  cognitive value of poetry 158
  cultural guide of Florence 158
  imitation of Dante in vernacular prose and poetry 156–59, 236
  judgement on Dante 159–60
  patriotic value of vernacular 158–59

Index

criticizes scholasticism 177
defence of poetry in 31, 64
first printing of vernacular works 242
imitation of Dante in Latin works 33–34,
  39, 243, 251
imitation of Dante in vernacular works
  38–39
influence on later humanist attitudes to
  Dante 40
legendary status as *dantista* 52
on Dante's use of vernacular 34–37, 41, 51,
  61, 233
on incompleteness of Statius' *Achilleid* 40,
  228, 251
representation in visual arts with Dante 52
revises Dante on Dido, Plato, and Ulysses
  39, 40, 251
superiority of Latin 35, 55
works: *Canzoniere* (*Rerum vulgarium
  fragmenta*) 37, 38, 39, 138, 250; *Rerum
  familiares libri XXIV* (x, 4) 31, 264;
  (XVIII, 5) 253; (XXI, 15) 32–37, 38, 39, 40,
  41, 51, 52, 55, 58, 61, 84, 249, 250, 253;
  (XVIII, 5) *Rerum memorandarum libri* 37,
  250; *Seniles* (IV, 5) 255; (V, 2) 37, 249; (IX,
  17) 251; *Trionfi* 38, 39, 40, 140, 151, 209,
  250, 251, 266
see also Benvenuto da Imola; Boccaccio,
  Giovanni; Bruni, Leonardo; *Comento
  sopra la Comedia*; Dante Alighieri:
  deficiencies in Latin language/culture;
  Greek: etymology of 'poet'; Landino,
  Cristoforo; Manetti, Gianozzo; Pico
  della Mirandola; rebirth/renaissance;
  Salutati, Coluccio; *terza rima*
Petrocchi, Giorgio 8, 241, 245, 255, 256
Petrucci, Armando 241, 254
Piana, Celestino 241, 253
Pico dalla Mirandola 266
  letter comparing Lorenzo de' Medici to
  Dante and Petrarch 266
Picone, Michelangelo 240, 245, 251, 282
Piemontesi, Ludovico and Alberto 242
Pier delle Vigne 139
Pierozzi, Antonino (Bishop of Florence)
  253
Pietro Alighieri 45, 48, 57, 73, 74, 108, 194,
  209, 213, 216–17, 220, 222, 224, 235, 241
  Dante commentary: *Comentum* 200, 209,
  223, 248, 262, 278, 279, 280–81
Pintor, Fortunato 242
Pisistratus 138
Pistolesi, Elena 242
Plato 107, 112, 142, 144, 145, 146, 180, 183, 186,
  187, 199–211, 224
  furor poeticus in 118, 156, 186
  myth of Er in 108

works: *Crito* 200; *Gorgias* 200; *Ion* 187, 200,
  274; *Laws* 200; *Letters* 200; *Parmenides*
  200; *Phaedo* 200, 207; *Phaedrus* 118, 187,
  200, 274; *Republic* 108, 200; *Symposium*
  146, 156, 183, 200; *Timaeus* 200
see also Aristotle; *Comento sopra la Comedia*;
  Dante Alighieri: as Platonist; Ficino
  Marsilio; Palmieri, Matteo; Petrarch;
  Platonism; Virgil: as Platonist
Platonism (Platonic tradition, Neoplatonism,
  Neoplatonists) 128, 142, 179, 199–211
  adapted to Christianity 201–2, 203, 210
  body as prison in 186
  descensus ad inferos 108, 202
  descent of soul into body in 108, 111, 201,
  205–7
  Phaedran chariot in 202
  pre-existence of soul in 150, 205
  revival in 15C Florence 134, 135, 145, 151,
  179, 183, 204, 234
  Two Venuses in 202, 204
Plautus 2, 184, 224
Pletho, George Gemistus 210
  work: *De differentiis platonicae atque
  aristotelicae disciplinae* 210
Pliny the Elder 180, 181, 227, 279;
  work: *Historia Naturalis*: 180, 212; its
  popularity with humanists 277
see also Landino, Cristoforo: works
Plutarch 112
  work: *Lives* 115
Poliziano, Angelo 134, 138–41, 150–56, 163,
  185, 236
  Dante mistakes Statius' birthplace in 227,
  283
  polemic with Cristoforo Landino 139,
  236
  imitation of Dante in vernacular and
  Latin: *Epistola* 139–40; *Stanze* 152–54;
  Sylva in Scabiem 154–56
  imitation of Dante's Earthly
  Paradise/*Purgatorio* 152, 269
  philological commentary in 195
  poetic theory/defence of poetry in 152
  use of Greek and Latin intertexts in 152,
  155
  works: *Commento alle Selve* 283; *Epistola* to
  Raccolta Aragonese 138–40, 178, 266;
  *Stanze per la giostra di Giuliano de'
  Medici* 151–54, 269; *Sylva in Scabiem* 151,
  154–55, 269
see also Benvenuto da Imola
Polizzotto, Lorenzo 284
prisca theologia see Ficino, Marsilio
Priscian, *see Institutiones*
Procaccioli, Paolo 166, 175, 213, 270, 272, 275,
  276, 277, 279, 281, 282, 284

Index

Propertius 2, 224, 226, 281
Ptolemy 212
    work: *Geographia* 212, 277
    see also Berlinghieri, Francesco
Pucci, Antonio 248
Pulci, brothers 147
Pulci, Luca 268
Pulci, Luigi 156, 268
Pulsoni, Carlo 247, 249
Pythagoreanism 106, 148, 179

Quint, David 260
Quintilian 56, 104, 105, 190
    work: *Institutio oratoria* 105, 250, 261,
    274

Rabelais, François 49
Raccolta Aragonese 138–41, 151, 158, 160,
    248
    Dante's works in 139
rebirth/renaissance
    applied to Dante 2–4, 28, 70–71, 91, 92,
        133, 138, 177, 178, 265
    applied to Bruni 105, 261
    applied to Florence 88, 105
    applied to Florentine sculpture 105
    applied to Petrarch 33, 85, 177
reception, theory of 6–7
Renaudet, Augustin 239
Resta, Gianvito 239
Rheinfelder, Hans 244
Ricci, Corrado 249
Ricci, Pier Giorgio 247, 258, 261, 266
Riccucci, Maria 251
Richardson, Brian 242, 284
Rinuccini, Alemanno 133
Rinuccini, Cino 78–82, 87, 88, 92, 101
    critique of Florentine humanism
    praises Dante's scholastic qualities 82
    works: *Invettiva* 78–83, 87, 89, 91;
        Responsiva 78, 87, 257, 258
Rizzo, Silvia 255
Robin, Diana 260
Rocco, Flavia 253
Rochon, André 269
Roddewig, Marcella 8, 241, 242–45
Rome
    development as humanist centre
    133
    see also Florence
Ronto, Matteo 241, 268
Rose, Paul Lawrence 273
Rossi, Aldo 245, 249, 267
Rossi, Luca Carlo 252, 253, 270, 283
Rossi, Roberto de' 83, 85
Rossi, Vittorio 245
Roush, Sherry 284

Rubinstein, Nicolai 257, 258
Ruini, Roberto 256
Russo, Vittorio 252

Sabbadini, Remigio 280, 282, 283
Sacchetti, Franco 35, 104
    work: *Il Trecentonovelle* 243, 248
Sallust 69, 281
Salutati, Coluccio 56–69, 72, 73, 74, 76, 77,
        78, 82, 83, 84, 85, 86, 87, 88, 91, 92, 101,
        132, 171, 172, 178, 185, 233, 236, 243
    attitude to monarchy 67
    Chancellor of Florence 56
    Dante-Petrarch comparison(s) in 58, 63
    defence of poetry 64, 74, 86, 188, 243,
        255
    defender of Dante 57, 78
    humanism of 56–57
    humanistic/classicizing treatment of Dante
        58–59, 62, 63, 82, 105, 233
    Latin translations of Dante 57, 60, 65, 66,
        254
    letter on Latin literature 60
    on spelling of Dante's family name 62–63
    on vernacular (especially in Dante) 57, 61,
        121, 233
    on Virgil's birth under Julius Caesar (*Inf.* 1,
        70) 59, 74, 228
    public letters 56–57
    textual emendation of *Comedy* 62, 69
    use of Dante as doctrinal source 57, 65
    vernacular verse 57
    works: *De fato et fortuna*; 57, 60, 65–66, 87,
        255, 256; *De laboribus Herculis* 57, 63–65,
        88, 188, 223, 251, 256, 264, 274; *De
        tyranno* 57, 66–69, 256; *Epistolario*
        (epistolography) 58–63, 254, 255, 256;
        *Invectiva in Antonium Luschum
        Vicentinum* 63, 68, 69, 255, 273; his
        vernacular verse 254
    see also Benvenuto da Imola; Bruni,
        Leonardo; Brutus and Cassius debate;
        Dante Alighieri: surpasses ancient
        writers; Florence: founded by Sulla;
        Greek: etymology of 'poet'
Sandkühler, Bruno 242, 245
Santagata, Marco 251
Santini, Emilio 259
Santoro, Mario 266
Sardi, Tommaso 150
    work: *De anima peregrina* 268
Savonarola, Girolamo 237
Scapecchi, Piero 269
scholasticism
    see Bruni, Leonardo; Dante Alighieri;
        Petrarch, Rinuccini, Cino
Scott, William O., 274

322

Index

science (natural philosophy)
   see also Comento sopra la Comedia; Dante
     Alighieri; Florence
Segre, Cesare 267
Selvaggia 38
Seneca 56, 64, 281
   works: *Hercules furens* 64; *Hercules oeteus* 64
Sennuccio del Bene 38
Sermartelli, Bartolomeo 248
Servius 27, 30, 226
Shaw, Prudence 267
Sicilian, school of poetry (Sicilians) 138,
   140
Siegel, Jerrold 87, 259
Silvestri, Domenico 256
Sixtus IV, pope 167
Socrates 116
Sottili, Agostino 282
Spain 3
Stadter, Philip A., 253, 258
Staico, Ubaldo 265
Statius 29, 75, 120, 155
   conversion to Christianity (in Dante) 3
   error regarding birthplace (in Dante) 3,
     227
   views on incompleteness of *Achilleid* (in
     Dante) 228
   works: *Silvae* 227, 228; *Thebaid* 119; (XII,
     816–19) 255
   see also Comento sopra la Comedia: on
     Statius as Tolosan; Petrarch; Poliziano,
     Angelo
Stinger, Charles L., 253
Storey, Christina 268
Strabo 212, 224
   work: *Geographia* 277
Strozzi, Palla 98
Suetonius 26

Tacitus 280
Tagliabue, Mauro 241
Tanturli, Giuliano 142, 257, 258, 259, 260,
   261, 262, 266, 267, 268, 269
Tasso, Torquato 258
Tavoni, Mirko 122, 264, 266, 267
Taylor, Karla 283
Tedaldi, Bartolino 156
Terence 2, 184, 214–224
terza rima
   imitation after Dante 11, 150, 246
   in Dante 5–6, 240
   in Boccaccio 39, 245
   in Lorenzo de' Medici 156, 158
   in Matteo Palmieri 147, 148
   in Petrarch 39
Theophrastus 227
Thompson, David 182, 263, 266, 273

Tomè Marcassa, Paola 281
Torini, Agnolo 258
Toscanelli, Paolo (Florentine Paolo) 176, 192,
   221
Toussaint, Stéphane 274
Traversari, Ambrogio 83, 97, 98, 178, 224
Trinkaus, Charles 255, 281
Trissino, Giovan Giorgio 242
Trovato, Paolo 251, 260, 263

Uberti, Maria Luisa 253
Ullman, B. L., 253, 254, 255, 258
Universal Judgement 49
Ursolo, Lucius Statius 227

Vallone, Aldo 247, 254
Varese, Claudio 243
Vasari, Giorgio 192, 274
Vasoli, Cesare 143, 242, 253, 259, 265, 267,
   274, 276
Veglia, Marco 247
Venchi, Innocenzo 253
Vergerio, Pier Paolo 57, 83
Verino, Ugolino 147, 268
   works: *Paradisus* 147; *Carlias* 147
Veronese, Guarino 277
Velli, Giuseppe 251
vernacular
   and Florence 56
   status raised in Medici Florence 16, 97, 131,
     134–60
   used by Italian princes 132, 179
   viewed as inferior to Latin and Greek by
     humanists 55
   volgarizzamenti (vernacular versions of
     Latin and Greek texts) 134, 135, 141–46,
     163
   see also Alberti, Leon Battista; Boccaccio,
     Giovanni; Bracciolini, Poggio; Bruni,
     Leonardo; Dante Alighieri; Ficino,
     Marsilio; Florence; humanism; Landino,
     Cristoforo; Medici, Lorenzo de';
     Palmieri, Matteo; Petrarch; Poliziano,
     Angelo; Salutati, Coluccio; Villani,
     Filippo; women
Vespasiano di Bisticci 99
   Le vite 258, 261, 268
Vespucci, Nastagio 156, 157
Villani, Filippo 10, 12, 69–76, 77, 78, 82, 88,
   92, 108, 132, 133, 177, 180, 233, 235, 241,
   253
   allegorism in 72–73, 74–75
   biographer of Dante 70–72
   defence of poetry in 73, 92
   influence on later Florentine writers/
     artists 70, 72, 175, 176, 178, 179, 180,
     257

323

CAMBRIDGE STUDIES IN MEDIEVAL LITERATURE